Tourism in the U.K.

Pat Yale

ELM Publications

First published in August, 1992 by ELM Publications, Seaton House, Kings Ripton, Huntingdon PE17 2NJ, Tel. 04873-254 or 238, Fax 04873-359.

Printed by St Edmundsbury Press, Bury St Edmunds, Suffolk and bound by Woolnough Bookbinding, Irthlingborough, Northamptonshire.

ISBN 1 85450 017 1

CONTENTS

LIST OF FIGURES

LIST OF TABLES

INTRODUCTION

This textbook is aimed primarily at students taking the Incoming and Domestic Tourism unit of the BTEC National Diploma in Travel and Tourism. However, some of its contents may also be useful to those studying the Visitor Attractions, Heritage Tourism and Passenger Transport Operations units and the City and Guilds units focusing on tourism in the UK.

It builds on work that students will have done in the first year BTEC National Travel and Tourism Environment unit and in some ways should be seen as an extended case study, building on the basics of Pat Lavery's *Travel and Tourism* in the same series; thus the chapter on the impact of tourism deals with the specific effects of tourism in the UK rather than on the theoretical framework for analysing them. What I have called the 'tourist geography' chapter, for want of a better name, does not set out to be an exhaustive study of the UK's physical or climatic make up. Instead it focuses on identifying the main natural and historic attractions the various areas of Britain have to offer tourists. More detailed information about the tourist attractions industry will be found in my own *From Tourist Attractions to Heritage Tourism*, (ELM Publications, May 1991 ISBN 185450.0171) also in the same series. Although marketing is an important function of the various UK tourist boards and tourist information services which are examined in this book, marketing as a subject in its own right is not covered here since students will be examining it in greater depth through the Selling and Marketing of Tourism unit.

Preparing this book in 1991 was an odd experience since the Gulf War and the recession had combined to devastate tourism at home and abroad, destroying trends established over previous years. I presume this was a temporary 'blip' and that in years to come 1991 will look like an aberration in the statistics. This, of course, remains to be confirmed.

Throughout the text I have used the conventional abbreviations BTA to refer to the British Tourist Authority, ETB for the English Tourist Board, STB for the Scottish Tourist Board, WTB for the Wales Tourist Board and NITB for the Northern Ireland Tourist Board.

In researching this book I have found the ETB publication *Insights* invaluable for its up-to-date summaries of current issues in domestic tourism. Also very useful was another ETB publication, *Tourism Enterprise*. Once again I am indebted to the staff of the

National and Regional Tourist Boards for providing me with a seemingly endless supply of useful information; without their help this book could never have seen the light of day. And once again thanks go to my Soundwell colleagues, especially Sharon North, Rachel Millward and Carol Calder. I am also indebted to the College's 1990 and 1991 travel and tourism students who were my guinea pigs while this book was being put together. Finally, special thanks are owed to Sean Taplin for tolerance beyond the call of duty while the word processor tapped away into the early hours and for help with the cover.

Pat Yale December 1991

CHAPTER ONE
INTRODUCTION TO TOURISM IN THE UNITED KINGDOM

Tourism is a boom industry in Great Britain. In 1989 the World Tourism Organisation (WTO) estimated that 4.3% of total tourist arrivals worldwide were to the United Kingdom and that Britain had a 5.4% share of total tourism expenditure. In the same year the International Passenger Survey indicated that about 17.2 million overseas visitor trips netted around £6,945 million for the UK; 109.5 million domestic trips brought in a further £10,865 million. Since 1970 tourism to the UK has risen by about 5.1%, slightly more than the average increase worldwide.

The Growth of the UK Holiday Market

There have been travellers in Britain for as long as records have been kept. However, until relatively recently most people left home because they had to, primarily for trade, but sometimes for reasons like desire to go on a pilgrimage, rather than for the sheer pleasure of doing so. Travelling was arduous and unpleasant. From the time that the Romans left England until the Industrial Revolution of the 18th century venturing onto the roads meant risking days of bumping over hardened ruts in summer or getting bogged down in mud in winter, with the ever-present risk of robbery by footpads to add to the problems.

In the 18th century the wealthy classes nevertheless began to take what are recognisable holidays in the modern sense of the word, frequently in spa towns like Bath which were regarded as healthy places to go. Gradually seaside resorts also became popular, and villages like the original Brighton grew rapidly to accommodate the new travellers.

The Industrial Revolution changed the transport situation drastically as the need to move the new factory products around the country led to rapid improvements to the roads, and then to the growth of canals and railways. As more and more people crowded into the new towns where the factories had grown up, a psychological need to escape back to the country seems to have developed. The railways also brought seaside resorts like Southend, Southport, Blackpool and Brighton within easy reach of many more people. In 1841 Thomas Cook introduced the concept of the package excursion when he laid on reasonably priced rail transport to get people from Leicester to Loughborough for a temperance rally. However, for most people holidaymaking as opposed to day tripping was still out of the question. It wasn't until the late 19th century that many people had sufficient spare money even to pay the train fare for day trips to the coast.

Interest in holidays to wilder parts of the countryside was slower to develop although an English climber was recorded at Mount Snowdon as early as 1639. Nevertheless by the end of the 18th century the Romantic poets and particularly William Wordsworth had drawn the public's attention to the Lake District. By the 1840s new railway lines were already bringing crowds to Windermere.

In 1871 the **Bank Holiday Act** introduced four public holidays in the year, paving the way for people to stay away from home for slightly longer. The resorts reacted by laying on accommodation to suit the pockets of their new visitors. The 1938 **Holidays With Pay Act** offered a further boost to tourism by empowering employers to provide paid holidays for the first time. In 1937 Billy Butlin set up the first holiday camp at Skegness to meet the needs of the new holidaymakers. By 1945 80% of the population had paid holidays, providing them with the time and money to take vacations. Holiday camps rapidly dotted most of the coastline.

In the early 1950s about 60% of all domestic holidays were taken at the seaside and most people travelled to their destination by coach or train. The British Travel Association, predecessor of the British Tourist Authority, was set up to encourage the burgeoning tourism industry. But from the 1960s onwards competition from the cheap sun, sea and sand resorts of the Mediterranean gradually reduced the popularity of domestic tourism. Relatively few people now take their long annual holiday at the seaside resorts.

Just as there have always been some domestic travellers, there have always been some overseas visitors too, including soldiers, diplomats or traders. Even in the 17th century there are records of these visitors touring some of the country's stately homes and castles. However, the number of overseas visitors couldn't really expand until there were better international transport links and until the concept of paid holidays became common all over Europe. In 1946 there were only 203,000 recorded overseas visitors to the UK and most of them had arrived by boat. By 1960 there were 1.7 million visitors and many of them had arrived by air.

THE OVERSEAS VISITOR MARKET

Overseas visitors are those who are permanently resident outside the United Kingdon and who visit it for periods of less than a year at a time. British citizens who live abroad or who only come home on leave are counted as overseas visitors for most statistical purposes.

In 1989 51.8% of overseas visitors to the UK came from other EC countries. A further 20% came from North America, 10% from non-EC European countries and 18.2% from the rest of the world. Since 1980

North Americans have made up a slightly increasing proportion of the market and EC residents a declining proportion. In the first six months of 1990 the UK received 9% more visitors from North America and 22% more from the rest of the world than in 1989. Visitor numbers from European countries were virtually unchanged. However, like other European countries, Great Britain suffered a drop in overseas tourist arrivals at the start of 1991 as a result of the Gulf War. Provided that numbers return to normal, the BTA estimates that there will be 22 million overseas visitors, spending £13.5 billion by 1995.

FIGURE 1 VISITS TO THE UK BY OVERSEAS RESIDENTS

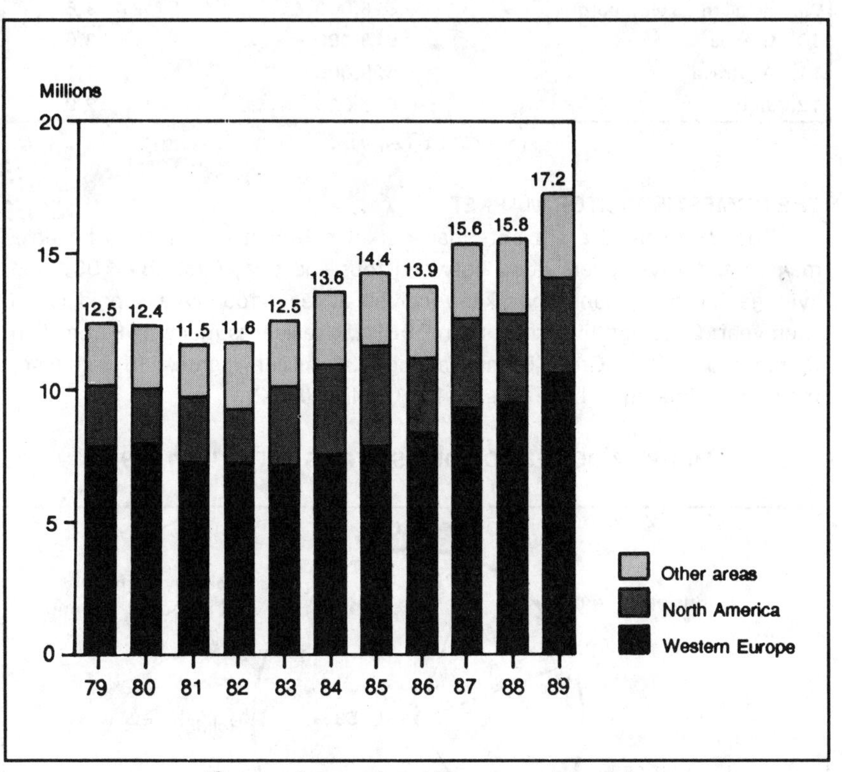

(Source: International Passenger Survey)

Since 1980 the number of visitors from the United States, Canada and Italy has risen, while the number of visitors from the Middle East, Belgium and Luxembourg has fallen slightly. The biggest percentage increases in visitor numbers between 1980 and 1989 were from Japan, Eastern Europe and Spain.

TABLE 1 MAIN COUNTRIES GENERATING TOURISM TO THE UK IN 1989

	Number of Visitors	Percentage of Total
1. The United States	2,814,000	16.4
2. France	2,254,000	13.1
3. West Germany	2,012,000	11.7
4. Irish Republic	1,302,000	7.6
5. Netherlands	945,000	5.5
6. Italy	700,000	4.1
7. Canada	633,000	3.7
8. Spain	622,000	3.6
9. Belgium/Luxembourg	616,000	3.6
10. Greece	613,000	3.6
11. Australia	529,000	3.1
12. Japan	505,000	2.9

(Source: BTA, 1989)

THE DOMESTIC VISITOR MARKET

The UK itself offers a potential market of roughly 38 million holiday-makers and day-trippers aged between four and sixty-five. By 1990 the average full time manual worker received at least four weeks paid leave each year; 27% had five weeks. In 1989 UK residents made 109.5 million tourist trips within Great Britain lasting 433 million nights. In doing so, they are estimated to have spent £10.9 million (Fig.2).

FIGURE 2 DOMESTIC TOURIST TRIPS IN THE UK 1989

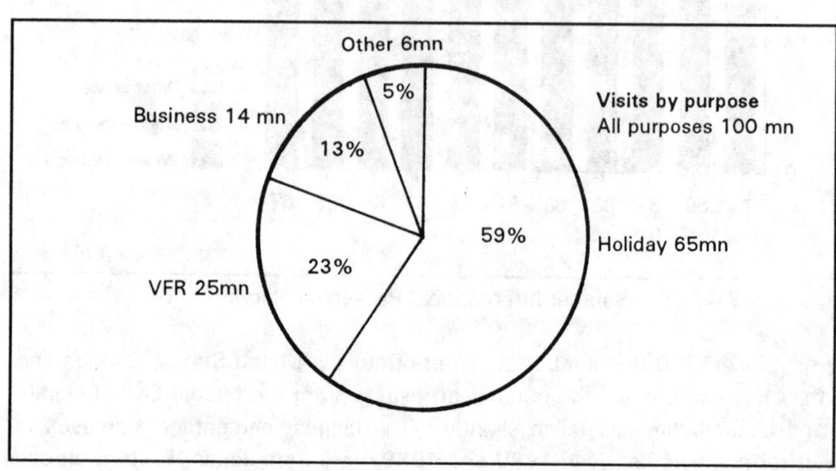

(Source: UK Tourism Survey, 1989)

The domestic market can be divided into the following categories:

The Youth Market (16-24)

Young people have fewest commitments and therefore the highest level of discretionary income, representing a potential £30 billion worth of expenditure. This situation was nevertheless threatened by an increasing level of youth unemployment in the early 1990s. The number of people in this age bracket is also shrinking; by 2000 the number of 16-24 year olds is expected to have declined by 12%. Young people are responsible for 12% of total tourism expenditure, but tend to be seen as fickle consumers of transitorily fashionable products. The younger end of this age range tend to holiday in peak periods to coincide with school/college holidays and may have little spending power. However, at the opposite end of the scale are the so-called 'dinkies' (dual income, no kids), frequently high spenders able to holiday at any time of year.

The Family Market (25-50)

The middle age bracket often has the highest level of actual income (perhaps £112 billion), but also the highest level of commitments in the form of mortgages, school fees, clothing for children, etc. They tend to holiday in peak periods to coincide with school holidays and are responsible for 45% of tourism expenditure.

The 50+ Market

The over-50s, or 'empty-nesters', represent a huge amount of potential spending power (perhaps £108 billion), largely because they have often paid off their mortgages and other financial commitments, and their children have usually left home. In addition the over-50s hold 70% of all savings, may be reaching the point when insurance policies mature and may inherit up to £8 billion a year, much of it in property form. An increasing number of over-50s are taking early retirement and/or may benefit from occupational pensions. This is a growth market; over-55s made up 26% of the population in 1990 but will make up 33% by 2027. Amongst domestic holidaymakers only the 55-64 and 65+ age groups take more holidays at home than abroad. They are also able to take their holidays at off-peak times of year and are responsible for 43% of all tourism expenditure.

Nevertheless, the market divides into those who are relatively young and healthy and those at the extreme end of the age scale who may be prevented from taking holidays by age and/or infirmity. There is also considerable poverty in this age range, especially amongst those who retired before 1979 and who live alone on a state pension in rented accommodation. What's more car ownership and usage declines as people age; according to the 1985 National Travel Survey non-working elderly people used their cars for holidays and day trips less frequently than younger working people.

Special Domestic Markets

Disabled Tourists

In 1989 the BTA/ETB launched their *Tourism For All* strategy which aimed to make holidaymaking easier for people with disabilities. In 1988 the Office of Population Censuses and Surveys *Survey of Disability in Great Britain* estimated that there were approximately 6.2 million over sixteen year olds (about 14% of the population) with physical or sensory disabilities, or learning difficulties. Many disabled people, especially the elderly, suffer from more than one disability.

TABLE 2 PREVALENCE OF TYPES OF DISABILITY IN THE UK IN 1988

	Adults (millions)	
Locomotion	4.3	(approx half use wheelchairs)
Reaching and stretching	1.2	
Dexterity	1.7	
Seeing	1.7	(approx. 150,000 are registered blind)
Hearing	2.6	(approx. 220,000 have severe or profound hearing loss)
Personal care (getting dressed unaided, etc)	2.5	
Intellectual functioning	1.5	
Behaviour	1.3	
Communication	1.2	

(Source: *The Disabled Visitor*, ETB Insights, 1991)

The OPCS survey suggested that about 2.7 million disabled adults take holidays in Britain. They make up almost 10% of the UK holiday market. What's more many disabled people travel with their carers or families, so there is a considerable multiplier effect. A 1982 ETB *Disabled People and Holidays Survey* suggested that the disabled are more likely than average to stay in this country, less frequently take short breaks and are more likely to opt for low season trips.

People with disabilities seem to have similar holiday aspirations to the rest of the population, although they are frequently doubly handicapped by low incomes which limit their freedom of choice. However, they often need extra information to help them decide where to go. Both the Holiday Care Service and RADAR (The Royal Association for Disability and Rehabilitation) can offer this extra help.

The following are some of the ways in which attractions, hotels, etc. can make life easier for the disabled:

* installing induction loops to amplify sound for the hard of hearing.
* providing ramps, lifts or chair-lifts alongside steps.
* edging steps in white or yellow to make them more visible.
* adapting toilets for easy disabled access and use.
* providing extra bright lighting.
* fitting wider doorways.
* fitting transport with lifts and/or wider doors for easier access.
* providing clear wheelchair access maps.
* providing detailed and accurate information about accessibility to avoid disappointment.
* providing wheelchairs and buggies for loan at attractions.
* devising special training to help all those who deal with the public take the needs of the disabled into account.

Incidentally it has been suggested that there is a large untapped market of potential disabled visitors from Europe, the USA and Canada, and Australia and New Zealand as well.

School Groups

In 1987 an ETB survey suggested that 5% of all sightseeing visits in England were made by school students. At a typical attraction school students made up between 5% and 25% of total visitor numbers. Historic buildings, art galleries and theatres in particular receive a lot of school groups, especially in late June/early July when exams are over but holidays haven't started. Since children sometimes return to attractions with their families and some teachers bring groups year after year school visits offer potential for valuable repeat business.

School visits to attractions had steadily risen since the 1944 Education Reform Act was passed. However, the 1988 Education Reform Act reasserted that education, including visits in term time, must be free. Under financial pressure, many schools had started charging for trips. As a result of the ruling many attractions, including theatres and zoos, reported a decline in school visits in 1989 although with the more practical, project-orientated GCSE exams they might have expected an increase.

Regional Breakdown of Tourism in the UK

England

In 1989 overseas visitors made 15.5 million trips to England, spending £6,300 million. In addition domestic visitors made 88.5 million trips to England, spending another £8 billion.

Overseas visitor trips were overwhelmingly concentrated in London, which received 9.9 million of the total trips and 41% of the staying visits. It also received 56% of all the tourism expenditure in 1989. In contrast 13.5 million of the domestic trips were to the West Country, with another 9 million each to London, the North West, Yorkshire and Humberside, and the Heart of England. Perhaps surprisingly the smallest number of domestic and overseas trips was to Cumbria.

Wales

In 1989 overseas tourists made 0.64 million trips, or 3% of the total, to Wales, spending approximately £118 million. UK residents made 9.5 million trips to Wales lasting 43 million nights. They are estimated to have spent £985 million. Overseas visitors represented only 6% of all staying visitors in Wales but were responsible for 10% of the expenditure.

South Wales was the most visited area of Wales in 1989, with 52 million trips. North Wales received 35 million trips. Mid Wales was the least visited area with only 14 million trips.

Scotland

In 1989 overseas tourists made 1.44 million trips, or 7% of the total, to Scotland, spending approximately £388 million. UK residents made another 10 million trips to Scotland, lasting 48.6 million nights. They are estimated to have spent £890 million. Overseas visitors represented 13.6% of all staying visitors in Scotland but were responsible for 27.4% of the expenditure. Thirty per cent of all Scotland's overseas tourists come from the USA.

The Strathclyde region was the most popular area with domestic tourists, while overseas visitors preferred Lothian. Edinburgh received about 1,500,000 domestic trips and 700,000 overseas trips. The least visited areas were the Borders, Central, Fife, and Dumfries and Galloway.

Northern Ireland

In 1989 overseas tourists made 137,000 trips, or 1% of the total, to Northern Ireland, staying for 910,000 nights. They spent approximately £26 million. In addition visitors from the British mainland made 1.5 million trips lasting 4.3 million nights. They spent nearly £165 million.

TABLE 3 OVERSEAS VISITS TO THE UK REGIONS

	Staying Visits %		Expenditure %	
	1978	**1988**	**1978**	**1988**
London	66.1	57.5	59.7	56.4
Rest of England	41.9	44.9	31.0	34.6
England	91.4	89.9	90.7	91.0
Scotland	9.7	8.6	5.8	6.2
Wales	5.2	3.7	1.8	1.6
Northern Ireland	0.8	0.4	0.5	0.4

(Numbers total more than 100 because of tours covering several areas)
(Source: ETB)

Visitors from the Irish Republic made a further 342,000 trips to the North, lasting 1,383,000 nights. They spent about £28 million. It was the first time total visitor numbers had exceeded one million since 1969. Revenue from visitors had also risen by 30% in real terms since 1988. In all in 1989 English visitors made up 43% of the visitors, Irish tourists accounted for 32% and North Americans made up only 5% of the market.

The Channel Islands

Jersey

In 1989 Jersey received 880,000 visitors, 589,000 of them between May and September when hotels reported an average 84% occupancy. This represented an increase of 5% on the 1988 figures. These visitors are estimated to have spent £270 million, a 10% increase on the 1979 figure, making tourism the second most important industry (after international finance) on the island. In 1990 80% of visitors to Jersey were from the United Kingdom.

Jersey also received 140,000 day trippers, many of them from France. In addition 8,095 yachts called into Jersey, 4,553 of them registered in France, 2,732 in the UK. Each yacht was thought to represent additional expenditure of about £310.

Guernsey

In 1989 Guernsey received about 250,000 staying visitors between April and October, an increase of 47% on the 1983 figures. Of these visitors 91% came from the UK. There has been a slight increase in the number of visitors from countries further afield, including Scandinavia, Southern Europe, North America and Australasia. Overall about £120 million was spent by Guernsey's tourists.

In 1988 13,524 yachts, 4,396 of them registered in France and 8,162 registered in England, visited Guernsey.

TABLE 4 COUNTRY OF RESIDENCE OF TOURISTS TO JERSEY, 1989

Country	Tourists
UK	732,000
France	80,000
Republic of Ireland	13,000
Germany	10,500
Sweden	10,000
Norway	7,000
Netherlands	6,000
Switzerland	4,000
Belgium	3,000
Others	14,500

(Source: Annual Report to the States, 1989)

Isle of Man

In 1990 there were 502,219 recorded passenger departures from the Isle of Man (Fig.3). However, 183,071 of these departures were by local residents. Of the other 319,148 departures, 160,040 were by visitors who had stayed in paid accommodation on the island, a marked decrease from 1985 when 243,327 visitors using paid accommodation had been recorded. Another 65,506 departures were by visitors who had been staying with friends and relatives, a figure which had increased since 1985 when only 54,323 had been staying with friends and relatives. There were 77,085 recorded business travel departures, a figure which had more than doubled since 1985. The number of day trippers has stayed remarkably stable in five years; in 1990 16,517 day tripper departures were recorded.

An increasing number of visitors (28% in 1990) are taking short breaks of between two and four nights on the island, and there are relatively fewer people staying for more than five nights. The majority of visitors come from North West England, the Republic of Ireland, South East England, Northern Ireland and the Midlands. There are very few overseas visitors to the island. Only 28% of the 1990 visitors were on package holidays.

Business travel is increasingly important to the Isle of Man; 15% of the 1990 departures were business travellers, compared with only 7% in 1985. Over 70% of business travellers spend at least one night on the island, while 27% spend a weekend there. The 1990 Passenger Survey also suggested that an increasing number of business travellers were from overseas.

FIGURE 3 ISLE OF MAN, RECORDED PASSENGER DEPARTURES

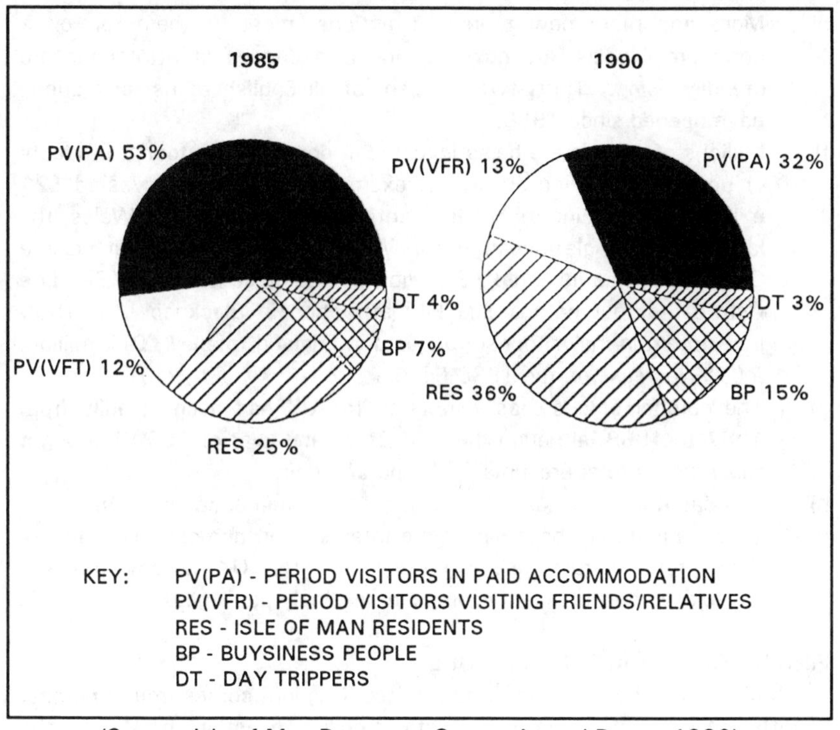

(Source: Isle of Man Passenger Survey Annual Report 1990)

Trends in Tourism in the UK 1980-1990

By 1991 the following trends in UK tourism were discernible:

a) The percentage of British adults taking a domestic holiday has fallen steadily since 1975, reflecting the increasing popularity of holidays overseas. In particular more young people, people from the AB socio-economic groups and residents of South East England are holidaying abroad.

b) Domestic holidaymakers are taking fewer long holidays of four nights or more in England. (The number had fallen by more than 20% in the 1980s.)

c) The overall number of short holidays of up to three nights taken by domestic holidaymakers in England remains static. However, the number of short breaks taken in commercial accommodation as opposed to staying with friends or relations is growing steadily.

d) Expenditure on short holidays is growing in real terms, while expenditure on long holidays is falling.

e) More and more new tourist attractions, most of them run on a commercial basis, are opening, and attendances at attractions are steadily rising. Thirty-two per cent of all English tourist attractions have opened since 1980.

f) Millions of pounds are being invested in opening new tourist products or upgrading existing ones. For example, Butlin's has invested £21 million in up-grading its holiday centre at Pwllheli in North Wales, the largest ever single investment in Welsh tourism, while First Leisure Corporation has invested £3 million in a joint venture with Sea Life Centre Ltd to create a Sea Life attraction in Blackpool. In 1989 investment in major tourism projects in England totalled £972 million, a 61% increase on the 1988 figure.

g) The number of overseas visitors to the UK had risen steadily from 1987 to 1989, although the Gulf Crisis and War of 1990/1 brought this process to a, presumably temporary, halt.

h) Self-catering is increasingly popular for long domestic holidays.

i) Travel agents are becoming more interested in domestic holidays as their profit margins are squeezed and the UK holiday product, especially short breaks, becomes increasingly packaged.

FINDING OUT ABOUT THE VISITORS

Information about tourism in the United Kingdom comes from a number of different sources. Some of the data is collected within the UK, by the regional tourist boards, conservation groups, etc. Some of it is collected on a worldwide basis by the **World Tourism Organisation (WTO)** and the **Organisation for Economic Co-operation and Development (OECD)**. Where different organisations are involved in collecting broadly similar information their different collection methods may lead to slightly different results. The statistical base on which many conclusions about tourism are placed is sometimes also alarmingly narrow.

When using the statistics it is important to understand the precise meaning being given to terms like 'tourist trips', 'nights', 'stays', etc.

The British National Tourist Boards, the World Tourism Organisation and the Organisation for Economic Co-operation and Development all define a *tourist trip* as a stay of one or more nights away from home for a holiday, visiting friends or relatives, business, attending a conference or any other purpose except boarding education or semi-permanent employment. *Tourist nights* are nights spent away from home on tourist trips, staying in any type of accommodation. *Tourist expenditure* is money spent while away from home on a tourist trip, and advance payment for things like fares and accommodation; expenditure by the tourist on other people (e.g. children) will be counted, but hire purchase or interest payments on equipment won't be.

Holidays are those tourist trips described by the participants as holidays, together with visits to friends and relatives mainly thought of as holidays by the visitor. *Leisure day trips* start and end at the same place on the same day, are of at least three hours' duration and take place entirely within Great Britain (journeys to work or for shopping are excluded).

International Passenger Survey (IPS)

This survey of tourism into and within the UK is carried out on a quarterly basis by the Department of Employment. It assesses the number of *visitor trips* and *nights* spent in Great Britain as a whole by questioning people departing from the UK. Data is collected at all four Heathrow terminals, at Gatwick and Manchester airports, and at Southampton, Tilbury and Dover ports by questioning a random sample of people crossing a specific line. About 182,000 people a year are questioned. The IPS also collects data on tourism expenditure; where the passenger has visited several countries their expenditure is attributed to the country where they spent most of the time. Difficulties can arise when a respondent's grasp of English is not good enough to answer the questions accurately. Figures are published on a quarterly and yearly basis.

Overseas Visitor Survey

Every year the British Tourist Authority supplements the IPS with its own survey which collects data on what visitors to the UK think about their trips amongst other topics.

United Kingdom Tourism Survey (UKTS)

Since 1989 the English, Scottish, Wales and Northern Ireland Tourist Boards have been collecting and publishing data on domestic tourism as a single, regionally consistent survey. UKTS measures the volume and value of domestic tourism trips involving at least one overnight stay on a national and regional level. It contains information on the following topics:

* the purpose of the trip
* the month of the trip
* the amount spent in total and by category
* the mode of transport
* activities undertaken during the stay
* any inclusive tours taken
* the duration of the stay
* the party size and its composition
* the country, region and place of destination
* the type of accommodation
* any use made of the travel trade
* any trips by unaccompanied children

Information is collected on a monthly basis and published yearly. The data comes from a random monthly sample of UK residents living in 540 constituencies. Every fifteenth name is picked from the electoral roll; people are then visited at home and interviewed about all domestic trips involving an overnight stay that they have taken in the previous two months. In a year about 80,000 residents are interviewed. However, this means that in a local authority area containing five constituencies only seventy-five people per constituency are being questioned each month.

In 1989 UKTS replaced the British Tourism Survey Monthly (BTSM) which had been collecting and publishing similar information since 1972. Because of the change in the way that statistics are collected, 1989 must now be taken as the starting point for accurate calculation of trends.

Leisure Day Visits Survey (LDVS)

From April 1988 to March 1989 the Department of Employment and the British Tourist Authority undertook a joint survey of all trips away from home of between three and twenty-four hours that interviewees had taken in the previous two weeks.

English Hotel Occupancy Surveys (EHOS)

These surveys are carried out on behalf of the different regional tourist boards by Howarth and Howarth. They collate confidential monthly reports from 550 hotels (fewer in winter when some hotels are closed) on room and bed occupancy, guests' average length of stay and the number of overseas visitors. The hotels selected are spread over twelve regions and all tariff levels which means that only fifteen hotels per tariff level in each region may be investigated each month. Data is published yearly.

British National Travel Survey (BNTS)

This periodic survey, commissioned by the BTA, investigates the travel patterns of 10,000 randomly selected British households. Data is collected by means of an interview and through a diary in which respondents are asked to record all the travel they undertake in a week. Interviewees are also asked about all domestic holidays of four nights or more that they have taken in the previous twelve months. The most recent National Travel Survey was conducted in 1985/6.

ETB Market Outlook Survey

Since 1987 the ETB has been carrying out telephone surveys of commercial holiday companies, hotel groups, holiday centres, agents for holiday homes, resort tourism officers and other interested parties to ascertain the forward booking situation for UK holidays, recent trends, etc.

Findings from the survey are published in the quarterly ETB publication, *Insights*.

Holiday Intentions Survey

Every Easter the ETB also conducts an annual survey of British adults' holiday plans. Although this survey helps with assessing likely trends it suffers from the drawback that it asks about 'intentions' rather than confirmed events; some people who say they intend to take a holiday may not actually do so, while others who did not plan to holiday may change their plans at the last moment.

Visitor Attractions Surveys

Each of the National Tourist Boards carries out an annual survey of attendances at attractions in its region. The different tourist boards all categorise attractions in slightly different ways. For example, the Wales Tourist Board collates statistics on theme and leisure parks and on preserved railways in separate categories, while the English Tourist Board lumps them together in a 'miscellaneous' category. This makes drawing direct comparisons between different regions difficult.

The States of Guernsey Tourist Board conducted detailed surveys of departing passengers in 1983 and 1989. The Finance and Economics Committee of Jersey also publishes detailed data on the number of visitors to the island collected from several different sources including the States Tourism Department. Since 1985 the Economic Affairs Department of the Isle of Man Treasury has been conducting a systematic *Isle of Man Passenger Survey* by interviewing passengers departing from Douglas Harbour and Ronaldsway Airport.

In addition to these regular surveys and sources of information the Regional Tourist Boards all carry out their own surveys, particularly about visits to local attractions. Every year each ETB region publishes **Tourism Fact Sheets** which contain detailed information about visitors to their particular area. The ETB also publishes the **English Heritage Monitor** which summarises information about visits to architectural and historic attractions and highlights relevant trends.

Why People Visit the UK

Overseas Visitors

According to the International Passenger Survey 7,237,000 overseas visitors came to the UK for *holidays* in 1989. Of these visitors 2,009,000 came on organised inclusive holidays while 5,228,000 were independent visitors. The number of independent travellers had risen by 15% since 1988, while the number of holidaymakers on inclusive packages had fallen by 4% in line with a general trend towards more independent holidays.

A further 4,323,000 overseas visitors came here on *business trips*, while 3,471,000 were *visiting friends or relatives*. Students and people coming to Britain to attend sporting events, go shopping or for medical treatment made up another 2,173,000 visitors, an increase of 16% since 1988. The number of people coming to Britain for business reasons has been rising by an average 6% a year since 1980, which is important since these visitors tend to generate the largest amount of income.

TABLE 5 THE MOST ENJOYABLE FEATURES OF A VISIT TO BRITAIN, 1977-1988

	1977	1988
The people	32	30
The countryside	17	15
Visiting historic places	15	6
Museums/art galleries	11	8
Theatres/concerts	7	5
Parks	5	5
Shopping	11	7
Sightseeing generally	6	5
Ease of travel	4	8
The pubs	4	5
No answer	18	17

(Numbers total more than 100 because some people cited more than one feature.)
(Source: Digest of Tourist Statistics)

Relatively few visitors (14%) to Northern Ireland go there for true 'holidays'. However, in 1989, which was an exceptionally good year for tourism in the province, this was the area of the UK which showed the biggest percentage increase.

When the West Country carried out a survey to discover why visitors came to their region the two main reasons cited were 'plenty of places of interest and heritage attractions to visit' and 'good area for touring holiday by car'. Table 5 summarises what overseas visitors in general find appealing about the UK as a holiday destination

In 1988 82% of overseas visitors to Scotland cited the scenery as what they liked best about their holiday, 67% cited the friendly people and 61% the castles, churches, museums and sites of historic interest. Forty-three per cent of all overseas visitors declined to mention anything they had 'disliked' (Table 6).

TABLE 6 WHAT OVERSEAS VISITORS LIKED/DISLIKED ABOUT SCOTTISH HOLIDAYS, 1988

Liked	Western Europeans	North Americans	All
	%	%	%
Scenery	73	88	82
Friendly people	63	76	67
Historic buildings	52	74	61
Peace and quiet	39	31	36
Wildlife	49	20	34
Range/quality of accommodation	27	30	28
Good food and drink	18	27	24
Disliked			
Poor weather	29	19	26
Difficulty travelling around	6	12	11
Poor quality food	11	9	9
Lack of wet weather facilities	10	3	8
Poor quality accommodation	2	3	3
No dislikes mentioned	40	57	43

(Source: Scottish Tourist Board, 1990)

The West Country Tourist Board survey suggested that additional visitors might be attracted if there were more all-weather facilities, more budget hotels, more accommodation with on-site leisure facilities, and better car parking and transport facilities. A London Tourist Board survey of visitor likes and dislikes also discovered that many tourists were upset by the amount of litter in the streets.

Domestic Visitors

In 1989 the United Kingdom Tourism Survey suggested that 59% of all British residents spending one night or more away from home were on *holiday*. A further 23% were *visiting friends or relatives.* Thirteen per cent were travelling on *business*. The other 5% were travelling for a variety of reasons to do with studying, their health, etc (Fig.4).

When UK Holidays Take Place

The 1989 International Passenger Survey showed that the majority of overseas visitors (35%) come to the UK in the third quarter (July-September) of the year when the temperature is likely to be highest and when most European schools and colleges close for holidays. Of a total

17.2 million visits, 5,957,000 of them took place in the third quarter and another 4,129,000 in the second (April-June). Only 3,344,000 visits took place in January, February and March.

FIGURE 4 DOMESTIC TOURIST TRIPS IN THE UK, 1989

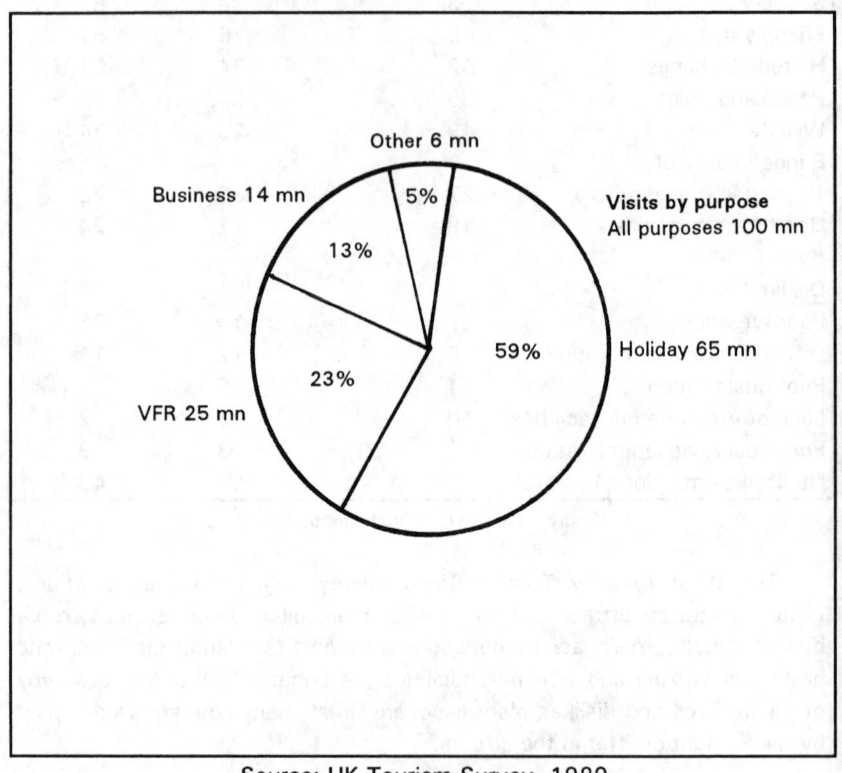

Source: UK Tourism Survey, 1989

In 1989 UKTS showed that 33% of domestic holidaymakers took their main holidays between July and September, 27% between April and June, 18% between October and December and 15% between January and March. Domestic short break holidays are more evenly spread throughout the year with only 29% taking place between July and September.

Business visits are also more evenly spread throughout the year; in 1989 there were 1,177,000 visits in the fourth quarter, 1,113,000 in the second and 1,071,000 in the third.

Only 7% of all visitors to Northern Ireland visit between January and March. The quietest months in Wales are from November to February, while in Scotland they are from January to March.

How Long Visitors Stay

Overseas Visitors

The 1988 International Passenger Survey suggested that the further a visitor has had to travel to reach the UK, the longer they are likely to stay. Thus visitors from France stayed for an average 7.1 days, while those from Canada stayed 13.6 days, those from the Middle East 17.4 days and those from New Zealand 30.1 days. The average European visitor stayed for 9.2 days, while the average visitor from the rest of the world stayed for 14.5 days. The overall average length of stay for all visitors was 10.9 days. Exceptionally, Japanese visitors only stay for an average 6.5 days, 2.6 of them generally in London.

FIGURE 5 DISTANCES TRAVELLED BY SHORT BREAK TAKERS

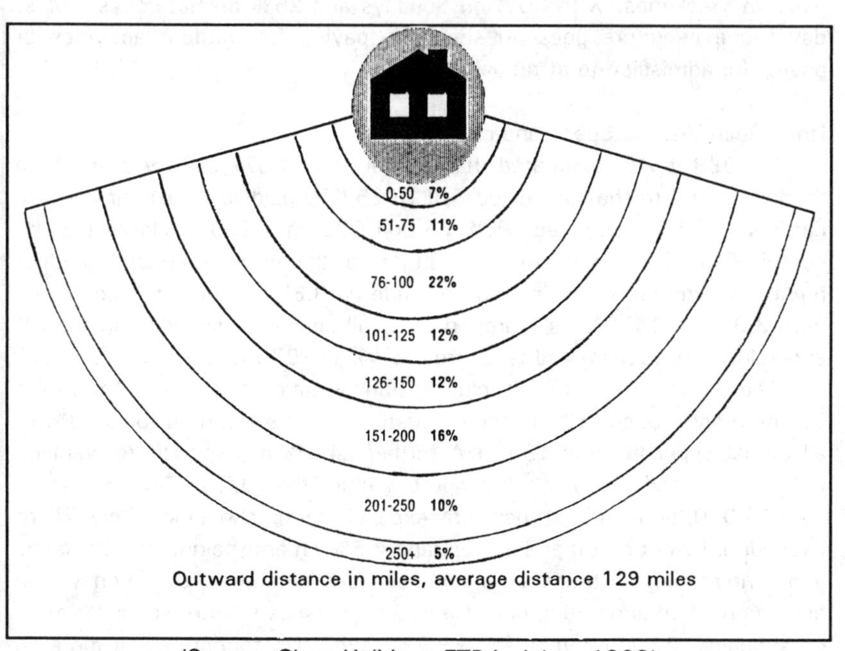

(Source: *Short Holidays*, ETB Insights, 1989)

Domestic Visitors

The United Kingdom Tourism Survey produces a different picture for domestic tourism, with short holidays of less than one week's duration making up an increasing proportion of the market. Thus the average domestic trip within the UK in 1989 lasted for only 4.1 days, with the shortest stays in England (4 days) and the longest in Scotland (4.9 days).

This is a marked change from the 1960s when many families took their annual two week break in the UK and has led to an increased interest in marketing special short break holidays, especially to the cities. Most short breaks are also taken relatively close to home. Fig.6 shows the distances from home people are prepared to travel for stays of one to three nights.

Day Trips

The 1989 Leisure Day Visits Survey suggested that the average domestic day tripper travels 68.4 miles to their destination, with inland destinations proving far more popular than coastal resorts. Eighty per cent of day trippers use private motorised transport to reach their destination, 5% use trains or the London Underground, 4% use coaches and 3% buses. Most people travel to take part in outdoor activities, to visit friends or relatives or to visit a tourist attraction. More than 50% of all day trips take place at weekends, with 30% on Sundays and 25% on Saturdays. Most day trip expenditure goes on shopping, paying for outdoor activities or paying for admission to attractions.

How Much Visitors Spend and on What

In 1989 it was estimated that a total of £19,377,000 was spent on tourism in and to the UK (including £1,625,000 paid to British air and sea carriers). This compared with £5,601,000 in 1970. However, the contribution of UK tourism expenditure to the gross domestic product remained fairly constant; in 1989 it made up 3.8% of the total, compared with 3.9% in 1970. As a proportion of all consumer spending in the UK expenditure on tourism had fallen from 6.4% in 1970 to 6% in 1989.

The biggest single item (excluding transportation costs to and from the UK) on most tourists' bill is accommodation which accounted for 31.8% of all tourist expenditure in 1989. A further 24.3% of expenditure went on eating out, and 19% on transport within the UK. Tourists spent £2,919,000, or 16.4% of their total expenditure, on shopping. Only 4% of expenditure went on other services, and 4.5% on entertainment. Domestic and international tourists spent similar amounts of money on accommodation and eating out. However, overseas visitors spent far more on shopping (27.1% compared to 9.7%), while UK tourists spent more on internal transport getting to other parts of the country than foreign visitors who often stay fairly close to their arrival point.

In 1989 the average overseas visitor spent £37 a day or £397 a trip. At current prices this was more than in 1988, but when inflation is taken into account the amount has actually fallen and was at its lowest real level for ten years. Some nationalities tend to spend more than others; the Japanese are particularly noted as high spenders (£75 a day or £488 a trip on average). Business travellers also spend conspicuously more than average (£85 a day or £465 a trip), while those visiting friends and relatives spend relatively little (£20 a day or £300 a trip).

The 1990 Isle of Man Passenger Survey showed that on average each visitor arriving by air and staying in paid accommodation had spent £257, while those arriving by sea spent an average £243. The average per head expenditure of those visiting friends and relatives was £130, while business travellers spent an average £232.

FUNDING FOR UK TOURISM

In the UK much of the funding for specific tourism developments like hotels, holiday camps and theme parks has come from the private sector. Private sector organisations may have adequate capital reserves to fund new projects, or may raise more capital through a new share issue. Failing that, they may be able to secure a loan from one of the clearing banks, merchant banks, building societies or insurance companies.

However, central and local government funding also supports some tourism ventures. Fig.6 shows how central government funds filter down to tourism projects through four different departments and several statutory agencies.

FIGURE 6 GOVERNMENT PROVISION OF FUNDING FOR TOURISM AND LEISURE THROUGH GOVERNMENT DEPARTMENTS AND STATUTORY AGENCIES

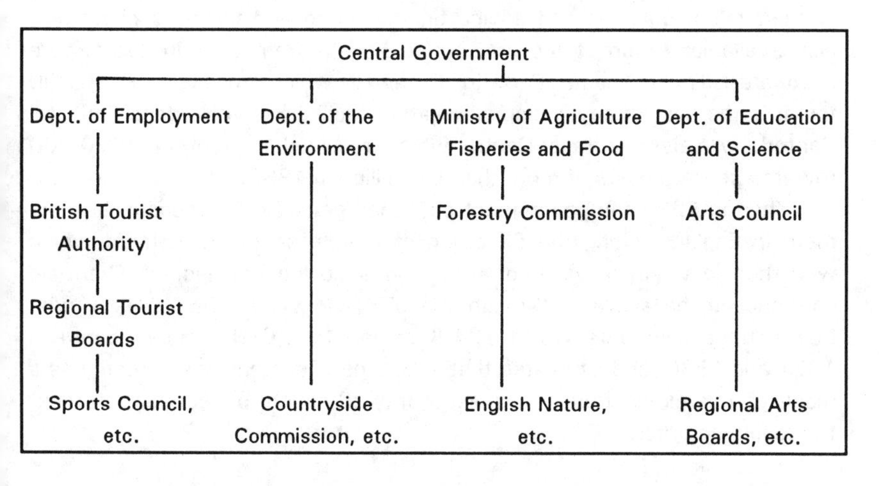

In the late 1980s a characteristic of tourism funding was the increasing emphasis on sponsorship as both central and local government attempted to reduce public expenditure on tourism and leisure. Businesses (and to a lesser extent individuals) were asked to sponsor everything from gates at the Wildfowl and Wetlands Trust, to theatre productions and art exhibitions. However, the recession of the early 1990s made such deals harder to arrange.

The cost of some tourism developments is so great that the public and private sectors need to work together to fund them. This is particularly the case in areas which have not traditionally been attractive to tourists where private developers may require incentives before agreeing to invest large sums.

Tourism Funding from within the UK

Section 4 Funding

Section 4 of the 1969 Development of Tourism Act (see Chapter Five) enabled the national tourist boards to administer funds to develop tourism projects in their area. In the first eight months of 1988 the ETB alone provided £8.5 million worth of assistance to 359 projects through this Tourism Grants Scheme. In 1983 a new four-year programme of grants throughout the UK made £47 million available to generate public and private sector investment in tourism of about £360 million. In 1987 a new five-year development plan, *Vision for England*, was launched. By the end of 1988 a further £21 million of Section 4 funding had generated about £167 million of other investment, creating approximately 13,500 new jobs. Section 4 funding was provided in the form of grants, loans, repayable grants and interest relief, but help and advice on marketing and business plans was also available. Amongst the projects to benefit from Section 4 aid were Flambards Triple Theme Park in Cornwall which received £190,000 towards the cost of developing all-weather facilities, and Heritage Projects' Canterbury Tales Heritage Centre which received a grant of £120,000 towards start-up costs of more than £1 million in 1988.

Then in 1989 the government abolished grant-aid for tourism development in England, citing the £2 billion of private sector investment which was then in progress as proof that it was no longer needed. Grant-aid continues to be available through the STB and WTB. The Wales Tourist Board made payments worth £34.8 million to 1,653 projects between 1971 and 1990, and estimated that 7,176 new jobs had been created as a result of this expenditure. It gives priority to capital projects which meet the following criteria:

a) the end products will be available to the general public
b) they will be likely to attract domestic and overseas visitors to Wales
c) they will provide full-time employment opportunities

d) they will help extend the tourism season
e) they will enhance the range and quality of local tourism amenities
f) they will provide significant benefit to the community in terms of income and job creation, improving the local infrastructure and preserving local landscapes
g) they will be of good standard and design
h) they will have sound marketing potential
i) they are viable projects in their own right

With limited resources available to it, the WTB also prioritises specific areas and fields. So in 1991 its grants focused on major new tourist attractions, activity centres (where it hopes to establish Wales as a market leader), hotels large enough to accommodate whole coach parties, upmarket country house hotels, quality caravan parks and large, all year round holiday villages.

In Northern Ireland public sector tourist projects may be eligible for grants from the Department of Economic Development as a result of Part III of the Development of Tourist Traffic Act. Grants to public sector attractions may also be available through the International Fund for Ireland Tourist Amenity Development Scheme. In both cases the NITB advises on the suitability of applications.

Tourism Development Action Programmes (TDAPs)

In the 1980s the ETB also provided money through three year Tourist Development Action Programmes in areas which were thought suitable for intensive development (Fig.7). By 1990 twenty such TDAPS had been created, although some of the older ones had come to the end of their life. The TDAPS were in 'heritage' towns (Lancaster, Nottingham, Carlisle, Norwich), seaside resorts (Bridlington, Torbay), rural areas (Exmoor, Kielder, the Forest of Dean, Shropshire, the North Pennines), combined rural and traditional areas (East Kent, the Isle of Wight, Cornwall) and industrial/maritime heritage centres (Bristol, Bradford, Portsmouth, Cleveland, Leicester, Tyne and Wear). The sums of money invested by the ETB were not large; typically Cleveland received £350,000. However, they were intended to encourage others to contribute more generously by giving projects a seal of approval. In 1991 a new TDAP was created around the seaside resort of Weston-super-Mare.

TDAPs attempt to bring together public and private sector brains and funding in short, sharp bursts of activity to kick-start tourism projects into action. The TDAP set up in East Kent was typical in bringing together all the following organisations: Ashford, Canterbury, Dover and Thanet local authorities; Kent County Council; the ETB; the South East Tourist Board;

British Rail; Sally Line; Dover Harbour Board; Eurotunnel; English Heritage; British Telecom; and Shepherd Neame Breweries. They concentrated their efforts on East Kent's maritime traditions and on developing heritage trails, etc. Carlisle's TDAP has resulted in better car parking facilities, two new coach pick up and set down points on the edge of the historic city centre, an improved Tourist Information Centre and the opening of Tullie House as a new tourist attraction.

FIGURE 7 TOURISM DEVELOPMENT ACTION PROGRAMMES IN ENGLAND, 1990

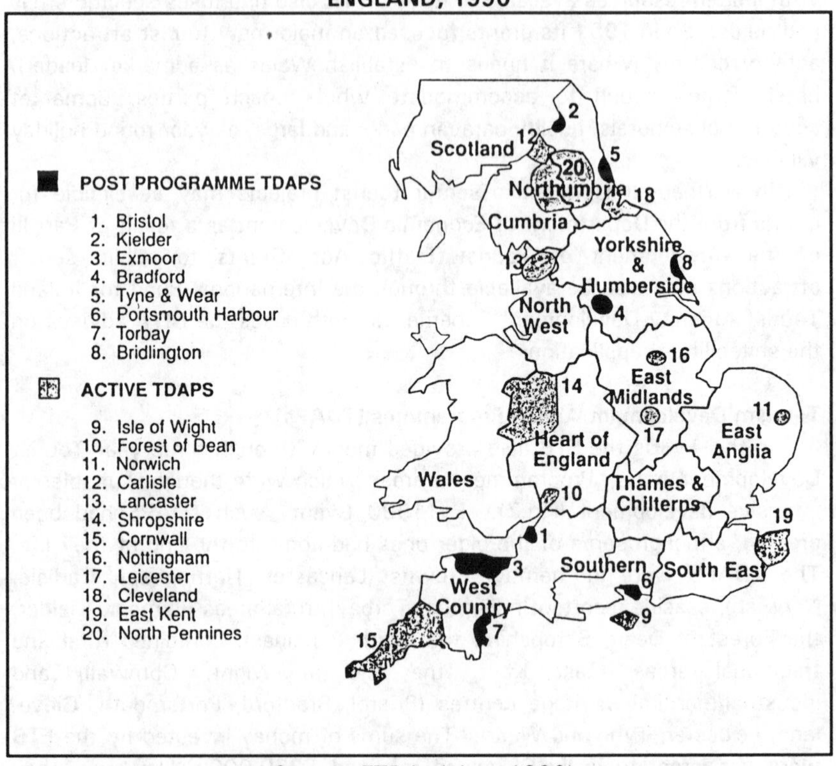

(Source: ETB Insights, 1990)

Tourism Action Plans (TAPs)

Tourism Action Plans involve several different local authorities working together to boost tourism in a particular area which is seen as undervisited. In 1989 the East Lancashire councils of Blackburn, Burnley, Hyndburn, Ribble Valley, Ravendale and Pendle got together to develop the concept of 'Lancashire's Hill Country'. In 1990 there were also TAPs in London Docklands and the Eden area of Cumbria.

Strategic Development Initiatives

Since 1985 local authorities have also entered into partnerships with private industry to boost funding for tourism development through concentrated, well-targeted projects chosen to capitalise on each area's potential. These Strategic Development Initiatives have been set up in Leeds, Manchester, Liverpool, Sheffield, Cleveland, Leicester, Nottingham, Plymouth, Carlisle and Lancaster. In Manchester in 1990 Salford, Trafford and Manchester district councils and Central Manchester and Trafford Park Development Corporations were working together on an SDI in the Castlefield area of the city.

Urban Development Corporations (UDCs)

In the 1980s Urban Development Corporations were set up to regenerate run-down inner city areas of Britain. Although tourism development was not an essential part of their remit, for most of them it soon became part of a strategy to bring new jobs and services to the designated areas.

The UDCs have been set up in three bursts and have operated in London Docklands (1980), Merseyside (1982), Central Manchester, Trafford Park, Teesside, Tyne and Wear, the Black Country and Cardiff Bay (1987), Sheffield (1988) and Bristol (1989). They usually run for between five and ten years, have budgets ranging from £15- to £160 million and have far-reaching powers to override local planning procedures in the interests of getting a lot done in a short period of time.

Tourism Funding from the European Community (EC)

European Community grants are sometimes available to help tourism development projects in under-developed or deprived areas of the Community or areas of high unemployment. Only areas which fit into tightly defined categories are eligible. The money is usually aimed at programmes of action rather than at individual projects. **The European Social Fund (ESF)** administers funds to pay for vocational training improvements; Wigan Pier Heritage Centre was helped with an ESF grant. **The European Agricultural Guidance and Guarantee Fund (EAGGF)** administers funds which can be used to help develop rural tourism through undertaking marketing studies, paying for the restoration of places of interest, and implementing programmes to encourage off-peak tourism. The **European Investment Bank** also provides general purpose loans (it loaned 100 million Ecus towards the cost of the second terminal at Stansted Airport), while the **European Coal and Steel Community** provides loans to create new jobs in areas hit by the closure of coal mines and steel factories.

The European Regional Development Fund (ERDF)

The ERDF administers funds for infrastructural developments. These may not amount to more than 75% of the total programme cost and are almost exclusively paid to public sector organisations. The ERDF can also supply backing for employment and tourist-related projects. In 1989 it is estimated to have contributed £386 million in grants to the UK. The National Fishing Heritage Centre in Grimsby, Wigan Pier Heritage Centre and Bradford's Alhambra Theatre have all received grants from the ERDF.

Tourism projects in Glasgow/Greenock, Fife, Middlesbrough/Langbaurgh, Tyne and Wear, and Plymouth are eligible for assistance through the ERDF RENAVAL programme to help areas hit by the collapse of shipbuilding. Northern Ireland and Kent are also eligible for grant-aid through the INTERREG programme to help develop tourism in border areas.

TOURISM IN THE UK AND THE TRAVEL TRADE

Although travel agencies have always handled bookings for car ferries, domestic flights and car hire arrangements, traditionally holidaymaking in the UK has been unpackaged. Package arrangements to the Channel Islands developed quickly, as did organised coach tours with companies like Wallace Arnold, but most other domestic holidaymakers tended to make their own reservations direct with the principals concerned. In the 1980s this situation started to change as some of those charged with developing domestic tourism began to appreciate the potential of selling holidays through Britain's 7,500 travel agencies. Because of the low levels of commission they earn on what can be quite complicated arrangements few agencies are interested in selling unpackaged domestic holiday arrangements. So creating packages inclusive of accommodation and transport was a first step to getting domestic holiday brochures on the racks. The Golden Rail packages were some of the first of the new range of packaged domestic holidays. Others available include Highlife Value Breaks, Rainbow Holidays and Shortbreaks, Shearings Holidays and Superbreak Mini Holidays. Companies like Hoseasons Holidays have been very successful in getting their brochures onto agency racks. Nevertheless, in 1989 UK holidays still only accounted for 5% of the average travel agent's business.

For smaller operators to produce their own brochures and pay commission direct to travel agents would not be realistic. Instead some of them, particularly the larger, city-based hotels, have made use of consortia like Stardust Holidays, despite the loss of individual identity involved in being packaged under a brand name. However, Victor Middleton has questioned whether the smallest operations are well-advised to turn to travel agents unless they have exhausted all other possible methods of direct marketing because of the increase in marketing costs this entails. Procter Naylor of the East Anglia Tourist Board has pointed out that there is also little that travel agents can do for domestic holidaymakers that they could not do just as well, or better, for themselves. This is not necessarily the case when it comes to overseas holidays.

Almost all the domestic tour operators are specialists of one kind or another. They may specialise in one region (the Channel Islands), one type of holiday (coach tours) or one type of product (city breaks or boating holidays). However, some diversification is taking place among the longer established companies. Hoseasons Holidays which started out offering just boating holidays now has a *Lodges, Cottages, Chalets and Caravans in Britain* brochure. Some companies like Wallace Arnold are members of ABTA. Others belong to more specialist trade associations like CITOG, the Channel Islands Tour Operators' Group. Others belong to no trade associations at all.

To meet the expectations of modern clients and to offer quicker and more efficient reservations services, some of the domestic tour operators have introduced computerised booking systems. Hoseasons Holidays, for example, has a Viewdata booking system which can be accessed by the 3000 travel agents stocking its brochure.

In the late 1980s accommodation providers like Butlin's also began to appreciate the advantages of using travel agencies. The Butlin's brochure was revamped and relaunched, and 55% of bookings are now made through agents rather than directly to the holiday centres. Many short break packages have now been put together by UK hoteliers in an effort to boost off-peak and weekend bookings.

Most overseas visitors to the UK also make their arrangements independently; in 1988 only 13% of overseas visitors arrived on an inclusive holiday compared with 29% who were holidaying independently. However, some groups of overseas visitors are more likely to take package holidays; for example, in 1988 38% of Japanese visitors arrived on inclusive holiday arrangements, compared with only 22% who were holidaying independently.

There are roughly 300 incoming tour operators who specialise in dealing with the overseas tourist market. Some are little more than handling agents, providing a 'meet and greet' and escort service for overseas tourists. Others put together proper package holidays, including special interest tours. Yet others concentrate on selling to specific markets where they can build up an expertise: Japanese visitors, for example.

Many incoming tour operators belong to the British Incoming Tour

Operators Association (BITOA), founded in 1977. BITOA has the following objectives:

a) to improve the quality of service provided, and to encourage the maintenance of a high standard of facilities by all providers of tourism services.
b) to develop and uphold a generally accepted code of conduct in the supply of services by members.
c) to establish and maintain a recognised status for members, by informing the travel industry, the British government and associated agencies, and the public of activities and objectives of members.
d) to provide a forum for the exchange of ideas and information relevant to members' activities.
e) to provide members with an opportunity to express a corporate voice on matters of common interest e.g on the exchange rate which can create the impression that the UK is an expensive holiday destination, and on the forthcoming EC Package Travel Directive which will make tour operators responsible for many more aspects of their packages than at present.

Associate membership of BITOA is open to the following: accommodation providers, arts and leisure providers, conference venues, ecclesiastical foundations, restaurants and caterers, services like printers and language schools, shops and stores, tourist boards/organisations, tourist attractions and transport providers.

Unlike the names of outgoing tour operators, the names of incoming tour operators are rarely well-known names. The following are some of the UK's incoming tour operators who are also members of BITOA:

American Express Europe Ltd
British Heritage Tours
CIE Tours International (UK) Ltd
CIT (England) Ltd
Destination Scotland Ltd
Eurowales Ltd (City Travel Ltd)
Evans Evans Tours Ltd
Frames Tours
Galleon Tours Ltd
Insight International Tours Ltd
Japan Travel Bureau (UK) Ltd
Kuoni Travel Ltd
Latin Travel Ltd
London Handling Ltd
Musgrove and Watson Travel Ltd
Northern Welcome (CWS Travel Group)
Panita Travel Ltd
Pilgrim's Progress Tours
P & O Travel Ltd
Quo Vadis Ltd
Reliance Tours (UK) Ltd
Sovereign Tourism
Spectra Travel Ltd
Supertravel Ltd
Swinards UK Ltd
Tailor Made Tours
Take-A-Guide Ltd
Tanners International
Travel Scotland Group
Wedgewood Travel Ltd

CHAPTER TWO
TOURIST GEOGRAPHY OF THE UNITED KINGDOM

The United Kingdom consists of four separate countries: England, Scotland, Wales and Northern Ireland. Since local government reorganisation in 1974 England has been divided into 45 counties, Scotland into twelve, Wales into eight and Northern Ireland into six (Fig.8). The Republic of Ireland, or Eire, while a geographical part of the British Isles, is an independent country.

FIGURE 8 ENGLAND, SCOTLAND, WALES AND NORTHERN IRELAND

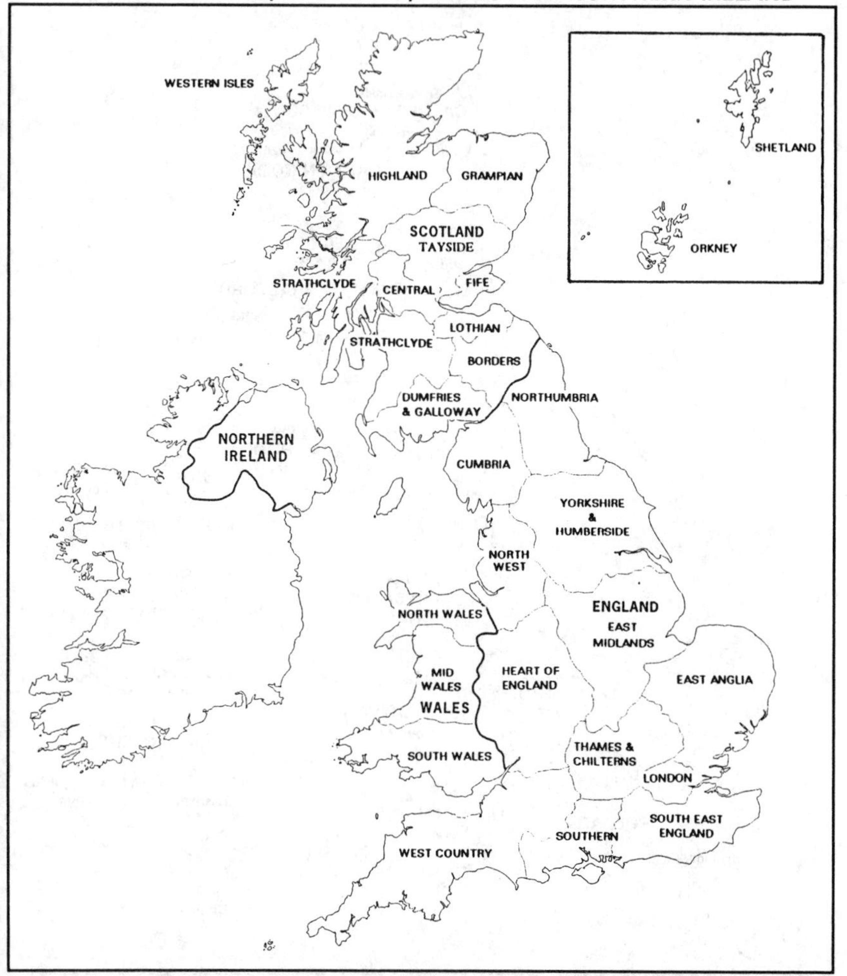

For the purpose of tourism promotion the counties of the United Kingdom are grouped together into different Regional Tourist Boards under the overall supervision of the English Tourist Board (ETB), Scottish Tourist Board (STB), Wales Tourist Board (WTB) and Northern Ireland Tourist Board (NITB). Jersey, Guernsey and the Isle of Man have independent tourist boards. During the 1980s the Regional Tourist Boards promoted the UK by creating a number of different 'country' themes (Fig.9).

FIGURE 9 THE 'COUNTRIES' OF ENGLAND

ENGLAND

London is by far the most popular destination with overseas tourists and received 9.5 million visitors in 1989. Eighty per cent of all overseas visitors to the UK arrive in London and two thirds of visitors stay in the capital. Almost 57% of all tourist visits in the UK are to London, and almost 41% of bed nights are passed in the capital. Just over 58% of all UK tourism expenditure takes place in London.

Next in popularity with overseas visitors in 1989 were the South East (1.9 million), West Country and Heart of England (1.3 million) and Thames and Chilterns (1.25 million) areas. The South East and Thames and Chilterns regions obviously benefit from their proximity to the capital (Table 7).

Domestic visitors prefer the West Country; in 1989 it received 13.5 million domestic visitors, compared with the 9 million received by London, the North West, Heart of England, and Yorkshire and Humberside. In contrast Cumbria received only 3 million domestic visitors and 0.24 million overseas visitors (Table 7).

TABLE 7 REGIONAL DISTRIBUTION OF UK TOURISTS, 1989

	UK residents		Overseas visitors	
Millions	Trips	Spending	Trips	Spending
Cumbria	3	£ 265	0.24	£ 35
Northumbria	4	£ 260	0.32	£ 86
North West	9	£ 855	1.01	£ 215
Yorks & H'side	9	£ 840	0.82	£ 154
Heart of England	9	£ 575	1.28	£ 277
East Midlands	7	£ 460	0.60	£ 119
Thames & Chilterns	6	£ 320	1.25	£ 317
East Anglia	8.5	£ 655	0.86	£ 206
London	9	£ 765	9.87	£ 4015
West Country	13.5	£ 1790	1.28	£ 269
South	6.5	£ 670	0.74	£ 179
South East	8	£ 565	1.88	£ 416
ENGLAND	88.5	£ 8020	15.48	£ 6308
N. IRELAND	1.5	£ 165	0.07	£ 26
SCOTLAND	10	£ 890	1.44	£ 388
WALES	9.5	£ 985	0.64	£ 118
UK	109.5	£10,865	17.3	£ 6,945

(Source: BTA)

London

As the UK's capital, London has the highest concentration of world-class museums, art galleries and other historic attractions. It is also home to the Royal Family and to the Houses of Parliament, both big tourist attractions in their own right. London also has more theatres than other British cities and is the base for many of the country's world-class orchestras, opera companies, dance troupes, etc. Although many of its attractions are long established and historical, new ones are still opening. Two recent success stories are the Museum of the Moving Image on the South Bank and Rock Circus in Piccadilly.

Most transport systems converge on London, which is the most easily accessible place in the UK.

Although London is one of the world's largest cities, tourist activity is concentrated within a relatively small part of it, particularly in the one square mile of the City of London, and in Westminster. However, tourism spills over into some of the other more attractive central boroughs, like Kensington and Chelsea, and into some of the leafier suburbs like Kew, Richmond, Hampstead, Wimbledon and Greenwich. The recent redevelopment of the East London docks will bring more tourists to that area too.

Although London is very built-up it does have many parks, including the Royal Parks, and other attractive open areas like Wimbledon Common and Hampstead Heath. The River Thames runs through the centre; until recently the river's tourism potential had barely been tapped but now the Port of London Authority is working to promote its use.

London has three cathedrals: St. Paul's, Southwark and Westminster. Westminster Abbey and Palace, and the Tower of London are designated *World Heritage Sites.*

TABLE 8 LONDON'S MOST VISITED ATTRACTIONS IN 1989

	Visitor Nos. (millions)
1. British Museum	4.4
2. National Gallery	3.4
3. Westminster Abbey	*3.25
4. Madame Tussaud's	2.6
5. St. Paul's Cathedral	*2.5
6. Tower of London	2.2
7. Natural History Museum	1.6
8. Tate Gallery	1.2
9. Chessington World of Adventures	1.2
10. London Zoo	1.2

(* approximate number)

(Source: London Tourist Board)

FIGURE 10 SOUTH EAST ENGLAND

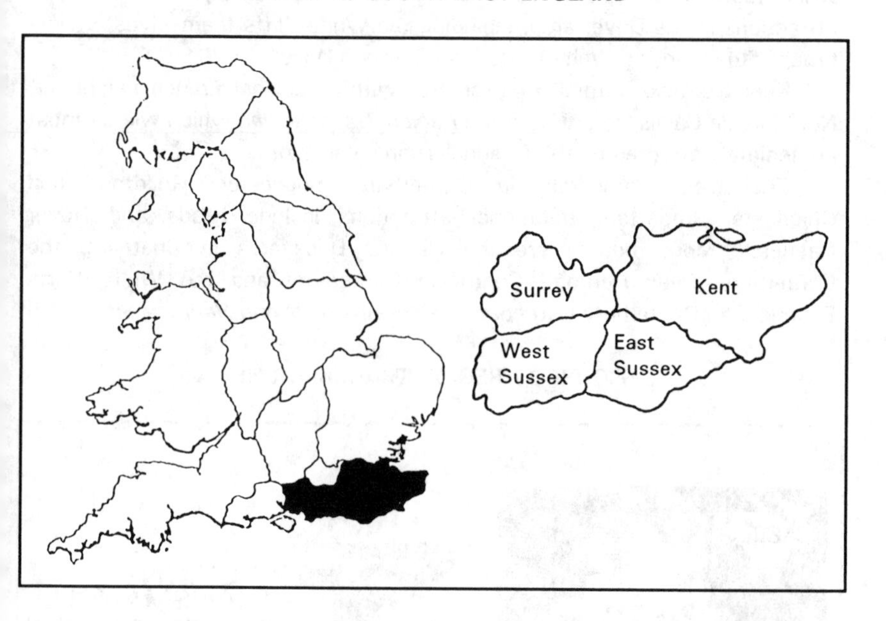

South East England

The South East England Tourist Board covers East and West Sussex, Kent and Surrey. It is a 'gateway' region, with 85% of overseas visitors either arriving in it or on its boundaries. Within this area are the Chichester Harbour, Sussex Downs, Surrey Hills, High Weald and Kent Downs *Areas of Outstanding Natural Beauty (AONBs)* and the Sussex, South Foreland and Dover to Folkestone stretches of *heritage coast*. The South Downs Way and North Downs Way *long distance footpaths* also cross this region. The main rivers are the Medway and the Thames.

South East England has a string of *seaside resorts*, some like Brighton dating back to the 18th century, most like Margate and Worthing dating back to the 19th century. Large towns include Canterbury, Guildford, Lewes and Chichester. There are major ferry ports at Ramsgate, Dover, Folkestone and Dieppe. The M2, M20 and M23 motorways link the South East with the M25 and London.

Kent, with its oast houses and orchards, is known as the Garden of England, but in 1990 Shepway District Council launched a new marketing campaign to identify the stretch of coast linking Folkestone, Hythe and Romney Marsh as the **Garden Coast**. The area around Battle and Hastings has also been promoted as **1066 Country** in memory of the battle which changed the face of British history. **Dickens Country** centres on Chatham, where the famous writer lived for six years as a child, and, Rochester which featured in three of his novels. **White Cliffs Country** focuses on the attractions in the Dover area, including the White Cliffs themselves, vividly brought to life in the White Cliffs Experience in Dover.

Kent has also formed a partnership with its closest French neighbour, Nord-Pas de Calais, to promote the *Region Transmanche* which will be most immediately affected by the Channel Tunnel (Fig.11).

There are cathedrals in Canterbury, Rochester, Guildford and Chichester. Important traditional attractions include Leeds and Hever Castles. More modern are the Historic Dockyards in Chatham, the Canterbury Tales Heritage Centre in Canterbury and the White Cliffs Experience. Canterbury Cathedral is a designated *World Heritage Site.*

FIGURE 11 REGION TRANSMANCHE

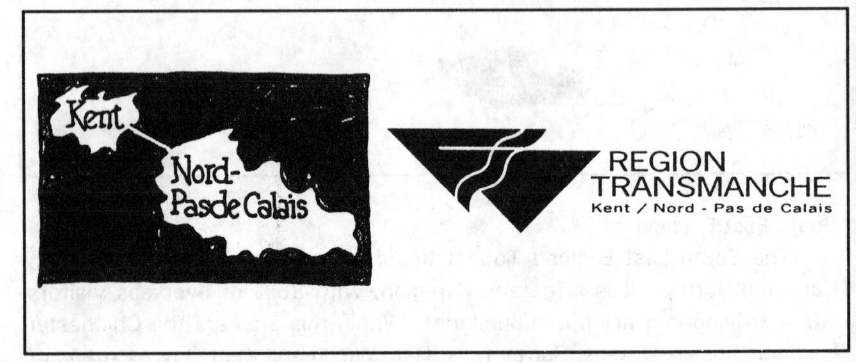

(Source: Kent County Council)

TABLE 9 THE MOST VISITED TOURIST ATTRACTIONS IN SOUTH EAST ENGLAND, 1989

		Visitor Nos
1.	Canterbury Cathedral	2,125,000
2.	Thorpe Park	1,300,000
3.	Smarts Amusement Park, Littlehampton	*750,000
4.	Leeds Castle	528,529
5.	Eastbourne Pier	*500,000
6.	Drusilla's Zoo Park	*350,000
7.	Eurotunnel Exhibition Centre	344,649
8.	Royal Pavilion, Brighton	321,990
9.	Brighton Aquarium and Dolphinarium	293,553
10.	Hever Castle	284,985

(* approximate number)

FIGURE 12 SOUTHERN ENGLAND/CENTRE SOUTH

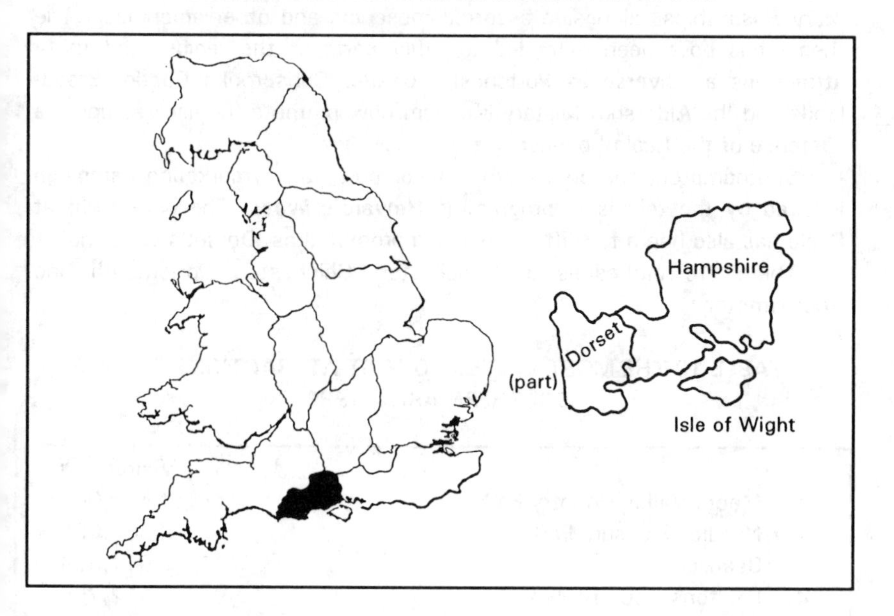

Southern England/Centre South

The Southern Tourist Board area covers Hampshire, South Wiltshire, east Dorset and the Isle of Wight. Included within the area are the Purbeck, Isle of Wight, South Hampshire Coast and East Hampshire *AONBs;* the Cranborne Chase and West Wiltshire Downs, and North Wessex Downs *AONBs* also overlap the boundaries. The Tennyson and Hamstead stretches of coast on the Isle of Wight are designated *heritage coastlines.* The main river, the Test, flows into the sea at the Solent which separates the Isle of Wight from the mainland. The M3 connects Southern England with London, and the M27 links Portsmouth and Southampton.

Southern England has a string of popular *seaside resorts* stretching from Swanage in the west to Southsea in the east. Many of them were established in the 19th century when the new railway lines brought them within easy reach of London. There are major ferry ports at Portsmouth and Southampton. The Isle of Wight, a 147 square mile island off Portsmouth connected to the mainland by ferries and catamarans and with its administrative centre in Newport, is particularly dependent on tourism; there are long-established *seaside resorts* at Sandown, Shanklin, Ryde and Ventnor.

Portsmouth Harbour has been the focal point of a *Tourism Development Action Programme* which focused on its maritime heritage and created the marketing tag 'the South's Historic Maritime Resort City'.

The Naval Base area now displays the *HMS Victory*, the *Warrior* and the *Mary Rose* ships alongside assorted museums and other amenities. The theme has now been extended to other parts of the region, and thirty attractions as diverse as Portchester Castle, Carisbrooke Castle, Broadlands and the Aldershot Military Museum now promote themselves under a 'Defence of the Realm' banner.

Southampton, the area's other major port, ran a marketing campaign inspired by the television programme **Howard's Way**. The waterfront at Poole has also had a facelift and is being promoted as 'Dorset's Lakeland'.

There are cathedrals in Winchester, Chichester, Portsmouth and Southampton.

TABLE 10 THE MOST VISITED TOURIST ATTRACTIONS IN THE SOUTHERN AREA, 1989

		Visitor Nos
1.	Moors Valley Country Park	*600,000
2.	Needles Pleasure Park	*580,000
3.	Beaulieu	511,994
4.	Paultons Country Park	412,700
5.	Winchester Cathedral	*400,000
6.	Queen Elizabeth Country Park	374,053
7.	Mary Rose, Portsmouth	*350,000
8.	HMS Victory, Portsmouth	302,875
= 9.	Alum Bay Glass, Isle of Wight	*300,000
= 9.	Bournemouth Exhibition Centre	*300,000

(* approximate numbers)

West Country

The West Country Tourist Board covers Cornwall, Devon, Somerset, Wiltshire, Avon, west Dorset and the Isles of Scilly. The *National Parks* of Exmoor (North Devon) and Dartmoor (South Devon) are within its borders, as are the Mendip Hills, Quantock Hills, Bodmin Moor, North, South and East Devon, and Isles of Scilly *AONBs*. The Cotswold Hills and West Wiltshire Downs *AONBs* also overlap into the West Country. The South West Peninsula Coast Path, a designated *long distance footpath*, runs all the way round the coast, from Dorset's Purbeck coast in the south to the eastern edge of Exmoor in the north. The following areas have all been designated *heritage coasts*: Lundy Island, Hartland, Pentire Point to Widemouth, Trevose Head, St. Agnes, Godrevy to Portreath, Penwith, Isles of Scilly, The Lizard, The Roseland, Gribbin Head to Polperro, Rame Head,

South Devon, East Devon and West Dorset. The Exmoor and North Devon coastline is also likely to be designated eventually. The West Country is separated from South Wales by the River Severn, crossed by the Severn Bridge just outside Bristol. Other important rivers include the Avon, Taw and Tamar. Amongst the largest towns are Truro, Exeter, Taunton, Bath, Bristol, Salisbury and Dorchester. The area is linked to London via the M4 and M5, with the A30 running the length of Cornwall.

FIGURE 13 THE WEST COUNTRY

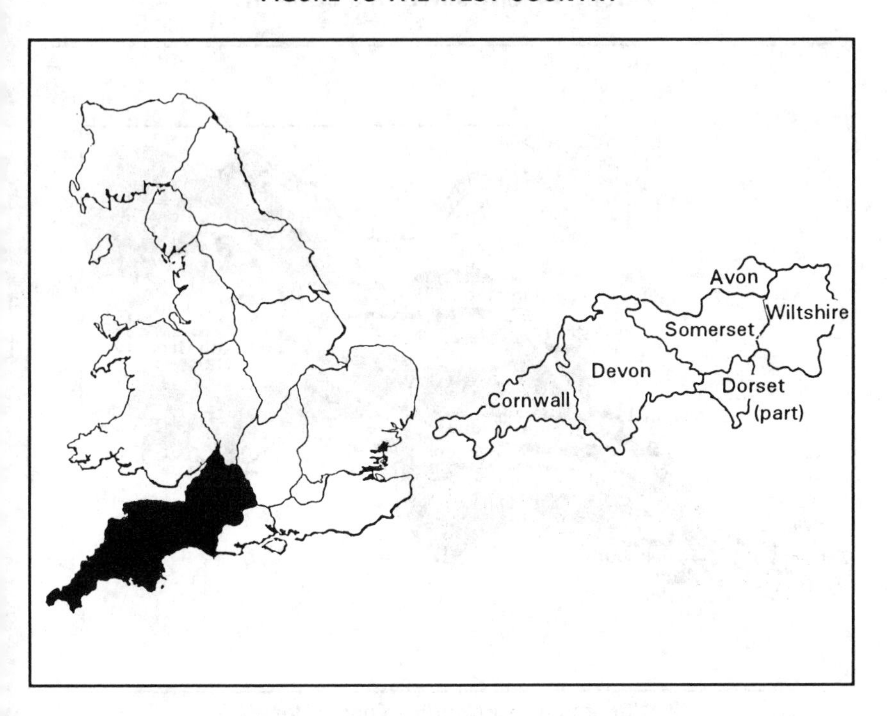

The area is ringed with *seaside resorts*. Some are picturesque ex-fishing villages set round rocky bays as at Clovelly, Mevagissey and Fowey, but others are more tacky. To counteract a rather downmarket image the southern resorts of Torbay (Torquay, Paignton and Brixham) with their mild climates successfully created the concept of 'the English Riviera'. Over 180 miles of still-unspoilt West Country coastline have been bought by the National Trust's Enterprise Neptune to safeguard them from future development.

England's most southerly (The Lizard) and westerly points (Land's End) are both in Cornwall. Land's End was developed as a theme park by entrepreneur, Peter de Savary, who has now sold it.

The Scilly Islands are a group of 140 small islands twenty-five miles south west of Land's End and connected to the mainland by ferries and helicopters to Penzance. Of the five inhabited islands St. Mary's is the largest, and Hugh Town is the capital of the Scillies as a whole. The other inhabited islands are Tresco, St. Martin's, St. Agnes and Bryher. Lundy is a small island in the Bristol Channel, accessible by boat from Bristol and Ilfracombe.

FIGURE 14 KING ARTHUR'S COUNTRY

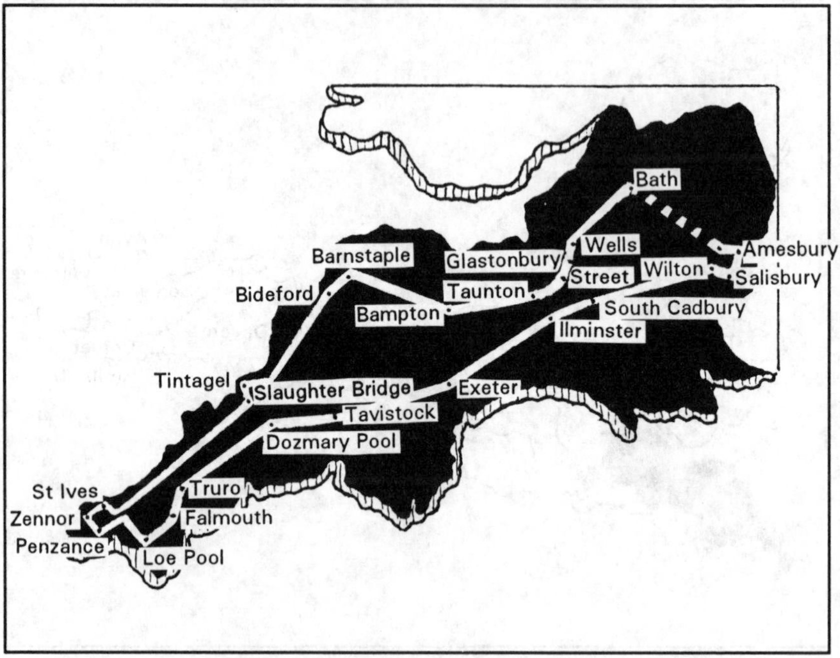

(Source: West Country Tourist Board)

Parts of the West Country are marketed as **King Arthur Country,** building on links with the mythical 6th century British hero who was supposedly born at Tintagel and buried at Glastonbury. He is said to have thrown his sword Excalibur away in Dozmary Pool on Bodmin Moor. At South Cadbury in Somerset an 18-acre Neolithic fort has also been identified as a possible site for Camelot, King Arthur's castle (Fig.14).

Parts of West Somerset and North Devon are marketed as **Lorna Doone Country** after the R.D. Blackmore novel which tells how the heroine Lorna Doone was kidnapped by the outlawed Doone family. Places mentioned in the novel include Dunster, Porlock, Barnstaple and Dulverton (Fig.15).

FIGURE 15 LORNA DOONE COUNTRY

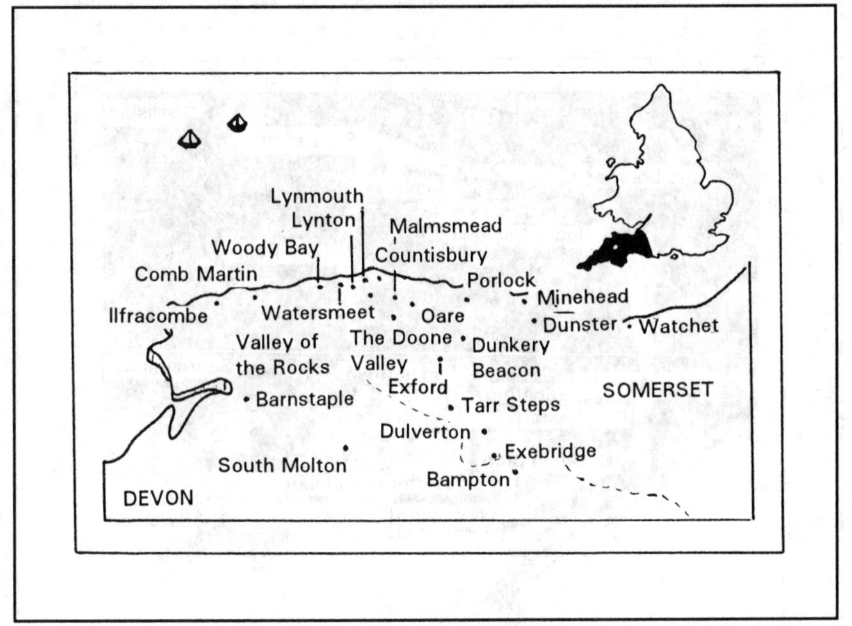

(Source: West Country Tourist Board)

The Dorset part of the West Country is marketed as **Thomas Hardy's Wessex** (Fig.16) after the famous 19th century novelist who was born and died near Dorchester and wrote many of his books while living in Weymouth. Hardy himself called the fictional area about which he wrote 'Wessex' after the Anglo-Saxon kingdom which used to occupy southwest England. Many Dorset towns and villages including Dorchester and Weymouth appeared in his novels with their names changed.

The Tarka Project, based on the the Taw and Torridge rivers in Devon, aims to diversify the local economy by developing small scale tourism, using a theme taken from Henry Williamson's popular novel about Tarka the otter. A *Tarka Trail* now runs along a disused railway line, and the Bideford to Exeter rail link is being promoted as the Tarka Line. Real life otters are also being protected as a result of the Project.

In 1988 the West Country town of Plymouth was the focus of a nationwide celebration of the 400th anniversary of the sailing of Sir Francis Drake's Armada.

There are cathedrals in Salisbury, Bristol, Wells, Exeter and Truro. Stonehenge and Avebury, and the City of Bath are designated *World Heritage Sites.*

FIGURE 16 THOMAS HARDY'S WESSEX

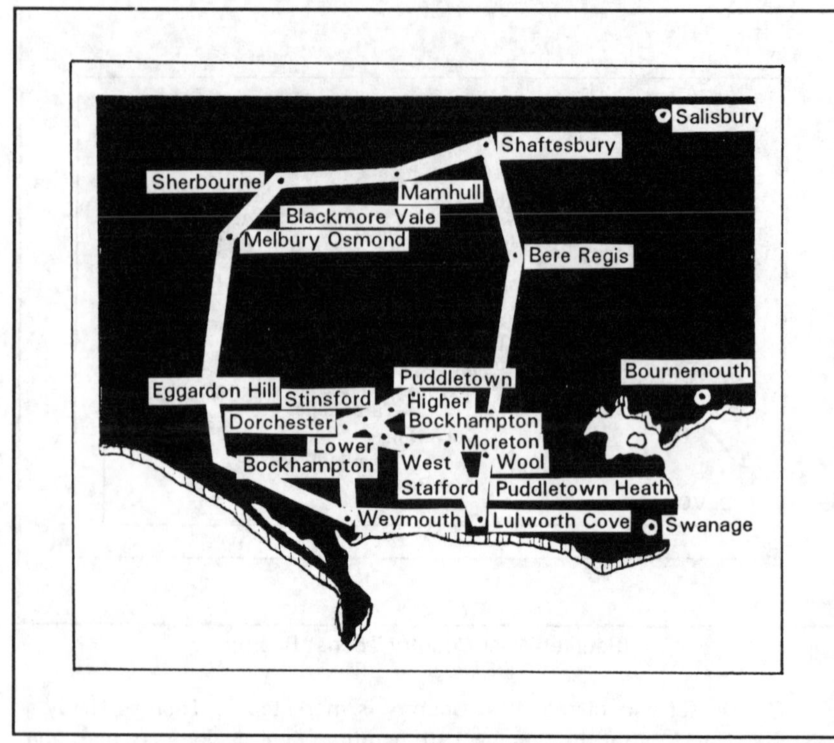

(Source: West Country Tourist Board)

TABLE 11 THE MOST VISITED TOURIST ATTRACTIONS IN THE WEST COUNTRY, 1989

		Visitor Nos
1.	Roman Baths and Pump Room, Bath	931,832
2.	Stonehenge	681,657
3.	English Riviera Centre, Torquay	*643,000
4.	Buckfast Abbey	551,413
5.	Dartington Cider Press Centre	511,394
6.	Salisbury Cathedral	*500,000
7.	Babbacombe Model Village	472,032
8.	Bristol Zoo	450,908
9.	Cheddar Caves	390,000
10.	Wells Cathedral	*356,200

(* approximate number)

FIGURE 17 THAMES AND CHILTERNS

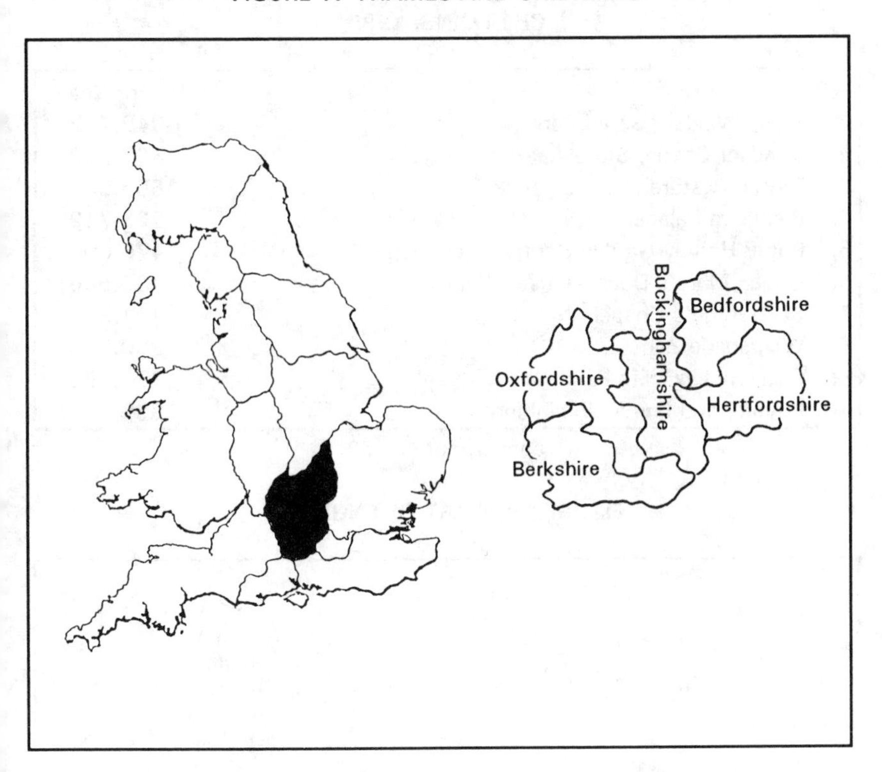

Thames and Chilterns

The Thames and Chilterns Tourist Board area covers Oxfordshire, Berkshire, Bedfordshire, Buckinghamshire and Hertfordshire. The Chilterns *AONB* runs across it, while the Cotswolds *AONB* touches the northwestern corner. The Ridegway *long distance footpath* also traverses Thames and Chilterns. Large towns include Oxford, Reading, Buckingham, Bedford and Hertford. The M1, M4 and M40 all connect this region with London.

The Thames and Chilterns region contains some particularly well-known traditional tourist attractions: Windsor Castle, Eton College, Henley, St. Albans, Hatfield House and the Oxford colleges.

Hertfordshire is promoted with the tag 'Herts...England's Best Kept Secret', while Berkshire, with its historic associations at Windsor, calls itself 'Beautiful Berkshire...the Royal County'. Cashing in on its proximity to London, the Thames and Chilterns Tourist Board also describes the region as a whole as **London's Country.**

There are cathedrals in St. Alban's and Oxford. Blenheim Palace is a designated *World Heritage Site.*

TABLE 12 THE MOST VISITED TOURIST ATTRACTIONS IN THAMES AND CHILTERNS, 1989

		Visitor Nos
1.	Royal Windsor Safari Park	1,049,722
2.	Windsor Castle, State Apartments	807,880
3.	Dinton Pastures Country Park	*656,000
4.	Blenheim Palace	523,712
5.	Roger Harvey Garden Centre, Stevenage	*475,000
6.	Queen Mary's Dolls' House, Windsor	400,556
7.	St. George's Chapel, Windsor	411,542
8.	Whipsnade Zoo	*380,000
9.	Cotswold Wildlife Park	373,780
10.	Royalty and Empire Exhibition	335,326

(* approximate number)

FIGURE 18 HEART OF ENGLAND

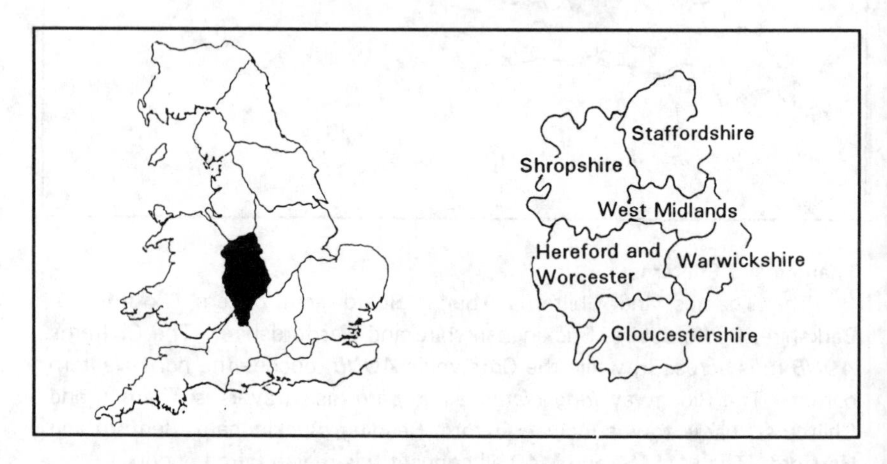

Heart of England

The Heart of England Tourist Board covers Gloucestershire, Herefordshire, Shropshire, Staffordshire, Warwickshire, West Midlands and Worcestershire. The Cotswolds, Malvern Hills, Shropshire Hills and Cannock Chase *AONBs* are all in this area, while the Wye Valley and Clwydian Range *AONBs* overlap it. The Peak District *National Park* also crosses its north-eastern corner. For some of its route the Offa's Dyke *long distance footpath* separates the 'Marches' area of the Heart of England from Wales. Important rivers in this region include the Severn and its tributary the Avon which flows through the Vale of Evesham. The Thames and its tributary, the Windrush, have their sources in Gloucestershire. The M6 links the Heart of England to London and the M5 links it to the West Country.

Large towns in the region include Gloucester, Stafford, Warwick, Birmingham, Wolverhampton and Stoke-on-Trent. Several of England's most popular tourist attractions, including Alton Towers, Warwick Castle, the Ironbridge Gorge Museum and Stratford-on-Avon, are in the Heart of England. Not surprisingly the area around Stratford, where Shakepeare was born, is marketed as **Shakespeare Country**. However, Coventry also cashes in on the Bard's fame by calling itself the 'City in Shakespeare Country'. In Staffordshire the area to the east of Alton Towers is marketed as **George Eliot Country** after the 19th century female novelist who renamed it Stonyshire in *Adam Bede*. Lichfield also makes much of its links with the famous 18th century dictionary-writer Dr. Samuel Johnson.

There are cathedrals in Gloucester, Hereford, Worcester, Coventry and Lichfield. England's first designated *World Heritage Site* was the industrial archaeological site at Ironbridge Gorge.

TABLE 13 THE MOST VISITED TOURIST ATTRACTIONS IN THE HEART OF ENGLAND, 1989

		Visitor Nos
1.	Alton Towers	2,382,000
2.	Clent Hills Country Park	*1,000,000
3.	Drayton Manor Park	908,000
4.	Warwick Castle	637,056
5.	Birmingham City Museum and Art Gallery	601,554
6.	Shakespeare's Birthplace, Stratford-upon-Avon	571,262
7.	Queenswood Country Park	*400,000
8.	Walsall Arboretum Illuminations	377,230
9.	Birmingham Science and Industry Museum	356,808
10.	Ironbridge Gorge Museum	350,310

(* approximate number)

East Anglia

The East Anglia Tourist Board area covers Essex, Suffolk, Norfolk and Cambridgeshire. The Norfolk Broads, an extensive area of flooded medieval peat workings, has been a national park in all but name since 1987. The area also includes the Dedham Vale, Suffolk Coast and Heaths, and Norfolk Coast *AONBs* and the Suffolk and North Norfolk *heritage coastlines*. The Peddars Way and North Norfolk Coast Path is a designated *long distance footpath*. Epping Forest is only twenty miles east of London.

FIGURE 19 EAST ANGLIA

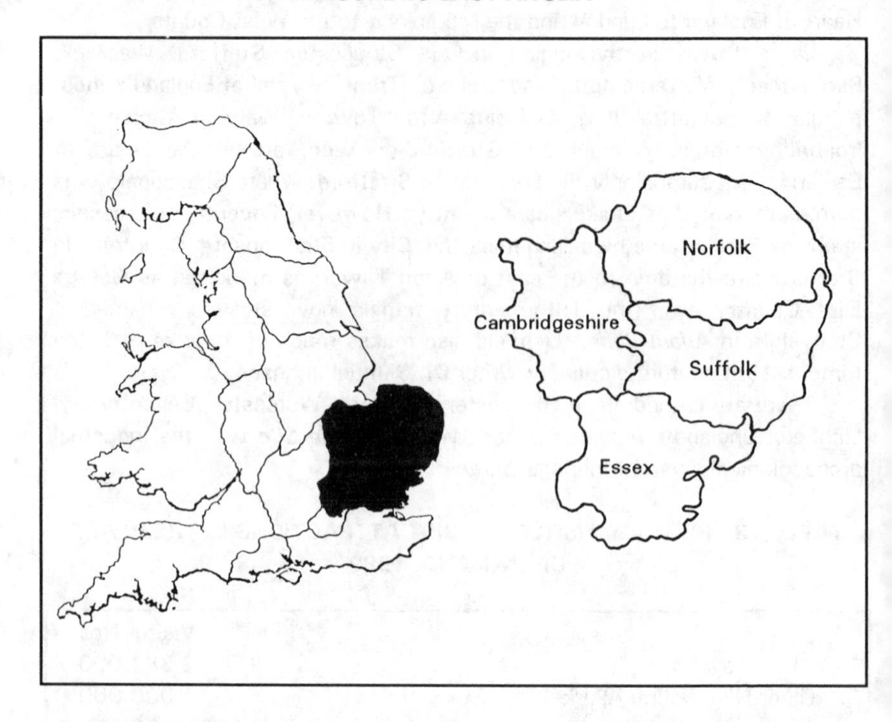

Much of Norfolk and Cambridgeshire in particular is very flat, with the Fens stretching north to meet the Wash. Along the 200-mile coastline there are long-established *seaside resorts* at Southend-on-Sea, Clacton-on-Sea, Lowestoft, Great Yarmouth, Cromer and Sheringham. There are major ferry ports at Harwich, Felixstowe and Sheerness. Other large towns include Norwich, Ipswich, Cambridge, Peterborough, Chelmsford and Colchester. The Thames, crossed by the Dartford Tunnel and Queen Elizabeth II Bridge at Dartford, divides East Anglia from South East England. Other important rivers include the Cam and the Great Ouse. The M11 links London and Cambridge.

The 'wool' towns of Suffolk (Lavenham, Long Melford and Kersey), with their pastel-coloured houses and thatched roofs, are very popular with visitors. Cambridge, with its medieval colleges, is another important traditional centre for tourism.

Part of Essex and South Suffolk has been marketed as **Constable Country** after the 19th century artist who painted some of his most famous landscapes in and around Dedham and the Stour Valley. Flatford Mill is in an *environmentally sensitive area*, the Suffolk River Valley. The district just south of the Wash known as the Fens has also been marketed as **Hereward**

the Wake Country after the 11th century Anglo-Saxon leader who held out against the Normans on the Isle of Ely.

There are cathedrals in Chelmsford, Norwich, Ely, Peterborough and Bury St. Edmunds.

TABLE 14 THE MOST VISITED TOURIST ATTRACTIONS IN EAST ANGLIA, 1989

		Visitor Nos
1.	Pleasure Beach, Great Yarmouth	*2,475,000
2.	Pleasurewood Hills American Theme Park	537,407
=3.	Charles Manning's Amusement Park, Felixstowe	*500,000
=3.	Marina Leisure Centre, Great Yarmouth	*500,000
=3.	Norwich Cathedral	*500,000
6.	Imperial War Museum, Duxford	392,069
7.	Southend Pier	*387,000
8.	Colchester Zoo	372,322
9.	Norwich Castle Museum	257,733
=10.	Sea Life Centre, Hunstanton	250,000
=10.	The Splash, Sheringham	*250,000
=10.	Wood Green Animal Shelters, Huntingdon	*250,000

(* approximate number)

East Midlands/The Shires of Middle England

The East Midlands Tourist Board area covers Derbyshire, Leicestershire, Lincolnshire, Northamptonshire and Nottinghamshire. England's first *National Park*, the Peak District, with the Derbyshire Dales to the south, fills the northwestern corner, while the Lincolnshire Wolds *AONB* lies to the northeast. The Peak District *long distance footpath* also starts in this area. There are long-established *seaside resorts* at Skegness and Cleethorpes on the Lincolnshire coast. Other large towns include Lincoln, Nottingham, Derby, Leicester and Northampton. The River Trent and its tributaries drain this region of England. The M1 runs through the middle of it.

Northamptonshire, 'the Rose of the Shires', is the most southerly of the counties. Southern Lincolnshire, to the east, is famous for the spring-time flowers grown around Spalding. North west Leicestershire has been marketed as **Ivanhoe Country** after Sir Walter Scott's famous novel which used Ashby-de-la-Zouch castle as the setting for a dramatic medieval tournament. Not surprisingly Nottinghamshire is marketed as **Robin Hood Country** after the medieval outlaw who was supposed to have hidden in Sherwood Forest and robbed the rich to give to the poor. The focal points are the town of Nottingham itself, with a brand-new 'Tales of Robin Hood' experience, and Sherwood Forest where Center Parcs now has an all-weather holiday park.

Traditional attractions in the area include Chatsworth and Burghley Houses. There are also cathedrals in Leicester, Lincoln, Southwell and Derby.

FIGURE 20 EAST MIDLANDS/THE SHIRES OF MIDDLE ENGLAND

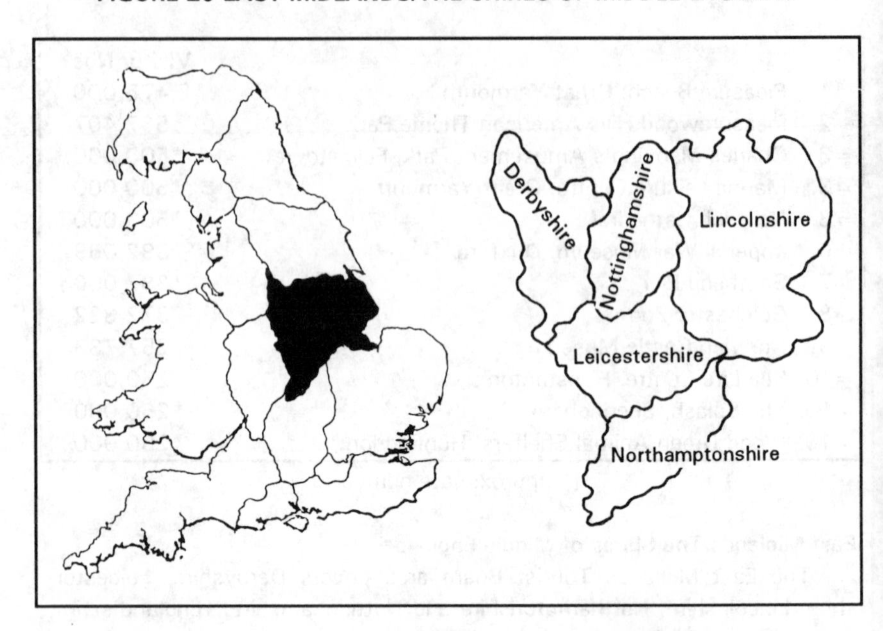

TABLE 15 EAST MIDLANDS' MOST POPULAR TOURIST ATTRACTIONS, 1989

		Visitor Nos
1.	Bradgate Park	*1,300,000
=2.	Clumber Park	*1,000,000
=2.	Sherwood Forest Country Park	*1,000,000
=2.	Shipley Country Park	*1,000,000
5.	Elvaston Castle Country Park	*930,000
6.	Nottingham Castle and Museum	601,983
7.	Rufford Country Park	590,330
8.	Rutland Water	*500,000
9.	Rufford Craft Centre	*472,000
10.	Irchester Country Park	467,491

(* approximate number)

Yorkshire and Humberside

The Yorkshire and Humberside Tourist Board area covers the counties of North Yorkshire, South Yorkshire, West Yorkshire and Humberside. It includes both the Yorkshire Dales and North York Moors *National Parks.* There are stretches of *heritage coastline* at Spurn Head, Flamborough Headland and along the North Yorkshire and Cleveland coast. The Pennine Way, Wolds Way and Cleveland Way *long distance footpaths* all pass through this region. The River Swale flows through the Vale of York, its tributaries, the Nidd, Wharfe, Aire and Calder, draining into it from the Dales. The Trent meets the sea at the Humber estuary where the Humber Bridge just outside Hull joins up Humberside's two parts. There are long-established *seaside resorts* at Saltburn, Bridlington, Filey, Scarborough and Whitby. Large towns in this region include York, Hull, Leeds, Bradford, Sheffield, Huddersfield, Halifax and Wakefield. The M1 connects London and Leeds, while the M62 crosses the Pennines to link Hull and Liverpool.

FIGURE 21 YORKSHIRE AND HUMBERSIDE

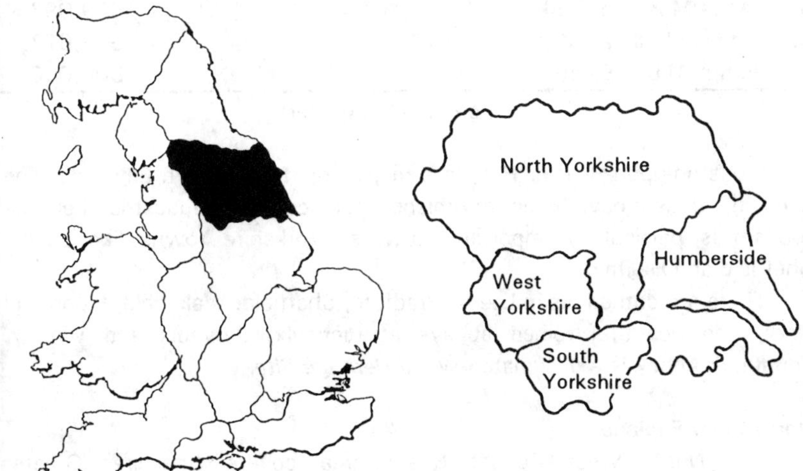

The Hambleton area just to the west of York has been marketed as **Herriot Country** after the successful television series about a vet's surgery,

All Creatures Great and Small, in turn taken from James Herriot's books. The town of Thirsk was the model for the fictional Darrowby. Television series' have also provided themes for **Last of the Summer Wine Country** focused on Leeds and Bradford, and **Emmerdale Farm Country** around Holmfirth. More traditional is **Bronte Country** based on the Parsonage at Haworth where the three Bronte sisters, Emily (author of *Wuthering Heights*), Charlotte (author of *Jane Eyre*) and Anne (author of *The Tenant of Wildfell Hall*) grew up.

TABLE 16 THE MOST VISITED TOURIST ATTRACTIONS IN YORKSHIRE AND HUMBERSIDE, 1989

		Visitor Nos
1.	York Minster	*2,300,000
2.	Flamingoland	1,006,000
3.	Jorvik Viking Centre,York	904,483
4.	Rother Valley Country Park	781,167
5.	National Museum of Photography, Film and Television	736,444
6.	Tropical World, Leeds	731,069
7.	Hornsea Pottery	*700,000
8.	Castle Museum, York	659,097
9.	National Railway Museum, York	542,677
10.	Bolton Abbey Estate	*500,000

(* approximate number)

Kingston-upon-Hull, or Hull, is a major port for northern England. The decaying docks have been refurbished for tourism. Industrial heritage tourism is particularly important to West Yorkshire towns like Leeds, Sheffield and Halifax.

There are cathedrals in Leeds, Bradford, Sheffield, Wakefield, Ripon and York, and beautiful ruined abbeys at Rievaulx, Jervaulx and Whitby. Fountains Abbey is a designated *World Heritage Site.*

North West England

The North West Tourist Board area covers Cheshire, Greater Manchester, Lancashire, Merseyside and the High Peak area of Derbyshire. The Peak District and Yorkshire Dales *National Parks* both overlap the area, and the Forest of Bowland is an *AONB.* There are long-established *seaside resorts* at Southport, Lytham St. Anne's, Blackpool and Morecambe. To overcome the area's industrialised image the boroughs of Blackburn, Hyndburn, Burnley, Pendle, Ribble Valley and Rossendale are marketed as **Lancashire's Hill Country**. The most important rivers in the region are the

Mersey and the Ribble. Large towns include Liverpool, Chester, Manchester, Salford, Runcorn, Wigan, Blackburn and Lancaster. The M6 links Liverpool to London, while the M62 links it to Hull via Leeds. The M61 and M55 link Manchester and Blackpool.

Industrial heritage, or 'smokestack', tourism has been important in the redevelopment of the declining industrial areas of the north west. Liverpool in particular has benefited from investment in the Albert Dock, now one of the country's most popular attractions. The development of the Granada Studios tour in Manchester and of Wigan Pier Heritage Centre are other examples of how modern tourist attractions can bring new life to an area. In contrast Chester has always been an important stopping point for tours heading for Scotland or the Lakes.

FIGURE 22 NORTH WEST ENGLAND

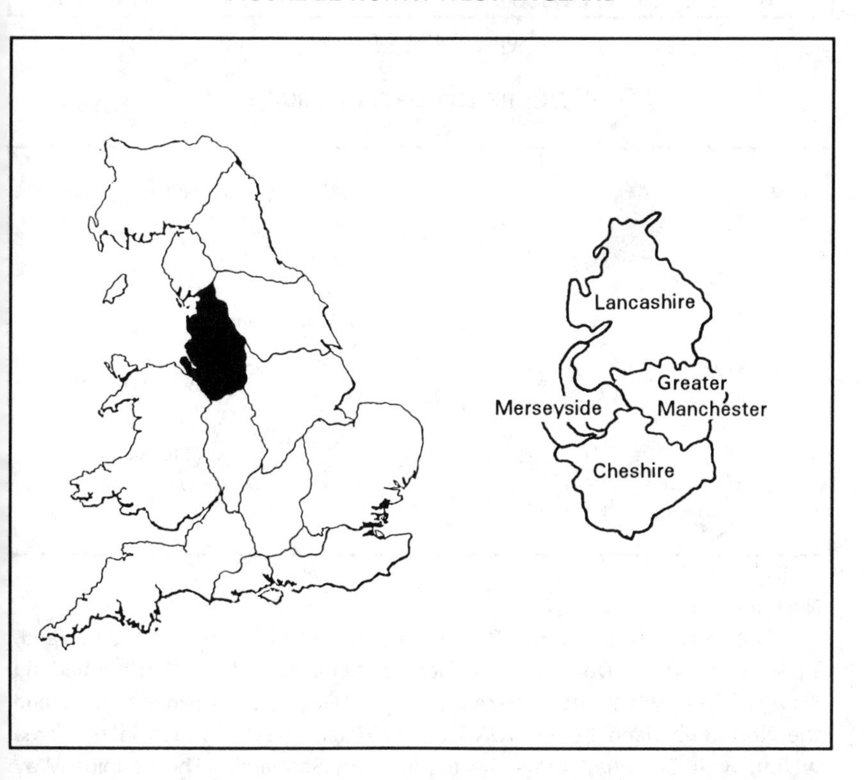

Traditional attractions include the medieval 'Rows' shopping arcades in Chester and the many black and white half-timbered houses around Chester, including Speke Hall. There are also cathedrals in Chester, Liverpool, Blackburn and Manchester.

TABLE 17 THE MOST VISITED TOURIST ATTRACTIONS IN NORTH WEST ENGLAND, 1989

		Visitor Nos
	1. Blackpool Pleasure Beach	*6,500,000
	2. Albert Dock, Liverpool	*5,100,000
	3. Pleasureland, Southport	*1,500,000
	4. Blackpool Tower	1,495,000
	5. Stapeley Water Gardens	*1,270,000
	6. Frontierland, Morecambe	*1,200,000
	7. Chester Zoo	904,251
=	8. Chester Cathedral	*750,000
=	8. Croxteth Country Park	*750,000
	10. Tate Gallery, Liverpool	687,352

(* approximate number)

FIGURE 23 NORTHUMBRIA

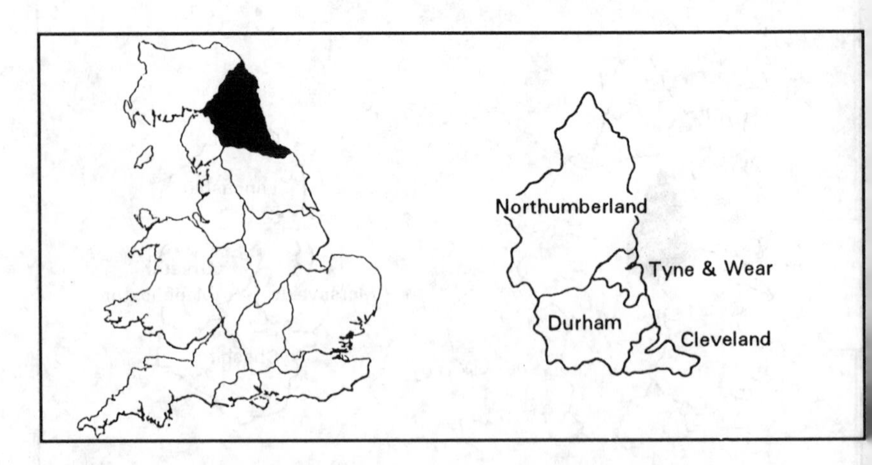

Northumbria

The Northumbria Tourist Board area covers the counties of Cleveland, Tyne and Wear, Durham and Northumberland. The Northumberland *National Park* (which includes the Cheviot Hills and the Kielder Forest) and the Northumberland Coast *AONB* and *heritage coast* are also in this area which, with Cumbria, forms the border with Scotland. The Pennine Way *long distance footpath* continues north through this region too, and the North Pennines are also an *AONB*. The most important rivers are the Tyne and Tees. Newcastle-upon-Tyne is a major ferry port. Other large towns include Gateshead, Middlesbrough and Durham. Although the A1 between

Newcastle and Scotch Corner is of motorway standard, no true motorways run through Northumbria.

South Tyneside has been marketed as **Catherine Cookson Country** after the best-selling novelist who was born in South Shields. Cleveland, a largely industrial area, also has a **Captain Cook Country,** centred on Middlesbrough where the explorer was born and which is now the starting point for a heritage trail along the North Yorkshire coast.

There are cathedrals in Durham and Newcastle. Durham Cathedral and Castle, and Hadrian's Wall are designated *World Heritage Sites.*

TABLE 18 THE MOST VISITED TOURIST ATTRACTIONS IN NORTHUMBRIA, 1989

		Visitor Nos
1.	Beamish North of England Open-Air Museum	486,565
2.	Preston Hall Museum	462,317
3.	Durham Cathedral	400,296
4.	Kielder Water	*300,000
5.	St. Aidan's Winery, Holy Island	*200,000
6.	Castle Eden Walkway	*150,000
7.	South Shields Museum and Art Gallery	139,558
8.	Housesteads Roman Fort	129,032
9.	Chantry Craft Centre, Morpeth	*129,000
10.	Sunderland Museum and Art Gallery	122,550

(* approximate number)

FIGURE 24 CUMBRIA

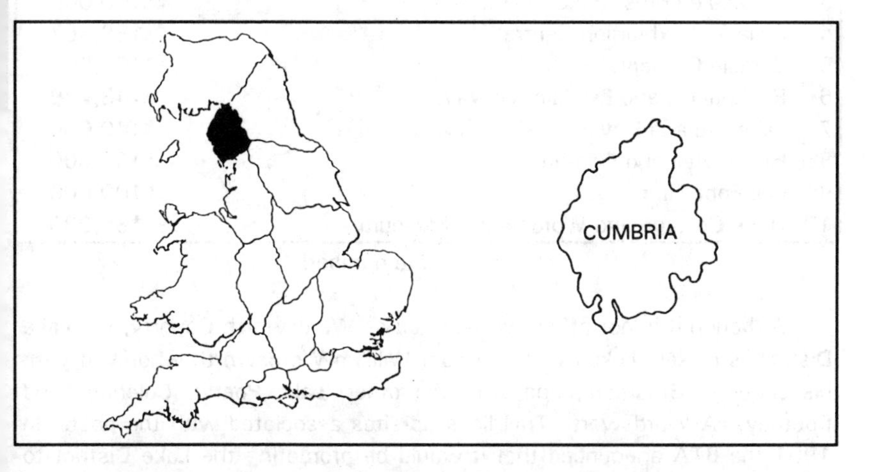

Cumbria

The Cumbria Tourist Board area covers only the county of Cumbria which forms half the border with Scotland and contains the Lake District *National Park* and part of the Solway Coast, Arnside and Silverdale, and North Pennines *AONBs*. The Yorkshire Dales also overlap southern Cumbria. St. Bees Head is *heritage coastline*. The main lakes are Windermere, Coniston Water, Wast Water, Lake Grasmere, Ennerdale Water, Lowes Water, Buttermere, Crummock Water, Derwent Water, Thirlmere, Ullswater and Hawes Water. At 978m, Scafell Pike is England's highest mountain. Large towns include Carlisle, Workington, Whitehaven, Barrow and Kendal. The M6 rings the Lakes to link Carlisle to the Midlands, while the A66 cuts across them to Workington.

Traditionally most tourism in Cumbria has been concentrated in the central region where most of the lakes and mountains can be found. However, Carlisle has been the centre of a *Tourist Development Action Programme*, aimed at encouraging tourism on the county's periphery. Eden District, Cumbria's 'best-kept secret', has also had its own *Tourism Action Programme* to promote rural tourism in the area, while West Cumbria has been subject to a *Strategic Development Initiative*. The coastal area around Morecambe Bay is sometimes called **Cumbria's Riviera.**

TABLE 19 THE MOST POPULAR TOURIST ATTRACTIONS IN CUMBRIA, 1989

		Visitor Nos
1.	Windermere Iron Steamboat Co.	572,616
2.	Talkin Tarn Country Park	*200,000
3.	Grizedale Forest Park	*160,000
4.	Sellafield Exhibition Centre	159,567
5.	Carlisle Cathedral	*150,000
6.	Ravenglass and Eskdale Railway	143,739
7.	Lakeside and Haverthwaite Railway	*140,000
8.	Holker Hall and Gardens	*102,000
9.	Fell Foot Park	*100,000
10.	Dove Cottage and Wordsworth Museum	*85,900

(* approximate number)

Although it is not officially marketed as Wordsworth Country, the Lake District is closely linked with the poet William Wordsworth who lived with his sister in Grasmere, and with the other 'Lake Poets', Coleridge and Southey. A Wordsworth Trail links up sites associated with the poet. In 1991 the BTA announced that it would be promoting the Lake District to the Japanese market as **Peter Rabbit Country** because of its connections with Beatrix Potter who lived for much of her life at Hill Top Farm in Near Sawrey.

There is a cathedral in Carlisle. Hadrian's Wall, which continues into Cumbria from Northumbria, is a designated *World Heritage Site.*

WALES

Since 1974 Wales has consisted of the counties of Gwent, South, West and Mid Glamorgan, Dyfed, Powys, Gwynedd and Clwyd. Cardiff is the capital of Wales. Wales has its own language, spoken by 20% of the population especially in Mid and North Wales. It also has its own stamps and its own flag which sports a red dragon on a green and white striped background. The Offa's Dyke *long distance footpath* stretches from near Chepstow in South Wales to near Prestatyn in North Wales.

FIGURE 25 THE REGIONS OF WALES

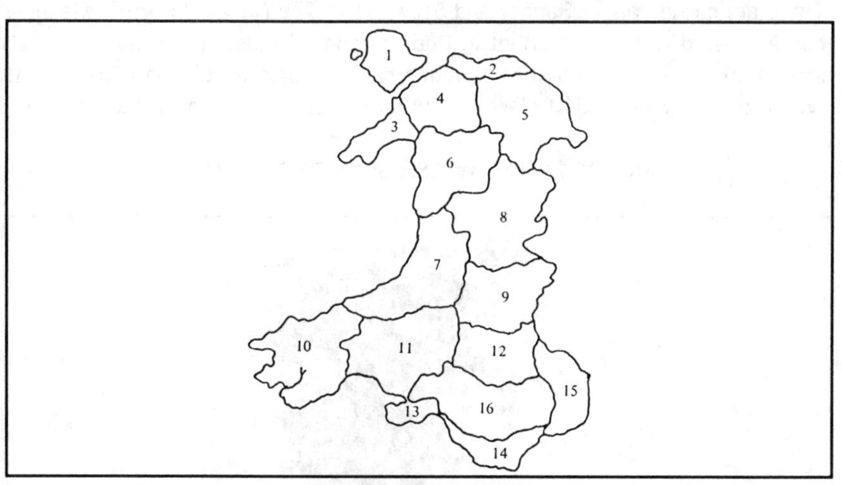

(Source: WTB, 1989)

North Wales

The Wales Tourist Board subdivides North Wales into (Fig.25):

Isle of Anglesey (1)
North Wales Coast Resorts (2)
Lyn Peninsula (3)
Snowdonia Mountains and Coastline (4)
Clwyd Country (5)

The vast Snowdonia *National Park* is in North Wales, as are the Lyn and Anglesey *AONBs*, and part of the Clywdian Range *AONB*. There are stretches of heritage coast around the Lyn Peninsula, Great Orme, Aberffraw Bay, Holyhead Mountain and North Anglesey. Holyhead on Anglesey is a major ferry port. The A55 which links Chester to North Wales has been upgraded to near motorway standard.

There are a string of long-established *seaside resorts* along the North Wales coast (Prestatyn, Rhyl, Abergele, Colwyn Bay, Llandudno, Pwlhelli) and on Anglesey which is separated from the mainland by the Menai Straits. However, many visitors come to North Wales to climb and walk in Snowdonia, an area of impressive mountains and lakes, including Mount Snowdon which is, at 1085m, the highest mountain in Wales. Llangollen is an important centre for water sports and is where the International Music Eisteddfod is held every July.

Edward I's castles and walls in Gwynedd (Caernarfon, Conwy, Harlech and Beaumaris) are designated *World Heritage Sites*. Other important castles (not all of them medieval) include Chirk, Criccieth and Penrhyn. There are cathedrals at Bangor and St. Asaph. The National Portrait Gallery has an award-winning offshoot in Bodelwyddan Castle. Industrial heritage attractions cluster round the slate-quarrying district of Blaenau Ffestiniog where the old workings of Llechwedd Slate Quarry are open to the public.

FIGURE 26 THE WELSH SEASIDE RESORTS

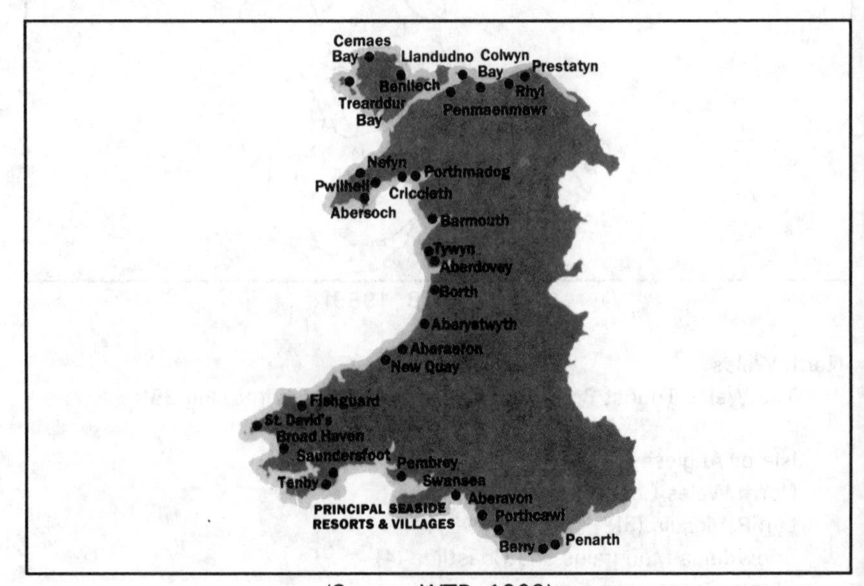

(Source: WTB, 1989)

Mid Wales

The Wales Tourist Board subdivides Mid Wales into (Fig.25):
Meirionnydd (6)
Ceredigion (7)
Montgomeryshire (8)
The Heart of Wales (9)

Part of the Shropshire Hills *AONB* lies within Mid Wales, and there are stretches of *heritage coast* on the Ceredigion Coast. *Cader Idris*, or Arthur's Seat, is a vast mountain area just inland from Barmouth. Road and rail access to Mid Wales has never been as good as to the North or South.

Tourism in Mid Wales has tended to focus on *seaside resorts* like Aberystwyth, Aberdovey, Barmouth and Tywyn, and on inland spa towns like Llandrindod Wells and Builth Wells. For a taste of the real Wales tourists can visit small market towns like Machynlleth and Dolgellau. Mid Wales has a strong 'alternative' feel. The Centre for Alternative Technology, just outside Machynlleth, introduces the public to non-conventional sources of power and farming methods; in 1991 it took the unusual step (for a tourist attraction) of selling shares in order to finance expansion of the site. Since 1985 the Festival of Wales has promoted tourism in this relatively undervisited area.

The border area with England ('The Marches') has attractive black and white half-timbered houses.

South Wales

The Wales Tourist Board subdivides South Wales into (Fig. 25):
Pembrokeshire (10)
The Coastline and Vales of Dyfed (11)
Brecon and the Beacons (12)
Swansea, The Mumbles and the Gower Peninsula (13)
Cardiff and the South Wales Coast (14)
The Vale of Usk and the Wye Valley (15)
The South Wales Valleys...Rhondda, Taff, Cynon, Rhymney, Neath (16)

South Wales contains the Brecon Beacons and Pembrokeshire Coast *National Parks*, and the Gower and parts of the Wye Valley *AONBs*. The following are stretches of *heritage coast*: Glamorgan, Gower, South Pembrokeshire, Marloes and Dale, St. Bride's Bay, St. David's Peninsula, Dinas Head and St. Dogmaels and Moylgrove. Pembroke and Fishguard are important ferry ports. The Pembrokeshire Coast *long distance footpath* is also in South Wales. The M4 connects Cardiff and Swansea with London.

Traditionally tourism in South Wales has focused on the coastal resorts of the south and west, and on the mountainous attractions of the Brecon Beacons National Park. The *Pembrokeshire Coast National Park* extends for 180 miles around the south westerly coast and takes in the island nature reserves of Skomer, Skokholm and Grassholm. Long established *seaside resorts* include Barry Island, Porthcawl, The Mumbles and Tenby.

The area around Laugharne has been promoted as **Dylan Thomas Country** after the Welsh poet best known for *Under Milk Wood* which he wrote in a boathouse (now open to the public every summer) overlooking the Taf Estuary.

In the late 1980s both Cardiff and Swansea began to promote themselves as tourist destinations; in both cases their restored waterfront areas were the focus for this activity. As coal-mining collapsed tourism was also seen as offering hope of future employment in the Welsh Valleys. The Big Pit Mining Museum was opened in Blaenafon, and the Rhondda Valley Heritage Park was developed just outside Pontypridd. In 1992 Ebbw Vale was also the setting for a Garden Festival.

TABLE 20 THE MOST POPULAR TOURIST ATTRACTIONS IN WALES IN 1989

		Visitor Nos
1.	Pembrey Country Park	*450,000
2.	Barry Island Log Flume	424,484
3.	Swallow Falls, Betws-y-Coed	306,626
4.	Portmeirion Italian Village	312,711
5.	Penscynor Wildlife Park, Cilfrew	290,000
6.	Caernarfon Castle	285,789
7.	Oakwood Leisure Park	270,000
8.	Welsh Folk Museum, St. Fagans	259,907
9.	Nova, Prestatyn	250,000
10.	Padarn Country Park, Llanberis	240,810
11.	Welsh Fusiliers' Museum, Caernarfon Castle	227,848
12.	Dan-yr-Ogof Showcaves	220,000
13.	Margam Country Park	219,038
14.	Conwy Castle	214,534
15.	Welsh Mountain Zoo	211,760
16.	Swansea Maritime and Industrial Museum	209,705
17.	Loggerheads Country Park	*200,000
18.	Llechwedd Slate Caverns	198,561
19.	Anglesey Sea Zoo	189,638
20.	Manor House Wildlife and Leisure Park	177,778

(* approximate number)

Particularly important castles in South Wales (not all of them medieval) include Caerphilly, Cardiff, Castell Coch, Kidwelly, Pembroke and Raglan. There are cathedrals in Cardiff (Llandaff), Newport and St. David's.

SCOTLAND

Since 1974 Scotland has been divided into the following regions: Borders, Dumfries and Galloway, Lothian, Strathclyde, Fife, Central, Tayside, Grampian, Highland, Western Isles, Orkney and Shetland. Edinburgh is the Scottish capital. Scotland has its own banknotes and flag. There are 90,000 Gaelic speakers in Scotland.

Geographically Scotland can be divided into the Highlands, the Islands (Shetlands, Orkneys and Hebrides), the Central Lowlands and the Southern Uplands. The largest towns, including Glasgow, Edinburgh, Dundee, Perth and Stirling, are in the Central Lowlands which is consequently by far the most densely populated part of the country.

Despite its great natural beauty Scotland does not, as yet, have any National Parks, although the *Cairngorms*, the *Ben Nevis-Glencoe area, Wester Ross* and the *Loch Lomond-Trossachs area* have been suggested as possible future National Parks or Scottish Wilderness/National Heritage Areas. Nor does it have protected Areas of Outstanding Natural Beauty. Instead there are designated **National Scenic Areas** (Fig.65), most of them in north and west Scotland and the islands and covering 12.9% of the land and inland waters.

The Highlands

The Highlands consist of the Western Highlands to the west and the Grampian Highlands to the east, with the Great Glen stretching between them. The most northerly point of mainland Britain, Dunnet Head, is just west of John o'Groats, in the Highlands. At 13547m Ben Nevis in the Western Highlands is not just the highest peak in Scotland but in the whole of Great Britain. Lochs Ness, Oich and Lochy run through the Great Glen, linked together by the Caledonian Canal. Renowned beauty spots include Glencoe, the site of an infamous massacre in 1692, and the many lochs and inlets along the west coast. Kyle of Tongue, North West Sutherland, Assynt-Coigach, Wester Ross, Glen Strathfarrar, Kintail, Glen Affric, the Cairngorms, Ben Nevis and Glencoe, Loch Shiel, Knoydart, Morar, Moidart and Ardnamurchan are all *National Scenic Areas.*

FIGURE 27 THE REGIONS OF SCOTLAND

(Source: STB, 1992)

Inverness is the largest town in the Highlands. Oban, Mallaig and Ullapool on the west coast are important ferry terminals for the islands as are Aberdeen and Scrabster to the north. Aberdeen ('the Granite City'), Peterhead and Fraserburgh are the largest towns in the Grampian Highlands.

The Highlands contain Scotland's ski resorts: Aviemore in the Spey Valley, Glenshee and Tomintoul. A *Malt Whisky Trail* links up eight Scotch whisky distilleries including Glenfiddich and Glenlivet in Grampian, while a *Fishing Heritage Trail* links fishing ports between Aberdeen and Nairn. Finally a *Castle Trail* links up Grampian castles and stately homes associated with royalty, including Balmoral Castle; the area around Balmoral is actually called Royal Deeside. Some Highland Games events, including those at Braemar, take place in this area.

There is a ruined medieval cathedral at Elgin. The Cairngorms have been proposed as a future *World Heritage Site.*

The Islands

The Scottish Islands divide into:

a) the Inner Hebrides or Western Isles:

(i) the Inner Hebrides:	Skye, Mull, Staffa, Tiree, Coll, Rum, Eigg, Muck, Iona
(ii) the Western Isles:	Lewis, Harris, North Uist, South Uist, Benbecula, Barra
b) the Orkneys:	Mainland, South Ronaldsay, Hoy, Rousay, Stronsay, Westray, Sanday, etc
c) the Shetlands:	Mainland, Yell, Fetlar, Whalsay, Unst, Bressay, etc

Most of the smaller islands in these groups are uninhabited. Shetland, Hoy and West Mainland, South Lewis, Harris and Uist, St. Kilda, South Uist, Machair, Trotternish, the Cuillins and the Small Islands are all *National Scenic Areas.*

Important prehistoric remains can be found on Lewis in the Western Isles and at Skara Brae in the Orkneys.

The Isle of Skye is associated with the romantic tale of Flora Macdonald's efforts to help Bonnie Prince Charlie escape capture. It is dominated by the Cuillins which are extremely popular with climbers. Iona, one of the earliest centres of Christianity in the British Isles, has the remains of a fine abbey. Staffa is thought to have inspired Mendelssohn to write the Hebrides Overture. The Shetlands are so far north that visitors can experience the midnight sun during the summer. St. Kilda, in the Outer Hebrides, is a designated *World Heritage Site.*

Central Lowlands

The Central Lowlands are made up of five regions: Tayside, Central, Fife, Strathclyde and Lothian. The River Tay, Scotland's longest river flows through Tayside, to the east of Scotland. Central Scotland, or **Rob Roy Country** after Sir Walter Scott's book, contains the Trossachs and Loch Lomond. Loch Lomond, the largest Scottish lake, is surrounded by mountains including Ben Lomond and Ben Vorlich. Loch Tummel, Loch Rannoch and Glen Lyon, the River Tay, the River Earn, the Trossachs, Loch Lomond, Lynn of Lorn, Loch na Keal, Isle of Mull, Scarba, Lunga and the Garvellachs,

Knapsdale, Kyles of Bute, Jura and North Arran are all *National Scenic Areas*. Near Stirling are several important battlefield sites, including Bannockburn and Stirling Bridge. The M8 links Glasgow and Edinburgh, the M9 Edinburgh and Stirling, and the M90 Edinburgh and Perth.

Dundee and Perth are the largest cities in Tayside and Stirling is the largest town in Central Scotland. Edinburgh, the largest city in Lothian, has been a tourism centre for decades. It is dominated by its castle overlooking Princes Street, but other permanent attractions in the city include the Cathedral, Holyrood House, the Scottish National Portrait Gallery, the Scottish National Gallery of Modern Art and Holyrood Palace. The annual Edinburgh Festival in August attracts thousands of people; during the course of it the Military Tattoo takes place in the Castle.

Glasgow, the largest city in Strathclyde, straddles the River Clyde and is a more recent touristic success story. Amongst its attractions are the Kelvingrove Museum and Art Gallery, the Hunterian Gallery, the Burrell Collection, the Cathedral and the beautiful city centre architecture, some of it Victorian, some of it by the early 20th century architect, Charles Rennie Mackintosh.

Ayr, a large town and seaside resort in Strathclyde, is near the birthplace of poet, Robert Burns. A *Burns Heritage Trail* starts nearby. The famous Royal and Ancient Golf Club is at St. Andrews on the coast of Fife, but there are other important golf courses at Turnberry, Troon and Prestwick on the south west coast and at Gleneagles, north of Stirling.

Famous castles in the area include Blair Castle, Scone Palace, Glamis Castle and Stirling Castle.

The Southern Uplands and Southern Islands

Dumfries and Galloway is separated from Cumbria by the Solway Firth. The Firth of Forth separates Fife and Lothian and is bridged by the Forth Road and Rail Bridges. Off the coast of South West Scotland are the islands of Arran, Bute, Gigha, Islay, Jura, Colonsay and Great Cumbrae. The *Mull of Kintyre* is a long finger of land on the south west coast enclosing the Firth of Clyde and the Isle of Arran. The *West Highland Way* and the *Southern Upland Way* are long distance footpaths. Upper Tweeddale, Eildon and Leaderfoot, Fleet Valley, the Nith Estuary, and East Stewarty Coast are all *National Scenic Areas*. Stranraer and Cairnryan are important ferry ports in this region, linking Scotland with Northern Ireland.

Jedburgh, Dryburgh, Melrose and Sweetheart Abbeys are romantic ruins in the southern area. Gretna Green just across the Scottish border is also famous as a place where eloping couples from England could marry in a blacksmith's shop.

TABLE 21 THE TOP TWENTY VISITOR ATTRACTIONS IN SCOTLAND, 1989

		Visitor Nos
1.	Glasgow Museum and Art Gallery	1,041,401
2.	Edinburgh Castle	1,033,697
3.	Magnum Leisure Centre, Irvine	1,010,260
4.	Royal Botanic Gardens, Edinburgh	914,748
5.	Perth Leisure Pool	662,263
6.	Museum of Transport, Glasgow	633,551
7.	Edinburgh Zoo	*555,000
8.	Burrell Collection, Glasgow	490,572
9.	Royal Museum of Scotland, Edinburgh	464,543
10.	Mariner Leisure Centre, Falkirk	385,603
11.	Glasgow Botanic Gardens	*350,000
12.	People's Palace Museum, Glasgow	345,559
13.	National Gallery of Scotland	341,337
14.	Aberdeen Art Gallery	339,841
15.	Palace of Holyroodhouse, Edinburgh	303,811
16.	Culzean Castle and Country Park	297,689
17.	Museum of Childhood, Edinburgh	261,764
18.	Stirling Castle	256,218
19.	Blair Castle, Blair Atholl	168,005
20.	Blair Drummond Safari Park	166,636

(* approximate number)

NORTHERN IRELAND

Northern Ireland consists of the six counties of Antrim, Armagh, County Down, Fermanagh, Londonderry and Tyrone. Although it is often referred to as 'Ulster', this is really the name of a historic province which included the counties of Cavan, Donegal and Monaghan in the Republic of Ireland as well. Belfast, capital of the Six Counties, and Londonderry are the largest towns. The most important port is Larne on the east coast.

Amongst the natural attractions of Northern Ireland are Lough Neagh, the largest lake in Britain, the Giant's Causeway, the Sperrin and Antrim Mountains, and the Mountains of Mourne along the east coast. Most of Northern Ireland's lakes are in Fermanagh where the River Erne links Upper and Lower Lough Erne, a popular sailing area. Of the many *seaside resorts* on the Ards Peninsula (separated from the body of County Down by Strangford Lough), the most popular is Bangor. Armagh, the smallest county, is sometimes called 'the Garden of Ulster'.

FIGURE 28 THE COUNTIES OF NORTHERN IRELAND

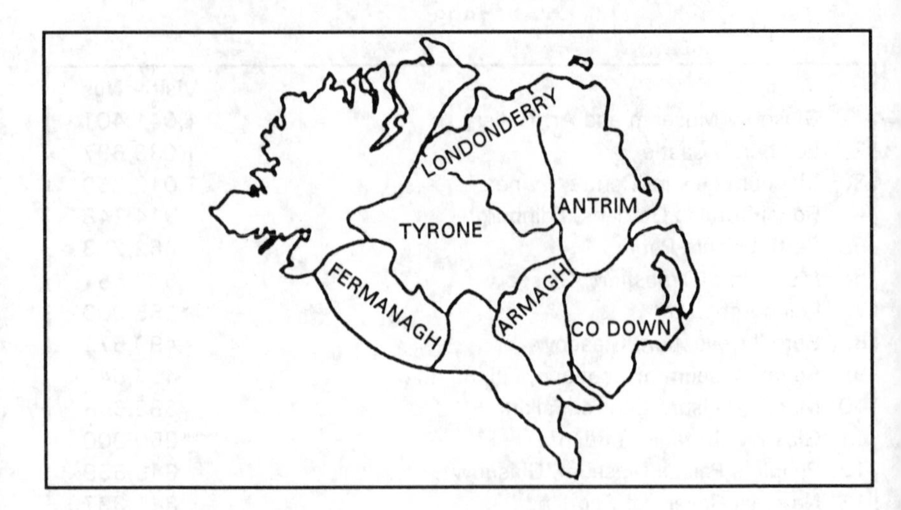

TABLE 22 THE TOP TWENTY VISITOR ATTRACTIONS IN NORTHERN IRELAND IN 1989

		Visitor Nos
1.	Giant's Causeway	300,000
2.	Ulster Museum	244,343
3.	Belfast Zoo	230,732
4.	Ulster Folk and Transport Museum	177,093
5.	Dundonald Old Mill	133,600
6.	Waterworld	123,978
7.	Ulster American Folk Park	102,445
8.	Causeway Safari Park	98,321
9.	Northern Ireland Aquarium	90,242
10.	Portstewart Strand	88,000
11.	Marble Arch Caves	65,000
12.	Armagh Planetarium	60,000
13.	Newry Arts Centre	58,743
14.	Carrickfergus Castle	57,024
15.	Tropicana	51,042
16.	Old Bushmills Distillery	48,830
17.	Castle Ward	45,000
18.	Florencecourt Gardens	44,895
19.	Butterfly House	49,946
20.	Bangor Visitor Centre	38,748

The Ulster Way is a 500-mile *long distance footpath* which will eventually ring Northern Ireland.

The area around Downpatrick is sometimes called **St. Patrick's Country** after the saint who landed in Ireland in 432 AD and is credited with bringing Christianity to the country.

The Giant's Causeway, a dramatic landscape made up of more than 38,000 mainly hexagonal basaltic columns created by volcanic activity, is on the north coast of County Antrim. It is a designated *World Heritage Site*. Important historical attractions include Carrickfergus Castle and the Round Tower of Antrim.

THE CHANNEL ISLANDS

The Channel Islands are a self-governing group of islands in the English Channel. The two largest islands are Guernsey and Jersey. St. Peter Port is the capital of Guernsey and St. Helier of Jersey. The smaller islands of Herm and Sark are quite close to Guernsey but Alderney is twenty miles away to the north; all three are part of the Bailiwick of Guernsey as are the tiny islands of Jethoou, Brecqhou and Lithou. All the islands are nearer to the coast of Normandy than they are to England; Jersey is only fourteen miles away from the French coast. The islands have their own stamps and coinage, although they are English-speaking. The Channel Islands are associate members of the EC but have their own taxation system which does not include VAT. The Islands are accessible by boat from Portsmouth, Weymouth and Torquay, or by air from Glasgow, Edinburgh, Belfast, Leeds/Bradford, Manchester, East Midlands, Norwich, Birmingham, Cardiff, Luton, Stansted, Heathrow, Gatwick, the City, Bristol, Bournemouth, Southampton, Exeter and Plymouth.

TABLE 23 THE MAIN TOURIST ATTRACTIONS OF JERSEY AND GUERNSEY

JERSEY	GUERNSEY
Jersey Zoo (Wildife Preservation Trust)	Guernsey Museum and Art Gallery
Covered Market	Castle Cornet
German Military Underground Hospital	Victor Hugo's House
St. Ouen's Manor	Dehus Dolmen
St. Ouen's, St. Brelade's and St. Aubin's Bays	St. Peter Port Harbour
Battle of Flowers	

FIGURE 29 POSITION OF THE CHANNEL ISLANDS

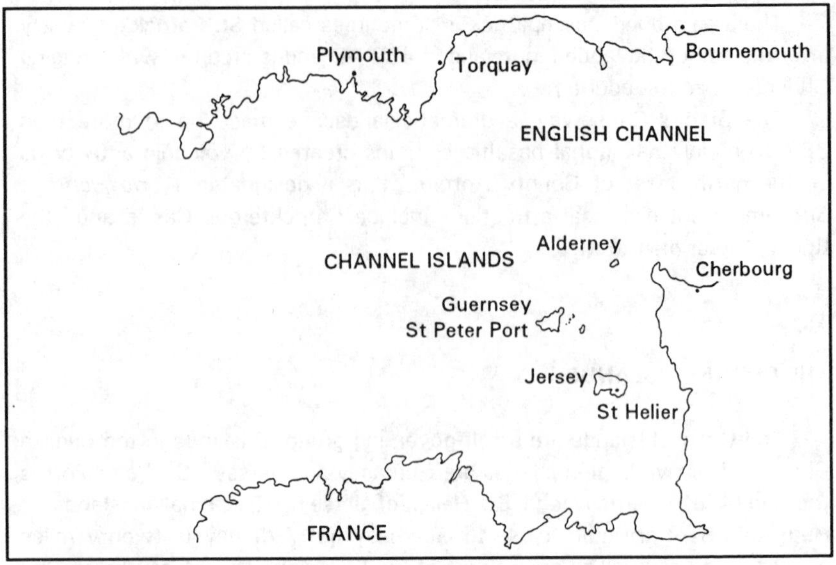

ISLE OF MAN

The Isle of Man is a self-governing island thirty-three miles long by twelve miles wide in the Irish Sea, accessible by boat from Liverpool, Heysham, Fleetwood, Workington, Belfast and Dublin, or by air from Heathrow, Luton, Dublin, Belfast, Cardiff, Newcastle, Manchester, Leeds/ Bradford, Birmingham, Liverpool, Blackpool and Glasgow. It has its own coinage and stamps. The island's capital is Douglas, seat of the Manx Parliament or Tynwald which was established in 979 AD and is therefore much older than Westminster. Manx pubs open all day and the island has a different taxation system to the mainland.

The Manx Government has designated seventeen *National Glens* which are preserved and maintained in a largely natural state. In 1979 the Isle of Man's first long distance footpath, the *Millennium Way* stretching from Ramsey to Castletown and following the route of a medieval highway, was opened to celebrate the millennium of the Tynwald. The ninety-mile coastal footpath or *Road of the Gull*, and fourteen-mile *Herring Road* following a route Manx fishermen used to walk were both created in 1986 to celebrate Manx Heritage Year. The Manx National Trust owns vast areas of countryside, including unspoilt stretches of coastline at the Chasms, Spanish Head and Maughold. It also cares for the *Calf of Man*, a tiny uninhabited island, separated from the southern tip of the mainland by the Manx Sound, which is home to a flock of rare native Loghtan sheep.

FIGURE 30 POSITION OF THE ISLE OF MAN

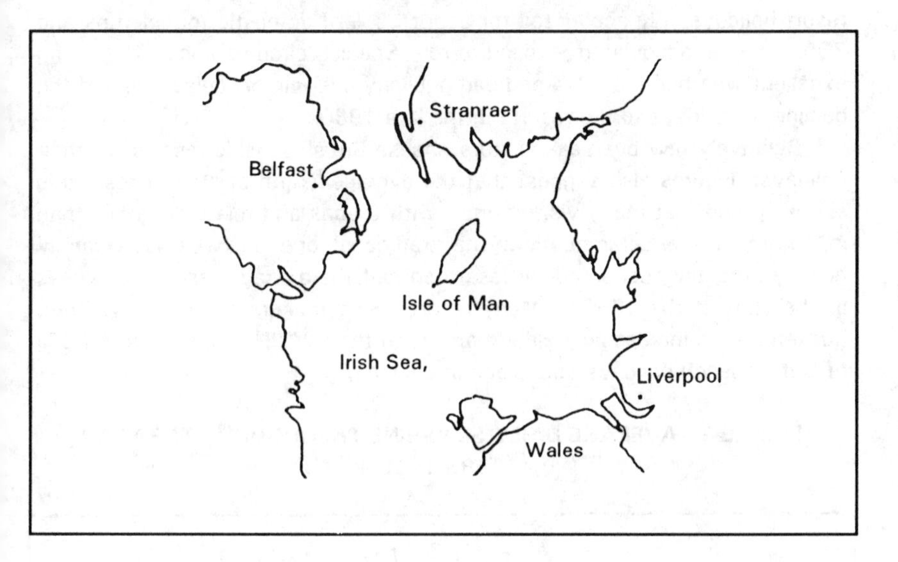

TABLE 24 THE MAIN TOURIST ATTRACTIONS OF THE ISLE OF MAN

Tynwald	Horse-drawn trams, Douglas (summer only)
Grove Rural Life Museum	Cregneash Folk Museum
Manx Museum	Castle Rushen
Peel Castle	Grand Union Camera Obscura
Manx Cattery at Knockaloe	Curraghs (Marsh) Wildlife Park
Isle of Man Steam Railway	Manx Electric Railway
T.T. (Tourist Trophy) Races	

HOLIDAYS BY THE SEA

There are an estimated 446 British seaside resorts (Figs. 26 and 33) and some of them were amongst the UK's first real tourist destinations. This was partly because the Prince Regent's faith in sea bathing made it fashionable, partly because the rapid spread of the railways in the 19th century brought resorts like Blackpool, Brighton and Bournemouth within easy reach of the working classes, and partly because growing incomes made day trips and holidays more feasible.

Until the early 1970s about 75% of British citizens holidayed in the seaside resorts. However, once cheap packages brought the guaranteed sun of the Mediterranean within reach of almost everyone the appeal of the resorts rapidly faded (Fig.31 shows the average hours of sunshine in the main British seaside resorts over a four year period). By 1990 seaside resort holidays only accounted for about 25% of domestic tourist trips and 33% of the associated expenditure. Special circumstances, including excellent weather in the UK and bad publicity over airport delays, halted the decline of holidays to the resorts in the late 1980s.

Relatively few overseas visitors choose British seaside resorts for their holidays. Figures also suggest that the average length of stay at resorts is shrinking and that many visitors stay with friends and relatives rather than in commercial accommodation; the traditional one or two week family holiday probably accounted for less than half the average resort's business at the start of the 1990s. Many resort holidaymakers are repeat visitors, but tend to be increasingly elderly and from the C2/DE groups. About 85% of British beach holidays take place in England.

FIGURE 31 AVERAGE DAILY SUNSHINE THROUGHOUT THE YEAR 1985-1988

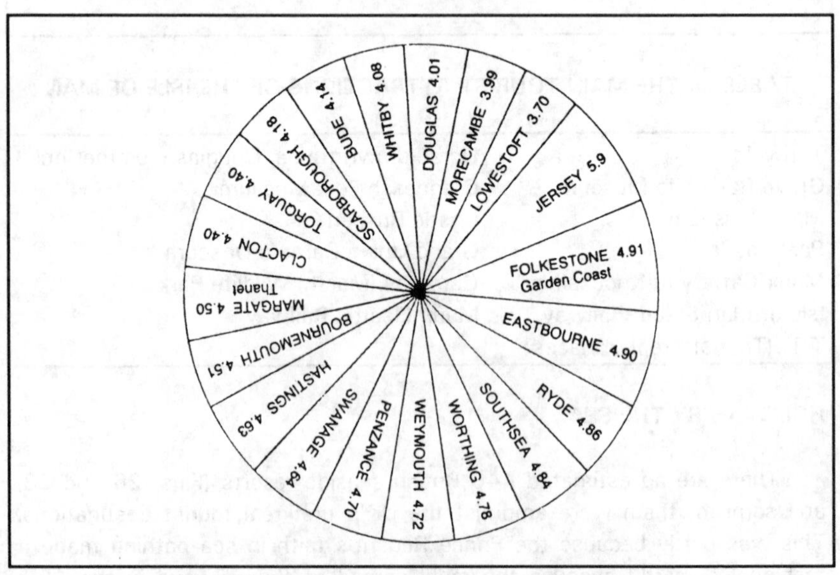

(Source: South East Tourist Board)

In the late 1980s many of the resorts invested in upgrading their facilities to try and improve their image. Brighton, Bournemouth and Blackpool marketed themselves successfully as conference destinations, while the Torbay resorts (Paignton, Brixham and Torquay) ran a successful campaign to cash in on their mild climate, reidentifying themselves as 'The English Riviera'.

In 1990 the following resorts could accommodate 500,000 people a year:

Scarborough	Torbay
Great Yarmouth	Newquay
Brighton	Tenby
Eastbourne	Llandudno
Isle of Wight	Rhyl
Bournemouth	Blackpool

Five resorts, including Blackpool and Bournemouth, can accommodate more than a million visitors a year.

In 1991 only thirty-five British beaches qualified for the European *Blue Flag* award indicating that the sand and water were clean, that there were proper toilets, that it was safe to bathe, that lifeguards and/or lifesaving equipment were available and that dogs were kept off the beach in summer (Fig. 32).

FIGURE 32 'BLUE FLAG' BEACH WINNERS 1991

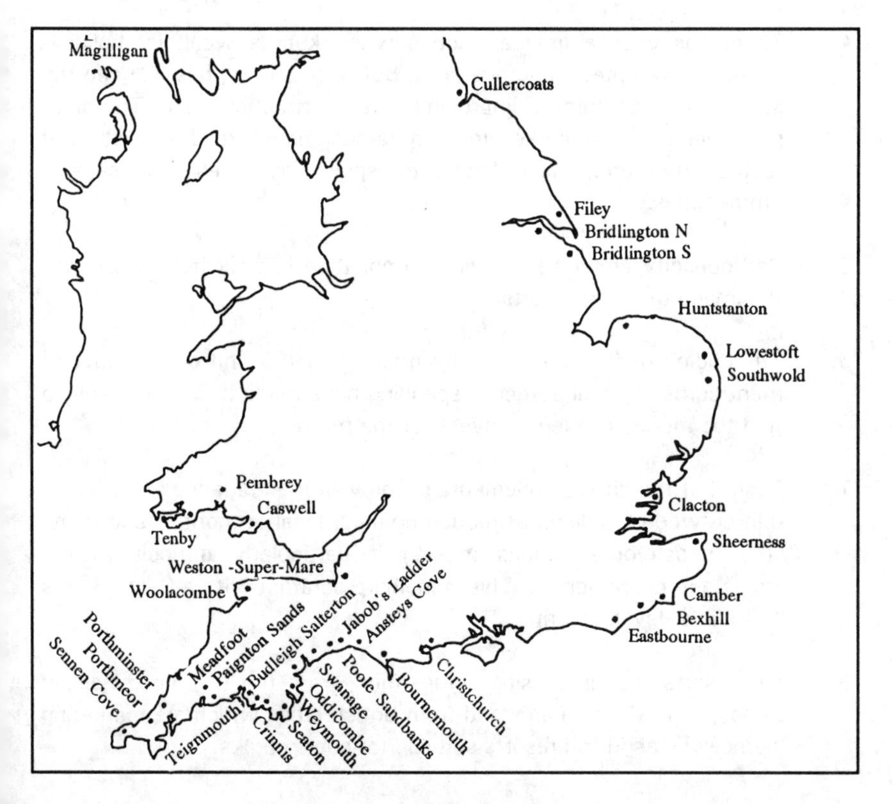

Problems facing the Seaside Resorts in the 1990s

Research suggests that most of the resorts faced the following problems by the early 1990s:

1. Many of them began life in Victorian times and have now lost their architectural coherence as more and more buildings have been added in piecemeal fashion to accommodate a growing residential population. Many are no longer as attractive to look at as they once were. What's more modern development often fails to make any distinction between seaside resorts and inland towns.

2. Most of the resorts also developed in the pre-private car era, and their once attractive sea-fronts have since been disfigured by busy roads and car parks.

3. Many resorts have a large elderly residential population whose needs often dictate what changes and improvements can be made.

4. There has been a gradual slide downmarket as wealthier holidaymakers have opted to go overseas. But price cutting has reduced the scope for investment in improving hotels, attractions, etc. The paraphernalia of downmarket tourism (amusement arcades, fast food restaurants, etc.) also tends to spoil once beautiful seaside promenades.

5. Bad publicity about beach and sea pollution has further undermined the image of many resorts.

6. The ending of Section 4 tourism grants in 1990 and central government curbs on local authority spending have made it more difficult to find the money needed to invest for the future.

7. Control of the different elements of the visitor experience in resorts is split between hoteliers, attraction owners, local authorities and many other people/organisations making it particularly difficult to co-ordinate improvememts. This is in sharp contrast with a Center Parcs or Butlin's development.

8. The resorts face increasing competition, from the revamped holiday camps, from Center Parcs and from British cities which are marketing themselves as inland resorts suitable for short breaks.

FIGURE 33 ENGLAND'S MAIN SEASIDE RESORTS (*indicates a pier)

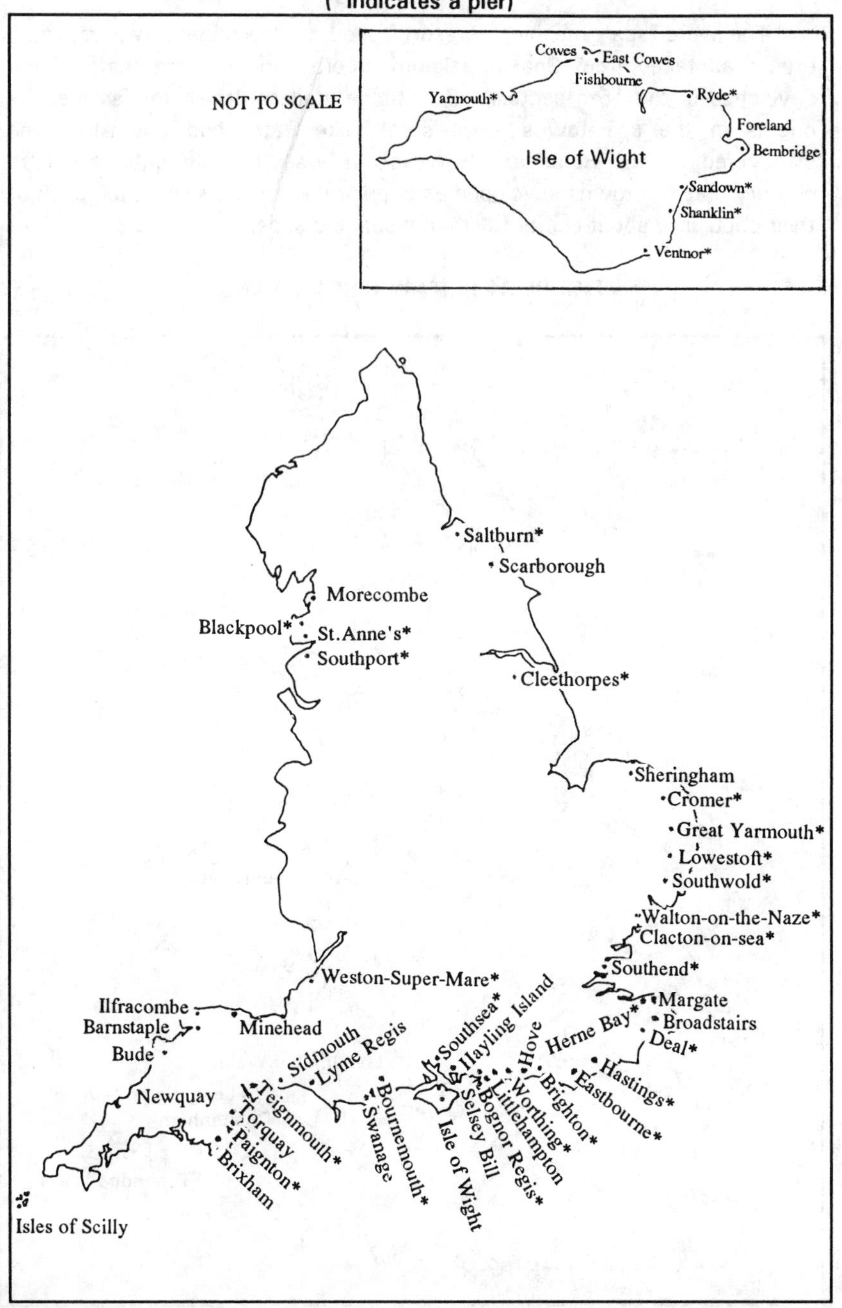

THE SPA TOWNS

The word 'spa', meaning a resort based around mineral waters, mud, etc., was taken from Spa in Belgium where mineral water baths were developed in the 15th century. In a sense modern British tourism had its origins in the spa towns since some, like Bath, had originally been discovered by the Romans. However, it wasn't really until the 18th century that spa towns developed as popular places to visit. At the peak of their popularity about eighty UK towns boasted spas.

FIGURE 34 BRITAIN'S SPA TOWNS

Since World War I traditional spas have declined in popularity. There are now only twelve left. Probably the best known are Bath, Cheltenham, Leamington Spa, Harrogate, Tunbridge Wells and Buxton. In the 19th century there were Welsh spas in Llandrindod Wells, Llanwrtyd Wells, Llangammarch Wells and Builth Wells; only Llandrindod Wells still has a spa, with a Spas of Wales Visitor Centre to explain its history. At Harrogate tourists can still swim in the Turkish Baths as well as visit a spa museum. Tourists can also visit the Pump Rooms in Bath, and in 1989 the City Council approved plans for LandLeisure plc to revive other features of the city's heyday; the Cross Bath, a Grade I listed building, is to be reopened as a spa bath with a 'Georgian Bathing Experience' attached. The Hot Bath will also be restored to offer hydrotherapy and other holisitic treatments. Finally the 19th century Beau Street Baths will be turned into a health and leisure centre.

In 1990 Heritage Projects invested £1.3 million in 'A Day at the Wells', an attraction focusing on Tunbridge Wells in the 1740s, housed in an old auction room in The Pantiles pedestrian zone.

CHAPTER THREE
THE BRITISH TRANSPORT NETWORKS

The transport infrastructure of Great Britain consists of a network of airports, ferry ports, railway lines, motorways and other roads, which, together, connect up even the remotest parts of the country. The planes and ferries are important in getting overseas tourists to the UK, while the railway, roads and rivers are more important in transporting them around the country after they arrive.

GETTING TO THE UK

THE AIRPORTS AND AIRLINES

TABLE 25 PASSENGER TRAFFIC THROUGH UK AIRPORTS, 1989

Airport	IATA Code	Terminal Passengers ('000s)	Passengers at all UK Airports (%)
1. Heathrow	LHR	39,588	40.0
2. Gatwick	LGW	21,150	21.4
3. Manchester	MAN	10,059	10.2
4. Glasgow	GLA	3,862	3.9
5. Birmingham	BHX	3,333	3.4
6. Luton	LTN	2,828	2.9
7. Edinburgh	EDI	2,363	2.4
8. Belfast	BFS	2,158	2.2
9. Aberdeen	ABZ	1,730	1.7
10. Newcastle	NCL	1,492	1.5
11. East Midlands	EMA	1,453	1.5
12. Stansted	STN	1,319	1.3
13. Leeds	LBA	866	0.9
14. Bristol	BRS	838	0.8
15. Cardiff	CWL	696	0.7
16. Isle of Man	IOM	510	0.5
17. Belfast City	BFS	507	0.5
18. Southampton	SOU	491	0.5
19. Liverpool	LPL	477	0.5
20. Tees-side	MME	332	0.3

(Source: Civil Aviation Authority)

(Figures include UK passengers leaving the UK, overseas passengers arriving in the UK and domestic passengers.)

In 1989 68% of overseas tourists arrived in the UK by air. Within the UK itself only one per cent of all travel was by air. However, domestic traffic was increasing faster than international traffic; in 1988 domestic airlines carried 11.8% more passengers than in 1987. Passenger movements through British airports were expected to grow by between 77% and 156% between 1987 and 2005. Table 25 shows the UK airports which received the largest numbers of passengers in 1989.

London, the main international gateway for the UK, has five airports: Heathrow, Gatwick, Luton, Stansted and London City.

FIGURE 35 THE POSITION OF LONDON'S AIRPORTS

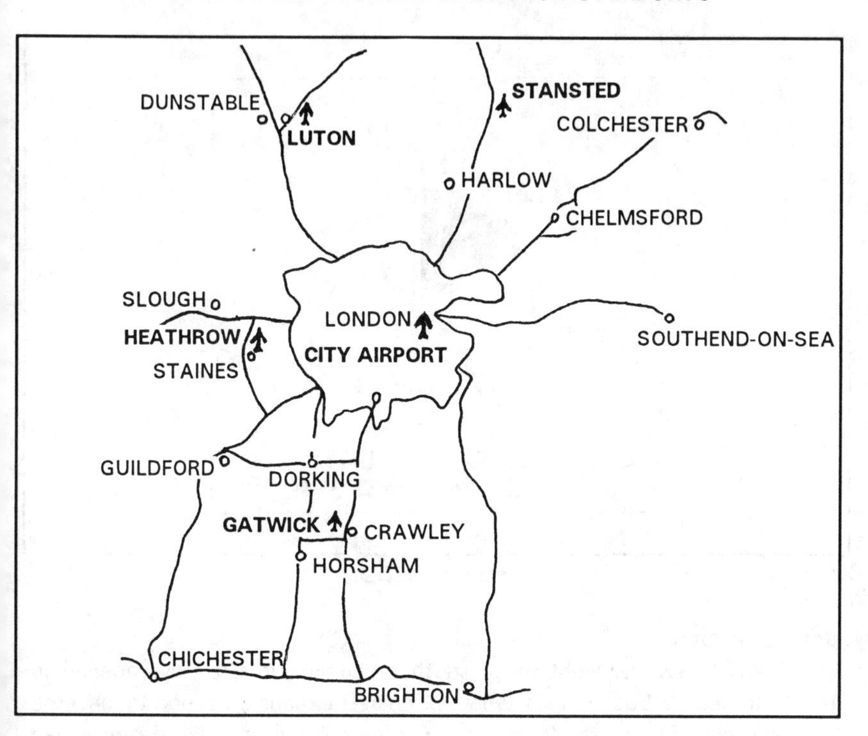

Heathrow Airport

Heathrow is in Hounslow, fifteen miles west of Central London, and was first opened in 1930. During the war it was used by the RAF, returning to civil operations afterwards. By 1973 it was already obvious that the three existing terminals wouldn't be able to cope with the projected increases in passenger and cargo traffic, and by 1991 a fourth terminal had been added. It is used by more than seventy airlines and is Europe's largest airport in terms of passengers handled. It is also one of the world's largest international airports. A fifth terminal is likely to be built at Heathrow eventually to enable it to handle 53 million passengers a year.

Heathrow is operated by BAA plc. Domestic air services operate out of Terminal One. The London Underground was extended to Heathrow in 1977, and there is a National Express interchange point there. In 1991 approval was given for a new British Rail link from London to Heathrow which is expected to open in 1992. Most of the funding will come from BAA plc. Fig.36 shows the modes of transport passengers use to get to Heathrow.

FIGURE 36 HOW PASSENGERS REACH HEATHROW

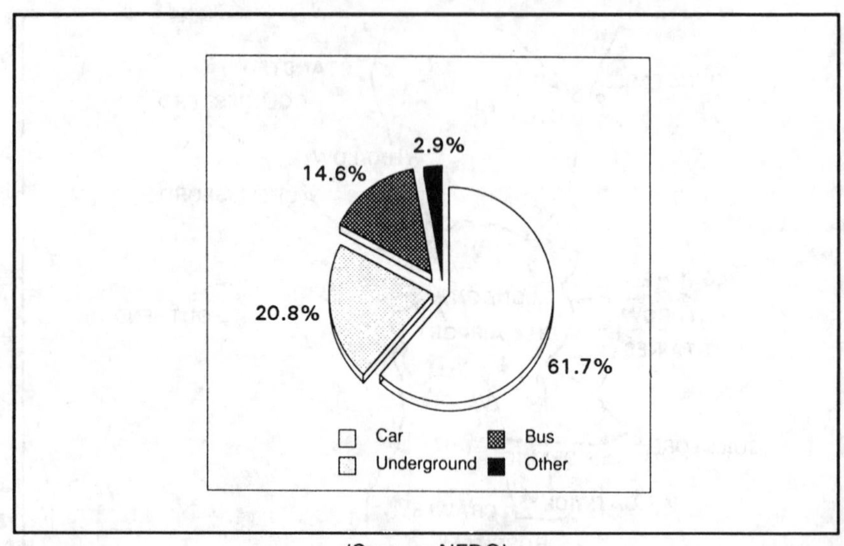

(Source: NEDO)

Gatwick Airport

Gatwick, twenty-eight miles south of London in Crawley, opened in 1936. In the 1950s it underwent extensive expansion work to become London's second airport. When this was completed in 1958 Gatwick had only one runway but a fine terminal building with a British Rail station just beside it. In the 1960s it handled much of the expanding charter holiday market, and in 1964 the runway was extended to accommodate larger aircraft. Before 1987 when it merged with British Airways, British Caledonian, the UK's second largest airline, used Gatwick as a base. Dan Air and several American scheduled carriers still do. In 1988 a second terminal, connected to the first by a rapid transit system, opened. Gatwick is operated by BAA plc.

London Luton Airport

London Luton Airport, thirty-two miles north west of London, first opened in 1938. In the 1960s, after the wooden terminal building was replaced and the runway extended, Luton's holiday charter business expanded and it became the base for the airline, Court Line. When Court Line collapsed in 1974 Luton's passenger figures slumped. However, in 1978 it was officially designated an international airport. Brand new facilities were opened in 1985 and efforts were made to boost traffic figures. Dan Air, Britannia and Monarch already used Luton but few scheduled carriers did. By the late 1980s British Midland, Ryan Air and Virgin Atlantic also offered ex-Luton services, as did charter airlines like Britannia Airways. In 1991 the airport changed in name to London Luton Airport to emphasise its position.

Stansted Airport

Until 1991 Stansted, thirty-four miles north east of London, was a relatively insignificant airport. Originally built in 1942 for military use, it had an unusually long runway making it suitable for larger planes when it reverted to civilian use. Stansted had a chequered history until 1986 when work started to turn it into London's third airport. (Schemes to develop a completely new site at Maplin or Cublington had by then been abandoned.) Stansted was relaunched in 1991 after architect Norman Foster had given it a £400 million facelift. Eventually it is expected to handle 15 million passengers a year.

London City Airport

A city centre airport had been talked about for many years, but it wasn't until 1987, the peak of the business boom in the City, that London City Airport opened in Docklands, six miles from the heart of the City. Initially only Plymouth-based Brymon Airways and Eurocity Express/London City Airways operated out of it, using small Dash-7 planes. At first the runway was only large enough for short take off and landing planes (hence its alternative title: the *stol*port) which meant it could only handle traffic for Paris, Amsterdam and Brussels. There was also initial bad publicity because the planes flew below air traffic control radar level where they were competing for airspace with private planes, gliders, etc. In 1991 the Airport was being adapted to take jet aircraft.

Fig. 37 shows the position of the UK's main airports. British Airways, the UK flag carrier, offers services to most provincial airports often timed to connect with international flights. It also operates the Shuttle services to Manchester, Glasgow, Edinburgh and Belfast which operate rather like train services, with short check-in times and no reservations required.

FIGURE 37 BRITAIN'S MOST IMPORTANT AIRPORTS, 1991

TABLE 26 SOME UK DOMESTIC AIRLINES & THEIR IDENTIFYING IATA CODES

Airline Name	Two Letter IATA Code
Air UK	UK
Aurigny Air Services	GR
British Midland	BD
Brymon Airways	BC
Dan Air	DA
Jersey European Airlines	JE
London City Airways	II
Loganair	LC
Manx Airways	UE

Until 1987 the British airports were owned by the government. BAA, plc (formerly British Airports Authority), the world's first privatised airport group, now owns and operates Heathrow, Gatwick, Stansted, Southampton, Glasgow, Edinburgh, Prestwick and Aberdeen airports. In 1990 these airports between them handled 74 million passengers; by 2005 they are expected to handle 148 million. In 1990 90% of BAA's profits came from running the airports. Other profits come from running a consultancy service, owning a small number of airport hotels, and cargo handling.

Other UK airports are owned and run by local authority airport companies. However, in 1991 the government was planning to privatise these as well. The larger ones like Birmingham, Manchester and East Midlands which have built up an international network should be able to continue operating. Others like Cardiff and Ipswich are too close to large towns to expand much more. Conceivably they could be sold for more profitable redevelopment. Fig. 38 shows the possible future of some British airports.

The Civil Aviation Authority (CAA)

The 1971 Civil Aviation Act established the **Civil Aviation Authority (CAA)** to regulate air services in the UK. Although the CAA is independent of the government, the Secretary of State for Transport appoints up to twelve Members of the Authority as a Board which then decides CAA policy. The CAA is expected to recover all its running costs and to make an 8% return on its capital so that the cost of essential civil aviation services falls on its users rather than on taxpayers as a whole.

FIGURE 38 THE FUTURE FOR BRITISH PROVINCIAL AIRPORTS?

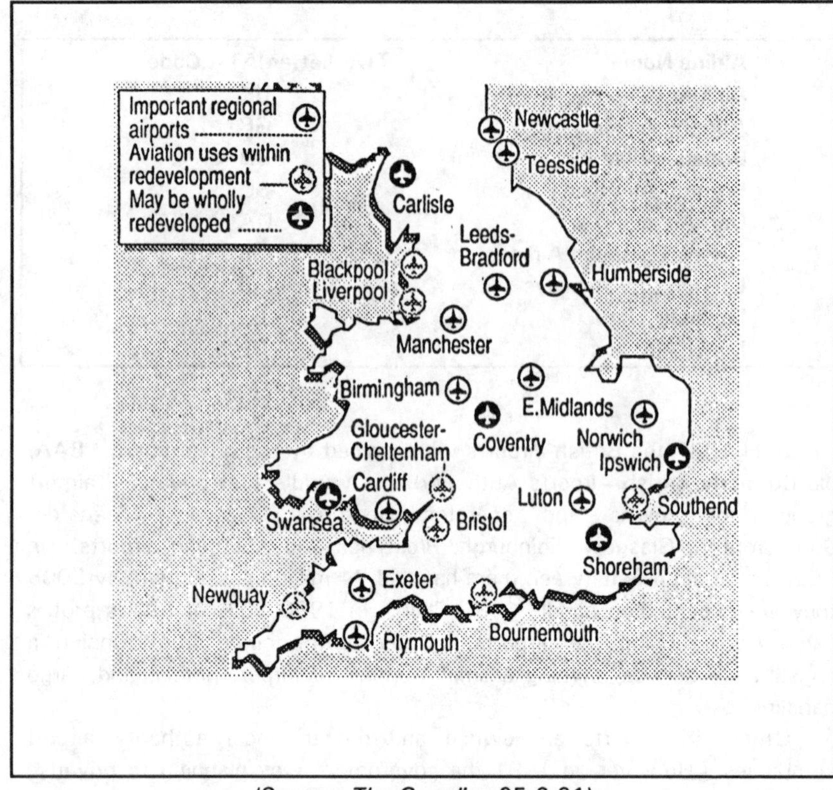

(Source: *The Guardian* 25.6.91)

The CAA has the following responsibilities:

* Provision of air navigation services with the Ministry of Defence through the National Air Traffic Services (NATS). NATS' function is 'to enable public transport, private, business and military aircraft to fly as far as is practicable when, where and how they wish, as safely as possible'. NATS provides navigational services for aircraft taking off and landing at most major UK airports.
* Economic regulation of the civil aviation industry, including air transport licensing. Before issuing licences for scheduled or charter services the CAA must check the financial and operational worthiness of applicants. Where another airline or third party raises objections to a licence the CAA must hold a public hearing to resolve the dispute. The CAA also approves international scheduled air fares. Domestic air fares are also filed although the CAA rarely intervenes in setting them. Since 1973

the CAA has also been responsible for issuing Air Travel Organiser's Licences (ATOLs) to air tour operators. Before granting these licences it has to be satisfied that the organiser's financial arrangements are sound. The organiser must also pay a bond which will be used to reimburse passengers in the event of financial failure (where the bond is inadequate to cover all the ensuing costs the CAA's Air Travel Reserve Fund can make up the shortfall).

* Air safety, air worthiness and operational safety, including the licensing of flight crew, aircraft engineers and aerodromes and the certification of UK airlines and aircraft.
* Advising the government on domestic and international civil aviation matters.
* Ownership and operation of Inverness, Benbecula, Islay, Tiree, Kirkwall, Stornoway, Wick and Sumburgh aerodromes in the Scottish Highlands and Islands, through the wholly owned subsidiary company, Highlands & Islands Airports Ltd. Apart from Sumburgh, these aerodromes have too little traffic to operate commercially but offer a vital link for remote rural communities, so the Scottish Office provides a grant to help maintain them.
* Regulating landing and similar charges and investigating claims of unfair trading practices at UK airports.
* Miscellaneous responsibilities including: looking after consumer interests; private aviation requirements; economic and scientific research; collecting and publishing statistics and economic data; and consulting and training overseas administrations.

Some of these functions involve the CAA in a delicate balancing act. For example, it tries to ensure that 'British airlines satisfy all major areas of public demand at the lowest possible charges consistent with the sound development of British air transport'. However, it also has to 'further the reasonable interests of air transport users and promote effective competition by British airlines with those of other countries'. It therefore has to try and balance what may well be the conflicting needs of the airline industry, air passengers and the UK as a whole.

The Department of Transport retains responsibility for the following civil aviation matters:

* International civil aviation relations.
* Investigating aircraft accidents.
* Developing policy on aircraft noise.
* Development policy for national airports.
* Co-ordinating aviation security.

Air Traffic Control in the UK

Air traffic control in the UK is the responsibility of the National Air Traffic Services (NATS) division of the CAA. British air traffic control services are provided from three bases: the London Air Traffic Control Centre (LATCC) at West Drayton; Manchester Airport; and the Scottish Air Traffic Control Centre (SCATCC) at Prestwick.

Air traffic controllers are equipped with radar displays, flight progress strips which show the position of individual aircraft, radios and closed circuit television sets. By 1995 a new system of control (Central Control Function or CCF) will have been introduced to the busy LATCC area, centralising landing and taking off control away from individual airports to West Drayton. A series of one-way 'tunnels in the sky' will then come into operation to simplify the air traffic controller's task.

Problems Facing the Airlines in 1991

Congestion in the Skies

As airline passenger traffic increased in the 1980s so the skies, especially above major airports like Heathrow, became very congested. This gave rise to some safety worries since improvements in the air traffic control system had not kept pace with the growth in the number of flights to be controlled. One unfortunate consequence was an increase in delays in take-offs because of competition for the available 'slots'; once an aeroplane had missed its scheduled 'slot', there might be a long delay before another was available, especially in the busy summer peak period. Charter passengers were left stranded in airports, sometimes for hours at a time, which led to bad publicity.

Safety Worries

The disaster over Lockerbie in December 1988 when a Pan Am plane was blown out of the sky by a terrorist bomb heightened fears about airport and aircraft safety. The airlines responded by introducing stricter airport checks, both of passengers' luggage and of those people allowed to move around the airport. Unfortunately the 1991 Gulf War exacerbated fears and resulted in a virtual collapse of air traffic during the first half of the year, with catastrophic consequences for airline profits.

Rising Fuel Prices

Airline profitability was threatened by sudden unexpected hikes in the price of fuel. These happened in 1973, and 1979, and then again in 1991 at the start of the Gulf War when the slump in passenger traffic made it difficult for the airlines to pass the increase on in the usual form of higher fares.

Competition

Before British Airways was privatised British Caledonian was large enough to provide it with competition. However, once British Caledonian and British Airways had merged and the airline had been privatised, the only domestic competition came from much smaller airlines like British Midlands which complained to the government that they were unable to compete on equal terms.

However, in the 1990s creeping deregulation of the European airlines, together with increased competition from big American carriers like United and American Airlines, put British Airways under pressure again. The conventional response of airlines in close competition has been to launch a price war. Although this benefits the consumer in the short-term, in the long-term it puts the airlines under economic pressure and may even threaten the existence of some of them.

Government Decisions

The government affects what the airlines can do in several ways. For example, it limits the number of traffic movements allowed in and out of the airports, dictates the hours when flights can take off and land, and has the ultimate say over whether a new airport can be built or an old one expanded. Although in the 1980s the government was inclined to lift all restrictions that affected business activities, British Airways was not always happy about its decisions.

THE FERRIES

Britain's position as an island has always meant that sea transport was very important. The Channel was first crossed by a steamship in 1816, and regular passenger services started in 1820. While the coming of aeroplanes has obviously affected the number of people arriving in the UK by boat, nevertheless in 1990 there were still several companies offering ferry services to and from the UK. In 1989 Department of Transport statistics recorded 28,925,000 passenger movements in and out of the British seaports, an increase of 16% on the 1988 figures which had been badly affected by an acrimonious strike at P & O European Ferries. Not surprisingly most traffic by boat was between the UK and neighbouring EC countries. However, 129,000 passenger movements involved cruise passengers.

Dover is Britain's busiest port. In 1989 Dover Harbour Board recorded 15,044,651 passenger movements through the port, an increase of 22.1% on the strike-damaged 1988 figures. In general the south-eastern ports are the busiest; 25% of visitors to Wales and 20% of visitors to Scotland still use these ports despite the distance to their final destination. Table 26 shows passenger movement figures for the main British ferry ports in 1988.

TABLE 27 PASSENGER MOVEMENTS THROUGH BRITISH FERRY PORTS, 1989

Name of Port	'000s
Dover	12,315
Portsmouth	2,071
Harwich	1,722
Ramsgate	1,549
Holyhead	1,528
Folkestone	1,128
Newhaven	878
Hull	724
Sheerness	674
Fishguard	474
Plymouth	431
Felixstowe	416
Pembroke	241
Weymouth	200
Swansea	125
Southampton	117
Poole	110

(Source: Department of Transport)

Thirty-four per cent of sea traffic between the UK and the Continent consists of EC residents visiting the UK. The remaining 66% is made up of UK residents visiting the Continent. The International Passenger Survey suggests that visitors from some EC countries are more ready than others to brave the seas; perhaps 25% of the traffic between France and the UK consists of French tourists travelling to England, while 66% of the traffic between West Germany and the UK consists of German tourists.

The most up-to-date source of information on ferry crossings is the bi-monthly ABC Passenger Shipping Guide.

In addition to the ferry routes, hovercraft services also operate between Dover and Calais and Boulogne, taking thirty-five and forty minutes respectively. Hovercrafts offer reserved seats and shorter crossing times but may be cancelled in bad weather. In 1990 Hoverspeed introduced high speed Seacats (catamarans) on the Dover to Calais/Boulogne, and Portsmouth to Cherbourg routes but these too may be cancelled in bad weather. Jetfoils operate between Dover and Ostend, taking one hour and forty minutes.

FIGURE 39 POSITION OF THE UK FERRY PORTS

Ferries are especially important to Scotland where they provide the cheapest and easiest access to many islands. Caledonian Macbrayne offer services to the Western Isles, Western Ferries to the Shetlands and P & O to the Orkneys and Shetlands.

In the early 1980s the ships used on the short sea crossings across the English Channel were often old and poorly equipped. In contrast those on the longer crossings had cabins, cinemas, swimming pools, discos and a choice of restaurants. In the late 1980s, with the threat of the Channel Tunnel looming, the ferry companies started improving their ships. In 1987 'superferries', which can carry 4,580 passengers, started service at Dover. Sally Line was the first of the short sea crossing companies to offer a 'cruise' experience across the Channel. By 1991 P & O European Ferries was promoting itself in a similar vein. In 1991 P & O and Sealink Stena Line also applied to the Monopolies and Mergers Commission for permission to pool their operations to compete against the Tunnel, although this application was turned down.

Problems for the Ferry Companies in 1991

In 1991 the ferry companies faced several problems:

* The threat from the **Channel Tunnel**

* The danger of a catastrophic drop in revenues if **duty-free shopping** within the EC is phased out. Apart from the loss of sales on-board the boats much day trip traffic to France could be lost without the lure of cheap shopping. However, some studies suggest people will still shop at the ports and on the boats because they are in a holiday mood.

* **Safety worries.** After the *Herald of Free Enterprise* sunk outside Zeebrugge harbour in 1987 the safety of the design of the roll on/roll off (roro) ferries was questioned. Their large, undivided hulls were ideal for boarding large numbers of cars quickly but dangerous if water got inside since nothing could stop it spreading. The ferry companies have since introduced tighter safety regulations, including issuing boarding passes to keep track of the number of people on board. Emergency procedures are also read out at the start of voyages, as at the start of flights.

* A **poor public image**, based on stories of appalling food and drunken, loutish behaviour by some passengers. Sealink Stena and P & O have invested large sums to bring their ships into line with those operated by Scandinavian Seaways and Brittany Ferries.

The Cost of Ferry Travel

Until 1979 the main ferry companies agreed prices through membership of the Harmonisation Conference in the same way as IATA airlines. In 1980 this system collapsed and companies set their own prices, leading to a loss-making price war. In 1982 prices were raised to realistic levels again.

Prices are usually based on:

a) the number of people travelling;

b) the size of accompanying vehicles;

c) the date of travel, with highest prices during the peak summer months, and over public holidays;

d) the time of travel, with cheapest prices on early morning sailings. Overnight prices on the longer crossings are sometimes high because accommodation must be booked and paid for;

e) the length of time which will be spent abroad, with special discounts for day trips, and short stays of three or five days.

Running ferries at a profit is not easy and depends on round the clock sailings and quick turnarounds at each end of the journey. By 1990 a ferry carrying 350 cars and 1,350 passengers could be turned around in one hour. The move towards larger ships also allows more space for revenue-generating 'extras' like shops, restaurants, bars, cinemas and discos.

GETTING AROUND THE UK

THE RAIL NETWORK

Great Britain's railway network was mainly built up in the 19th century. In 1825 the Stockton to Darlington line began to operate the first fare-paying passenger service. This was followed in 1830 by the opening of a service from Liverpool to Manchester, signalling the start of the Railway Age. At first train services were operated by a number of competing private companies. By the Second World War these had been reduced to four main companies: the Great Western Railway (GWR), the London North-Eastern Railway (LNER), the London Midland Service (LMS) and Southern Region (SR). In 1948 the Labour government nationalised these companies and they became one new company, British Rail (BR), with 19,600 miles of track, 8,294 stations and 20,000+ steam locomotives.

FIGURE 40 THE BRITISH RAIL INTERCITY NETWORK, 1991

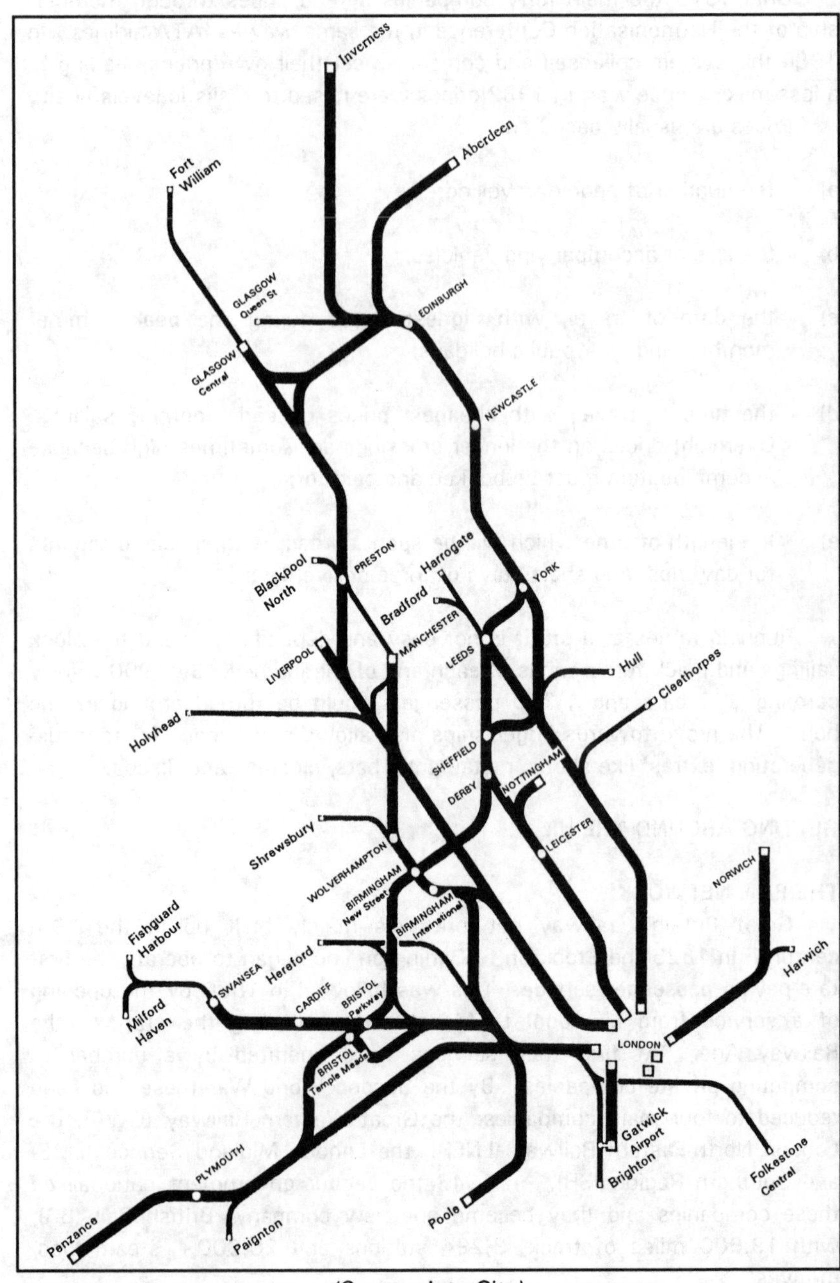

(Source: InterCity)

Since the Second World War British Rail has gradually shed routes and stations as its market has been eroded by competition from coaches, private cars and domestic airlines. Particularly crucial was the 1963 Beeching Report *The Reshaping of British Railways* which recommended the closure of 2,128 stations and a quarter of the railways lines, including all those north of Inverness, most of those in north and central Wales and those in the West Country. These cuts, implemented in 1964, entailed the loss of thousands of jobs. The routes closed were frequently in rural areas where they couldn't be run as profitable commercial operations. During the 1980s British Rail was once more under pressure to contract as the government steadily withdrew its subsidies. By 1990 only 10,500 miles of track remained, together with 2,600 stations. Only 7% of all passenger transport in the UK is now by train.

In 1980 British Rail still had a number of subsidiary businesses which have since been sold. These included several Victorian station hotels and the Sealink ferries. In 1988 Travellers' Fare, the BR-subsidiary which produced station and train meals, was also privatised.

The Rail Network in 1991

London forms the hub of the current British Rail network and is ringed with main-line stations which also connect with London Underground services. The following are the main-line stations and the areas of the country they serve:

Name of Station	Area served
Paddington	South Wales, the West Country
Euston	North West Region, Scotland
King's Cross	North East Region, Scotland, parts of East Anglia
St. Pancras	Sheffield
Liverpool Street	East Anglia
Waterloo	Portsmouth, Southampton, commuter belt
Victoria	Brighton, commuter belt
Charing Cross	South East Region, commuter belt
Marylebone	Commuter belt
Moorgate	Commuter belt
Fenchurch Street	Commuter belt
Cannon Street	Commuter belt
London Bridge	Commuter belt

In 1991 British Rail reorganised its services. The old London Midland, Western, Eastern, Anglia, Southern and Scottish regional management structure was abandoned and British Rail itself was reconstituted as a holding company. The management and operation of the railways was divided into six separate businesses with each station and train allocated to one of them. The six businesses are:

a) Network SouthEast serving London and the south-east commuter routes.
b) Regional Railways which operates local services in the rest of the country, commuter services to other big cities like Birmingham, and 'cross-country' services, including many tourist routes.
c) InterCity services, often operated by 125 trains travelling at speeds of up to 125 miles per hour or by brand-new 225 trains travelling at 140 mph, on main trunk routes. These are some of British Rail's most profitable services.
d) European Passenger Services Ltd which will operate international services through the Channel Tunnel
e) Freight
f) Parcels

TABLE 28 INTERCITY OPERATIONS, 1990

Customers	200,000	per day
Trains	750	per day
Stations	83	
Locomotives	200	
Carriages	1,900	+
InterCity 125 trains	87	
Passenger miles	8,500	million annually
Train miles	51	million annually

(Source: InterCity)

British Rail handles several different categories of railway user:

a) Commuters who use rail services on a daily basis from Monday to Friday to get to work. The majority travel in the peak periods between 0700 and 0930, and between 1600 and 1830. Many use *season tickets* which offer discounted prices for weekly, monthly, quarterly or yearly travel. The commuter market is especially important to Network SouthEast.
b) Business travellers who use the railways as an alternative to driving or flying to business appointments. They often use first class services and are rarely price conscious. First class Pullman services were developed primarily with business travellers' needs in mind and offer extra comfort, including meals served at passengers' seats.

c) Leisure travellers who mainly travel at weekends and off-peak periods. Much of this business is generated in the summer months and over other holiday periods (Christmas, the New Year, Easter, school half-terms). Leisure travellers usually use standard class and are very price conscious. British Rail has developed a range of fares to suit their needs and to discourage leisure travellers from travelling during the congested peak periods. Shoppers, day trippers, holiday-makers and students travelling between their homes and their places of study are all leisure travellers who make up 70% of InterCity passengers.

TABLE 29 BRITISH RAIL ASSETS, 1989/90

Rolling Stock		
Locomotives	diesel	1,835
	electric	260
High Speed Trains	power units	197
Passenger carrying vehicles	locomotives hauled	2,465
	diesel multiple units	2,134
	electric multiple units	7,197
	high speed trains	718
(includes 301 catering carriages and 194 sleeping cars)		
Non-passenger carrying vehicles		1,319
Freight vehicles		21,970
Total seats/berths in passenger carriages		878,450
Stations		
Passenger		2,470
Parcel traffic only		1
Freight traffic only		125
	TOTAL	2,596
Route Miles Open for Traffic		
Passenger traffic only		1,057
Passenger and freight traffic		7,834
Freight traffic only		1,423
	TOTAL	10,314
which includes electrified	overhead systems (AC)	1,531
	third rail systems (DC)	1,188

(Source: British Railways Board Annual Report and Accounts, 1989/90)

TABLE 30 THE LONDON COMMUTER MARKET, 1989/90

(Total market: 473,000 daily commuters into London)

Network SouthEast	42%
London Underground	34%
Car	14%
London buses	6%
Motorcycle/cycle	2%
Private coach	2%

(Source: Network SouthEast)

Problems Facing British Rail in the 1990s

Financial Difficulties

In Europe no railways operate without government subsidy, and the British government has subsidised rail services in the UK since 1947. Although in the 1980s British Rail was under political pressure to reduce its costs as its subsidy was gradually reduced, by 1990 only InterCity was operating profitably without a government grant and even that profitability disappeared during the 1991 recession.

TABLE 31 NETWORK SOUTHEAST'S FINANCIAL PERFORMANCE, 1986-1990

	1986-7	1989-90
Total income	£818m	£930m
Deficit	£232m	£143m
Investment	£152m	£370m

(Source: Network SouthEast)

Between 1987 and 1989 a boom in the economy and soaring land values helped British Rail cope with the cuts. But by 1990 recession had set in and trading conditions became tougher as companies and individuals economised on travel just as land values started to fall again.

Despite the need to improve the rail network to meet the challenge of the Channel Tunnel, British Rail was hampered by a requirement to produce an 8% return on its investments and by a ban on borrowing money from the private sector. However, in 1991 the government signalled a change of heart in favour of moving more freight from the roads to the railway which offered hope of more funding, particularly to help with building the new Channel Tunnel rail link to East London. In October 1991 it also announced the route of the rail link which will approach London from the east rather than the south, British Rail's own preferred route.

In 1991 BR's priorities for investment were: further electrification of tracks, particularly along the East and West Coast lines; refurbishing stations including Gatwick, King's Cross and Liverpool St.; building an international passenger terminal at Ashford so Kent travellers can join the Channel Tunnel line there; building new links between Paddington and Heathrow, and between Manchester and its airport; and providing a televised information service to warn passengers of delays and problems.

Towards Privatisation

By 1990 it was clear that the Conservative government planned to privatise British Rail. There were several ways in which this could be done:

(i) The entire network could be turned into a private company, as happened with British Telecom and British Airways. This would mean replacing a public monopoly with a private one and was not, therefore, the most likely option to be adopted.

(ii) The tracks could be sold separately. Individual rail companies would then pay to use the track, allowing for competition and a range of different services. (The luxury Venice-Simplon Orient Express company already pays BR to use its lines.) This is more like what happened when electricity was privatised and might allow a return to something like the pre-War railway companies. For customers it might lead to less integration of services than at present.

(iii) Individual services could be sold separately. So InterCity services could be privatised while the government continued to support less profitable services.

Safety Concerns

In general British Rail has an admirable safety record. However, in 1988 several accidents, including a serious one at Clapham Junction, raised questions over whether safety procedures were falling victim to the economy drive. In particular it was clear that more needed to be spent on new signalling equipment. There were also fears that increasing congestion on the trains, as more passengers crowded onto reduced services, could lead to worse injuries and fatalities after a crash.

The Cost of Travelling

Fares on the first train journeys were calculated according to a flat rate formula, with each mile costing the same regardless of where it was travelled. By the 1980s BR's charging system had become more sophisticated. Different sums were charged depending on the route to be travelled, the time of day and the time of year. This led to a proliferation of fare types. By 1991 the usual categories were:

(i) first and standard class **singles**, valid for three days (except in the London/Network SouthEast region).
(ii) first and standard class **returns**, valid for one month, except in Network SouthEast area where they are valid for the day of issue only.
(iii) **saver tickets**, for journeys of more than twenty-five miles, valid on any day of the week, and **supersavers** which may not be used on Fridays or summer Saturdays. Savers from provincial cities to London are cheaper than savers from London to the provinces. They are valid for one month.
(iv) **Apex tickets** which must be bought at least one week in advance and can only be used on the dates on the ticket.
(v) **cheap day returns** for short, off-peak journeys.
(vi) **season tickets.**
(vii) **weekend first class tickets** which allow standard class passengers to upgrade to first for a small supplement at weekends and Bank Holidays.
(viii) **Network AwayBreaks**, for standard class journeys of more than thirty miles in Network SouthEast region. The are valid for five days.

Railcards offering discounts were available to senior citizens, young people under twenty-four, families and disabled travellers. There were extra charges for seat reservations.

Despite the range of tickets available, steady cuts in BR's government subsidy led to regular price rises, often in excess of the rate of inflation. By 1992 an annual season ticket from Bristol to London cost £4,632. With coach fares usually half the rail fares, many people were priced off the railways in spite of increasing concern about the adverse environmental impact of road transport.

Customer Relations

British Rail suffers from a poor public image. Common criticisms include:

* delays and cancellations without notice or explanation.
* overcrowding resulting in standing room only, even on long-distance routes. (BR's stated aim is that no one should stand for more than twenty minutes except by choice.)

* failure to anticipate the climate so that trains are cancelled after snow or autumnal leaf falls.
* poor catering standards.
* prohibitively expensive fares.
* rude and ill-informed station staff.
* dirty trains.

To counteract its poor image BR employed Saatchi and Saatchi to run an advertising campaign which the Advertising Standards Authority later criticised. In 1992 British Rail introduced a 'Passenger's Charter' which would entitle customers to compensation when the service did not meet the preset standards.

TABLE 32 NETWORK SOUTHEAST: THE ACTUAL PERFORMANCE

	Objective	1986-7	1989-90
Punctuality			
Trains running on time +/- 5 mins	90%	91%	90%
As above, in peak periods	87.5%	N/A	83.3%
Train Service Provision			
Minimum percentage of services to run	99%	98.4%	96%
Enquiry offices			
Percentage of calls answered in 30 secs	95%	77%	89%
Ticket offices			
Off-peak maximum queuing time	3 mins	N/A	97.8%
Peak maximum queuing time	5 mins	N/A	97.8%
Carriage Cleaning			
Interior and exterior daily	100%	87%	*77%
Heavy interior	100%	83%	90%
Load Factors			
Sliding doors...maximum in peak period	135%	139.2%	138.5%
Slam doors...maximum in peak period	110%	114.2%	113.5%

* exceptional circumstances applied

(Source: Network SouthEast)

The London Underground

In 1863 the Metropolitan Railway Company opened the world's first underground railway between Paddington and Farringdon St. The first 'tube' line which required deep drilling was completed in 1890 and ran from the City to Stockwell. Between 1905 and 1907 American companies financed the Baker St and Waterloo line, the Great Northern, Piccadilly and Brompton line, and the Charing Cross, Euston and Hampstead line. In 1908 the name 'Underground' was formally adopted.

Much of the current Underground network was built between the Wars. However, work halted in 1939 and the stations were turned into overnight bomb shelters. There was further work on the Central Line in 1949, and then another pause until 1969 when the Victoria Line from Walthamstow to Warren Street (later extended to Brixton) was laid. The Piccadilly Line Heathrow link was built in 1977, with a link to Terminal Four completed in 1986. The last completely new underground line to be laid, the Jubilee, was completed in 1979 (Fig. 41).

In 1984 the London Regional Transport Act transferred London Transport, which ran the city's underground and bus services, from the control of the Greater London Council (GLC) to that of the Secretary of State for Transport. London Transport became London Regional Transport (LRT). In 1985 LRT formed a separate company, London Buses Ltd (LBL) to run London bus services. In 1991 London Underground Limited was a wholly owned subsidiary of London Regional Transport, owning 500 trains and 250 stations, and employing 22,000 staff. Each of its ten lines was run as a separate business unit.

Like British Rail the Underground suffers from a poor public image, brought about by overcrowded trains, unexplained cancellations, neglected and dirty stations, erratic lift and escalator services and inadequate public communications. The King's Cross fire in 1987 also highlighted safety concerns at a time when some stations were having to be closed in peak periods because of the crowds on the platforms. In 1982 approximately 500 million Underground journeys were made each year, but by 1990/1 the number had risen to 775 million, with a further 20% increase forecast by the end of the century. An extension to the Jubilee Line, a new Cross-rail line from near Paddington to Bethnal Green, and a Chelsea to Hackney Line are planned to alleviate the congestion.

Ticket prices have risen steadily since a brief period in 1983 when the GLC operated a 'Fares Fair' policy of cheaper fares to encourage use of public transport. The average six mile journey now costs £1.40 in London compared with £0.32 in Paris. However, overseas visitors can buy three, four and seven day **Visitor Travelcards**, provided they do so before they arrive in London.

FIGURE 41 LONDON UNDERGROUND SYSTEM, 1991

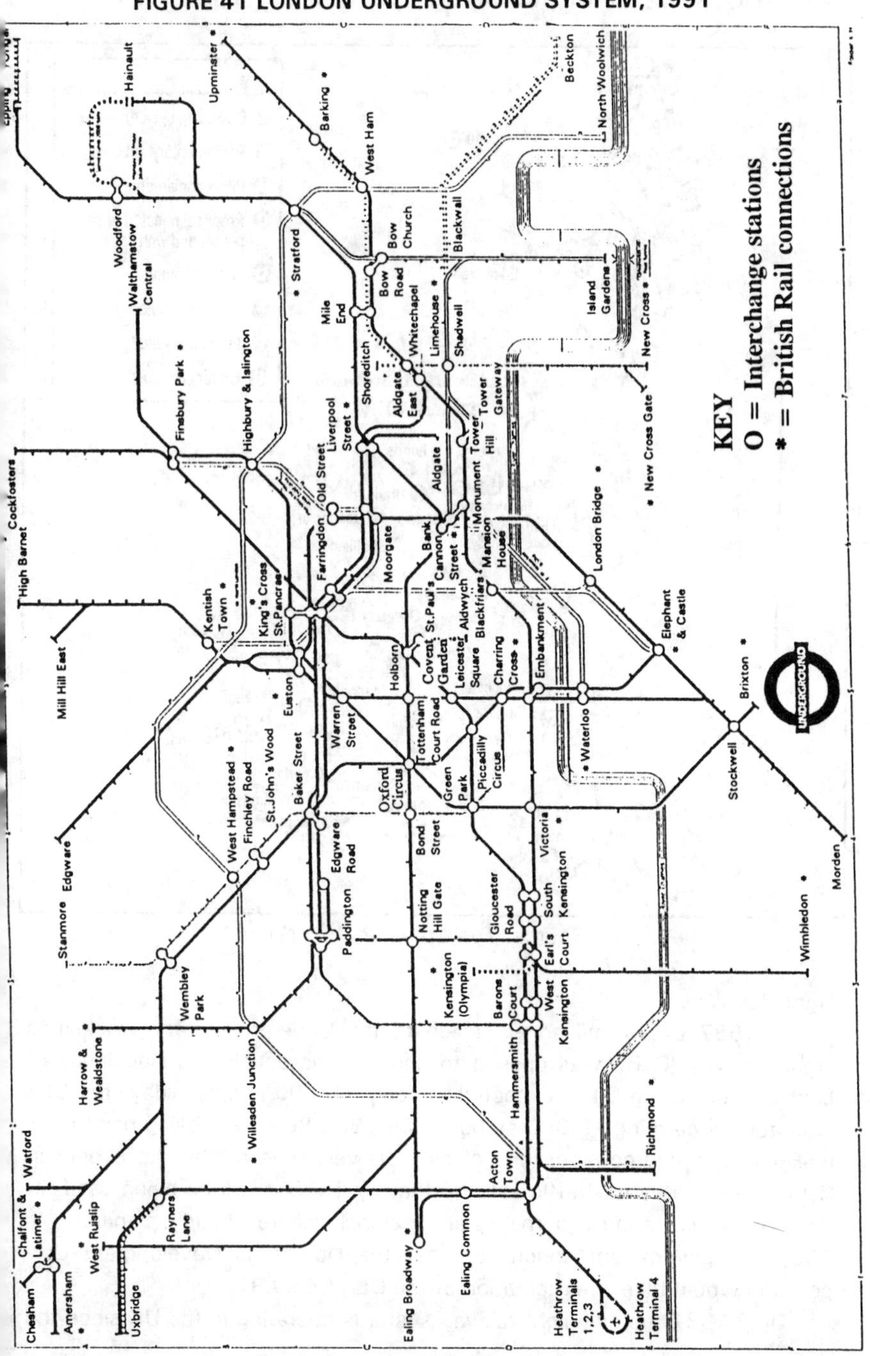

FIGURE 42 RAPID TRANSPORT SYSTEMS IN THE UK, 1991

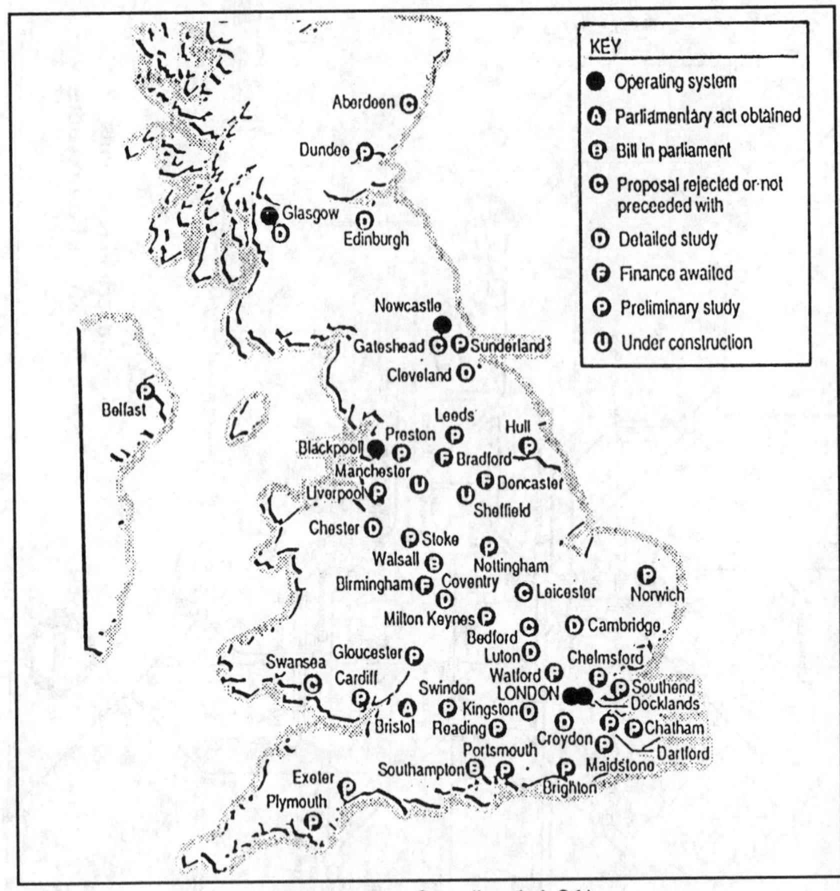

(Source: *The Guardian* 4.4.91)

Light Railways

In 1987 a £77 million extension to the Underground, the Docklands Light Railway (DLR), was opened to connect the developing Docklands of East London to the City. Expected to carry 15,000 people a day, the DLR was quickly carrying 15,000 an hour. By 1989/90 it was being used for 8 million annual journeys, despite closing at weekends and in the evenings. Revised estimates for traffic assume that by 1995 it will be being used for over 50 million annual journeys, and extensions are already planned. In 1991 the government announced that the Docklands Development Corporation would take over operation of the DLR from LRT.

Until 1987 the only light railway systems operating in the UK since the late 1960s had been the tourist tram service along Blackpool sea front and the Newcastle Metro. However, by 1987 traffic congestion in the larger British cities was such that the success of the DLR was pounced on as offering a reasonably cost-effective way of improving public transport while also revitalising town centres. Manchester and Sheffield in particular saw it as a possible way forward. By April 1991 studies of light railways and other rapid transit systems were under way all over the UK (Fig.42), although in the absence of central government funding work had actually started on very few. In 1992 the first new trains went into service in Manchester.

The Preserved Railways

In addition to the British Rail network the UK has many privately operated preserved railways which have been developed in response to line closures since 1948. The first preserved railway was opened by enthusiasts at Talyllyn in West Wales in 1951 and there is a concentration of similar railways in Wales, eight of them grouped together for marketing purposes as the 'Great Little Trains of Wales' (Fig. 43). Some preserved lines, like the Watercress and Bluebell Lines, operate on the standard gauge and could link into main BR services. Others, like the Ravenglass and Eskdale Line, run on a narrow gauge. Most now operate as registered charities, ploughing all their takings back into the railway. Many are run by volunteers or a skeleton staff. A few, like the Bluebell Railway, offer year-round services but most run only special services like 'Santa Specials' in winter.

The preserved railways, many of them running through spectacular countryside, should probably be seen as visitor attractions rather than as an integral part of the transport network.

The Railways and Tourism

In the 19th century the railways were vital in the development of mass market seaside resorts like Brighton and Bournemouth. They also played an important part in opening up areas of beautiful countryside to the public; after branch lines to Windermere, Coniston and Keswick from the main London to Carlisle line were opened in the 1840s the number of people visiting the Lake District soared.

However, in the 20th century the railways gradually shed their role in tourism as cars, coaches and planes became more popular. The Beeching Report in particular led to the closure of many lines to seaside resorts with only enough traffic to justify services during the short summer holiday period. Then in 1972 Golden Rail, a BR subsidiary based in York and offering short break rail and hotel packages, was developed. By 1986 174,000 Golden Rail holidays were being sold either directly through BR stations or through travel agents. In 1990 the ETB estimated that 10% of domestic tourist trips were made by train.

FIGURE 43 THE PRESERVED RAILWAYS OF WALES

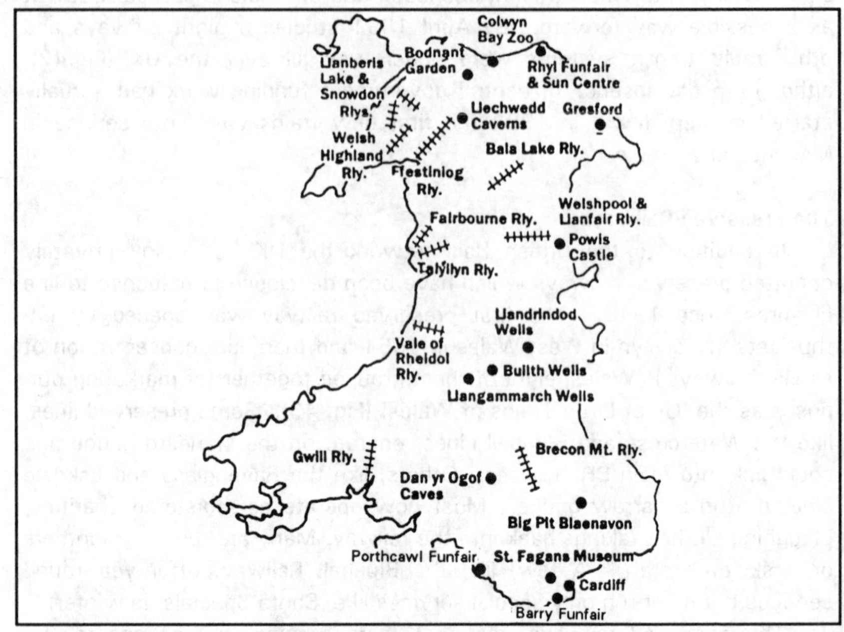

(Source: Wales Tourist Board)

In 1987 British Rail and the BTA produced a series of special leaflets promoting 'Scenic Rail Journeys' through exceptionally beautiful countryside like the Inverness to Mallaig and Shrewsbury to Aberystwyth routes. The new Regional Railways are also promoting scenic routes like the Tamar Valley Line in Devon. BR also offers summer rail rover tickets aimed at the tourist market. These allow unlimited travel within specific areas, like the North East, North West or East Midlands. **BritRail Passes,** which can only be bought abroad, allow overseas tourists between four days and one month of unlimited travel in either class for one fixed price. In 1990 over 100,000 BritRail Passes were sold, about 50,000 of them through travel agents in the USA.

BR also leases its lines to the private company, Venice-Simplon Orient Express, which uses them not only to reach the continent but also for up-market day excursions in Pullman carriages to Leeds Castle, Hever Castle, Salisbury, Bath, Bristol and Folkestone and to the races at Goodwood, Newmarket and Ascot.

FIGURE 44 BRITISH MOTORAIL NETWORK

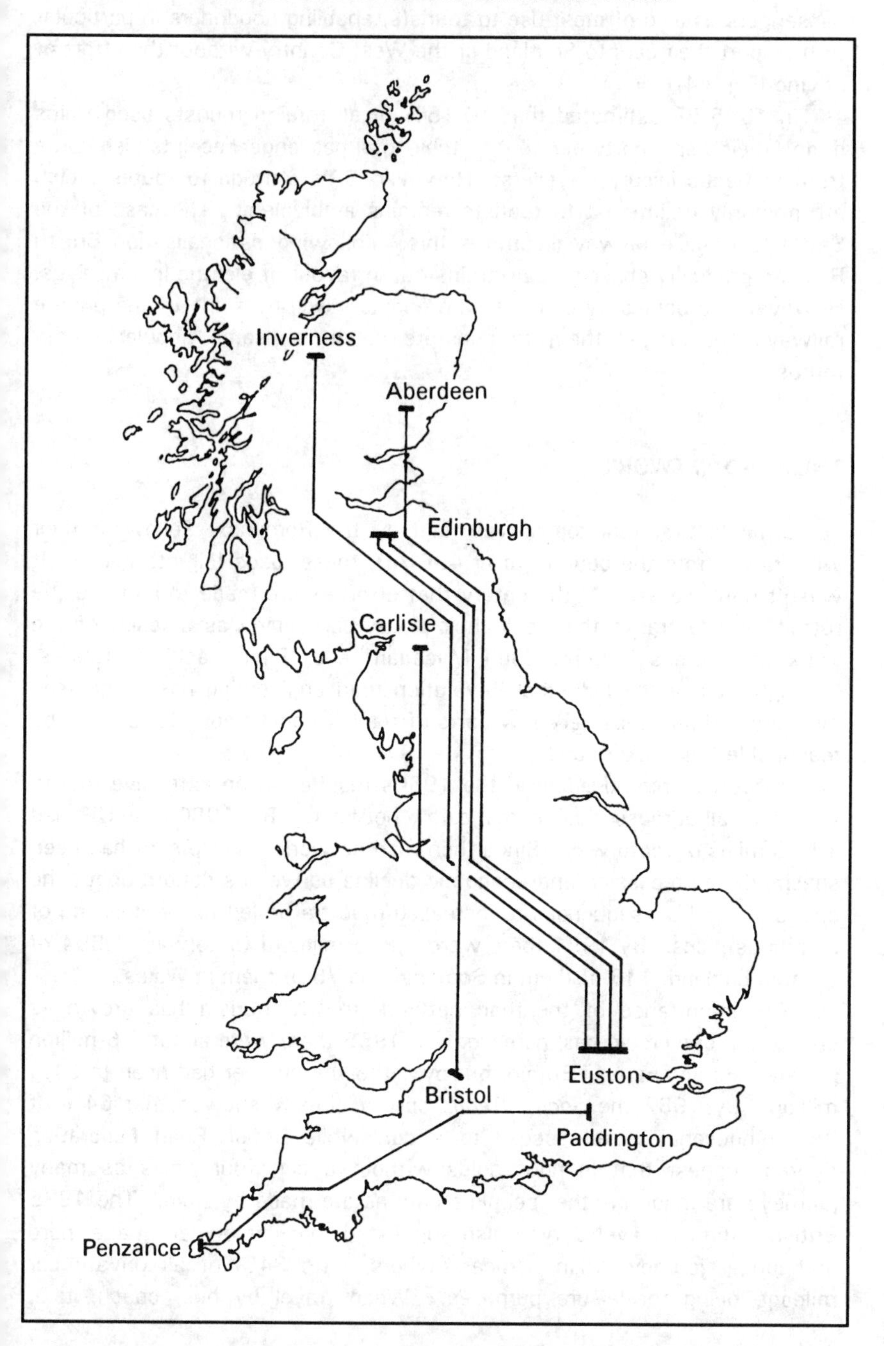

The UK Motorail network, with trains carrying cars as well as passengers, is also of most use to tourists, enabling Londoners in particular to transport their cars to Scotland or the West Country without the effort of driving (Fig. 44).

In 1986 BR estimated that 10-15% of all foreign tourists used trains during their visit. Forty per cent of their total passenger receipts also came from domestic leisure travellers. However, BR's attitude to routes which are primarily of interest to tourists remains ambivalent. The case of the Settle to Carlisle railway illustrates this. Following nationalisation British Rail had gradually phased steam trains out in favour of electric locomotives. However, the popularity of the steam engines used by some of the private railways encouraged them to reinstate steam on some popular tourist routes.

THE ROAD NETWORK

Britain's first real roads were laid by the Romans. Following their withdrawal from the country after 436 AD, these roads fell into decay. It wasn't until the early 19th century that efforts were made to improve the rutted, muddy tracks that took their place, particularly as a result of the work of Thomas Telford, John Macadam and 'Blind Jack' of Knaresborough. Since the Industrial Revolution road engineering has progressed by leaps and bounds. Very few parts of the UK cannot now be reached by reasonable, tarmacked road.

A spurt of road-building in the 1960s resulted in an extensive motorway and all-purpose dual carriageway network. By 1980 the UK had 1,500 miles of motorway. Since then road network development has been spasmodic as recession and economic decline as well as doubts about the environmental consequences of increased road traffic led to the shelving of ambitious plans. By 1991 there were 1,815 miles of motorway, 1,594 of them in England, 146 of them in Scotland and 75 of them in Wales.

The importance of the road network to UK tourism has grown as private car ownership has increased. In 1955 there were about 3.6 million private cars and vans in Britain, but by 1989 the number had risen to 21.3 million. By 1987 the *Social Trends* survey already showed that 64% of British households had access to a car, while British Road Federation figures suggest that in households without a car, four times as many journeys are made in other people's cars as are made by train. The 1985 British National Travel Survey also suggested that car owners make more and longer journeys than non-car owners, with 34% of all private car mileage being for leisure purposes. When travel by bus, coach, taxi, motorcycle and bicycle is taken into account, 92% of all passenger journeys within the UK are now made by road.

Government policies on road-building can affect tourism in several ways. For example, where roads are significantly improved or upgraded they may offer quicker, easier access to potential holiday spots. This has been the case with the A55 linking Chester to North Wales, and with the A303/A30 to Devon and Cornwall. In addition building by-passes can make the centres of historic towns much more appealing both for residents and visitors, despite the damage they may do to surrounding countryside; roughly half England's historic towns now have by-passes.

The British road network consists of the following:

a) Trunk roads. These are a national network of through roads, including the motorways which are 'special roads reserved for certain classes of traffic'. The Secretary of State for Transport (England) and the Secretaries of State for Scotland and Wales are highway authorities for the trunk roads.

FIGURE 45 HOUSEHOLDS WITH REGULAR USE OF A CAR, 1989

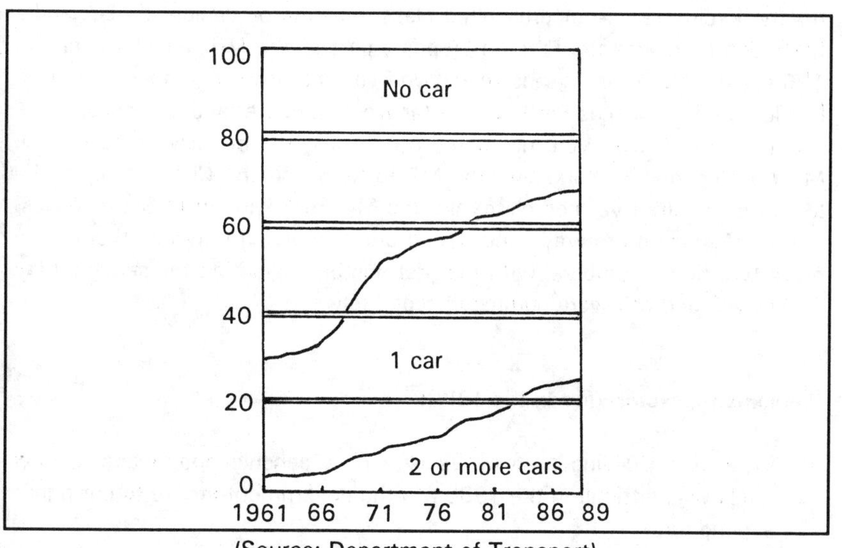

(Source: Department of Transport)

b) Non-trunk roads for which local authorities have responsibility. These are divided into classified and unclassified roads which are local distributor and access roads. Classified roads are further subdivided into:

(i) principal roads which are regionally and strategically important. A few local authority motorways come into this category.

(ii) non-principal roads which distribute traffic to urban and rural areas. These are often numbered B and C roads.

TABLE 33 BRITAIN'S ROAD NETWORK, 1992

Type of Road	Length (miles)	% of Network
Motorway	1,908	0.9
Trunk (exc. motorways)	7,877	3.6
Principal (exc. motorways)	21,845	9.8
Classified non-principal	68,709	30.9
Unclassified	122,215	54.8

(Source: British Road Federation, 1992

The Motorways

The most important roads are the motorways linking the main population centres. A motorway can be defined as 'a limited access dual carriageway road..., completely fenced in, normally with hard shoulders... for the exclusive use of prescribed classes of motor vehicles.' England's first such road was the Preston by-pass, part of the M6, which opened in 1958. By 1991 an extensive network of motorways fanned out from London, as far north as Perth and as far west as Exeter and Swansea.

The motorways were numbered by dividing the country up, using the M1 from London to Yorkshire, the M2 to Kent and the Channel Ports, the M3 to Exeter (not yet complete) and the M4 from London to South Wales. Spurs off these motorways and new motorways lying between them were given two figure numbers, with the first number indicating the section it lay in. The M5 and M6 were numbered separately.

Problems for Motorways in the 1990s

(i) **Expense.** Building motorways is very expensive and financing new roads was difficult in the 1980s as the government strove to cut public expenditure.

(ii) **Over-use.** By 1980 some motorways were already overloaded at peak periods. The problem worsened during the 1980s, and the volume of traffic meant motorways needed repair and reconstruction faster than expected. Building new roads simply seems to encourage more traffic; almost as soon as the M25 London ring road was opened it was overloaded.

FIGURE 46 BRITISH MOTORWAY NETWORK, 1991

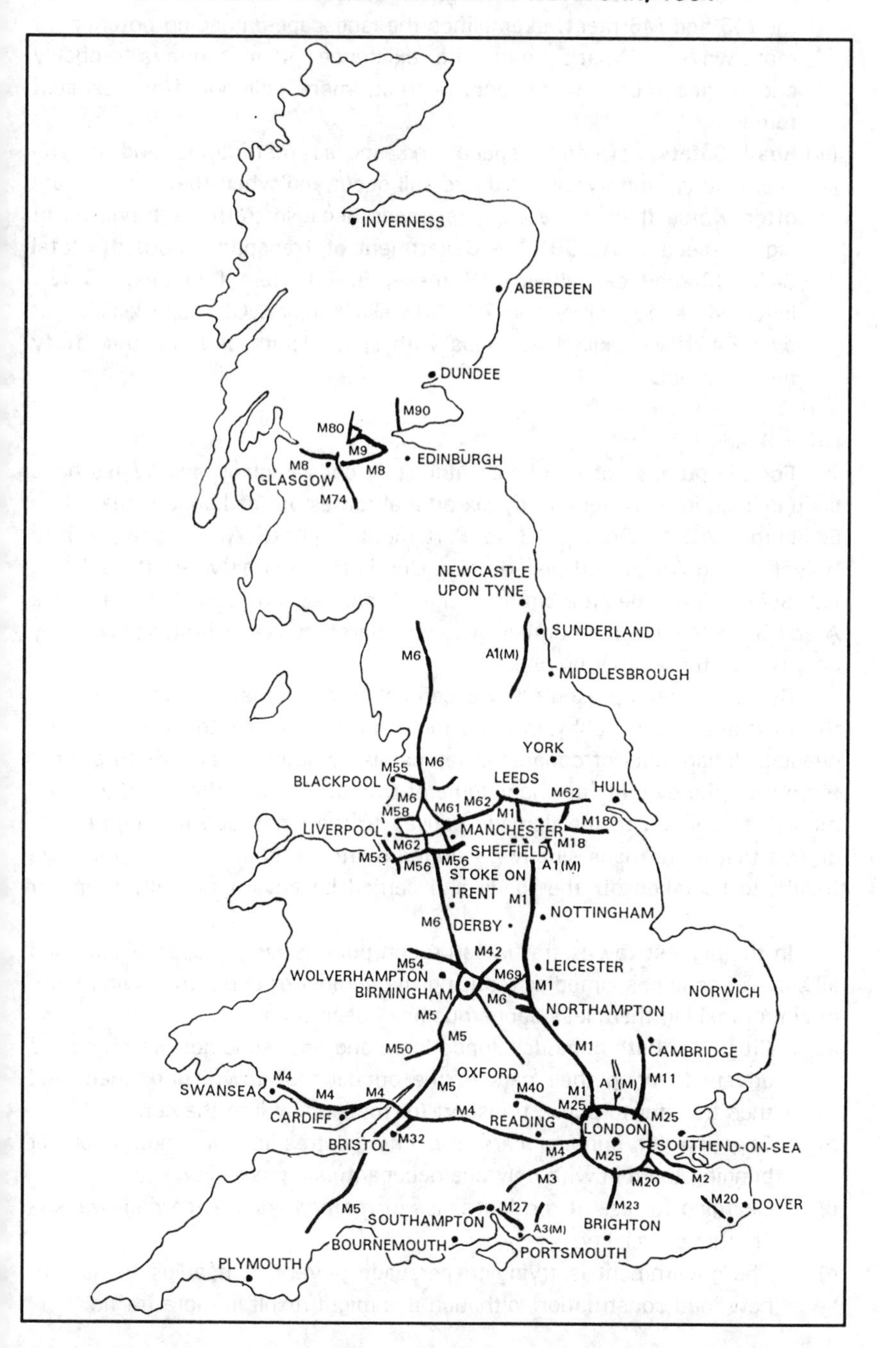

(iii) **Environmental Concerns**. 'Spaghetti Junction' at Birmingham, where the M5 and M6 meet, exemplifies the landscape-damaging potential of motorways. What's more the existence of motorways probably encourages more driving and, with it, more pollution from exhaust fumes.

(iv) **Road Safety**. Despite speed and access restrictions and careful signposting, motorway accidents still occur and when they do they are often worse than those on other roads because traffic is travelling at higher speeds. In 1991 the Department of Transport recorded a total 340,103 road casualties. Of these, 5,104 were fatalities, 60,435 involved serious injury and 274,563 slight injury. Of those killed, just over 54% were killed on roads with speed limits of more than forty miles per hour.

Other Roads

For the purpose of numbering principal roads England and Wales have been divided into six sectors by six arterial routes out of London: the A1 to Edinburgh, A2 to Dover, A3 to Portsmouth, A4 to Avonmouth, A5 to Holyhead and A6 to Carlisle. Section One is the area between the A1 and A2, Section Two the area between the A2 and A3, and so on. Other Class A and B roads have the number of the section they are in first, followed by one, two or three other numbers.

By 1991 roads presented two conflicting problems. On the one hand the road and freight lobby insisted more motorway and trunk roads were needed. Inhabitants of congested towns also wanted by-passes to protect them from the ever-increasing volume of traffic. On the other hand environmentalists pointed to the damage caused to the landscape by huge roads, argued that more roads simply generated more traffic and lobbied for more freight to be taken off the roads and carried by environmentally friendlier rail.

In the biggest towns traffic saturation point is rapidly approaching and all sorts of schemes aimed at reducing the number of cars, at slowing them down, or making them less dangerous have been tried:

a) Cities like Bath have developed 'park and ride' schemes which enable drivers to bring their cars to the outskirts of town, park them and then transfer to public transport for the journey into the centre.

b) Charging for bringing cars into city centres in peak hours, or for bringing them in with only one occupant, is a possibility.

c) Charging for use of the fast lanes of motorways/dual carriageways is another possibility.

d) The government is trying to persuade private companies to pay for new road construction, although this might result in more traffic.

e) Some local authorities are trying to develop new public transport systems, using metros or trams as part of an integrated transport system, as in Newcastle.

f) Exclusive bus lanes attempt to speed up public transport and make it more attractive.

g) In parts of London 'red routes' where no parking at all is allowed attempt to speed the flow of traffic.

h) 'Sleeping policemen' (bumps in the road) and road narrowing are used to slow traffic down in urban areas.

Bus and Coach Travel

Although stagecoach services could be seen as the forerunners of modern coach services, the first coach service in the modern sense of the word was introduced on the Bournemouth to London route in 1919. However, this was an infrequent service and the first daily, all year round express service was introduced on the Bristol to London route in 1925. Other operations quickly followed, including George Reddings' successful Black and White Motorways services out of Cheltenham which began in 1926.

Until 1930 bus and coach companies could operate whatever services they wanted. However the 1927-9 Royal Commission decided that this encouraged such roguish activities as speeding to stops to try and snatch passengers from rivals. As a result the 1930 Road Transport Act split the country into thirteen regional traffic areas, each with a Ministry of Transport-appointed Transport Commissioner to control routes. Individual bus and coach services could operate in monopoly conditions, although some pooled their resources to offer passengers a better service.

In the days before private cars, coach travel was very popular, but by the 1960s passenger numbers were declining even though the new motorways enabled companies to offer express services. The coach companies gradually amalgamated their services until in 1968 there were two main operators: the state-owned Tilling Group and British Electric Traction Group. In 1968 the government brought both under the control of the Transport Holding Company.

The 1968 Transport Act, which aimed to create an integrated public transport system, set up the National Bus Company (NBC) to take over from the Transport Holding Company and run English and Welsh services. By 1969 NBC controlled 93 bus companies and a fleet of 21,000 coaches, and employed 81,000 people, making it the biggest road passenger transport operation in Europe. The Scottish Bus Group was to handle Scottish services. New Passenger Transport Executives controlled services in the six English metropolitan counties and in Strathclyde.

By 1972 the NBC was marketing itself as 'National' and had adopted the present-day white livery. By 1973/4 it was also offering a comprehensive, integrated coach timetable in place of the frequently overlapping services that had preceded nationalisation. In 1974 the name 'National Express' was adopted, first appearing on the coaches in 1978. However, passenger numbers continued to decline; between 1978 and 1981 traffic fell by 26%. Since then it has remained fairly constant.

After 1979 controls over bus and coach services were gradually reduced. Fare fixing was removed in most situations and the 1980 Transport Act introduced a new system for licensing long distance express services. The 1983 Transport Act limited the amount of subsidy Passenger Transport Executives could provide for bus services. In 1984 National Express became a separate limited company, although still part of the NBC. The 1985 Transport Act also permitted anyone to register to operate a local bus service. Local authorities were required to restructure their revenue support for bus services towards unprofitable routes offering a social service. By 1988 the National Bus Company's seventy-two subsidiary companies had all been sold as required by the 1985 Act; National Express was bought by its management in March, 1988. Local authority bus services became independent Passenger Transport Companies and by 1988 the first of these had also been sold. In 1991 plans to privatise and deregulate London Buses Limited (a wholly-owned subsidiary of London Regional Transport responsible for most Greater London bus services) were announced, leading to fears that joint bus and Underground travel-cards might vanish along with the traditional red London bus.

Deregulation of bus and coach services has made it harder to obtain overall statistical information about the industry's size. However, by the end of the 1980s buses and coaches were probably carrying over 5.5 billion passengers a year (which is seven times as many as British Rail). There were between 6,000 and 6,500 operators and perhaps 73,000 buses and coaches offering several different types of service:

a) **Local (Stage) Services**, where all the passengers are travelling *less* than fifteen miles and everyone is paying a separate fare.
b) **Long Distance (Express) Services**, where all the passengers are travelling *more* than fifteen miles and everyone is paying a separate fare.
c) **Local Excursions and Tours,** where the passengers are all paying separate fares but are travelling together, with or without breaks, from one or more places for *less* than fifteen miles.
d) **Non-Local Excursions and Tours**, the same as (c) but where all passengers are travelling *more* than fifteen miles.

e) **Contract Hire Services** where services are arranged and paid for by a third party; for example where a local authority provides buses to ferry pupils to and from college.

f) **Private Hire Arrangments**, where a group of people hires a coach on a one-off basis and then divides the cost of using it amongst those using it; for example, when a sports club charters a coach to take members to a sports fixture and everyone contributes to the cost.

Department of Transport statistics suggest that although buses and coaches are clocking up more miles, the number of passengers is actually falling. This discrepancy is explained by the fact that more operators are using mini (9-16 seat) and midi (17-35 seat) vehicles instead of full-length or double-decker buses.

TABLE 34 WHO USES LOCAL BUSES?

	16-19	20-29	30-59	60-64	70 and over	All ages
Male	70%	42%	25%	35%	43%	35%
Female	78%	62%	48%	61%	50%	54%

(Source: Department of Transport, 1985)

The 1985 National Travel Survey concluded that 37% of bus and coach travellers used them to go shopping or for personal business trips, 23.7% used them to get to and from work, 22% used them for social, recreational or holiday purposes, and 17.3% used them to get to and from school or college.

National Express surveys suggest that coach passengers are primarily young (16-24) or old (55+), that they are disproportionately female, and that only 19% come from socio-economic groups A or B. Not surprisingly the vast majority are leisure travellers. The main reason given for choosing to travel by coach is the relatively low price.

National Express/Caledonian Express

In 1984 National Express became a separate limited company, although still part of the National Bus Company. From 1986 it began contracting its coaches from the NBC and became responsible for its own profits and losses as a first step towards privatisation. In 1988 National Express was bought from NBC by its management. The parent company, National Express Holdings Ltd, now owns a number of subsidiary companies, most notably Caledonian Express which runs the routes to Scotland. It also manages Eurolines UK Ltd which offers services to 190 European destinations. National Express and Caledonian Express also operate their own UK package coach tours. Between them National Express and Caledonian Express account for 80% of the entire UK coach travel market.

In 1991 National Express served 1500 destinations and carried about 14 million passengers a year. It is busiest during the summer when 900 daily coaches travel over 90 million miles around the UK. Almost all these coaches are contracted from other companies who must operate them to National Express specifications. National Express also operates the coach stations in Birmingham, Leeds, Manchester and Bournemouth, although London Regional Transport has run Victoria Coach Station, which is used by roughly 11 million passengers a year, since 1988. Other than in London, there are major coach interchange points in Bristol, Cambridge, Edinburgh, Glasgow, Leeds, Leicester, Manchester, Nottingham, Oxford, Perth, Preston and Sheffield.

On forty-four of their routes National Express/Caledonian Express operate 'Rapide' services, sometimes in double-decker coaches, with fitted toilets, reclining seats and hostesses/stewards to serve light refreshments. Advance seat reservation is usually possible. Special discount fare cards are available to senior citizens (over sixty) and young people (16 to 23).

Coaches and Tourism

Coaches are vital to UK tourism not just as a way for individuals to get from A to B but also as the basis for many organised tours and day trips. Coach operators therefore work in close co-operation with the hotel and visitor attractions sectors of the tourism industry.

Operators tend to favour hotels which are big enough to accommodate an entire coachload of visitors, have parking near the entrance, offer good food and are able to deal with the sudden rushes of activity associated with a tour group's arrival: being able to pre-allocate rooms avoids queues in reception; and being flexible about last minute confirmations may make the difference between profit and loss for the coach company.

Most tourist attractions want to encourage coach parties which means providing adequate coach parking, rest facilities and food for the driver, and being able to deal with sudden rushes by, for example, providing tickets in advance.

British companies offering coach excursions include Wallace Arnold, Frames, Rickards, Evan Evans Tours and National Express Holidays.

Many coach operators also put together ad hoc itineraries as and when required. These have to fit within EC regulations on driving hours which state that no driver should be on the road for more than eight hours in one fourteen hour period, and that s/he should have at least one forty-five minute break during that time.

FIGURE 47 NATIONAL EXPRESS NETWORK, 1991

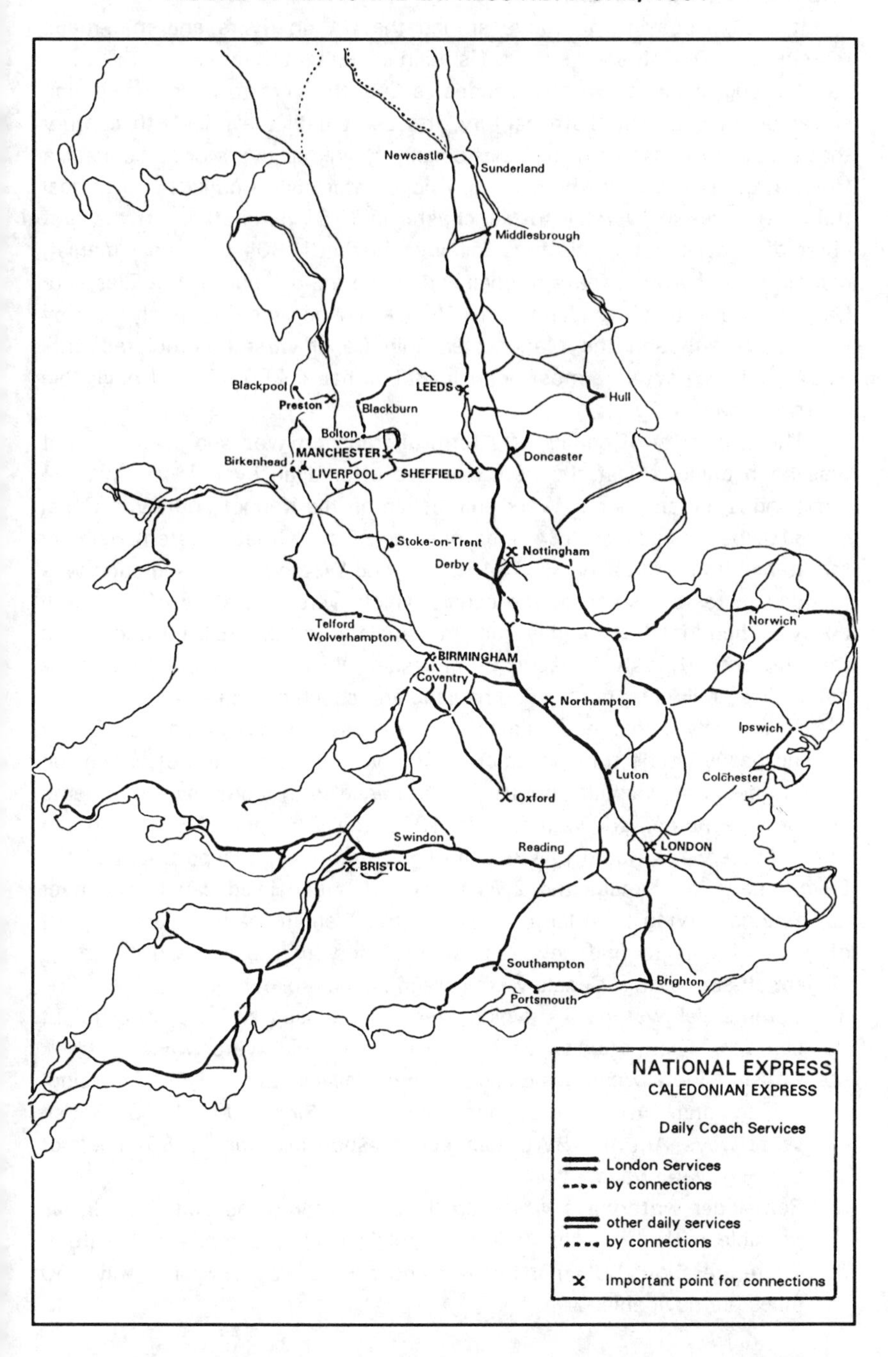

THE RIVERS AND WATERWAYS

It is also possible to move around the UK on rivers and man-made waterways. Fig. 48 shows the UK's main inland waterways.

Although locks were being added to English rivers to make navigation easier as early as the 16th century, it wasn't until the mid-18th century that true canals started to be built, usually to link up rivers or to connect a town to the sea. When the Duke of Bridgewater built a canal to carry coal from the mines at Worsley to Manchester in 1761 he sparked off the first burst of canal fever. This was followed in the 1780s by 'canal mania', characterised by great feats of engineering like the building of the Ellesmere Canal from Nantwich to Llangollen. The Canal Age was effectively over by the 1830s although the Manchester Ship Canal wasn't completed until 1894. When they were most popular, Britain had 4,250 miles of navigable rivers and canals.

The popularity of canals as a form of transport was shortlived since it was soon obvious that the new railways offered an even better way to move industrial products. Work only began on the Kennet and Avon Canal in 1810, but already by 1841 the opening of the Great Western Railway threatened its profitability. In 1946 the Inland Waterways Association was founded to restore some of the canals which were in a state of complete decay. Then in 1948 roughly half the canals were nationalised and put in the care of the British Transport Commission which also handled the newly nationalised railways, ports, road haulage and coach companies.

Fortunately canal enthusiasts, like railway lovers, could see a life beyond heavy goods transportation for the waterways, many of which run through areas of unspoilt countryside, are lined with industrial monuments and provide homes for wildlife. In 1962 the Transport Act set up the British Waterways Board (BWB), now sponsored by the Department of the Environment, to manage the 2,000 miles of nationalised canals and river navigations varying from large rivers like the Trent to narrow canals. Part of its brief was to find new recreational uses for those which were no longer self-supporting. Canals were categorised as follows:

a) **Commercial waterways** which were to be used primarily for freight carriage. There are now 380 miles of commercial waterway.

b) **Cruising waterways** which would be available primarily for cruising, fishing and other recreational activities. Since the 1983 British Waterways Act the BWB has been responsible for 1,185 miles of cruising waterways.

c) **Remainder waterways** which are to be dealt with as economically as possible within the constraints of public health, amenity and safety. There are about 600 miles of remainder waterway of which only 250 miles are navigable.

FIGURE 48 INLAND WATERWAYS OF ENGLAND, SCOTLAND AND WALES

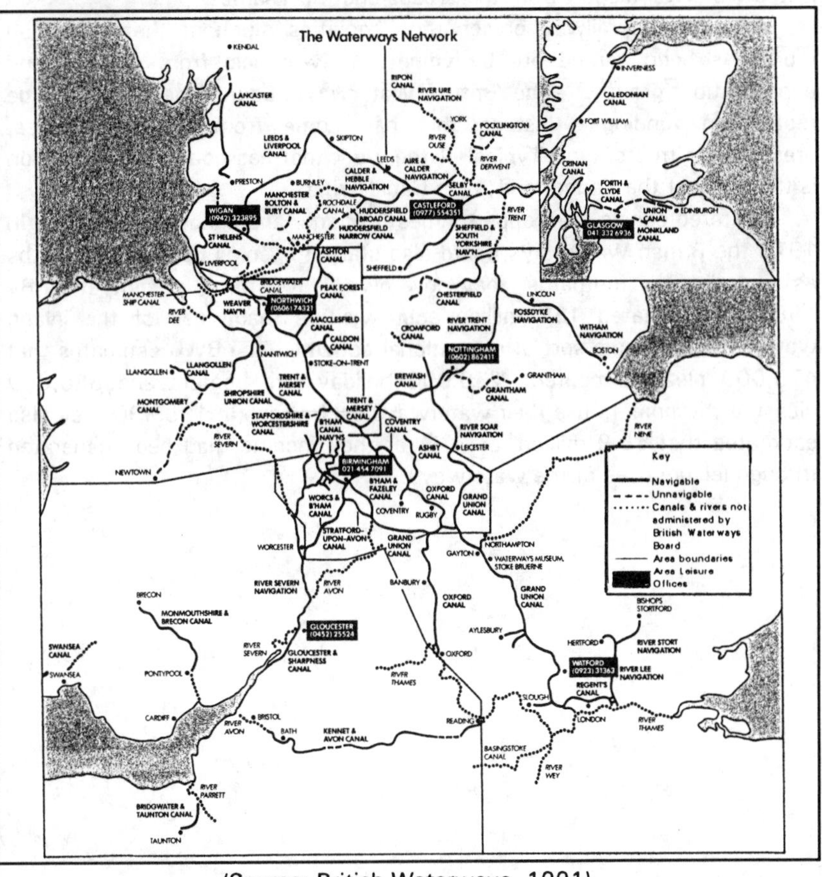

(Source: British Waterways, 1991)

TABLE 35 INLAND WATERWAYS BY REGION, 1991

British Waterways Board Region	Miles of Canal
North West	472,48
Midlands	431.75
North East	433,74
South East	296.80
South West	199.33
Scotland	145.00
TOTAL	**1,979.10**

(Source: British Waterways Board, 1991)

The BWB is now responsible for the majority of Britain's navigable inland waterways apart from the Broads and the Thames.

As with the railway preservation societies much of the restoration work has been carried out by volunteers with help from amenity and conservation groups. The British Waterways Board does not provide restoration funding. Instead this has come from local authorities, preservation trusts, etc. Typical of the work that has gone into restoration is the story of the Kennet and Avon Canal Trust.

Restored canals offer opportunities for barge and canoeing holidays. In 1978 the British Waterways Board also started opening up canal towpaths as long-distance footpaths; they now own 1,500 miles of footpath. By 1989 an estimated 132 million adult visitors made use of the inland waterways for some sort of recreational activity. The BWB estimates that 470,000 pleasure boaters, 250,000 holiday hire boaters and 580,000 pleasure trip boaters use their waterways each year. In 1989/90 they also estimated that £5.9 million, or 36% of their income, had been generated through leisure uses of the waterways.

CHAPTER FOUR
ACCOMMODATION IN THE UK

Visitors to the UK can stay in five star hotels, motels, timeshare apartments, guest houses, pubs, bed and breakfasts, farms, self-catering cottages, caravans and camp-sites. Of a total £17,810 million spent on tourism in the UK in 1989, the BTA estimates that £5,655 million was spent on accommodation.

Accommodation is often categorised as *serviced* i.e. with staff to change beds, prepare meals, etc., or *non-serviced* i.e. self-catering properties. It may also be categorised according to *geographical position*: resort hotels, those in large towns, those in small towns, rural hotels and those in London. Finally it may be categorised as *commercial*, or *quasi- or non-commercial* depending on whether it is operated with a view to making a profit or simply to cover costs (as is the case with Youth Hostel Association hostels), or to contribute to the running costs of something larger (as when university rooms are sub-let in the vacations).

FIGURE 49 TOURIST ACCOMMODATION IN THE UK

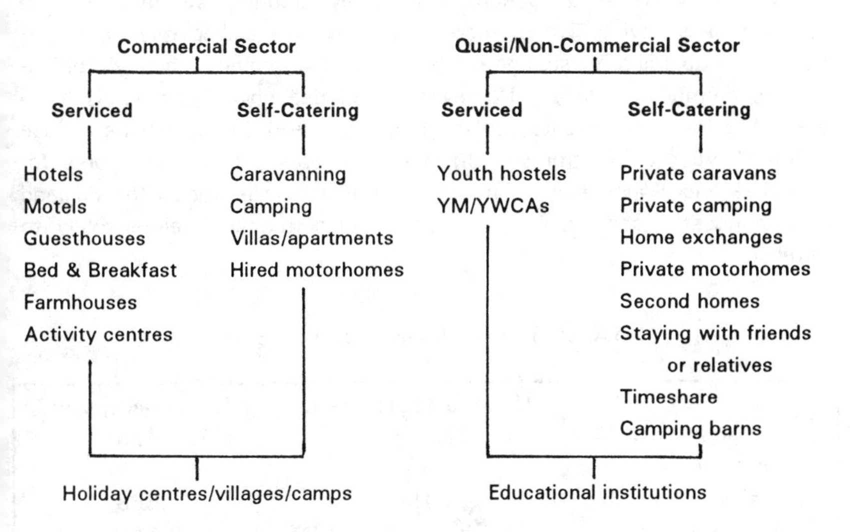

It is difficult to give precise figures for the number of tourists staying in the different types of accommodation because the four national tourist boards collate them into slightly different categories. In addition Northern Ireland counts visitors from the British mainland as overseas visitors, and counts as domestic holidaymakers only those from the Six Counties.

TABLE 36 ACCOMMODATION USED BY DOMESTIC TOURISTS, 1989

Type of accommodation	England	Scotland	Wales	Northern Ireland
	%	%	%	%
Hotel/motel/guesthouse	23	30	17	14
Farmhouse	1	1	2	1
Bed and breakfast	3	5	3	1
Self catering in rented:				
flat/apartment	2	3	3	1
house/chalet/villa/bungalow	4	5	7	4
Holiday camp/village	3	1	3	2
Camping	3	4	7	3
Touring caravan	4	4	5	7
Static caravan	6	5	16	14
Staying with friends/relatives	47	41	34	46

HOTELS

The English Hotel Occupancy Survey defines a hotel as 'an establishment having five or more bedrooms, not calling itself a guest-house or a boarding house, and not being listed as providing bed and breakfast accommodation only.' However, calculating how many hotels there are in the UK is complicated by the fact that the different regions include different types of accommodation in their figures. Thus the figures for Scotland and Wales include motels and inns, while those for England include guesthouses. Only the Northern Ireland figures relate solely to hotels.

TABLE 37 HOTELS IN THE UK, 1989

	No. of establishments	No. of bedspaces
England	22,936	751,475
Scotland	2,907	92,217
Wales	1,456	48,668
Northern Ireland	120	6,142

(Source: BTA)

Development of Hotels in the UK

Britain's first hotels opened in 18th century spa resorts like Bath. In the 19th century, as sea bathing became popular, others opened at the seaside resorts. The railway companies, which carried an increasing number of holidaymakers to the sea, also developed hotels at their termini. (Many of these railway hotels still survive, although they are now privately owned.) In 1910 the British Hotels, Restaurants and Caterers Association (BHRCA) was formed to represent hoteliers' interests.

After the Second World War, Trust Houses, British Transport Hotels, Lyons and several breweries provided Britain with Europe's first chain hotels. Although local authorities sometimes encouraged new hotel building as part of their plans to redevelop city centres in the 1950s and '60s, by the late 1960s there was a shortage of hotel bedspace. In 1969 the government introduced the **Hotel Development Incentive Scheme (HDI)** which resulted in 60,000 new rooms, mostly in three or four star hotels, being made available by the mid 1970s. Centre, Crest and Golden Egg Hotels also started to develop the middle and economy markets.

In 1973 the HDI was scrapped, and the high price of land and planning constraints meant there was little further hotel building. During the 1960s and '70s several big brewing (Scottish and Newcastle) and catering companies (Grand Metropolitan) acquired hotel chains as part of diversification plans. In the mid 1980s there was another spurt of hotel building since hotels were seen as good long-term property investments. But by the late 1980s it was clear that profitability was actually declining, partly because of the high cost of developing and refurbishing hotels. As a result the value of shares in hotels started to decline, while high interest rates simultaneously forced up the cost of loans taken out to finance development. Not surprisingly, although upmarket hotels were still being snapped up when they came on the market, in 1988 Scottish and Newcastle sold Thistle Hotels to Mount Charlotte Investments, and Grand Metropolitan sold the Intercontinental and Forum chains to a Japanese company, Seibu Saison.

There are a wide range of hotels in Great Britain, some of them small and privately owned, others huge and owned by well-known national or international hotel chains.

Hotel Chains

About one-third of British hotels with eleven or more rooms, including almost all the largest hotels, are operated by big hotel chains, the majority of them UK-owned. Until the late 1980s these chains concentrated almost exclusively on the middle and top end of the market. During the 1970s and 1980s when there was little new hotel building larger hotel groups battled to buy out smaller chains and independent hotels; Mount Charlotte Thistle Hotels and Queens Moat Houses expanded in this way. In 1987 London Tara Hotels bought Copthorne Hotels, but retained its group identity. In

1989 Copthorne Hotels in turn bought the 122-room Effingham Park Hotel which is only six miles from Gatwick and has south-east England's best conference facilities. Other hotel groups, including Holiday Inns, expanded by operating a franchise system.

Being part of a chain offers many advantages. Firstly, it makes brand and image development easier. Then it offers bulk purchasing power for fixtures and fittings, and economies of scale in terms of staff training and recruitment. Central reservations systems (CROs) which make for easier booking also become cost effective. To share in these advantages some independent hotels have formed themselves into consortia where, in return for a membership fee, they too can have bulk purchasing power, a group identity and other benefits (e.g. Consort Hotels, Prestige Hotels, Best Western Hotels).

TABLE 38 THE UK'S TOP TEN HOTEL GROUPS, 1990

Group	UK	AA Star Grading				Unclassified	No. of Rooms
	Hotels	5*	4*	3*	2/1*		in UK
Forte Hotels	265	3	39	123	25	75	23,843
Mount Charlotte Thistle Hotels	114		15	46	2	51	13,787
Queens Moat Houses	94	1	15	52	1	25	9,061
Hilton United Kingdom	33	1	4	13		15	6,658
Crest Hotels	49		2	43		4	5,641
Holiday Inns International	20		12	2		6	4,242
Swallow Hotels	34		5	26		5	3,856
Mecca Leisure Hotels	52		3	13	3	33	3,788
Stakis Hotels and Inns	27		4	11		12	3,257
Embassy Hotels	41		3	33	2	3	3,153
TOTAL:	**717**	**5**	**102**	**362**	**33**	**229**	**77,286**

(Source: *Caterer and Hotelkeeper*)

The Top End of the Market

In the late 1980s the hotel market started to diversify into distinct segments. Until then most hotel development was concentrated at the top end of the market, but as existing hotels were refurbished and upgraded, a shortage of three star hotels developed. Most new hotels were built in the larger towns where there is now little suitable land with planning permission available for future development.

Several country houses have now been refurbished as top class hotels, sometimes with golf courses attached, as at Goodwood Park Hotel, Golf and Country Club.

New Hall (see Fig. 50), which stands in extensive grounds in Sutton Coldfield, is typical of a country house that has been converted into a hotel. Although most of the existing building dates from the 16th century and later, New Hall started life as a medieval manor house and still has its moat which is fed by seven springs. There are three meeting rooms and some of the bedrooms have four poster beds, marble-tiled bathrooms and moat views. New Hall is marketed as a 'luxury country house hotel, run...as a grand family home which welcomes guests'.

FIGURE 50 NEW HALL... A TYPICAL COUNTRY HOUSE HOTEL

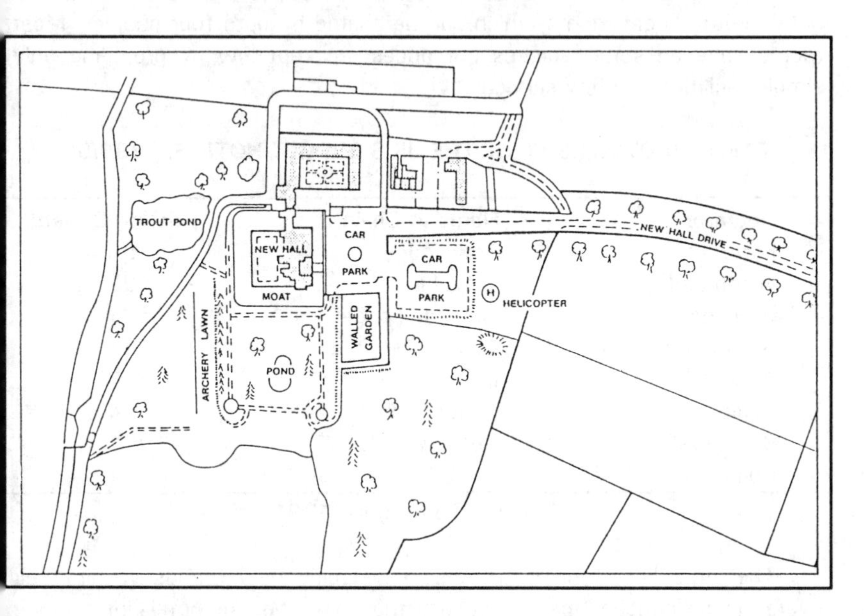

Top class hotels provide not only beautifully furnished and equipped rooms, but also a wide range of facilities and excellent service. Whereas chain hotels have distinctive corporate images, owners of country house hotels often prefer to emphasise the individual properties' unique features. So some of Wales' best country house hotels advertise together in the *Welsh Rarebits* brochure, with each described as an individual entity.

The United States has led the way in developing new hotel concepts. For example, at the top end of the market Marriott has introduced suite-only hotels, branded as Mariott Suites (with restaurants), and Residence Inns (with kitchens in all suites). These have proved particularly popular with travelling businesswomen. The Hilton Corporation's Hotel Conrad Chelsea Harbour in London is one of the UK's first all-suite hotels.

The Middle and Economy End of the Market

In the late 1980s new chain hotel products aimed at the middle and lower part of the market were developed, particularly by catering companies which already owned suitable sites. Typical of this development are Granada Lodges and Beefeater Travel Inns. Travelodge opened its first budget inn next to the Little Chef at Barton-under-Needwood in 1985. By late 1990 THF (now renamed Forte) had opened more than sixty-five inns, with double rooms costing about £27.50 and singles about £22.50. Greenall Whitley plan to add Ambassador hotels to their inns and pubs. The French companies Accor (Ibis Hotels) and Campanile have also introduced hotels with budget rooms which can be shared by upto four people. Most rooms have en suite facilities but prices are kept low by providing only simple facilities and few services.

TABLE 39 OWNERSHIP OF THE UK'S BUDGET HOTELS, 1989/90

Operator	Name of Chain	Existing Outlets
Forte	Travelodge	88
Whitbread	Travel Inns	22
Granada	Granada Lodge	21
Societe du Louvre	Campanile	11
Accor	Ibis	6
Rank	Motor Lodge	4
Brent Walker	Country Lodge	1
Budgotel	Sleep Inn	1

(Source: ETB Insights, 1991)

The large hotel chains are also developing new brands within their overall chain concept, partly because they have bought hotels of a lower grade. Holiday Inns International has already opened two Garden Courts, aimed at the middle market, in England. Quality International plans to develop thirty-five Sleep Inns which will offer no meals other than buffet breakfasts. Marriott Hotels is planning a chain of Courtyard Inns; in the United States these middle market hotels have about 150 rooms big enough to live and work in, a restaurant and lounge, and a swimming pool, whirlpool and exercise room set round a courtyard.

However, the London Tourist Board believes London is still very short of budget accommodation, partly because the cost of land makes it difficult to put up anything other than four star hotels, and partly because of the government policy of housing homeless families in what was bed and breakfast accommodation.

Hotel Grading Systems

The 1969 Development of Tourism Act allowed for compulsory classification and grading of British hotels, but a voluntary register of hotels was only introduced in 1975. Until 1987 the AA and RAC were the most familiar graders of UK hotel. Both use a 'star rating' system which awards hotels one to five stars depending on their facilities and service. Then in 1987 the English, Scottish and Welsh tourist boards introduced a new system which graded hotels with one to five 'crowns', depending on their facilities. There was also a 'listed' category for the most basic properties. The system was voluntary, unlike those operated by most tourist-receiving European countries. However, hotels taking part in the system were visited annually so their facilities could be checked. Only those taking part in the scheme can advertise in Regional Tourist Board publications. Once graded, hotels can display a blue and white signboard.

In 1989, by which time 16,000 properties were involved in the crown grading scheme, it was improved by the introduction of 'quality' grading, piloted in Scotland. Hotels offering the highest quality services can now have 'De Luxe' or 'Highly Commended' added to their crown grading. Others have 'Commended' or 'Approved', as appropriate. Lack of facilities need not be a barrier to a high quality grading; a 'listed' property with simple facilities but offering excellent service can still receive the 'Highly Commended' accolade. By July 1990 thirty-five establishments, or just under one per cent of crown classified hotels, had been awarded 'Highly Commended' status.

FIGURE 51 THE 'CROWNS' OF QUALITY ACCOMMODATION

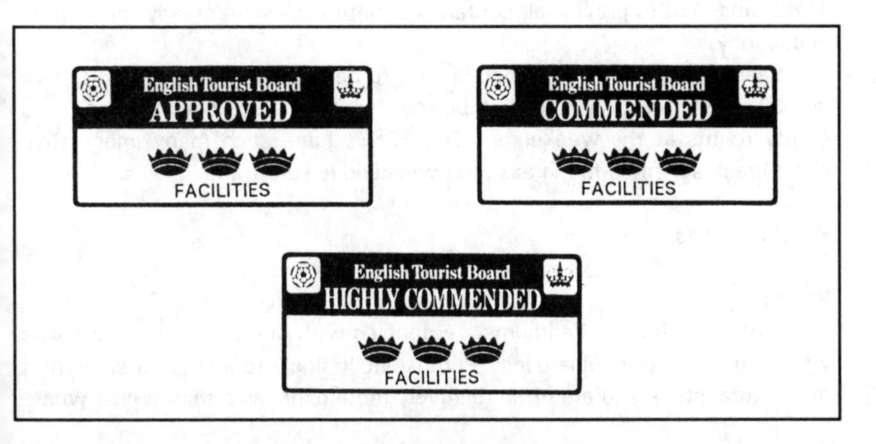

The Isle of Man Department of Tourism introduced a compulsory accommodation registration system in 1978. In 1986 the registration process was extended to include a grading system. As on the mainland, this now includes a qualitative assessment. Between one and five 'keys' are awarded to hotels, self-catering accommodation, hostels and camp-sites. Those which have only the minimum facilities required to be registered receive no keys.

Bed and Room Occupancy

The 1989 English Hotel Occupancy Survey (EHOS) calculated the average room occupancy throughout the year to be 57%, but with only 45% bed occupancy (reflecting the fact that twin or double rooms can be let for single occupancy i.e. 100% room occupancy but only 50% bed occupancy). The room occupancy rate had declined slightly since 1988 but the bed occupancy figure had stayed the same since 1987. London had the highest average room and bed occupancy, the traditional seaside resorts the lowest. South East England experienced the biggest increase in hotel occupancy in 1989.

In 1989 EHOS divided hotels into different tariff categories. In London 'lower tariff' hotels were those charging under £44.50, 'higher tariff' hotels those charging between £44.50 and £67.50, and 'premium tariff' hotels those charging over £67.50. Outside London 'lower tariff' hotels charged under £29.50, 'higher tariff' hotels charged between £29.50 and £56.00, and 'premium tariff' hotels charged over £56.00. The highest room and bed occupancy rates were recorded in the higher and premium tariff hotels, even in seaside and countryside areas where fewer business travellers would be expected.

Room occupancy was best in hotels able to deal with large conferences of 200 or more delegates (68%) and small conferences (62%). Between 1986 and 1989 provincial conference hotels saw a steady growth in occupancy.

Seaside and countryside hotels tend to be busy at weekends, but town hotels experience an exodus of business guests on Friday mornings and empty rooms at the weekends. The 1980s have seen many imaginative short break schemes to increase the weekend leisure trade.

Hotel Facilities

Rooms

Most British hotel bedrooms are doubles with one double bed, or twins with two single or double beds. Purpose-built single rooms are a small part of the total stock and are often relatively more expensive than twins; where no single room is available, a single visitor may be given a twin and charged extra for single occupancy on the basis that the hotel would have made more money if it had been let to a couple. An increasing number of hotels offer four-poster beds which are very popular with honeymoon couples.

At the top end of the market rooms have en suite bathrooms with bath, shower and toilet articles like shampoo and bath foam provided. Large colour televisions, often with satellite or cable channels, are standard. There will usually be a settee and comfortable chairs, a coffee table and a writing desk equipped with stationery. All beds will have bedside lamps and clock-radios. There will usually be a telephone although the cost of making outside calls may be very high. Kettles will be provided, with tea, coffee and biscuits. Most rooms have trouser presses, a few have irons. Some, particularly those meant to appeal to women, will have hair-driers. Many rooms have fridges or mini-bars; guests are charged for whatever the chambermaid replaces each day. **Suites** are sets of rooms, with perhaps a bedroom, lounge, kitchen and bathroom and all these facilities.

Access to rooms may be by means of a conventional key. However, increasingly it will be via a unique computer card which can also be presented in restaurants, bars, etc, to keep a tally of what is being spent. In the newest hotels these computer keys may also operate the lights. From the hotel's point of view these key systems are initially more expensive to introduce but reduce the cost of replacing all the keys guests forget to return. Some hotels offer lone women guests extra protection by booking them onto a floor to which access can only be gained by computer key.

A room's cost will reflect its facilities, with views of the sea, mountains, historic attractions, race-courses, etc. attracting either an in-built premium or a supplementary charge.

Restaurants and Bars

The best hotels have several restaurants offering à la carte meals and set menus. Some may have self-service buffets as well as table service. Sometimes different in-house restaurants may have 'themes'; alternatively they may concentrate on different cuisines. Some may also offer banqueting facilities. Most hotels are licensed, and some will have a separate cocktail bar and/or coffee lounge.

Public Areas

Large hotels have spacious reception areas, staffed twenty-four hours a day. Billing arrangements are usually computerised and there may be express check-in and check-out facilities for business travellers and conference groups.

The ground floor or the foyer will often have one or more shops. Sometimes there may be a complete shopping mall, with shops selling clothing and souvenirs as well as newspapers, books, toiletries, cigarettes, confectionery, etc.

Leisure Centres

In the 1980s many top class hotels, especially those aiming for the conference trade, built sports and health centres offering swimming pools, gymnasia, jacuzzis, saunas, solaria, squash courts, etc. To increase their profitability some hotels operate their leisure centres as private health clubs with membership open to non-residents. However, research carried out by Schroder Asseily and Co. Ltd in 1990 suggested that it was difficult to make money out of purpose-built leisure centres because of the high building and maintenance costs involved. Instead it concluded that a leisure centre's main benefit might be 'its viability...as a bedfiller' for the hotel as a whole.

Conference and Business Facilities

Hotels wishing to host conferences need a range of meeting rooms to accommodate anything from half a dozen to several hundred people. Sometimes screens which can be folded back to increase the room's size are used. Meeting rooms need back-up audio-visual equipment, flip-charts, writing paper, pencils, etc. Sometimes the meetings area will be entirely separate from the rest of the hotel, as in the Chester International Hotel.

Hotels concentrating on business travellers may also provide business centres with secretarial and translation services, and back-up telex, fax and computer services.

Hotel Services

The higher a hotel's grade, the more services it will be expected to provide. These will range from uniformed staff at the main entrance and lift staff, to twenty-four hour room service, newspaper delivery, laundry and shoe-cleaning services. Hotels priding themselves on service will also have reception staff who can help with theatre bookings, advice on what to visit, etc. Many hotel receptions offer bureaux de changes, although their rates usually compare badly with those in banks.

Problems for Hotels in the 1990s

Seasonality and periodicity

Many city centre hotels suffer from *periodicity:* all year round they may be full of business travellers during the week and empty at weekends. In contrast resort hotels suffer from *seasonality*: they may have many more week-round bookings, but the majority of their business may be squeezed into June, July, August and September.

This is a particular problem since hotels suffer from high fixed costs. Both buildings and land in the prime central positions that visitors favour are expensive. Other costs for business rates, maintenance, etc. will continue even if the hotel is closed in winter to save on heating, lighting and staff costs.

Staffing difficulties

Many hotels are having increasing difficulty in attracting and keeping good staff. This is a reflection of the long hours, shifts and poor pay involved in much hotel work, and is not helped in resort areas where hotels close in winter so that only temporary employment can be offered.

Abolition of Section 4 grants

Since 1969 the Development of Tourism Act had enabled the regional tourist boards to provide financial help to tourism ventures, including hotels, through Section 4 funding (see Chapter One). Typical of hotels which received help through the scheme is Bradford's Guide Post Hotel which received an £80,000 ETB grant to help with building costs, and then a second repayable grant to extend it. The owners of the Tudor Rose Original in Blackpool were typical of many private hoteliers who used an ETB grant to improve their facilities and achieve a higher grading. However, in July 1989 the government dropped this form of funding in England. It continues in Scotland and Wales.

Uniform Business Rate (UBR)

In April 1990 business rates were replaced with 'uniform business rates', calculated on a standard basis for the whole country. (This system was introduced a year earlier in Scotland and not at all in Northern Ireland.) Many hoteliers, especially in southern England, found themselves facing much higher bills, albeit phased in over a period of five years. These seemed likely to force prices up by as much as 20%. Businesses started after 1 April 1990 faced paying the higher rate immediately.

Recession and the Gulf War

In 1990 the impact of record interest rates began to cut into the domestic holiday market. The same interest rates also made the cost of building or expansion prohibitively expensive and made it difficult to service debts for costly developments like new leisures clubs. Incipient recession was then aggravated by the Gulf Crisis and War. Large companies grounded their travelling personnel for the War's duration, and many overseas tourists, especially Americans, opted to stay at home. Hotels countrywide reported a drop in bookings of up to 30% and entire floors empty. Some had to lay off staff or cut their working hours. Others had to reduce prices to try and lure guests. The War ended in March, 1991, but the recession deepened and hotel chains reported significant drops in profitability.

Marketing Hotels

Given the need to fill hotels all year round, marketing is becoming increasingly imaginative. Many hotels now offer special weekend breaks, with inclusive prices for transport, accommodation and meals, sometimes packaged in brochures and retailed through travel agencies. Themes can be used to make the packages more interesting; 'murder weekends' where the guests act out a scenario and have to try and identify a 'killer' have been especially successful. Other weekend breaks offer participants the chance to learn new skills like painting or orienteering.

People usually decide where they want to go and only then pick their accommodation, so most hotels have to concentrate on marketing the area in which they are located rather than just their own property.

MOTELS

Motels are hotels which have been designed with the motorist's needs in mind. Consequently they are usually by main roads and have large car parks. The UK has about 150 motels.

GUESTHOUSES/BED AND BREAKFAST ACCOMMODATION

As well as the larger hotels, the UK has an extensive network of approximately 30,000 privately owned and managed guesthouses, including about 11,700 bed and breakfast establishments. Bed and breakfast is also offered in many farmhouses and large pubs. Guesthouses are graded with the same crown symbols as the larger hotels, but their main selling points are may be their friendly, personal service and their good value for money.

Most bed and breakfasts open all year round but are fullest from June to September. Usually thay are entirely financed by their owners and run by just one or two people. Many have no more than three rooms. Perhaps 30% of bed and breakfast occupants are business travellers, but most aim mainly at tourists. As a result most stock literature about local attractions, transport services, etc., perhaps in looseleaf 'What Shall We Do Next?' booklets in the bedrooms.

Crown graded bed and breakfasts can be listed in Regional Tourist

Board publications and in annual 'Bed and Breakfast Touring Maps' which give address and telephone numbers and map locations.

The introduction of the uniform business rate and the **100 Day Rule,** which said that wherever rooms were let to paying guests for more than one hundred days in the year the owners were liable for the UBR as well as the personal community charge, led to uncertainty in 1990. Some guest-houses seemed likely to go out of business, or stop taking part in the grading schemes which had done much to improve overall standards. Following protests the government agreed to review the rule. Houses in which rooms are let to no more than six guests, where the owner lives on the premises and where the building's use for bed and breakfast is secondary to its domestic purpose are likely to be exempted from the business rate.

Government policies on housing the homeless have affected the availability of bed and breakfast accommodation in city centres. During the 1980s much council housing was sold and little more was built. Local authorities are required by law to house homeless families where they are not intentionally homeless. With fewer council properties to let they often fell back on paying for bed and breakfast in guesthouses and private hotels. Since hoteliers are guaranteed payment from the DSS, many are happy to swap from offering conventional holiday bed and breakfast. In London, in particular, this has contributed to the shortage of cheap accommodation.

FARM HOLIDAYS

Farms have always accommodated tourists, whether as bed and breakfast guests or as campers or caravanners. However, in the late 1980s farm tourism became more importance as EC subsidies to farmers to produce stockpiled food began to be phased out. To make ends meet even more farming families are taking in guests, especially in Wales where 1,208 farms were letting 6,976 bedspaces in 1990; of all the British counties Gwynedd has the most farm tourists. Perhaps 10,000 British farms offer farmhouse accommodation, while another 10,000 offer self-catering in adjacent cottages or converted farm buildings.

Farmhouse accommodation is generally subject to the same grading procedures as other types, but Wales also has a yellow dragon *Farmhouse Award* for extra-special standards of furnishings, facilities, comfort and surroundings.

The Farm Holiday Bureau promotes holidays on working farms and produces the *Stay on a Farm* guidebook listing over a thousand serviced and self-catering farm properties.

HOLIDAY CENTRES/VILLAGES

Billy Butlin set up the first British holiday camp at Skegness in 1936, supposedly after he spotted miserable holidaymakers in a bus shelter on a typically wet British summer day. Fred Pontin and Harry Warner were quick to pick up his idea. By the 1960s about 150 holidays camps ringed the British coastline, mostly attracting a local working-class clientele. When the advent of cheap package holidays in the 1960s started to reduce the number of holidaymakers, amenities were rapidly improved. In particular more self-catering units were built.

By the 1980s the biggest holiday camp operators were Butlin's (Rank Organisation), Pontin's (Bass) and Warner/Ladbroke's (Mecca Leisure Group). In 1988/9 21% of all UK domestic holidays were based in holiday centres, the new name for holiday camps. However, the new more up-market Center Parcs villages in Sherwood Forest and Elvenden presented a threat to the traditional camps.

TABLE 40 BRITISH HOLIDAY CAMPS IN 1990

Company Trading Name	Ownership	Number of Camps/Centres
Ladbroke's/Warners	Mecca Leisure Holidays	36
Haven	Rank Organisation	29
Pontin's	Bass	20
Butlin's	Rank Organisation	5

SELF-CATERING ACCOMMODATION

In the 1960s and '70s self-catering holidays became more popular because they were cheaper than hotels and offered greater flexibility, particularly for families with young children. Many holiday camps and farms offer self-catering units, but there are also about 50,000 holiday cottages which can be rented, usually for a week at a time. Some of these are second homes let on a casual basis, but others are let regularly through professional letting agencies. The National Trust, Landmark Trust and Forestry Commission also let cottages to bring in extra income.

In 1990 3% of domestic holidays seem to have been taken in holiday cottages but few overseas visitors use this type of accommodation. Rented cottages seem more popular with the AB social groups.

The biggest letting agencies for holiday cottages are Blakes, Cottage Directory, Country Holidays, English Country Cottages, Hoseasons and Mackays who handle about 16,000 properties between them.

The ETB grades self-catering accommodation with between one and five 'keys' for facilities and equipment. Standards of service are recorded in the same 'approved', 'commended' and 'highly commended' categories as hotels.

FIGURE 52 'KEYS' TO GOOD SELF-CATERING ACCOMMODATION

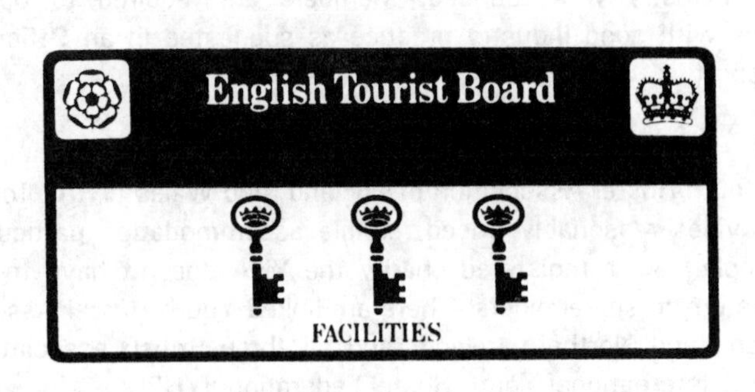

SECOND HOMES AND TIMESHARE

Some holidaymakers who like to return to the same spot each year buy second homes in their chosen destination. However, there can be practical difficulties over leaving a property empty for long periods, particularly in areas where local people object to second-homers.

Timeshare evolved as an alternative to second homes. The owner buys not the entire property, but a fixed part of it for a fixed period in the year (say, two weeks in July) in perpetuity. The price paid reflects the popularity of the chosen time of year and the quality/situation of the actual property.

The first UK timeshare development opened in Loch Rannoch in Perthshire in 1974. By 1990 there were eighty-five sizeable timeshare resorts in the UK and Ireland, ten of them actually built in 1990. Most are in the Lake District, Scotland, and Devon and Cornwall. Some resorts consist of villas and apartments, while others are converted country houses or hotels. Many have their own leisure facilities which may include swimming pools, gymnasia, golf-courses, shops, jacuzzis, saunas and tennis, squash and badminton courts. By 1990 there were 220,000 timeshare owners in the UK and Ireland. However, of the 460,000 owners in Europe, only 7% own properties in the UK, compared with 28% in the Canary Islands, 21% on the Algarve and 19% on the Costa del Sol.

British timeshare developments are mostly owned by UK residents and could therefore be seen as part of the domestic holiday market. However, in future it may be easier to swap shares with other owners, allowing owners to take holidays in different places as well, so the idea has potential for international tourism too.

On the continent some complex developers' hard sell tactics have given timeshare a bad name. However, in the UK development has proceeded more slowly and there have been fewer problems. In 1991 a Timeshare Council dedicated to promoting, developing, representing and regulating the timeshare industry was founded. Members are required to operate in accordance with good industry practice as suggested in an Office of Fair Trading report in 1990.

HOSTELS

The Youth Hostel Association of England and Wales (YHA), founded in 1930, provides reasonably priced, simple accommodation particularly for young people. As a registered charity the YHA doesn't have to make a profit to return to shareholders. There are linked Youth Hostel Associations for Scotland and Northern Ireland, and all three British associations are linked to the International Youth Hostel Federation (IYHF).

In England and Wales the YHA has about 250 hostels, many of them in remote and beautiful countryside, but others in busy town centres. Only Association members can stay in them but in 1991 there were 320,000 members. Hostel prices start at £2.60, and hostellers are provided with simple dormitory beds and basic bedding. Cooking facilities are usually available, and some hostels provide simple meals and have shops. There are a further 80 hostels in Scotland.

Until the late 1980s hostels discouraged car drivers in favour of walkers, climbers, etc. but by 1990 this attitude had changed, and rooms offered more privacy and attractive decor in keeping with people's higher expectations.

The YMCA and YWCA also offer some hostel accommodation, although they tend to prefer long-stay tenants. In the 1980s more hostel accommodation was being made available as old barns were converted into 'camping barns' offering simple accommodation suitable for walkers.

CAMPING AND CARAVANNING

Some people enjoy camping or caravanning holidays despite the British climate. Camping first became popular in the 1880s, but it wasn't until car ownership became the norm that camping and caravanning really took off as holiday options. Their popularity grew rapidly in the 1970s but had stabilised by the late 1980s. In 1988 the 6.7 million camping and caravanning holidays in England made up 9% of all holiday trips, although few overseas visitors were involved. About half these holidays were short breaks. Almost 92% of all camping and caravanning holidays take place between April and September.

Camping can be one of the cheapest holiday options. It also offers freedom, making it popular with younger people. In Britain most people camp on sites where they must take along all the equipment. Many British camp-sites are also more basic than those on the continent, with only simple sanitary and washing facilities and no shops.

There are two types of caravan: touring caravans which are usually owned by the holidaymaker and can be taken from site to site, and static caravans which never leave their sites. Most static caravans belong to the site owner, although sometimes they may belong to individuals who rent the site. Caravanning is particularly popular with older age groups, although many families also choose it, perhaps because it can be fairly cheap.

Many UK sites are used for camping and caravanning. In 1990 there were an estimated 3,500 sites for tents and touring caravans, with perhaps 300,000 pitches in all. New sites require licences (under the 1960 Caravan Sites and Control of Development Act) and planning permission. Most are privately owned, although some are owned and operated by local authorities or by the Camping and Caravan Club or the Caravan Club. The National Trust, the Forestry Commission and the National Park Authorities also provide some camouflaged camping and caravanning sites on their land. In areas like the Lake District temporary summer sites also exist under the '28 Day Rule'; this permits three caravans on a five acre site or one caravan on any piece of land for no more than two consecutive nights provided the site is not used for more than twenty-eight days in the year. A special licence is not needed to allow tent camping alone if this only takes place on 42 consecutive days or 60 days in total in any one calendar year. Sites owned by the Caravan or Camping and Caravan Club don't need special licences.

Two thirds of British camping/caravan sites are in England, with perhaps a quarter of the pitches in Devon and Cornwall. Cumbria, Norfolk, Dorset, Hampshire, North Yorkshire and other coastal areas also have many sites.

Wales has many static caravan sites, and WTB data shows that average occupancy increased between 1988 and 1989 in all three areas of the country, with the highest average occupancy in North Wales (75% in 1989). Not surprisingly sites are most full (86%) in August. Touring caravan pitches have a much lower average level of occupancy (32% in 1989). The WTB has been examining ways to camouflage sites to reduce their impact on the landscape.

To improve standards at static caravan parks the National Tourist Boards, together with the British Holiday and Home Parks Association (BH & HPA), now award ticks (shown within the letter 'Q' for quality) to approved parks; the more ticks the better the park. Four and five tick parks may also be given rose, thistle or dragon awards for providing a high standard of facilities, and having first class caravans for hire. By 1991 more than 1,000 UK caravan parks had received the 'quality' award.

FIGURE 53 'TICKS' FOR QUALITY CARAVAN PARKS

The Rose Award
For the growing number who enjoy staying on a holiday caravan park, look out for those with a Rose Award. These are awarded each year to those parks which not only provide facilities to a high standard but also have first class caravan holiday homes for hire.

ACCOMMODATION AND DISABLED VISITORS

For accommodation to be accessible to disabled visitors the following adaptations may be required:

a) Ramps at all public entrances.

b) Lifts large enough for wheelchairs to be manipulated wherever there are steps. Alternatively, chair-lifts can be attached to the wall or stair-rail so guests can be moved up and down without their chairs.

c) Ground floor bedrooms set aside for those with mobility problems.

d) Public areas made accessible by avoiding unnecessary platforms and steps in restaurants and bars.

e) Bedrooms with enough space to turn wheelchairs round.

f) Suitably adapted bathrooms. Where they are en suite, doors can be taken off their hinges to make access easier; sliding doors are another possibility. Bars should be provided beside baths and toilets to help people get up and down. Non-slip mats should be placed in the bath itself. Waterproof seats should be provided in showers.

g) Long strings on bedroom light switches.

In 1990 the National Tourist Boards produced accessibility symbols (Fig. 54), to be displayed by accommodation which the Holiday Care Service had approved as suitable for disabled people. Saga Group plc, which specialises in organising holidays for older people, also helped produce a handbook, *Providing Accessible Accommodation*, which offers advice on how hotels can make the disabled welcome.

FIGURE 54 SIGNS OF ACCESSIBILITY

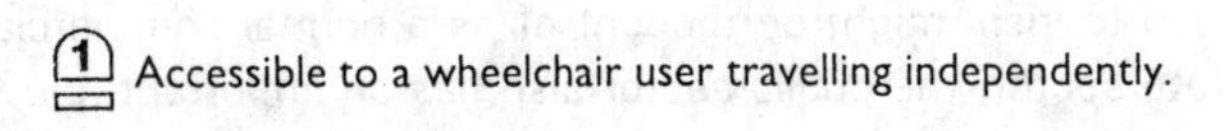

1 Accessible to a wheelchair user travelling independently.

2 Accessible to a wheelchair user travelling with assistance.

3 Accessible to someone with mobility difficulties, but able to walk a few paces and up a maximum of 3 steps.

CHAPTER FIVE
THE PUBLIC SECTOR AND TOURISM

Although tourism might be thought of as a normal commercial activity in the private sector, the public sector also has an important role to play in providing the framework for tourism development. It is, for example, responsible for the provision of the transport infrastructure which is fundamental to the development of tourism. It is also important in providing information services for the public through the network of National Tourist Boards, Regional Tourist Boards and Tourist Information Centres.

The public sector is also responsible for providing much of the training for tourism. In 1991 513 colleges and polytechnics were providing courses in travel and tourism, business studies for travel and tourism, hotel management and hospitality, and catering.

Tourism and Central Government

In general the Conservative government of the 1980s saw its role in relationship to tourism as 'promoting a general economic climate favourable to the industry's growth' and as 'removing unnecessary restrictions or burdens'. Its views were set out at length in the 1985 report *Pleasure, Leisure and Jobs: The Business of Tourism*, produced by the Enterprise Unit of the Cabinet Office with Lord Young at the helm.

More specifically it believed in giving special assistance to economically weak areas of the country and helping to promote year-round tourism to all parts of the country. The Department of the Environment provides more than half the government's investment in tourism, although development grants and advice also come from other departments and agencies.

Until 1985 tourism policy was the responsibility of the Department of Trade and Industry. Following the publication of Lord Young's report which recognised the industry's importance as an employer, it was transferred to the larger Department of Employment. The Department of Employment now funds the British Tourist Authority and English Tourist Board, and liaises with them on broad funding and policy issues. In 1990/1 the government spent about £530 million on tourism and leisure-related actvities in the UK.

In 1988 the first Minister for Tourism was appointed. The post has since been held by John Lee MP, Lord Strathclyde and Viscount Ullswater. The Minister's role is to ensure that the industry's views are represented in government. (The only other industry that has a Minister specifically to represent it is agriculture.) The Minister for Tourism works with a team in the Department of Employment, while the Employment Secretary represents the industry at Cabinet level. S/he has overall responsibility for tourism in the UK as a whole and in England, while the Secretaries of State for Scotland, Wales and Northern Ireland are responsible for tourism policy within their own areas.

Central government is involved in tourism in many ways. It owns most of the national museums and art galleries, it grant-aids bodies to preserve ancient buildings and monuments and the countryside and to support the arts, and it provides the basic transport infrastructure which facilitates tourism (the airports, seaports, roads, railways amd waterways). It also sets many of the rules within which the tourism industry operates: on licensing and shopping hours, on advertising and on employment.

At present central government is responsible for setting the VAT rate and deciding which services it should be levied on. Increases in the VAT rate can have damaging consequences for those providing tourist services. Increasingly these decisions are likely to be made through the European Community. For example, passenger transport is not currently liable for VAT. However, when European rates are eventually harmonised it is likely to be levied at a rate of between four and nine per cent which will push up ticket prices and the cost of coach and rail tours. If VAT is also imposed on publications (zero rated at present), the cost of preparing promotional materials is likely to rise.

The government is also in charge of Customs and Immigration arrangements and thus of foreign visitors' first impression of the country. It is their decision, for example, that Channel Tunnel passengers must undergo Customs and Immigration procedures at the point of entry to Britain even though in most of Europe such procedures will now be completed only once, at the point of departure.

The Development of Tourism Act

The 1969 Development of Tourism Act established the British Tourist Authority (BTA) and the English (ETB), Wales (WTB) and Scottish (STB) Tourist Boards. A Northern Ireland Tourist Board (NITB) had already been created by the 1948 Development of Tourist Traffic Act (Northern Ireland). The five tourist authorities are completely independent of each other and financed directly by the government, although in practice the BTA often works in collaboration with the four National Tourist Boards. The BTA and ETB are responsible to the Department of Employment, while the STB and WTB are responsible to the Secretaries of State for Scotland and Wales respectively Fig. 55.

The Isle of Man Tourist Board, and the States of Jersey and Guernsey Tourist Committees have comparable functions to the mainland tourist boards but are completely independent of them.

FIGURE 55 TOURIST BOARD STRUCTURE IN THE U.K.

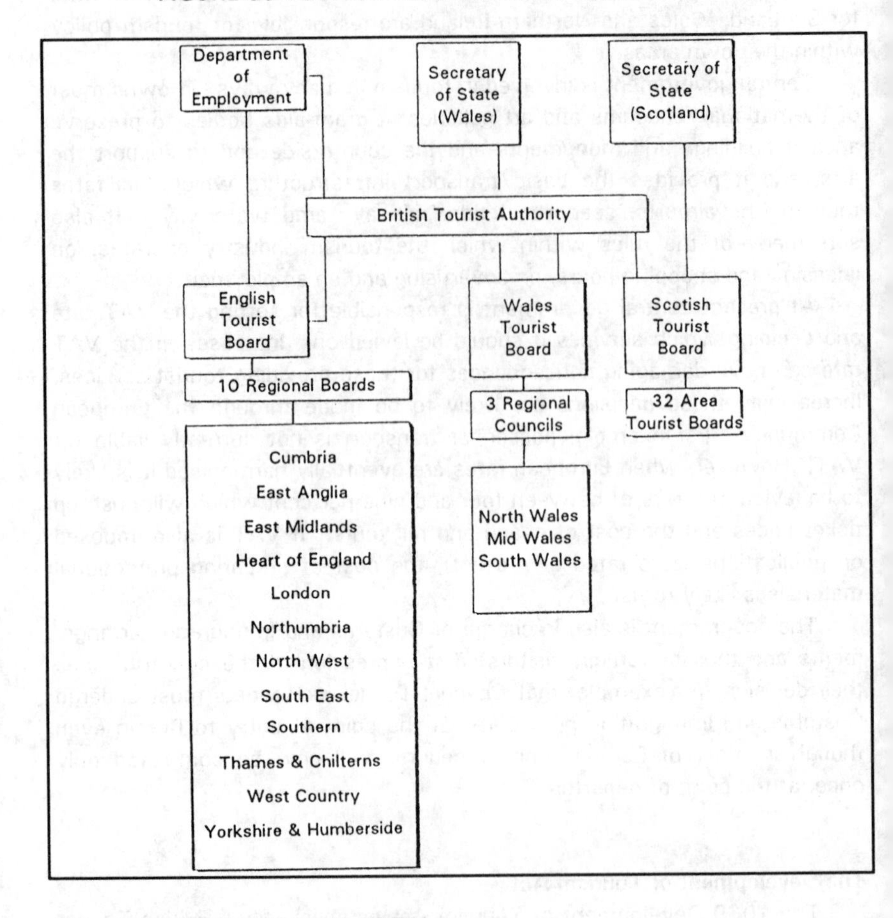

The British Tourist Authority (BTA)

The British Tourist Authority is funded by the Department of Employment. In 1991/2 it received £29.5 million in grant-aid. It has responsibility for promoting the UK as a holiday destination for overseas visitors. It also advises the government on tourism matters that relate to the UK as a whole and collects statistics on tourism to and within the UK. In 1989 it published *Strategy for Growth 1989-1993* in which it identified its main objectives as:

a) maximising Britain's foreign currency earnings from tourism.
b) identifying foreign tourists' needs and evolving product improvements to meet them.
c) spreading tourism nationwide and throughout the year.

The BTA has overseas offices in Argentina, Australia, Belgium, Brazil, Canada, Denmark, France, Germany, Hong Kong, Ireland, Italy, Japan, Mexico, the Netherlands, Norway, Singapore, South Africa, Spain, Sweden, Switzerland and the USA, and works with overseas companies wishing to offer packages to the UK. Where there is no overseas office, liaison with overseas operators is channelled through the marketing executives of London-based 'Desks'.

The BTA provides familiarisation trips for foreign tour operators and journalists. It produces newsletters aimed at specific overseas markets and compiles profiles of individual markets. It also helps UK tourism businesses promote themselves overseas and can assist with brochure distribution. The Business Travel Department advises conference and exhibition organisers looking for an overseas market.

The BTA publishes the monthly upmarket *In Britain* magazine, and the multilingual *Hello Britain* magazine, aimed at independent travellers. It also produces US and Canadian Sales Guides. Central Information Services produce information guides and directories for the overseas offices. The BTA also produces some films, videos and radio programmes, and has a conventional library, and film and slide library. The Sales Promotions Department produces shell folders which can be used to make reasonably priced brochures.

The Product Marketing Department also develops and promotes 'themes' to sell Britain. Recent themes have included 'Britain For All Seasons', 'Family Fun in Britain', 'Britain's Treasured Landscapes' and 'Waterfront Britain'. In 1990 it produced a 'Movie Map' of the UK, showing sites which are linked to films or television.

The BTA also sponsors the annual 'Come to Britain' trophy for outstanding new attractions or amenities for tourists.

In 1986 the BTA and British Rail opened the British Travel Centre in London's Lower Regent Street. The Centre offers information services and rail bookings and contains an American Express foreign exchange bureau, a travel bookshop, a souvenir shop, interactive video information points and a 'video wall' showing images of the UK.

The National Tourist Boards (NTBs)

According to the Development of Tourism Act the functions of the National Tourist Boards were to promote domestic tourism in their area by:

a) encouraging British residents' tourism within their own country,
b) encouraging the provision and improvement of attractions and facilities for domestic (and overseas) tourists in the UK,
c) administering government grant schemes for tourism projects, and
d) advising the government on UK tourism matters.

In pursuance of these functions the Act empowered the NTBs to undertake the following activities:

a) all forms of promotional and publicity activity
b) providing advisory and information services to the tourism industry
c) offering financial assistance to significant tourism projects likely to provide or improve tourist amenities
d) promoting or undertaking research
e) advising on policy matters to do with tourism

In 1988 the ETB interpreted its role in terms of the following main tasks:

* providing leadership for the industry by linking up private companies, local authorities and central government.
* identifying trends and working to spread product knowledge.
* carrying out essential but non-profitable tasks like: providing tourist information; offering guidance on important developments like the Single Market, the Channel Tunnel, the Sunday Trading Act and the Local Government Finance Act; research; and promoting areas with high unemployment as potential tourist destinations.
* co-ordinating collective marketing of England
* stimulating investment in both old and new projects to improve England's competitiveness as a tourist destination.
* providing a national framework and marketing support for the regional tourist boards
* improving standards by encouraging education and training and by promoting accommodation grading schemes.
* protecting consumers by providing unbiased advice and assistance.

In 1991/2 the ETB received £14.7 million in grants from the Department of Employment but devolved £6.8 million of this to the twelve regional tourist boards.

The NTBs all collect and publish statistical data on tourism and undertake a range of marketing and promotional activities. Until 1989, under Section 4 of the Development of Tourism Act all the NTBs administered funds to help tourism projects in their area. In 1989 the government abolished grant-aid for tourism in England, although it continues to be available through the STB, WTB and NITB.

The NTBs produce strategy proposals for future developments. In 1988 the ETB launched *Vision for England,* its strategy for tourist development upto 1993, with a target of achieving investment of between £3-4 billion and 250,000 tourism jobs by the early 1990s. In 1991 it published *Planning For Success...A Tourism Strategy for England, 1991-1995.* The ETB has run campaigns focusing on particular aspects of tourism. Two important ones have been:

* **Tourism For All**, aimed at encouraging everyone involved in tourism to take the needs of the disabled into account.
* **Tourism For Tomorrow**, aimed at encouraging sustainable tourism development which takes the environment into account.

To encourage higher standards and quality development the ETB launched the *England For Excellence* award scheme in 1988.

The NTBs have become major information sources. In 1990 the ETB published the following:

a) *Where To Stay* guides to: hotels and guesthouses; farmhouses, bed and breakfasts, inns and hostels; self-catering holiday homes; and camping and caravanning parks in Britain.
b) *Let's Go.* Guide to short breaks in England.
c) *Stay On A Farm.* Guide to British farm holidays.
d) *Countryside Directory.* A guide to farming museums, pick your own fruit and vegetable farms, agricultural shows, farms offering afternoon teas, etc.
e) *Britain At Work.* A guide to industrial tourism in Britain.
f) *Let's Do It.* A guide to activity and hobby holidays.

The ETB also produces the *England Holidays* brochure in which hoteliers and tourist attractions can advertise alongside copy produced by the tourist board itself.

The NTBs synthesise information from other sources and distribute information provided by other principals. Visitors to the BTA Travel Centre can pick up leaflets produced by attractions, hotels and transport undertakings.

Marketing is a major activity for the NTBs. From 1985 the ETB marketing department organised the two-day annual MOOT show, the largest domestic travel trade event. The 300-odd exhibitors saw it as a chance to launch new products and reach important buyers, about 1500 of whom, including coach tour operators, incoming tour operators and handling agents, usually attended MOOT. In 1992 the ETB, WTB and NITB worked together to set up the British Travel Trade Fair (BTTF) at the National Exhibition Centre to replace MOOT.

Like the BTA the NTBs are working to disperse tourism away from 'honeypot' or over-visited destinations to less popular areas, and away from the peak summer months to the less congested times of year.

In the 1990s the NTBs were under pressure to raise more money from non-governmental sources. The ETB has suggested the following possibilities:

* Expanding its publication range, perhaps in collaboration with private publishers.
* Creating high street English Holiday Shops to operate as domestic holiday travel agencies.
* Charging for inspections to grade accommodation.
* Marketing the ETB database of 80,000 establishments, attractions, events, etc.
* Providing paid consultancy services.

In the late 1980s the possibility of privatising the NTBs was discussed. A 1989 review of the ETB's functions resulted in a decision to scale them down and devolve some of the responsibilities to the Regional Tourist Boards. The functions to be devolved included:

(i) local development work, including involvement in tourism development action programmes.

(ii) responsibility for the accommodation grading schemes.

(iii) responsibility for tourist information services and networking the TICs.

(iv) local marketing and encouragement for training.

In addition the promotion of trade events and the production and publication of accommodation guides were to be contracted out to other bodies.

The Regional Tourist Boards (RTBs)

Although it was not required by the 1969 Act, in 1970 the English and Welsh Tourist Board created a network of Regional Tourist Boards to share their workload and to promote tourism within smaller areas. The RTBs are funded by the ETB/WTB, the local authorities and private contributions (Fig. 56).

The 1982 **Local Government and Planning (Scotland) Act** resulted in the creation of thirty-two Area Tourist Boards or ATBs (Fig. 57). Most ATBs are funded by the STB, the local authorities and private contributions. However, the City of Edinburgh, Kirkcaldy and Moray District Councils have retained full control over tourism development in their areas.

FIGURE 56 THE ENGLISH AND WELSH REGIONAL TOURIST BOARDS

(Source: BTA, 1992)

The RTBs produce regional accommodation/attractions guides, run advertising campaigns, and organise workshops and exhibitions focusing on their particular area. They also conduct their own surveys and give local councils and commercial operators advice on tourism matters. They provide information direct to the local TICs, and in popular tourist destinations may even operate their own information bureaux. The RTBs also develop local tourism strategies, often in co-operation with bodies like the Countryside Commission.

FIGURE 57 SCOTTISH AREA TOURIST BOARDS

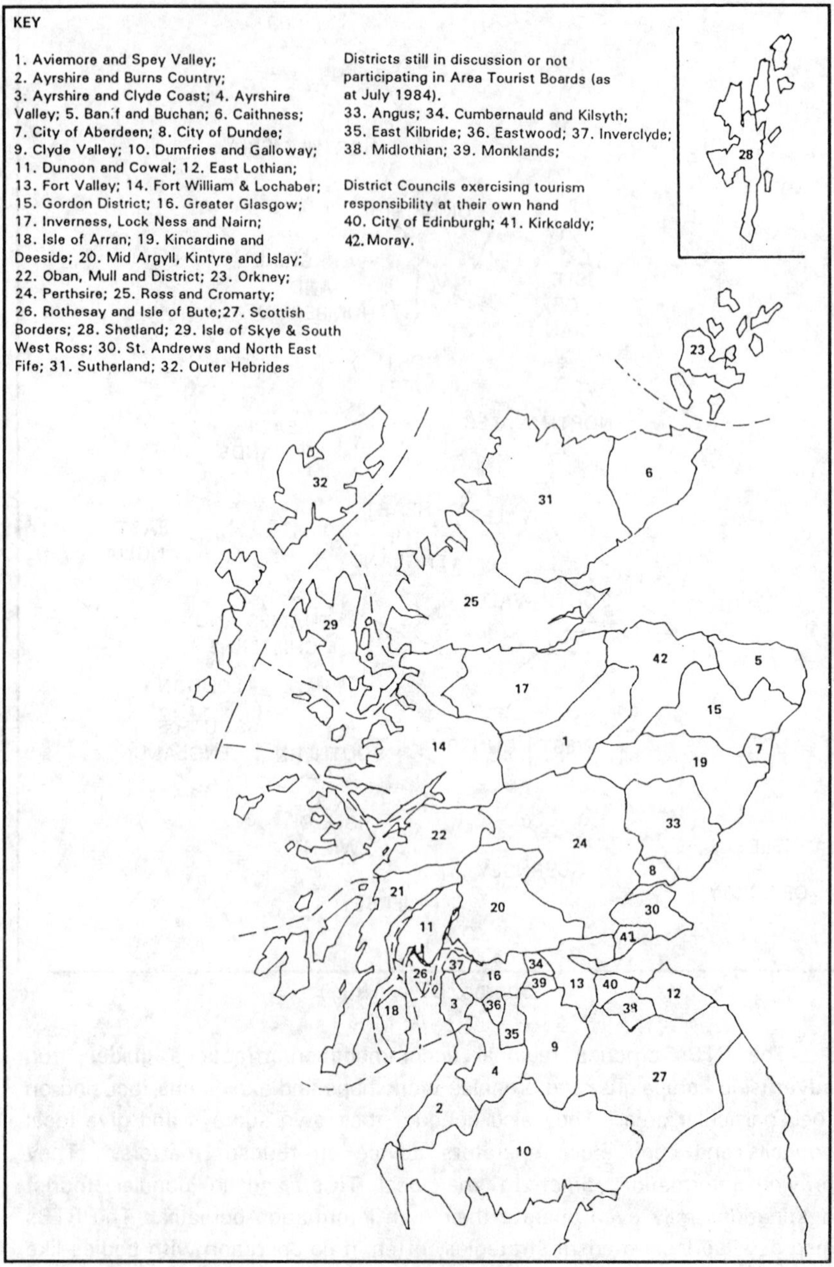

KEY

1. Aviemore and Spey Valley;
2. Ayrshire and Burns Country;
3. Ayrshire and Clyde Coast; 4. Ayrshire Valley; 5. Banff and Buchan; 6. Caithness;
7. City of Aberdeen; 8. City of Dundee;
9. Clyde Valley; 10. Dumfries and Galloway;
11. Dunoon and Cowal; 12. East Lothian;
13. Fort Valley; 14. Fort William & Lochaber;
15. Gordon District; 16. Greater Glasgow;
17. Inverness, Lock Ness and Nairn;
18. Isle of Arran; 19. Kincardine and Deeside; 20. Mid Argyll, Kintyre and Islay;
22. Oban, Mull and District; 23. Orkney;
24. Perthsire; 25. Ross and Cromarty;
26. Rothesay and Isle of Bute; 27. Scottish Borders; 28. Shetland; 29. Isle of Skye & South West Ross; 30. St. Andrews and North East Fife; 31. Sutherland; 32. Outer Hebrides

Districts still in discussion or not participating in Area Tourist Boards (as at July 1984).
33. Angus; 34. Cumbernauld and Kilsyth;
35. East Kilbride; 36. Eastwood; 37. Inverclyde;
38. Midlothian; 39. Monklands;

District Councils exercising tourism responsibility at their own hand
40. City of Edinburgh; 41. Kirkcaldy;
42. Moray.

(Source: STB, 1992)

Tourism and Local Government

Local government first became involved in tourism in the late 18th century when it started to play a role in providing regional infrastructure, developing facilities like museums and theatres, and providing information for visitors. This work was gradually consolidated throughout the 19th century. Then the **1948 Local Government Act** empowered local authorities to set up tourism information and publicity services. The **1972 Local Government Act** also gave them the right to encourage tourists and provide suitable facilities for them. During the 1970s local government reorganisation tended to preoccupy the authorities. However, in the 1980s, with industry in decline all over the country, they once again turned their attention to tourism. Of Britain's 453 local authorities, perhaps 200 were actively involved with tourism by 1991.

Local authorities tend to be involved with tourism in the following ways:

a) **Infrastructure Development.**

(i) Communications...road, railways, airports, car/coach parking

(ii) Planning and Development...local structure plans, local strategic plans, conservation, land use controls, development controls, sign-posting, planning permission, etc.

(iii) Creative Planning and Development...urban redevelopment, economic development, partnerships leading to shopping/leisure developments, conference centres, grant funding to encourage private developers.

b) **Providing Facilities.**

Theatres, concert halls, arts centres, museums and art galleries, parks and gardens, sea-front promenades, outdoor sports facilities (golf courses, tennis courts), indoor sports facilities (leisure centres, swimming pools, squash courts), public toilets, street cleaning, refuse collection, etc.

c) **Providing Tourism Services**

Tourist Information Centres, publicity and promotion activities, marketing partnerships with the private sector, events and festivals, and general support services (deckchairs, beach cleaning, etc.).

Many local authorities employ Tourism Officers who are responsible for advising on matters affecting tourism in their particular area. Marketing and public relations are usually important roles for these officers who will represent their area at exhibitions, conferences and workshops in the UK and abroad. Some also manage their local Tourist Information Centres. Other local authority jobs can also be seen as tourism-related; for example, electrical engineers at Blackpool work on the Illuminations, and archaeologists are employed on local excavations. One survey has suggested that as many as 9,090 local authority jobs in thirty-seven different areas are in some way related to tourism. Ninety per cent of these jobs are full-time, year-round posts which is atypical of tourism-related jobs as a whole.

Local government officials play a major role in developing local tourism strategies which analyse the state of play, look ahead to the future and set out what should be done to ensure that tourism develops in a controlled and beneficial fashion. Local authorities usually have control over all local planning applications, and responsibility for crucial matters like the provision of coach, car and caravan parks, public toilets, etc. Refusing planning permission can be a way of trying to control what is seen as unsuitable tourism development; for example, the proliferation of land-scape-marring caravan sites. In places with Urban Development Corporations, planning applications have been taken out of local authority control.

Local authorities may also own and run some tourist attractions, including local museums and art galleries, some theatres, and most parks. They may also manage the beaches and promenades. Some of the facilities provided for local residents (sports centres, playing fields, golf courses, picnic sites, etc.) will also be used by visitors. However, local authority funds were increasingly squeezed in the late 1980s. The new community charge meant that cuts to all non-statutory services became more likely, threatening such things as the provision of sports facilities and free admission to museums.

The Tourist Information Centres (TICs)

The 1969 Development of Tourism Act paved the way for the creation of a network of Tourist Information Centres by saying that the National Tourist Boards had the power '...to provide advisory and information services'. Britain now has more than 800 official TICs in England, Scotland, Wales, Northern Ireland, the Channel Islands and the Isle of Man, almost 600 of them in England. Many have evolved out of information centres already offered by local authorities, and funding for the TICs continues to come from local authorities in the main.

The ETB has compared its relationship to the TICs with that of a franchise operation. It has devised a unified image and system of presentation for the TICs and provides some centralised publicity, promotional and other materials with a 'corporate' image. It also provides some support services to the TICs through the Regional Tourist Boards. In return TICs have to agree to accept the ETB's standards of service, presentation, etc. in order to receive its approval.

In general TICs offer the following services:

* information on places to visit within a fifty mile or day trip radius.
* information and sometimes a booking service for local accommodation
* information about what's on locally, where to eat, what sports facilities are available, etc.
* a selection of brochures and leaflets.
* travel information.
* a register of approved Green and Blue Badge guides.

At the start of the 1990s the National Tourist Boards tightened up their criteria for recognising information centres as 'networked TICs'. For example, volunteer staff were no longer regarded as acceptable. From April 1992 the following minimum standards for recognition will apply and RTB inspectors will make annual visits to ensure they are being applied:

a) TICs must abide by agreed minimum summer and winter opening hours. Those in large towns must open for at least 48 hours a week all year round. Those in major resorts must open for 56 hours a week from Easter to 31 October and for 42 hours a week in winter. Rural TICs must open for 35 hours a week in summer and 15 in winter. They must also open during lunch-hours on working days.

b) They must maximise access by providing car parking and suitable ETB-approved signposts for pedestrians and drivers (Fig. 58) whenever possible. The needs of the disabled must also be taken into account in designing the buildings.

FIGURE 58 ETB-APPROVED SIGNS FOR TICs

c) They must provide a telephone information service and list its number in the British Telecom phone books. They must also publicise the TIC as widely as possible to ensure maximum use.

d) During closing hours, they must provide basic tourist information, including details of the opening hours of neighbouring TICs, both on an external display (perhaps an EMU display) and on a pre-recorded telephone message.

e) They must provide a comprehensive, impartial information service; stock a range of local, RTB, ETB and private literature; reply to all enquiries; and keep records of relevant information.

f) They must run a bed booking scheme, using classified and graded accommodation wherever possible.

g) They must employ one full time paid member of staff in charge of operations and at least one full time paid member of staff to deal with counter enquiries. This staff member must wear a uniform or an ETB-approved name badge and hold or be studying for the Certificate of Tourist Information Centre Competence (COTICC). In areas with many overseas visitors there should be 'sufficient' counter staff with appropriate language proficiency.

h) They must have a budget adequate to cover the required opening hours, and must keep such records as the ETB recommends.

i) Wherever possible, they should install the ETNA computer system to provide the most efficient service to their customers.

In return for accepting these standards TICs get ETB support in the form of guidance notes, publicity, signposting, information services, uniforms and staff training. Limited financial assistance is sometimes available too.

The WTB, STB and NITB are currently agreeing similar guidelines for TICS in their areas.

To improve the standard of service offered in TICs it has been suggested that some should offer a Holiday Information Service to help local people plan holidays elsewhere in the UK. It has also been suggested that TICs should be established in continental ferry ports to provide information to overseas visitors en route for the UK.

In addition to having to meet the new minimum standards, TICs are also having to try and generate more income because most are dependent on local authority funding, which is under increasing pressure. Providing tourist information services is not one of a local authority's statutory duties, so this is an area where they could consider economising. The TICs are therefore having to prove that they are trying to reduce their running costs.

Most TICs can make money from providing posters, postcards, books, camera films, AA/RAC membership, stamps and phonecards. Other possibilities include:

* becoming a booking agent for British Rail, National Express, car hire companies, etc.

* becoming a ticket agent for local theatres, attractions, etc.
* selling appropriately designed merchandise.

The Book A Bed Ahead (BABA) Scheme

Some TICs only provide information on accommodation possibilities. Others can book beds in their own area, usually for a fixed service charge or for a percentage of the cost (normally 10% of the first night's cost, paid by the hotelier rather than the client). Yet others charge for booking beds elsewhere in the UK. In future TICs may also book self-catering accommodation, camp-site space, etc.

A few TICs, including those in airports or motorway service stations, may be restricted by the terms of their lease from undertaking some of these commercial ventures, particularly if they might compete with other operations in the same area.

Tourist Information Points (TIPs)

Tourist Information Points are like mini tourist information centres. Usually unstaffed, they are stands equipped with information primarily about local attractions. Often they can be found in the foyer of other tourist attractions or in hotel receptions. Leaflet distribution may be organised by the attractions involved or contracted out to specialist distributors.

Technology and the TICs

English Tourist Network Automation (ETNA)

During 1990 the ETB and the RTBs worked together to introduce ETNA to the recognised TICs. In 1991 ETNA2, an updated package taking into account the experience of those operating the first generation system, was introduced.

ETNA has been designed to run on the Apricot Qi350ti system and is supplied to the TICs through approved regional re-sellers. It offers the following features:

a) **Accommodation Search** which allows counter staff to match clients' specific needs (vegetarian meals, accommodation for pets, etc.) to a database of accommodation. The computer-generated listing will show availability. The counter clerk can then make a telephone booking, type in the client's details and print out a booking form.

b) **Details of attractions and events**. The counter clerk can feed in the attraction/event's name, the desired location or the type of attraction/event. The computer will generate a suitable list and details can be printed out for clients.

c) The **Mailing System** collects the names of clients who book accommodation through the TIC. Additional names can be added manually and the database thus formed used to create labels or provide mailing lists for promotions, etc.
d) The system can also generate **statistics** on topics like the number of enquiries received in the TIC.
e) **A word-processing package.**
f) Access to **videotex services**, including Prestel, through telephone lines. Counter clerks can use these services to order brochures, check details of British Rail services and car hire companies, etc. and to access EXTRA, the National Express booking system.

Much of ETNA's information is drawn from the all-England **National Tourism Resource Database,** compiled by the ETB/RTBs through questionnaires sent to hoteliers, facility managers and event or activity organisers. TICs are also expected to compile their own database of local information and make it available to the RTBs. Most ETNA users are only supplied with access to data for their own RTB, although TICs in 'gateway' areas may be able to access data from several areas.

FIGURE 59 TECHNOLOGY IN PUBLIC SECTOR INFORMATION PROVISION

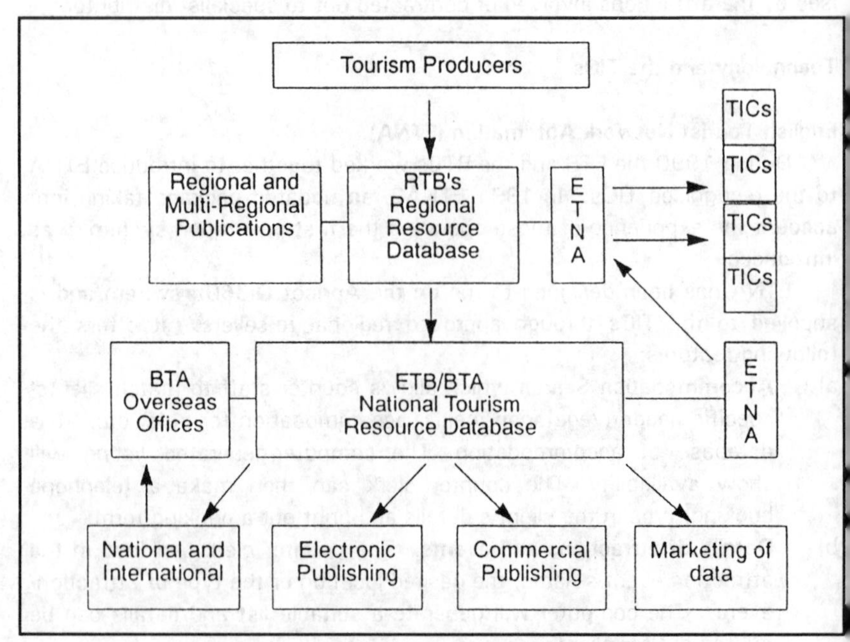

(Source: *ETB Technology Now*, Nov. 1990)

Tourism Resource Information Processing System (TRIPS)

During 1991 the ETB and BTA worked together, with Department of Employment backing, on the TRIPS project which would integrate the National Tourism Resource Database with the BTA's own databases.

Public Access Systems

Commercial organisations also provide TICs with public-access computerised information databases like the EMU system, often on the external wall of the building where it can be accessed when the TIC is closed. These databases usually contain information on local accommodation, restaurants, attractions, etc. In 1992 the ETB and RTBs were trying to devise a co-ordinated system.

Guide Services

Tourist Information Centres keep lists of registered **Blue** and **Green Badge** guides for their area. *Blue Badge Guides* are qualified to guide individuals or groups of all ages around a whole tourist board region. *Green Badge Guides* are only qualified to show people round a specific town, except in Wales where normal 'Blue Badge' guides wear green badges instead. Registration involves passing examinations (on foot, on site, on coaches, and in writing) at the end of a course recognised by the relevant tourist board. Separate endorsement is required to act as guides in the Palace of Westminster and in the City of London, and in York, Lincoln and Wells cathedrals.

The **Guild of Guide Lecturers**, the professional association for guides, was established in 1950 and currently has 1,200 members in England, Wales and Scotland. Between them they speak over thirty-five languages ranging from Afrikaans to Welsh. Individual guides are self-employed and may be specialists in specific areas e.g. guiding children or the disabled, or talking about local commerce, local ghosts and so on.

The Guild publishes an annual list of registered guides for England and Wales. Included in this are the names of registered driver-guides.

CHAPTER SIX
THE UK TOURIST ATTRACTIONS INDUSTRY

Despite the hot summers of 1989 and 1990 the British climate generally has none of the appeal that turned countries round the Mediterranean into holiday paradises. Nor does the UK boast the palm-fringed beaches and warm seas that guarantee the Caribbean its tourist trade. Instead it is dependent on a range of *tourist attractions* to bring in its visitors; the 1987 Overseas Visitor Survey showed that 69% of respondents had visited heritage or cultural attractions during their stay, while in 1989 an ETB survey revealed that 41% of foreign visitors to the UK said that desire to visit historic sites had influenced their choice of Britain as a holiday destination. In 1989 the BTA estimated that more than 50 million people visited a tourist attraction in Britain, with a total of 300 million visits in all. In the course of those visits over £700 million was spent at British tourist attractions, £359 million of it coming from admission charges.

The National Tourist Boards define a visitor attraction as 'a permanently established excursion destination, a primary purpose of which is to allow public access for entertainment, interest or education; rather than being principally a retail outlet or a venue for sporting, theatrical or film performances. It must be open to the public, without prior booking, for published periods each year, and should be capable of attracting tourists or day visitors as well as local residents'. In *Sightseeing in 1988* the English Tourist Board divides tourist attractions into the following broad categories: historic buildings, museums and galleries, wildlife attractions, gardens, country parks, workplaces, steam railways, leisure parks and 'other' attractions.

Categories of Tourist Attraction

Tourist attractions are often sub-divided according to distinguishing features. This can be done in several ways:

(i) The simplest distinction can be made between *indoor* and *outdoor* attractions. Indoor attractions include historic buildings (castles, palaces, stately homes), museums, art galleries and theatres. Outdoor attractions include zoos, safari parks, parks, gardens, archaeological sites and permanent funfairs like Blackpool Pleasure Beach.

(ii) A further distinction can be made between *man-made* and *natural* attractions. Man-made attractions include buildings like castles and museums but also archaeological sites and permanent funfairs.

Natural attractions include beaches, mountains, rivers and other beauty spots. However, few natural attractions remain completely natural. For example, Britain's National Parks are clearly 'natural' in origin, but the facilities like car parks that enable people to visit them are obviously man-made.

iii) A third division is between *site* and *event* attractions. Site attractions are all those, whether man-made or natural, indoor or outdoor, that are permanent and fixed to one spot. Event attractions are phenomena that may occur in the same place at a regular time each year but which are only ever temporary and could, at least in theory, move to a different site. Some event attractions draw just as many people as famous site attractions like Blenheim Palace. Examples are the Chelsea Flower Show and the Lord Mayor's Show.

(iv) The English, Scottish and Northern Ireland Tourist Boards also subdivide attractions into those with *admission* charges and those that are *free* (Table 41).

TABLE 41 BRITAIN'S TOP TWENTY TOURIST ATTRACTIONS, 1989

	Free Attractions		Attractions with Entry Charges	
1.	Blackpool Pleasure Beach	6,500,000 *	Madame Tussaud's	2,609,000
2.	Albert Dock, Liverpool	5,100,000	Alton Towers	2,382,000
3.	British Museum	4,600,000	Tower of London	2,214,000
4.	Strathclyde Country Park	3,900,000	Blackpool Tower	1,495,000
5.	National Gallery	3,368,000	Natural Hist. Museum	1,490,000
6.	Pleasure Beach, Great Yarmouth	2,475,000	Thorpe Park	1,300,000
7.	Bradgate Park, Leics	1,300,000	Chessington World of Adventures	1,2636,000
8.	Stapeley Water Gardens	1,270,000	London Zoo	1,221,000
9.	Tate Gallery, London	1,234,281	Kew Gardens	1,207,000
10.	Frontierland, Morecambe	1,200,000	Science Museum,	1,121,000

(* aproximate number)
(Source: British Tourist Authority)

(v) A final distinction is sometimes drawn between *nodal* and *linear* attractions. Nodal attractions are those which form the focus for a staying visit: the Pump Rooms in Bath, for example. In contrast linear attractions tend to be visited in a series of touring stops. The Cotswold villages, the 'wool' churches of East Anglia and the highlands of Scotland are good examples.

What Makes A Tourist Attraction Successful?

However enticing an attraction it will only achieve large visitor figures if it is also easily accessible and supplied with suitable amenities.

Accessibility

By 1987 the *Social Trends* survey showed that 64% of households in the UK had access to a car. Consequently access by road is generally more important for an attraction than access by public transport. Many overseas visitors also travel to attractions by coach which makes easy road access even more important. Ideally the attraction should be within an hour's drive of a motorway since journey time tends to dictate the visitor catchment area. Roads near the site must also be able to cope with the traffic generated and there must be adequate parking facilities (see below).

Nevertheless, the ideal site will also be within easy reach of the main rail and bus networks. For this reason MCA, which wants to open a Universal Film Studios Theme Park at Rainham Marshes in Essex, was interested in the proposed routes for the Channel Tunnel rail link, preferring one that would pass round the north-east of London giving easy access to its site.

However, Alton Towers shows that a sufficiently appealing and well marketed attraction may be able to succeed when it doesn't exactly match these requirements. An hour away from the motorway network and without a direct rail link, it still managed to draw 2,382,000 visitors in 1989, perhaps benefitting from a traditional British willingness to travel to leisure destinations.

In the UK few potential attractions are completely cut off. In fact in some areas like parts of the Lake District access is having to be restricted to prevent the sheer number of visitors ruining the peace and beauty they have come to experience (see Chapter Eleven).

Opening Hours

Attractions need to open at times that suit their visitors. Consequently most open at weekends, but may close on Monday or another week day when lower attendances could be expected. Traditionally most state-owned properties including the national museums and art galleries were closed on Sunday mornings. However, most newly-opened attractions treat Sunday as a normal working day.

At attractions where there is no attendant, including many English Heritage properties, visitors may be allowed into the site from dawn to dusk. Most cathedrals are also open from very early in the morning until dusk, as are those churches which are not kept locked. Where there is an attendant attractions are usually open from 0900 to 1700 or 1800, with shorter opening hours in winter. Only half the attractions in the UK open in January, but some, like the large theme parks, open all year round. The average attraction in England was open for 230 days in the year in 1988.

Amenities

Tourist attractions need many amenities in order to fulfil their potential. Some will be provided *on-site* (toilets, lifts, cafes, bookshops, restaurants, etc.) while others will be *off-site* (hotels, signposts, etc.).

The USA has led the way in showing what can be provided to make a visitor's stay enjoyable, and Disneyworld pioneered ideas like short-term camera loans. The UK is quickly catching on, and most new tourist developments now have lavatories with access for the disabled, mother and baby rooms, etc. The 1980s 'enterprise culture' also encouraged more imaginative attitudes. With most attractions under pressure to pay their way, profit-generating 'extras' like souvenir shops and restaurants began to be included automatically.

On-Site Amenities

Parking

Because so many visitors arrive at tourist attractions by car or coach providing adequate parking space is essential. Sometimes it is provided by the owner of the attraction, as at Beamish North of England Open-Air Museum, Thorpe Park and Alton Towers. Sometimes it is provided by the local authority to prevent traffic jams forming, as at Housesteads, the most popular Roman fort on Hadrian's Wall, which is owned by the National Trust but where Durham County Council provides the car park.

Parking space is usually provided free to encourage people to use it rather than clog up side streets. Where visitors are likely to park away from official sites, ditches can be dug, low fences erected or big stones placed along the roadside to prevent this without marring the landscape with garish yellow lines.

Parking sites can be very ugly. Ideally they should be screened from view by trees. Alternatively they can be positioned a little way away from the actual attraction in which case it is sensible to make the route from car park to site as interesting as possible. Since more space is usually needed in the high season it may be possible to lay gravel for parking over a relatively small area and then use adjacent fields in summer to reduce the impact on the scenery. At particularly busy sites carpark attendants are employed to direct drivers to empty spaces. Separate entrances and exits may also be needed for safety reasons.

Visitor Centres

Several factors have converged to ensure that most attractions now have Visitor Centres providing information to help tourists make more of their visits. Firstly, they are a good way to deal with the UK's unhelpful climate, ensuring there is somewhere for visitors to go when it rains. Secondly, Visitor Centres enable site owners to levy a charge where previously there was none on the basis that they are providing better facilities and therefore value for money. This is often the case with countryside attractions where charging is particularly difficult; a Visitor Centre not only provides an 'excuse' for a charge but also a way of collecting it. Thirdly, providing a Centre sometimes makes it possible to turn a non-site into something interesting: for example, at some battlefield sites.

Different Centres offer different types of information. For example the National Trust for Scotland Visitor Centre at Glenfinnan explains the historical events associated with the site, while the one at Torridon concentrates on local wildlife. Others are more like glorified shops-cum-restaurants with all the revenue-generating extras brought together under one roof. They may also house lavatories, information desks, audio-visual displays and rangers' offices.

Sometimes humble buildings can be reused to provide Visitor Centres. Others are purpose-built. Siting is particularly important. Where it is to act as a ticket office the Centre must be conspicuously positioned, preferably within easy reach of the car park. However, in the countryside or at an archaeological site it may be better to camouflage the building with trees to limit its impact on the scenery.

Deciding how large it should be may be difficult. Where coach parties are expected the Centre must be big enough to accommodate sudden rushes of people, although that may mean it will look bleakly empty at other times. Where few visitors are expected a mobile Centre may be appropriate; although this will not encourage visitors to linger and spend money it will be less obtrusive than a permanent building.

Signs and Labels

Within attractions signs perform several different functions. While some sites are laid out so that the best route round them is obvious (e.g. the Captain Cook Birthplace Museum in Middlesborough), in others there are several possible routes and directional signs are needed. At large sites like Alton Towers or Beamish the signs simply direct people towards the different attractions which can be viewed in any sequence. But in many museums and art galleries they indicate the best or most logical sequence for viewing. Zoos use temporary signs to draw attention to recent births. Museums and art galleries use them to direct people to new acquisitions.

Other signs give instructions. Sometimes these will be about safety: many English Heritage sites have signs warning visitors of the dangers of crumbling walls. Others indicate timed events that visitors may want to see: for example, feeding times at a zoo. They may also point out what is and isn't allowed: for example, bans on touching or photographing objects. However, since too may rules can seem off-putting attractions often try to phrase most of their notices in positive terms...telling visitors what they *can* do rather than what they can't.

Wherever overseas tourists are expected there should be signs in languages other than English. Symbols or pictograms are often as good as written signs and can be understood by overseas visitors as well. Signs, other than those required for safety reasons, should also be as unobtrusive as possible. Simple arrows are often adequate, and where it's not immediately clear what is needed temporary signs should be used at first.

Labelling is important at sites which aim to educate as well as entertain. Nowadays shorter messages which people are more likely to read and remember are preferred to offering lots of information. It helps if colour and graphics are used as well as words. Some attractions provide 'talking' labels as an addition to or even an alternative to written labels; London Zoo has provided 'talking' labels for many years.

Guides and Guidebooks

Relatively few British attractions employ official guides. Where there are guides, as at some National Trust properties, they are often volunteers. Apart from providing information for visitors guides also serve as custodians, dissuading their charges from touching exhibits, taking flash photographs and so on.

Many attractions provide guidebooks to help tourists make the most of their visit. These range from simple sheets of paper costing only pence in many churches to the definitive texts costing upwards of £20 published to accompany many temporary exhibitions in the national museums and art galleries. The vast majority of guidebooks fall somewhere in between. The largest attractions offer a range of guidebooks suitable for different ages and languages.

Shops

Commercial pressures have ensured that most tourist attractions now have retail outlets. Large sites like theme parks have many different shops, but even archaeological sites in the care of English Heritage sell key-rings and mugs in addition to the more traditional guidebooks and postcards.

What the shops sell is dictated by the number of likely visitors, the length of the average stay and the types of visitor expected. Ideally they will offer a range of goods from pens costing less than 50p and aimed at school groups to more expensive designer items for the AB socio-economic groups. To charge high prices they need to offer upmarket sales environments and employ professional sales-staff. They will also need to sell high quality goods, preferably with a clear link to the attraction. The Wedgwood Visitor Centre cashes in on the company's worldwide reputation for providing quality goods that have stood the test of time; its pottery is expensive but nevertheless sells well.

Ideally attractions have their own *merchandise*, bearing a distinctive advertising logo. However, where few visitors are expected this is unlikely to be economically feasible unless several attractions band together to design their goods, as the Treasure Houses of England group has done. The National Trust produces a wide range of goods which can be sold in all its on- and off-site shops. However, attractions need not actually own and run all the shops on their premises; open-air museums like Beamish and St. Fagan's lease space to outsiders to sell produce which is in keeping with the attraction.

Siting of the shop is important if it is to achieve maximum business. Many planners have followed the Disneyworld model where there are shops dotted all round the site and then a 'Main Street' of shops right by the entrance. The hope is that visitors who do not buy at the first opportunity will succumb when they see something for the second time on their way out. In long-established attractions the shops are being moved into more prominent positions.

Refreshments

Most attractions now offer refreshments, whether the simple cup of tea and home-made cake at National Trust properties or the choice of cooked meals at the major theme parks. The largest attractions offer a range of eating options to suit all tastes. Old stable blocks and outhouses attached to historic buildings often make ideal eating places and can be hired out for private parties, banquets, etc. Few tourist attractions have drinks licences, but theatres are always licensed.

Public Toilets

Health and Safety regulations require everywhere that serves food or drink to the public to provide separate male and female lavatories. These should be clean, supplied with toilet paper and hand-drying facilities and positioned so they can be found without difficulty, perhaps near the car park. Where lavatories are outdoors the entrances should be on the sheltered side and porches should be provided. Units should be light and well-ventilated, easy to clean and as vandal-proof as possible. There should be more female than male cubicles since women's lavatories are usually used by children as well and queues tend to be longer. Ideally cubicles should be fitted with waste disposal bins and with hooks for outdoor coats and bags. At many stately homes lavatories are housed in outbuildings like adapted stable blocks.

A separate 'mother and baby' room with nappy-changing table and waste disposal facilities should also be provided separately or inside the female lavatories.

Litter Bins

The more popular a tourist attraction is the more litter bins will be required. In the countryside these should be designed to be as unobtrusive as possible; wire mesh bins without linings and plastic dustbins look ugly, whereas bins surrounded by wooden palisades can look almost natural. Where mesh is used it should be narrow enough to prevent birds and animals pulling the contents out, and lids should be strong enough to resist wind and rain. Ideally bins should be sited where most people congregate: at car parks and picnic spots, next to benches and near the lavatories.

At sites where entertainment is the lynch-pin bins can be designed to amuse, making it more likely that children will use them. At some sites they are constructed in the shape of animals; at the American Adventure Theme Park at Ilkeston bins are shaped like giant grizzly bears.

However, even where plenty of bins are provided litter will still be dropped and the biggest sites like Alton Towers run regular litter patrol vans through the park to ensure it is kept clean. In general people seem to drop less litter at sites with high standards of cleanliness.

Seating

Seating is particularly appreciated at beauty spots where people want to stop and soak up a view. However, it should be designed to blend in with the surroundings, preferably by using natural materials, like local wood. Ideally it should be positioned along the edge of the view so that the seat itself doesn't obtrude into it. The same goes for associated litter bins, telescopes, etc.

Lifts, Escalators and Moving Pavements

In the UK many attractions provide lifts to help the disabled. However, escalators are rare, moving pavements even more uncommon although they have considerable potential for keeping people moving at very crowded sites. The 'time cars' first introduced at the Jorvik Viking Centre successfully perform this function in several British heritage centres.

Provision For the Disabled

In 1949 the Science Museum in London pioneered the ideas of 'hands-on' exhibitions and braille labelling for the blind. Sadly such innovative thinking has not always been followed up although an increasing number of attractions, particularly museums, now provide lifts, ramps and specially-fitted toilets for the disabled.

While some alterations to make places accessible to the disabled are costly, others are not. For example it is easy to reserve the parking bays closest to the entrance by marking them with wheelchair symbols. Wooden ramps can usually be introduced into churches and cathedrals to make them accessible to wheelchairs, although at some stately homes and castles the number and slope of the stairs mean that installing lifts would be essential. Major sites like theme parks can also lend/hire wheelchairs or buggies to visitors who need them.

At some Wildfowl and Wetlands Trust sites braille trails enable the visually handicapped to identify the birds they will hear. Several museums, including the Victoria and Albert, have organised special exhibitions where all the objects on show have been selected for their tactile qualities and can be handled. The Cathedrals Through Touch and Hearing project at Lichfield and Coventry Cathedrals has also provided wooden scale models of the buildings and their ground plans which the visually handicapped can feel. They also provide braille guidebooks, cassette commentaries and large print materials.

Some cathedrals have installed induction loops which amplify sound and make it easier for people with hearing aids to make out what is being said by a guide or to listen to the music.

It is especially important to the disabled that attractions provide accurate information so they can assess how easy a visit will be. For example the Beamish Museum's information for visitors points out that the site's steep paths may make visits tiring for those in wheelchairs. This is arguably more helpful than claiming the site is accessible to wheelchairs when only very small parts of it really are.

Off-Site Amenities

Signposts

Until the mid-1980s the signposting of tourist attractions was often arbitrary. Then in 1986 the Department of Transport (DOT) introduced white on brown pictographic signs representing the different categories of attraction to direct people to them. These are now commonplace throughout Britain (Fig. 60). As well as indicating specific castles, theme parks, etc. they also mark out scenic drives like the Northumbrian Coastal Route and linked attractions like farm trails. However, garden centres, pick-your-own farms, sports stadia, theatres, shops, leisure centres, golf courses and conference/exhibition centres are not normally eligible for these signs. Craft centres are only eligible where the public can watch demonstrations during at least 50% of the summer opening hours.

The signs serve three purposes. Their intended aim is to direct people to their planned destination by the best possible route. However, they are also distinctive enough to attract the attention of passers-by and can bring in visitors who might not have known there was anything worth seeing. Finally they can give a quick identity to a town; Cheltenham is signposted as 'Regency Cheltenham', offering an immediate reason why passers-by should deviate for a visit. Towns with by-passes are permitted to add brief descriptions to their signs to explain why people should divert; for example, Ancient Cathedral City. However, in 1991 the DOT reiterated that signs may not be used purely to advertise and announced that towns with just a few old buildings could no longer signpost themselves as 'historic'.

A property owner who wants a white on brown sign erected must first approach the local Regional Tourist Board which will check whether it meets the minimum criteria for a signpost before advising the highway authority responsible for erecting it of their decision in writing. Sometimes the RTB may agree that the attraction meets the criteria, but a sign may still be refused because it is in an environmentally sensitive area or because of concern about proliferating signs.

To meet the minimum criteria for white on brown signs an attraction must:

a) be permanent and a place to which people make excursions for sightseeing, entertainment or historical/cultural visits.
b) already be promoting itself to the tourist market through printed materials with clear travel descriptions, etc.
c) have car/coach parking, toilets, etc. appropriate to its size, location and character. Where appropriate, interpretation of the site must also be provided.
d) not have retailing or catering as its main purpose.
e) be open to people visiting on impulse within normal opening hours.
f) be open for at least 200 hours over at least 50 days in the year, and receive at least 5,000 annual visitors. For signposts on motorways 250,000 visitors a year must be expected except in Cumbria and Northumbria where the figure is 150,000.

FIGURE 60 TOURIST ROAD SIGNS

Fig 3: The New Tourist Road Signs

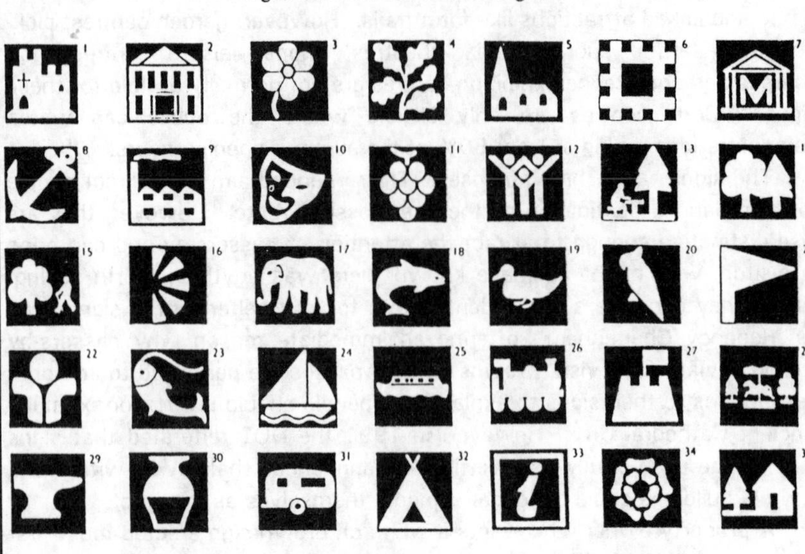

1. Castle
2. Historic House
3. Flower Garden
4. National Trust Property
5. Church of Intertest
6. English Heritage
7. Museum and/or Art Gallery
8. Historic Dockyard
9. Industrial Heritage
10. Theatre
11. Vineyard
12. Country Park
13. Picnic Area
14. Woodland Recreation Area
15. Woodland Walks
16. Viewpoint
17. Zoo
18. Aquarium
19. Nature Reserve
20. Bird Garden
21. Golf Course
22. Sports Centre
23. Fishing
24. Water Sports Activities
25. Canal Feature
26. Steam Railway
27. Beach
28. Pleasure Park
29. Forge or Craft Centre
30. Pottery
31. Caravan Park
32. Camping Site
33. Tourist Information
34. English Touris Board Rose (other attractions)
35. Youth Hostel

(Source: Department of Transport)

In addition to these general criteria there are others which relate specifically to motorways or to all-purpose trunk roads. If an attraction is not eligible for white on brown signs the local highway authority still has the discretion to provide local black and white direction signposts. The local authority will also need to decide how many signs are required for any one site, and try to co-ordinate signs for different sites to avoid unnecessary proliferation of boards

While permission for a permanent sign is being sought the AA or RAC can provide temporary signs although the local highway authority must still give permission first. The motoring organisations regularly provide sign-posting for event attractions which only need short-term directions.

FIGURE 61 NATIONAL CODE OF PRACTICE FOR VISITOR ATTRACTIONS

The owners and management have undertaken:

1. To describe accurately to all visitors and prospective visitors the amenities, facilities and services provided in any advertisement, brochure or any other printed means, and to indicate on all such promotional material any significant restrictions on entry.
2. To display clearly at public entry points any charges for entry (including service charges and taxes where applicable) and whether there are any additional charges for individual attractions.
3. To manage and, where appropriate, staff the attraction in such a way as to maintain a high standard of customer care, cleanliness, courtesy and maintenance to ensure visitor safety, comfort and service.
4. Where appropriate to the nature, scale and location of the attraction, to provide adequate toilet facilties, coach and car parking and catering arrangements.
5. To give due consideration to access and other provision for people with impaired mobility and for others with special needs, and to make suitable provision where practicable.
6. To deal promptly and courteously with all enquiries, requests, reservations, correspondence and complaints from visitors.
7. To provide public liability insurance or comparable arrangements and to comply with all applicable planning, safety and other statutory requirements.

(Source: ETB, 1991)

Hotels

Few UK tourist attractions can afford to offer their own accommodation for guests. However, attraction owners frequently work closely with local hoteliers, stocking hotel and bed and breakfast foyers with their marketing materials. In this way they get extra publicity, and accommodation owners are able to offer their clients a better all-round service.

Health and Safety at Tourist Attractions

Those in charge of tourist attractions owe a 'common duty of care' to visitors under the **1957 Owners' Liability Act** which means that they must operate the site in such a way as to keep risks to the public to a minimum. They can protect themselves by putting up warning notices where these are 'reasonable' and do not contravene the terms of the **1977 Unfair Contract Terms Act**. Conditions for use of the site can also be listed on the back of tickets, again provided they conform to the Unfair Contract Terms Act.

Site owners are also liable to be sued for negligence, even vicariously when an employee was responsible for the incident giving rise to the claim. This makes rigorous procedures for the selection and training of staff particularly important.

The **1974 Health and Safety at Work Act** also says that those who control premises and the activities that take place in them must ensure that they are safe for all who attend them. It states that 'it shall be the duty of every employer to conduct his undertaking in such a way as to ensure, so far as is reasonably practical, that persons not in his employment who may be affected thereby are not exposed to risks to their health and safety.' Everyone, from the company director down to the humblest worker, has an obligation to look after the health and safety of everyone else using the site. To comply with the Act attractions should have first aid facilities available and should take such precautions against fire as are advised by local fire officers.

The Health and Safety at Work Act is enforced by the Health and Safety Executive, and its inspectors may suggest improvements, post prohibition notices and prosecute where necessary. The Health and Safety Commission creates codes of practice for individual sections of the industry; these don't have the force of law but are admissible in court if an accident occurs and there have been omissions on the part of the attraction owner. Local authorities also appoint inspectors to visit sites and ensure that they are being operated safely. Special sections of the Health and Safety Act deal with the management of zoos, circuses and fairgrounds, and there is a code of conduct to regulate the running of theme parks.

Most UK tourist attractions have good health and safety records, although there have been some serious accidents at private zoos. In 1989 some visitors to Alton Towers were left suspended in a cable-car for an hour but were eventually brought down to the ground again safely. Fires at

Hampton Court Palace in 1988 and Uppark in 1989 damaged the properties involved, but visitors were not affected.

Originality

While all attractions need to be accessible with good amenities, other factors can also contribute to success. It helps, for example, to offer something unique. There is only one Big Ben and its silhouette is recognisable all round the world. There can hardly be a visitor to London who hasn't heard of it and who doesn't want to see it, without any hard selling or promotional activity on anyone's part.

Fashion

Fashion is also important. In the 1970s safari parks were extremely popular in Britain; new ones were constantly opening, and old ones made record profits. However, in the 1980s some, like Loch Lomond Bear Park, actually closed down while others, like Chessington Zoo (now the World of Adventures) and Flamingoland, have become leisure parks to suit changing tastes.

In the early 1990s the UK's most popular types of tourist attraction were:

* wax exhibitions (e.g. Madame Tussaud's)
* animated displays (e.g. Rock Circus)
* visitor centres linked to natural attractions (e.g. Loch Ness Exhibition)
* visitor centres linked to industry (e.g. Wedgewood Visitor Centre)
* zoos and wildlife parks (e.g. London Zoo)
* theme parks and large-scale leisure complexes (e.g. Thorpe Park, Granada Studios)
* audio-visual shows (e.g. London Experience, Light Fantastic)

The Attraction Providers

In the 1970s most UK tourist attractions were looked after by the State or conservation bodies like the National Trust and the Ministry of Public Buildings and Works (now English Heritage). Ecclesiastical buildings remained the responsibility of the Church and some stately homes were still in private hands. For many reasons there was only minimal private sector involvement:

* Creating a new attraction can involve enormous capital costs. The pioneering Jorvik Centre had cost £2.7 million when it opened in 1984, while Britannia Park, which opened and closed again in 1985,

cost £50 million to set up and lost £9 million in one season. Many attractions can recoup their running costs from admission fees, but few can recoup capital costs on this scale.

* A long tradition of free admission to parks, museums and cathedrals meant visitors were reluctant to pay to visit attractions.
* Because so few private sector companies had been involved with attractions, those that did want to get involved had little UK experience to draw on. Instead they had to use American businesses like Disneyworld as models.
* The UK climate also causes problems. When it's good people prefer to visit beaches and the countryside where most activities are traditionally free. Conversely outdoor attractions like leisure parks lose visitors in bad weather.
* Traditionally the UK tourist attraction business was also seen as seasonal, with four-tenths of visits concentrated into July and August.

As a result most companies involved in UK tourism preferred to concentrate on hotels, holiday centres, casinos, catering and producing merchandise for tourists.

The Entrepreneurs

In the 1980s changes took place, partly because the government wanted to reduce public subsidies wherever possible. The 'enterprise culture' encouraged entrepreneurs to create new tourist attractions. In 1973 John Broome married the daughter of the owner of Alton Towers, a crumbling Pugin building with a funfair in its grounds. Over the next ten years he proceeded to turn it into a successful theme park. He then bought Battersea Power Station in London for £1.5 million, intending to turn that too into a theme park.

Peter de Savary also moved into tourist attractions. In 1991 he owned Land's End and John O'Groats (both since sold) as well as Falmouth and Hayle Harbours. He has bought and sold land in Bristol and Weston-super-Mare with apparent plans to develop them for tourism.

In 1989 Lord Montagu of Beaulieu was awarded the ETB award for the most outstanding 'long-term contribution to UK tourism'. In 1951 he inherited Beaulieu Abbey and opened it to the public, creating the world's first Motorcycle Museum and the National Motor Museum in its grounds. Lord Montagu was soon involved in both public and private sector tourism. In 1980 he chaired a government working party on 'Britain's Historic Buildings: A Policy for their Future Use'. He has since been Chair of the

Museums Association, the Historic Houses Association and English Heritage. In 1989 he was also Chair of the Southern Tourist Board.

The Companies

In 1989 the largest public limited companies involved in the UK tourist attractions industry were Granada (Granada Studios Tour, and Camelot and American Adventure Theme Parks) and Pearson (Madame Tussaud). First Leisure Corporation also owned many seaside resort attractions, including Blackpool Tower and the Central and North Piers, Eastbourne Pier, Rhyl Amusement Park, etc.

By 1989 the ETB estimated that there were 1,783 historic buildings and monuments open to the public in England. Of these 43% were privately owned, 24% were owned by local authorities, 21% were owned by the government or its agencies and 12% belonged to the National Trust. In contrast, of 113 attractions (more than half of them historic buildings and monuments) surveyed by the NITB, 69% were owned by central or local government, 19% by private companies or individuals and 12% by the National Trust.

The Visitors

Attractions usually aim to pull in as many people as they can. However, sometimes too many people want to visit, posing a threat to the fabric of the attraction itself and to its visitors' safety. When too many people crowd in much of the pleasure of a visit may be lost anyway. So at places like Lindisfarne Castle in Northumberland, which regularly attracts capacity numbers of visitors, restrictions have been placed on the number who can be let in at any one time.

1. Overseas Visitors

In 1988 overseas visitors made up 29% of those visiting historic properties, 20% of visitors to museums and art galleries, and 6% of those visiting gardens and wildlife attractions in England. Perhaps not surprisingly only 9.5% of the 5.3 million visits to tourist attractions in Northern Ireland in 1989 were made by non-residents of the province.

To encourage overseas tourists to visit more attractions during their stay the BTA sells **British Heritage Pass Cards** which can be brought overseas or in the UK on production of a passport. These entitle their holders to free entry at properties owned by the National Trust/National Trust for Scotland, the Historic Houses Association, the Treasure Houses of England group, the Department of the Environment, English Heritage, the Scottish Development Department and Cadw.

2. The Domestic Market

Amongst domestic tourists it is, not surprisingly, mainly the young who visit theme parks, while older people make up the majority of visitors to stately homes and castles. Arts attractions tend to be most popular with the higher socio-economic groups, with ballet audiences predominantly made up of women.

Table 42 shows the total number of visitors to each category of tourist attraction in the UK in 1987:

TABLE 42 VISITORS TO TOURIST ATTRACTIONS (BY TYPE), 1987

Type of Attraction	Number	Percentage of Total	Millions	Percentage
Historic Buildings	1072	32	55	25
Museums and Galleries	1135	34	57	26
Wildlife	188	6	20	9
Gardens	225	7	10	4
Country Parks	83	2	19	9
Workplaces	119	4	5	2
Steam Railways	46	1	3	1
Leisure Parks	37	1	24	11
Other Attractions	422	13	30	13
Total	**3327**	**100**	**223**	**100**

(Source: ETB/BTA):

3. School Parties

Some attractions, like Ironbridge Gorge Museum, do especially well out of school visits. In 1988 Ironbridge hosted 80,000 students and teachers whose visits generated £8 million in admission fees, in spite of group and student discounts.

School parties are not usually big spenders and can be labour-intensive. They also create noise and can be disturbing for other visitors, a problem usually got round by publicising the times when children are most likely to be visiting. Attractions which are keen to encourage students often provide picnic areas where they can eat their packed lunches. Alton Towers also provides special picnic hampers and vouchers for set lunches. Many also publish special teaching packs and offer free reconnaissance visits for teachers.

In a 1988 ETB survey to discover how different attractions believed they had increased their visitor numbers, 28% cited better marketing, while 22% attributed the increase to new facilities. Others said they had been helped by special events/exhibitions, better signposting, longer opening hours and more group visits. Amongst reasons given for a drop in visitors were bad weather, lack of money for advertising, increased competition, staffing problems, roadworks, lack of coach parking facilities, shorter opening hours, strikes and structural alterations to the buildings.

The Employees

Tourist attractions are providing an increasing number and range of jobs. The number of staff at individual attractions varies depending on how many visitors are expected; on average where only 1,000 people a year are expected only one permanent job will be provided, whereas when 200,000 are expected there will be seventy-eight permanent jobs. The ETB estimates that the average wildlife attraction provides twenty-one jobs, the average historic building or museum ten jobs and the average garden seven jobs. Not all these posts are full time or permanent.

The number of jobs at individual attractions varies enormously. For example, in 1988 the Tate Gallery provided 330 full time, and six part time permanent jobs. Chessington World of Adventures had 150 full time permanent posts and 400 part time permanent ones. In contrast the popular Jorvik Viking Centre only needed twenty-seven full time permanent staff to handle more than 850,000 visitors.

In the 1980s attractions as diverse as nature reserves, open-air museums and archaeological sites were able to benefit from the government's job creation schemes, in particular from the MSC's Community Programme which enabled them to employ people for small sums of money on short-term contracts to carry out specific projects, frequently development schemes. When the Community Programme was replaced by Employment Training in 1988 attractions found it much harder to offer suitable placements to trainees.

Jobs available range from those for which high academic qualifications are essential (for example, as keepers in the national museums and art collections) to more menial jobs serving in on-site shops and restaurants where the fact that the work is at a tourist attraction is more or less incidental. Nevertheless, all jobs which involve contact with the public require sophisticated customer contact skills, and the most successful theme parks demand high standards of dress and behaviour from all their employees.

Modern attractions provide new types of employment both for designers and for costumed 'interpreters' who have replaced the traditional custodians in places like the Museum of the Moving Image and Beamish. Many attractions, particularly churches, cathedrals, National Trust properties and steam railways, also make use of volunteers.

Tourist Attractions and the Wider Environment

Tourist attractions lie at the very heart of the tourism industry, providing the reason for people to leave home in the first place. They also exist within the wider environment and have an influence beyond their own walls. In particular they play a vital role in local economies since most visitors spend considerably more than what is needed to see the site, in local shops, hotels, restaurants, bars and so on; the turnover of shops in tourist towns like York and Chester can be as much as 16% higher than in non-tourist destinations like Crawley and Blackburn.

Attractions are also affected by external factors. For example, in 1986 many site owners reported a drop in visitors as North Americans reacted to terrorism in Europe and the bombing of Libya by staying at home. In 1988 the relative strength of the pound against the dollar and the presidential elections had a similarly detrimental effect on visitor numbers. Conversely when the pound is weak the number of visitors from the States tends to increase. Many site owners, particularly in the south of England, hope the opening of the Channel Tunnel will bring more visitors from EC countries, reducing their dependence on the volatile American market. The relatively small number of non-Irish visitors to Northern Irish attractions is an obvious consequence of continuing political problems there. Nevertheless in 1989 the 68 attractions in the province with entrance fees still generated a joint revenue of £1,764,000.

The fate of the tourist attractions industry is also closely entwined with the work of British conservation and amenity groups. Although many theme parks, wax exhibitions and heritage attractions are entirely man-made and modern, other UK attractions are the result of the survival of historic buildings and artefacts, works of art and stretches of unspoilt countryside. For that reason conservationists work hand in hand with the tourism industry even if they can't be regarded as part of it. In some cases the continued existence of an attraction is dependent on the work of the National Trust/National Trust for Scotland or English Heritage and its regional equivalents. Amenity groups like the Georgian Group, Victorian Society and Civic Trust also ensure the survival of the sort of attractive environment in which tourism can flourish, while more of the countryside would rapidly vanish were it not for the efforts of groups like the National Trust, the Countryside Commission and the Wildfowl and Wetlands Trust. Without the National Heritage Memorial Fund and National Art Collections Fund more historical artefacts and works of art would be lost to British museums and art galleries and therefore to UK tourism.

'Heritage' Tourism

If 'enterprise' was the business buzz-word in the 1980s, 'heritage' was its touristic equivalent. It was already creeping in in the 1970s: in 1971 the Museums Action Group adopted the title 'National Heritage'; 'heritage coasts' were first designated in 1972; and Heritage in Danger was formed in 1974 and SAVE Britain's Heritage in 1975. European Architectural Heritage Year took place in 1975 when the first heritage centres were set up. Then the pace hotted up. In 1979 a National Heritage Act relaunched the National Land Fund as the National Heritage Memorial Fund. In 1983 another National Heritage Act renamed the Historic Buildings and Monuments Commission for England English Heritage. In 1986 the Wigan Pier Heritage Centre opened, followed by Edinburgh's Whisky Heritage Centre in 1989. Now every town and village, however small, seems to have its heritage trail. Even the shop run to support the Jorvik Viking Centre in York (set up, of course, by a company called Heritage Projects) calls itself simply 'Heritage'.

According to the Oxford English Dictionary 'heritage' simply means 'what is or may be inherited'. The current understanding of the word 'heritage' first developed in the United States. In the UK 'heritage' was originally thought of in terms of values, traditions and ideas, rather than in terms of paintings, historic houses, machinery, etc. However, in 1980 a report on the first year of the National Heritage Memorial Fund said that 'the national heritage of this country is remarkably broad and rich. It is simultaneously a representation of the development of aesthetic expression and a testimony to the role played by the nation in world history. The national heritage also includes the natural riches of Britain...the great scenic areas, the fauna and flora'. In 'The Heritage Industry' Robert Hewison claimed that heritage 'means everything, and it means nothing, and yet it has developed into a whole industry'. Clearly the UK tourist industry is heavily dependent on the country's history. At the same time 'history' and 'museum' are seen as dead words, lacking marketing pizzazz. 'Heritage' sounds much less dry, more homely, even more patriotic. At the same time nostalgia is big business in all areas of business, as if the faster modern life moves, the more people want to look back and cling to their roots. 'Heritage' seems to encapsulate their mood.

So the fashionable concept of 'heritage tourism' really means little more than tourism centred on what we have inherited, which can mean anything from historic buildings, to art works, to beautiful scenery.

CHAPTER SEVEN
HISTORICAL ATTRACTIONS

During the decade from 1981 to 1991 visiting historic attractions became increasingly popular with British tourists. In the same period there was a 25% increase in the number of historic buildings and a 34% increase in the number of museums open to the public.

Historical attractions can be divided into the following main categories: museums and heritage centres, archaeological sites, castles and stately homes, cathedrals and churches, and industrial heritage sites.

MUSEUMS AND HERITAGE CENTRES

The Oxford Dictionary defines a museum as 'a building used for storing and exhibition of objects illustrating antiquities, natural history, art, etc.' In 1990 the UK had almost 2,500 museums.

In Britain a distinction is usually drawn between *museums*, which house objects whether from history or the natural sciences, and *art galleries* which house paintings. However, the decorative arts are also housed in museums in England; hence the Victoria and Albert Museum contains one of the world's finest collections of art objects. Museums often contain books and printed documents but differ from *libraries* in that most of their printed materials are unique and form the raw materials for research. For example, the British Museum houses the earliest manuscript copy of the old English poem 'Beowulf' which forms the basis for the translation copies available in most libraries.

TABLE 43 GREAT BRITAIN'S MOST VISITED MUSEUMS, 1988

1.	British Museum	3,838,848
2.	Science Museum	2,436,048
3.	Natural History Museum	1,367,197
4.	Glasgow Museum and Art Gallery	926,804
5.	National Museum of Photography, Film and Television, Bradford	824,811
6.	National Maritime Museum	707,399
7.	Museum of Transport, Glasgow	671,821
8.	Castle Museum, York	640,705
9.	Birmingham City Museum	598,856
10.	Liverpool Museum	585,222

Not surprisingly, four of 1988's most visited museums were in London. Of these, only the British Museum still had free admission, although the

Science Museum had only just introduced charges and their effect had not yet been felt. All the other most visited museums were in cities with big resident markets. The Glasgow museums probably did particularly well in 1988 because of the Garden Festival, while the Bradford Museum of Photography had received extra publicity as a result of becoming 'Museum of the Year'.

The first museums were mainly seen as educational institutions. However, increasingly they are regarded as places of entertainment, competing for visitors with theme parks, stately homes and safari parks. As a result many have been forced to change, often drastically. In particular they have had to become more market-oriented and less inward-looking. Actors are used to bring the past to life, videos and slide shows have proliferated and cluttered showcases have been replaced with streamlined displays, owing much to modern shop-window display trends. Some of these changes are summarised in Fig. 62.

The Evolution of Museums

Most of the older British museums started life as private collections. It wasn't until 1656 that any English collection was formally named a museum. This eventually became the Ashmolean Museum, the first English example of a museum built to house a specific collection, which opened to the public in 1683.

Museums first became fashionable in the second half of the 19th century and almost one hundred museums opened in the UK in the 1870s and 1880s. These early museums saw themselves as primarily educational. As more opened and technology offered new opportunities design improved enormously; imaginative curators introduced dioramas to set objects in context. Gas and then electric lighting made longer opening hours possible.

Until the end of the Second World War museums tended to concentrate on the needs of a few well-informed visitors, often researchers. However, the War changed attitudes. Many exhibits were put into storage and the empty buildings allowed curators to improvise with temporary exhibitions. By the time they reopened many curators were ready to experiment with design and to work with specialist conservators. Elitist ideas gradually became unfashionable and the need to encourage a wider audience was recognised.

However, most museums were still state-run and based on the often idiosyncratic collections of private individuals. Some faced considerable problems with shortage of space and lack of funds to purchase items to make their displays more coherent. Since the 1960s there has been a second wave of museum openings with more emphasis placed on entertainment and profitability. There has also been a boom in specialist and often privately-funded exhibitions.

FIGURE 62 THE CHANGING FACE OF MODERN MUSEUMS

Area	Type of Museum	Change
Name	History	Heritage Centre
	Science	Exploratory
Setting	Folk	Outdoors
Entrance	All	Charges introduced even in public sector
Contents	History/Science/Specialist	More modern and ephemeral items displayed
Contents	All	Increasingly specialised
Presentation	History/Science/ Heritage Centre	Employment of costumed interpreters, craftworkers and actors
Display	All	Use of audio-visuals (videos, slides, sound recordings)
Display	Science/Natural History	'Hands-on' approach
Visitor comfort	All	More chairs, restaurants, shops
Publications	All	More attractively designed Easier to read Exhibition catalogues as definitive texts with prices to match
Marketing	All	Increasingly professional Distinctive logos Links with other local attractions e.g. in heritage trails and brochures More advertising

Ownership of the Museums

National Museums

In the UK many museums include the word 'national' in their title because they house the largest collection of something or even a unique collection: for example, the National Motor Museum at Beaulieu houses the UK's largest collection of motor vehicles. However, there are also true 'national museums', directly funded by the government through the Office of Arts and Libraries. These are:

British Museum (including Museum of Mankind)
Natural History Museum (including the Geological Museum)
Victoria and Albert Museum/National Museum of Art and Design (including the Theatre Museum; the Bethnal Green Museum of Childhood; the Wellington Museum; Ham House; and Osterley Park House)
Science Museum/National Museum of Science and Technology (including National Railway Museum, York; National Museum of Photography and Film, Bradford)
Imperial War Museum
National Army Museum, Chelsea
National Maritime Museum, Greenwich
Royal Air Force Museum, Hendon
Royal Armouries/National Museum of Arms and Armour
National Museums and Galleries on Merseyside
National Museums of Scotland
National Museum of Wales, Cardiff (including St. Fagan's)
Ulster Folk and Transport Museum
Ulster Museum

The **1983 National Heritage Act** established boards of trustees, funded by central government, for all national museums. Some of the British Museum's trustees are still appointed by academic bodies like the Royal Society, the British Academy and the Society of Antiquaries, but the government appoints all the Victoria and Albert Museum's trustees who are often selected as much for their business acumen as their academic credentials. Trustees are responsible for the finances of the national museums and develop policies for them. Increasingly they also undertake fund-raising activities to supplement government grants.

In 1988 the national museums took over the freeholds of their buildings from the government's Property Services Agency which had previously looked after them.

Local Authority Museums

The **1845 Museums Act** permitted local authorities in areas with populations of more than 10,000 to spend money from the rates on creating and administering museums. The **1850 Libraries Act** also allowed them to collect artistic and scientific objects and books. The **1964 Libraries and Museums Act** confirmed these rights, although it did not oblige local authorities to set up museums. Some local authorities run their museums as public services and don't charge for admittance. However, in the 1990s, with many authorities looking for ways to economise, museums were a likely target.

Municipal museums usually have governing bodies which appoint a Director to look after the day to day running of the museum and to liaise between staff and the governors.

Independent Museums

Independent museums were where the most rapid expansion took place in the late 20th century, with new ones opening in Great Britain almost once a fortnight; by 1990 65% of all Scottish museums were independent. Some independent museums operate as commercial concerns, while others, like Beamish, are non-profit-making charities. Some, like the Ironbridge Gorge Museum complex, have huge administrations; others, like Sally Lunn's House in Bath, have a tiny staff and very little administration at all. Independent museums are sometimes able to obtain financial assistance from local authorities and other sources; for example in 1990 the Wolfson Foundation and the government both contributed to a new £12 million Museums and Galleries Improvement Fund which could make grants to independent museums as well as those in the public sector.

University Museums

The British universities also finance and administer some museums and art galleries, including:

Ashmolean Museum, Oxford
Fitzwilliam Museum, Cambridge
Barber Institute of Fine Arts, Birmingham
Courtauld Institute, London
Sainsbury Centre for the Visual Arts, University of East Anglia

Trusts

Many British museums are run as charitable trusts, enjoying significant tax benefits. Ownership of the museum is then vested in a body of trustees. To qualify as trusts they must be able to prove that their existence involves some substantial social advantage, usually through their educational role. So the Leeds Castle Trust gives one of its objectives as to 'preserve the beauty of the castle and its grounds for the enjoyment of the public in perpetuity and without commercialisation'. In 1990 the Horniman and Geffrye Museums, which had been in the care of the Inner London Education Authority before its abolition, became independent charitable trusts.

Funding the Museums

Museum costs can be divided into three separate areas:

a) the **capital costs** of starting up the museum.
b) day to day **running costs** for staff, electricity, gas, telephones, stationery, fuel, publishing, etc.
c) the **one-off costs** of new purchases.

The national museums used to be funded entirely from central government who provided one grant for running costs and another for purchases. The British Museum was strapped for cash from the day it opened, and for many museums the problems have got worse as their buildings have aged and became more expensive to run. The rising price of art and antiquities has also made it increasingly difficult for them to make new purchases.

Between 1984 and 1991 the national museums found their purchase grants frozen just as prices were rising most steeply. Their grants for staff costs in 1988 only rose by 2.5% although salaries (which were linked to civil service pay scales) rose by between 8 and 10%. In 1988 the Commons Public Accounts Committee warned that the museums and art galleries were becoming unable to care for their exhibits, pointing to a backlog of conservation work at the Victoria and Albert Museum and in the British Library. By 1989 the Victoria and Albert Museum's staff costs accounted for 98% of its grant for running costs. In the light of these problems the government agreed to increase museums and art galleries' grants for running costs by 8.5% in 1991. The grant to the National Heritage Memorial Fund was also raised from £1.5 million to £5.5 million to make it easier for it to help museums with purchases.

Local authority museums are often funded from the community charge or poll tax (which replaced the rates in 1988 in Scotland and 1989 in England and Wales). In 1991 many of them faced cuts in their budgets as authorities struggled to cope with charge-capping; Manchester City Art Gallery alone lost £154,000 from a £1 million budget in 1989.

Even university museums were under financial pressure as cutbacks in overall university funding affected their ability to pay for them. Some independent museums were also concerned about the impact of the new uniform business rate on their profitability.

Faced with such problems museums can economise in several ways:

a) They can close for one day a week or close early.
b) They can close entire galleries, or close them on a rotational basis to save staff costs.
c) They can make staff redundant.
d) They can introduce or raise admission charges.
e) They can sell items from their collections.

Alternatively they can try and raise more money by selling publications and merchandise, by charging for temporary exhibitions or by renting out their premises for private functions. Almost all museums now have shops and restaurants; indeed almost the entire ground floor of the British Museum is now given over to fund-raising activities.

The Entrance Fee Debate

It used to be generally accepted that independent museums would charge for admission, but that the national museums and art galleries would not. Then in 1972 the government passed the Museums and Galleries Admissions Charges Act which permitted national museums to introduce charges. In January 1974 the Natural History Museum started charging 10p a head in July and August. This scheme had to be dropped after only three weeks when attendances slumped; the experiment had cost about £34,000. In 1974 the new Labour government withdrew the prospect of charges altogether.

When the Conservatives returned to power in 1979 the question of charges was inevitably raised again because of their policy of reducing public expenditure. In 1984 the National Maritime Museum in Greenwich introduced charges to enable it to open on Mondays and restore services cut as its income had fallen. The short-term result was a 36.6% fall in attendances. However, in January 1985 a MORI poll for the Royal Armories suggested that 61% of the public were prepared to pay to visit museums; only 27% totally opposed the idea.

In November 1985 the Victoria and Albert Museum introduced a controversial scheme for 'voluntary' entrance charges. Since 1976 the Museum had been closing on Fridays to economise and had also had to abandon its Circulating Exhibitions Department which loaned objects to provincial museums. Its parlous state was highlighted in 1986 when poor maintenance resulted in water flooding a basement and damaging items being stored for the planned Theatre Museum. In the scheme's first year attendances fell by 40% and only 55% of visitors actually paid; £400,000 was raised through fees, but the cost of collection (installing and manning turnstiles, printing tickets, etc.) might have been as high as £100,000. In the ten years to 1988 the number of visitors to the Victoria and Albert fell by 500,000.

Both the National Maritime Museum and the Victoria and Albert Museum aim for an adult market. However, in 1987 the Natural History Museum, a long-time family favourite, introduced compulsory charges, anticipating a £2.5.million deficit by 1990. Charges were to safeguard jobs and prevent the closure of exhibitions. Once again they led to an immediate 40% fall in admissions. In October 1988 the same thing happened when the Science Museum introduced charges (Fig. 63).

A short-term decline in visitor numbers is sometimes reversible. By 1990 visitor numbers at the National Maritime Museum had recovered, perhaps because of publicity generated by the 1988 Armada Exhibition and because it is so far from the centre of London that visitors will have made a special trip to visit and will not baulk at paying when they arrive. However, admissions to the Victoria and Albert remain 30% down.

FIGURE 63 IMPACT OF ADMISSION CHARGES ON ATTENDANCES AT NATIONAL MUSEUMS AND GALLERIES

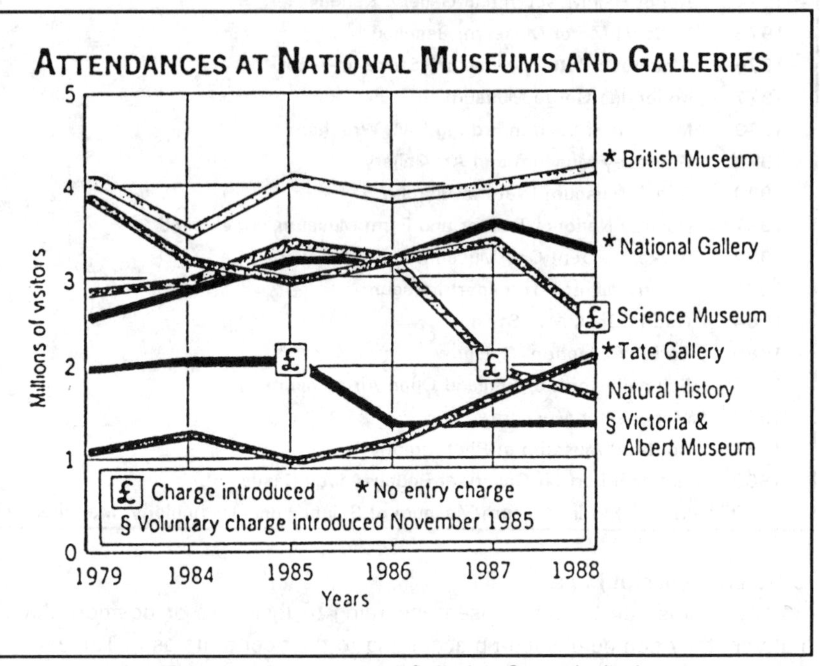

(Source: Museums and Galleries Commission)

Marketing and Publicising the Museums

Increasingly museums need to employ modern marketing methods to attract larger audiences. Despite their relatively small budgets many independent museums have led the way because their dependence on admission fee revenue makes it essential for them to attract as many visitors as possible.

Some museums have worked with the tourist boards to take advantage of their advertising budgets. Others have introduced techniques like devising immediately recognisable logos which can be stamped on merchandise to keep the museum in the public eye. So the Victoria and Albert

Museum has 'V & A' stamped on all its merchandise and publications, while the Natural History Museum has a design like a schematic twig.

One way a museum can attract media attention is by winning an award. Perhaps the most prestigious is the Museum of the Year Award given by National Heritage (Table 44).

TABLE 44 WINNERS OF THE NATIONAL HERITAGE MUSEUM OF THE YEAR AWARD

Year	Winner
1974	Abbot Hall Museum and Gallery, Kendal
1975	National Motor Museum, Beaulieu
1976	Gladstone Pottery Museum, Stoke-on-Trent
1977	Ironbridge Gorge Museum
1978	Museum of London/Erdrigg Hall, Wrexham
1979	Guernsey Museum and Art Gallery
1980	British Museum (Natural History)
1981	Hunday National Tractor and Farm Museum, Stocksfield
1982	Stoke-on-Trent City Museum and Art Gallery
1983	Ulster Folk and Transport Museum
1984	Quarry Bank Mill, Styal
1985	Burrell Collection, Glasgow
1986	Beamish North of England Open-Air Museum
1987	Manchester Museum
1988	Bradford Museum of Photography
1989	National Portrait Gallery at Bodelwyddan Castle
1990	Imperial War Museum/Museum of Science and Technology, Manchester

Different Types of Museum

Museums can be categorised according to their size or position. Alternatively they can be divided up according to their contents as in Table 45.

TABLE 45 TYPES OF MUSEUM

Type	Examples
Comprehensive	British Museum; Bristol City Museum and Art Gallery
Local History	Sheffield City Museum; Colchester City Museum; Museum of London
Science/Technology	Science Museum, London; Bristol Exploratory
Natural History	Natural History Museum, London; Colchester
Ethnography	Museum of Mankind, London; Pitt-Rivers Museum, Oxford; Horniman Museum, London

Open-Air	Beamish; St. Fagan's; Blist's Hill; Weald and Downland
Film/Photography	Bradford Museum of Photography, Film and Television; Museum of the Moving Image (MOMI), London; Lacock Abbey
Fine Arts	Victoria and Albert Museum, London; Barber Institute, Birmingham
Industrial Heritage	Ironbridge Gorge Museum; Bristol Industrial Museum; Camden Works, Bath
Historical/Literary Associations	Haworth Parsonage; Dove Cottage; Captain Cook Birthplace Museum
Archaeology	Corinium Museum, Cirencester
Children and Toys	Bethnal Green Museum of Childhood, London
Military	Imperial War Museum, London; Yeovilton Fleet Air Arm Museum; Stoke-on-Trent Spitfire Museum
Maritime	National Maritime Museum, London; Portsmouth Maritime Museum; Bristol Maritime Heritage Centre; Merseyside Maritime Museum
Transport	London Transport Museum; National Railway Museum, York; Great Western Railway Mueum, Swindon; National Motor Museum, Beaulieu
Specialist	Museum of Advertising and Packaging, Gloucester; Harvey's Wine Museum, Bristol; Clark's Shoe Museum, Street
Private Collections	Wallace Collection, London; Sir John Soane Museum, London

Temporary Exhibitions

There have been temporary exhibitions in England since 1851 when the Great Exhibition at Crystal Palace in London was a resounding success, attracting 6 million visitors to inspect more than 100,000 exhibits of industrial products. Increasingly museums have seen temporary exhibitions as a way of showing excess collections, focusing on specific topics or themes and raising extra money from admission fees and sales of associated merchandise. However, they present several problems which include:

a) the high cost of staging short shows in terms of staff time and effort, employing outside contractors to set them up, preparing catalogues, etc.

b) the prohibitive cost of insuring masterpieces on loan. The Museums and Galleries Commission administers a Government Indemnity Scheme to help smaller museums cope with this cost.

c) the risk of theft.

d) the reluctance of some museums to loan desirable objects.
e) the fact that the public can be very disappointed if they've travelled a long way to see something which is on temporary loan elsewhere.

Some museums like the British Museum now have a gallery specifically devoted to temporary exhibitions. Such galleries can be designed to be flexible, and other galleries need no longer be disrupted. Outside sponsorship is frequently sought to cover the extra costs. This can come from foreign governments, the Arts Council or commercial com-panies who hope to benefit from having their name on publicity materials.

Heritage Centres

In some ways the word 'museum' is a victim of its long history since it all too easily brings to mind images of dusty collections unimaginatively displayed and clearly assembled many years ago. Consequently the term 'heritage centre' is now preferred by some attractions which would once have been called museums.

The Civic Trust defines heritage centres as 'permanent exhibitions with the evolution of the whole community as their theme'. An increasing number have opened in the last twenty years. Some concentrate on the architectural history of a particular area, while others focus on a particular date, event or tradition; there is a Shipwreck Heritage Centre in Hastings, and a National Fishing Heritage Centre in Grimsby.

The first heritage centre opened in June 1975. Typically, it was housed in St. Michael's, a redundant Chester church. It was funded by Chester City Council and the Department of the Environment and presented the city's history with the aid of expensive audio-visuals.

Considerable capital investment is needed to create a heritage centre from scratch. To be successful it will need a central position which is likely to be expensive to rent or buy. While some of the older heritage centres display conventional museum exhibits, the newer ones tend to be completely artificial, with fibreglass models rather than original artefacts which minimises the risk of theft. Some differ very little from traditional museums, but others make use of the sort of imaginative techniques pioneered at the Jorvik Viking Centre. So visitors to The Tales of Robin Hood in Nottingham travel round in metal cars based on those used in an abbatoir.

Wigan Pier Heritage Centre is an example of what can be achieved in the most unpromising circumstances.

ARCHAEOLOGICAL SITES AND ANCIENT MONUMENTS

The word 'archaeology' means the study of human antiquities, regardless of their age. Great Britain is rich in relics of the past, ranging from the prehistoric causewayed camp at Windmill Hill in Wiltshire which dates from around 4000 BC to more recent survivals like the 19th century Sibsey Trader Windmill in Lincolnshire. Windmill Hill is an example of a traditional archaeological site, Sibsey Windmill of an industrial archaeological site.

That the expressions 'archaeological site' and 'ancient monument' are effectively interchangeable was illustrated by the **1979 Ancient Monuments and Archaeological Areas Act** which defined the word 'monument' so that it encompassed most archaeological sites as well. According to the Act a monument is:

a) any building, structure or work whether above or below the surface of the land and any cave or excavation, or

b) any site comprising the remains of any such building, structure or work or any cave or excavation.

In 1977 the English Tourist Board surveyed 11,789 'ancient monuments' and divided them into the following categories which indicate the scope of the term and the clear overlap with archaeological sites:

TABLE 46 TYPE OF ANCIENT MONUMENT

Type of Ancient Monument	% of surviving total number of monuments
Burial mounds and megalithic monuments	29
Camps/settlement sites	15
Linear earthworks	3
Roman remains	6
Crosses/inscribed stones	5
Ecclesiastical ruins	6
Castles/fortifications	10
Deserted villages/moated sites	7
Ancient bridges	4
Industrial monuments	2
Other secular sites/buildings	13

Ancient monuments can be divided into those that are *upstanding,* where little or no excavation is needed before they can be shown to the public, and those that are *below ground* where excavation is essential. The majority of pre-Saxon remains lie below modern ground levels and need to be excavated. Upstanding monuments are usually of most interest to tourists. However, some below-ground ruins are also of interest because of their great age. For example, the Roman palace at Fishbourne was very much a below-ground site which required extensive excavation to reveal its ground plan and mosaics. Nevertheless it attracted 250,000 visitors within six months of opening to the public in the 1960s. The Jorvik Viking Centre would be no more than a particularly unusual below-ground site were it not for the imaginative presentation that has turned it into an award-winning attraction.

In England most monuments are looked after by English Heritage (the Historic Buildings and Monuments Commission for England). In Wales they are cared for by Cadw (the Welsh Historic Monuments Commission), in Scotland by Historic Scotland and in Northern Ireland by the Department of the Environment. A few monuments remain in private hands.

TABLE 47 THE MOST VISITED ARCHAEOLOGICAL SITES IN GREAT BRITAIN, 1988

(excluding castles, ecclesiastical ruins and industrial archaeological sites and those for which there was no admission charge)

	Site	Visitors
1.	Roman Baths, Bath	954,142
2.	Jorvik Viking Centre	865,909
3.	Stonehenge	640,416
4.	Housesteads Roman Fort (Hadrian's Wall)	121,743
5.	Fishbourne Roman Palace	92,791
6.	Flag Fen Bronze Age Excavations, Peterborough	85,006
7.	Vindolanda Roman Fort (Hadrian's Wall)	77,000
8.	Chesters Roman Fort (Hadrian's Wall)	70,214
9.	Chedworth Roman Villa	59,918
10.	Old Sarum earthworks	48,977

Protection of Monuments in Great Britain

Archaeological sites and ancient monuments, once uncovered, are often fragile and depend for their survival on adequate protection. The laws relating to the protection of ancient monuments were consolidated into the **Ancient Monuments and Archaeological Areas Act** in 1979. In 1987 protection was extended to cover 12,800 sites in the UK, still only a tiny percentage of approximately 635,000 archaeological sites identified in the country.

In June 1989 English Heritage started a Monuments Protection Programme which will survey each county in detail with a view to offering protection to a further 50,000 sites. In 1990 Scotland had 4,700 protected monuments, Wales had 2,750 and Northern Ireland 1,100. There were no plans to resurvey these areas to expand the number.

Under current legislation ancient monuments can be protected in several ways:

* Those that are of national importance are taken into **guardianship** by English Heritage or its equivalents. Most such monuments are upstanding remains like Stonehenge, Tintern Abbey and Dover Castle.

* Other monuments deemed worthy of protection because of their fine state of preservation or academic significance can be **scheduled**. This prohibits building, farming or forestry work that is likely to damage them being carried out without notice being given to the Department of the Environment.

* Finally, monuments that are in imminent danger of destruction can be covered by an **interim preservation order** which should delay the work being carried out.

Presenting Ancient Monuments as Tourist Attractions

When the first excavations took place in the UK the sites were usually left much as they had been found and no attempt was made to interest the public in them. Not surprisingly archaeological sites were often thought of as dull. However, in the latter part of the 20th century much more effort is being put into making the sites both accessible and interesting to visitors.

Controversy has raged over whether some archaeological sites should be reconstructed so that they are easier for the public to understand. In 1970 the Vindolanda Trust started rebuilding a stretch of the turf wall, rampart walk and timber palisade of Hadrian's Wall. In 1974 the project was extended to include the reconstruction of a stone turret and timber milecastle gate. Opponents of ideas like this claim that it is unhistorical since some of the work must be based on speculation. Supporters say it performs a useful educational function and may divert people from more fragile original structures. Perhaps the crucial factor is that no deception should be involved. At Vindolanda it is perfectly clear which parts of what is on show are reconstructions. Elsewhere different building materials can be used to indicate sections of a monument that have been reconstructed.

Sometimes archaeological digs serve as temporary attractions before being filled in again and visitors can be allowed to walk around the trenches, perhaps on temporary wooden walkways to protect them from the mud. Archaeologists may act as guides, perhaps on a rota basis. In cities where access may not be practical viewing platforms can be provided to let people watch what is going on from a safe distance. It helps to provide maps and diagrams to explain the various structures that are being uncovered, and an information board to set the site in context. Ideally viewing platforms should be sited against the sun and sheltered from the wind.

The presentation of archaeological sites should aim to safeguard the remains, while also presenting them safely and intelligibly to the public. Even where the site is unsupervised information boards can help visitors understand the ruins. Main structures should be discreetly labelled. Colour-coded plans can be used to indicate the dates of different parts of the site.

The public are admitted to all monuments in guardianship unless there are safety problems. However, there is no automatic right of public access to scheduled monuments unless the local authority or Secretary of State for the Environment has reached agreement with the local landowner.

CASTLES AND STATELY HOMES

Castles and stately homes are often thought of together, but the word 'castle' actually means a large, fortified building or set of buildings, while 'stately home' means a large, magnificent house. In fact the two types of building belong, with some exceptions, to two different periods of history. Castles belong to the Middle Ages, to a time when life was uncertain and outbreaks of fighting could be expected at any time. Consequently they are found in greatest concentrations in towns which needed defending, along coasts and in areas which were regarded as potentially rebellious like the Scottish and Welsh borders. In contrast stately homes belong to the more settled, post-medieval world. Those built in the 16th century sometimes look as if their owners weren't quite sure about this, but by the 18th century the descendants of the medieval knights were building what were clearly houses for all their grand scale. What's more they were usually building them well away from towns.

Castles

Many of Britain's castles are preserved as ancient monuments and some, like Pleshey Castle in Essex, are little more than earthworks. Others, like Corfe Castle in Dorset, are pictureque ruins, sometimes deliberately destroyed by the victorious Parliamentary forces at the end of the Civil War in 1649 because their owners had supported King Charles. A few, like Arundel, Windsor and Warwick Castles, are still intact. Sometimes this was the lucky result of historic accident and sometimes because they were restored in the 19th century when medieval architecture was once again fashionable. Castles which have been continuously occupied up to the present are obviously more likely to be in one piece than those whose owners long ago abandoned them.

Ownership of British Castles

Most English castles are now looked after by English Heritage and make up a large proportion of the properties in its care. Most Scottish castles are owned by the Historic Buildings and Monuments Division of the Scottish Development Department. By far the most visited British castle is the Tower of London which is now in the care of the Royal Historic Palaces Agency. Its popularity stems in part from its important and colourful role in history but also from its situation beside the Thames in London.

Other castles are cared for by local authorities. Of these the most visited in 1988 was Norwich Castle which, like the castles in Colchester and Newcastle, now houses a museum. Durham Castle is owned by Durham University. The National Trust also looks after a few castles; in 1988 the most visited were Bodiam and Corfe Castle, both picturesque ruins.

Some castles are still privately owned. These include Berkeley Castle which has been lived in by the same family since the reign of Henry II, and Alnwick and Bamburgh Castles in Northumberland. In 1988 the most visited privately owned castles were Windsor and Warwick, but Hever, Arundel, Skipton, Belvoir and Mountfitchet also attracted more than 100,000 tourists each. Leeds Castle is now a charitable trust for medical research and an important international conference centre.

TABLE 48 THE MOST VISITED CASTLES IN GREAT BRITAIN IN 1988

1.	Tower of London	2,181,707
2.	Edinburgh Castle	957,584
3.	Windsor	699,836
4.	Warwick	645,000
5.	Leeds	488,501
6,.	Caernarvon	297,653
7.	Norwich	277,965
8.	Culzean	276,511
9.	Hever	256,950
10.	Stirling	218,883

Castles probably play a more important role in tourism in Wales than anywhere else; of the twenty most visited historic properties in Wales in 1988, sixteen were castles. They are also very important to Scottish tourism where sixty-three castles attracted 3,226,384 visitors in 1989. Carrickfergus Castle was Northern Ireland's most visited historic property in both 1988 and 1989.

The Appeal of Castles

Some of the most popular castles owe their popularity to aesthetics; Leeds and Bodiam in particular are everybody's idea of fairy-tale moated castles. Caerphilly, Conway and Carnarvon Castles in Wales, and Blair Castle and Eilean Donnan in Scotland are also strikingly beautiful.

Other castles, like Windsor, Hever (childhood home of Anne Boleyn) and the Tower of London, benefit from royal connections. The castles at Norwich and Lincoln probably gain from being close to particularly popular cathedrals, while Clifford's Tower, not in itself the most impressive of castles, has drawn more visitors since it took part in a joint marketing campaign with other York attractions. Tintagel owes much of its popularity (134,386 visitors in 1988) to romantic associations with the half-mythical/half-historical King Arthur. Apart from its links with Charles I, Carisbrooke on the Isle of Wight probably benefits from being on an island with large numbers of vistors where sightseeing possibilities are relatively limited.

Presentation of Castles as Tourist Attractions

Most of the castles in English Heritage's care are ruins and are shown to the public as such. However, wooden drawbridges may be replaced to provide access in its original form, and moats may be cleared of rubbish and refilled. New roofs may also be added to protect structures like the fireplaces at Tattershall and Caernarvon. Castles usually had thicker walls than abbeys and therefore often survived even deliberate destructive attempts fairly well; few have had to be as extensively excavated as ecclesiatical ruins. When restoration work has been carried out different materials are sometimes used to avoid confusion over what is original and what replacement. Further alterations may be needed to ensure visitors' safety and to provide access to towers or walls.

Increasingly English Heritage/Cadw castles offer programmes of special events including music through the ages, summer concerts, falconry displays, flower festivals, craft fairs, re-enactments of historical events and dramas.

Privately owned castles which are still lived in tend to be shown in much the same way as stately homes, with visitors invited to ponder a privileged way of life, now almost vanished. However, sometimes much has been done to make them more interesting. At Bamburgh in Northumberland there are waxwork prisoners in the 'dungeon', lavatories in the stables and a large restaurant and shop. The castle's floodlighting has also won it awards.

Stately Homes

According to the Historic Houses Association Britain still had about 3,500 country houses which retained their land and contents in 1990. Of these perhaps 2,000 were still owned by families with long-standing connections with the house.

Although there were always small numbers of visitors to stately homes, it was only after the First World War that the private motor car brought most of them within reach of ordinary people, leading to a boom in country house visiting.

TABLE 49 ENGLAND'S MOST VISITED STATELY HOMES, 1988

1.	Beaulieu Abbey	537,750
2.	Blenheim Palace	335,055
3.	Osborne House	247,873
4.	Polesden Lacey	185,627
5.	Harewood House	177,493
6.	Bowood House	165,963
7.	Hatfield House	141,000
8.	Lanhydrock House	127,246
9.	Haseley Manor	*125,000
10.	Knebworth House	*125,000

(* approximate number)

(precise figures not available for Castle Howard, Chatsworth or Woburn Abbey but presumed to be more than 200,000 each.)

Blenheim Palace, Polesden Lacey, Hatfield House, Haseley Manor and Knebworth House are all within easy reach of London, while Beaulieu Abbey, Osborne House and Lanhydrock House are all in popular holiday areas. Polesden Lacey, Bowood House and Lanhydrock House all belong to the National Trust and may therefore benefit from its membership scheme which encourages people to visit more than one attraction. Beaulieu, Hatfield and Knebworth are all stately homes which are almost as well-known for their 'other' attractions which guarantee them higher visitor figures than they might get if they were simply impressive houses.

Beaulieu, Blenheim and Harewood House are also members of the Treasure Houses of England marketing consortium whose other members are Castle Howard, Broadlands, Warwick Castle, Woburn Abbey and Chatsworth House. The eight properties produce a joint leaflet with details of each property and a map showing its position vis-a-vis the other ones. A visitor to any one of the houses can therefore pick up literature advertising the other seven and containing vouchers offering discounts for taking in the others as well.

Financial Problems For Stately Home Owners in the 20th Century

In 1894 the British government introduced death duties, signalling the start of financial difficulties that have plagued country house owners throughout the 20th century and have resulted in many houses becoming tourist attractions first and foremost. By 1919 the amount owed could amount to 40% of the value of an estate worth £2 million or more. Inevitably the only way to release the money to pay these debts was to sell parts of the estate. Under such pressure many owners allowed their houses to be demolished; between 1918 and 1945 458 country houses were demolished, amongst them Drayton Manor and Agecroft Hall.

In the 1920s and 1930s the National Trust lobbied Parliament for tax concessions for owners who would agree to public access to their properties. Eventually this pressure led to the **1937 National Trust Act** which permitted the Trust to accept a country house with its contents and enough land to maintain it so that it could be opened to the public even if the original owner continued to live in it as a tenant. By the early 1950s the National Trust was caring for 98 country houses, which attracted 700,000 visitors between them.

It wasn't until 1946 that the 'listing' of historic buildings offered routine protection to the most important stately homes. In 1948 a survey of all the country houses still standing led to the 1950 report, *Houses of Outstanding Historic or Architectural Interest*. This in turn resulted in a clause in the 1953 Historic Buildings and Ancient Monuments Act which allowed Historic Buildings Councils to make grants for repairs and maintenance of houses which were opened to the public.

The huge cost of maintaining these houses meant that yet another 712 were demolished between 1945 and 1974, 431 of them in England, 175 in Scotland and 23 in Wales. Age was no guarantee of protection; in 1965 16th century Rawtensall Manor was demolished. Even the work of renowned architects disappeared; in 1964 Hawksmoor's work at Panton Hall was also pulled down. However, the value of land was rising so fast that some house owners like the Duke of Devonshire at Chatsworth who had previously moved out actually went back home again. Enterprising owners also turned their minds to alternative ways of bringing money into their estates: in 1949 the Marquis of Bath introduced lions to Longleat; in 1952 Lord Montagu opened the National Motor Museum at Beaulieu; and in 1955 the Duke of Bedford instituted nudist camps and jazz festivals at Woburn Abbey.

In 1975 pressure from the Historic Houses Association helped ensure that death duties were replaced with Capital Transfer Tax, giving tax exemptions to owners who opened their houses to the public on at least sixty days in the year. The first charitable trusts were also set up to 'own' houses and their estates. But in 1977 the sale of the Rothschilds' old home at Mentmore highlighted the continuing difficulty faced by those who thought such houses should be acquired for the nation. Lord Rosebery offered the house, its contents and the grounds to the government for £2 million at a time when the National Land Fund (set up to buy properties for the public as a reminder of those who had died in the wars) had a balance of more than £17 million. However, the government refused to release the necessary funds and the house was eventually sold privately and turned into a meditation centre. The public outcry eventually led to the clause in the **1980 National Heritage Act** which replaced the National Land Fund with the National Heritage Memorial Fund (NHMF). Unlike its predecessor the NHMF could not only buy land, properties and artefacts but could also make endowments which made it easier for the National Trust to take over any houses it saved. Since then the NHMF has been instrumental in saving Belton House, Fyvie, Kedleston Hall, Nostell Priory and Weston Park. (In Northern Ireland the Ulster Land Fund serves a similar function to the National Heritage Memorial Fund.)

Heirs to country houses continue to face difficulties in maintaining them. Faced with a huge Capital Transfer Tax bill in 1982, Henry Harpur-Crewe, the heir to Calke Abbey in Derbyshire, offered the Abbey with its contents and enough land to maintain it to the government (who would then give it to the National Trust). However, the Treasury refused to accept the land, and the National Trust wouldn't take the house without it. Calke Abbey was remote and little-known. However *Country Life* magazine ran a series of illustrated features highlighting it, and SAVE Britain's Heritage launched a campaign to save it. Finally in the 1984 Budget the Chancellor agreed to give the National Heritage Memorial Fund enough money to buy Calke and hand it to the National Trust. Altogether £4.5 million was then spent on its restoration. In 1989 it won the ETB Visitor Attraction Development Award.

The Costs of Running Stately Homes and Ways to Defray them

Maintaining a country house is tremendously expensive. The age of the buildings means that large sums may need to be spent on repairing them. The fittings may also need similar sums spent on delicate, specialist conservation work which can't be done cheaply. Heating large buildings is expensive and, of course, if they are to remain in use, they must be suitably lit and ventilated as well. If the building is open to the public security guards may be needed, together with alarms to protect the fittings.

Even if the building is closed some protection against vandals or squatters will be needed. Opening to the public brings in money to help defray the costs but initially involves further investment: in printing tickets, guidebooks and other materials, in installing lavatories, litter bins, car parks and other amenities, in salaries for guides and custodians. Capital investment may also be required, for example to renovate stables for use as a shop or restaurant.

The National Heritage Memorial Fund

The National Heritage Memorial Fund is the successor to the National Land Fund which was set up in 1946 to act as a memorial to the dead of both World Wars. The 1979 National Heritage Bill converted the Fund, which had not been entirely sucessful in its aims, into the NHMF. This had capital of £12.4 million which was to be topped up each year by grants from the Department of the Environment and the Office of Arts and Libraries. The NHMF has been described as a 'fire engine for the heritage' which can step in when there is danger of loss, whether through export, dilapidation or damage. It can give grants to help secure anything which is regarded as important to the national heritage, including works of art. By 1986-7 it was dispensing grants worth almost £40 million a year. Sometimes it makes joint purchases with the National Art Collections Fund (see below). Amongst the beneficiaries of grants have been stately homes (Calke Abbey, Kedleston Hall), churches (Jarrow, Little Stanmore), cathedrals (Ely), museums (Ironbridge Gorge, Museum of London), art galleries (National Gallery, Tate Gallery), gardens (Biddulph Grange), industrial heritage sites (Quarry Bank Mill, Big Pit Mining Museum), ships (SS *Great Britain*) and piers (Clevedon). Grants vary in size from the £4,000 given to buy Stanley Spencer's *Chestnuts* for Wolverhampton Art Gallery in 1984, to the £900,000 given to help the Tate buy Picasso's *Weeping Woman* in 1987.

Owners of stately homes have shown great imagination in dreaming up cash-generating schemes.

a) Luckily the houses are often the centre of large estates, with plenty of space for other activities; the grounds of Knebworth House are regularly used for pop concerts and the grounds of Longleat House now contain a safari park (a holiday village may eventually be added to the estate too). Other houses have grouse or pigeon-shooting in the grounds, and there are falconry displays at Sudeley Castle and jousting at Chilham Castle. Most such ventures are obviously commercial. However, even the National Trust uses its estates for other activities, like the Classical music concerts in the grounds of

Parham House. At Kentwell Hall in Suffolk the public are even invited to take part in large-scale annual recreations of the past.

b) Medieval banquets are held at Caldicot Castle and Elizabethan ones at Hatfield House. Some historic properties are also used as original conference venues. Others, including Althorp, Hatfield, Hagley, Belle Isle and Ripley Castle, offer corporate entertainment.

c) Turning stately homes into hotels often protects the external and/or internal features. In 1988 American Bob Paynton (the ETB's 1990 'Tourism Personality of the Year') turned 18th century Stapleford Park in Leicestershire into an upmarket country house hotel with individually designed bedrooms. Such houses are not real visitor attractions but are still accessible to tourists, with much of their appeal (and the justification for their high prices) coming from their architectural beauty and historic interest.

The grounds of Beaulieu Abbey are a show-case for what is possible. The core of the Beaulieu site is a ruined medieval abbey, now overshadowed by Palace House which displays costumed figures in keeping with the Montagu family history. A monorail links various attractions in the grounds. Foremost amongst these is the National Motor Museum with its collection of vintage cars and commercial vehicles. Within it 'Wheels' is a Jorvik-style exhibition with time cars to take visitors past the history of the car. The grounds also contain an audio-visual exhibition called Transporama.

Some properties like Chatsworth House have become charitable trusts. In 1986 and 1990 the Duke of Marlborough hosted 'at home' parties in Blenheim Palace for wealthy Americans prepared to pay between £6,000 and £30,000 each for a ticket. All proceeds went to the Blenheim Foundation, a private trust set up to maintain the palace.

Presenting and Caring for Stately Homes

While castles are often presented to the public as ruins, country houses are usually shown as homes with their furnishings intact. Unlike museums country houses display the fine and decorative arts side by side.

Fittings and furniture can require almost as much maintenance as the building itself and the National Trust employs an army of conservators to carry out the necessary work. Furnishings must be protected against pests like death-watch beetle. Humidity levels must also be carefully controlled; if it is too dry paint and wood may crack, while if is too damp mould may grow on books and fabrics. Sudden changes in humidity can also cause paintings to flake. Ideally it's best to keep a low, steady temperature or to put dehumidifiers into every room to remove excess moisture from the air.

Fabrics, furnishings and paintings can also be damaged by too much light. At the brightest times of day blinds may need to be pulled fully or halfway down or ultra-violet filters must be fitted. When the house is closed blackout curtains can be pulled across or shutters used to protect the contents.

To safeguard furnishings and paintings against damage caused by constant touching visitors must often follow a route through the rooms marked out with low, unobtrusive ropes. Modern carpet is often laid over antique carpets where the public will walk, and extra carpeting supplied near entrances. Sometimes tourists are provided with felt or plastic slippers to wear during their visit.

Many stately homes' outhouses have potential for conversion, often allowing more blatantly commercial activities to be carried out away from the house itself. Stable blocks often become ticket offices, shops, restaurants or lavatory blocks. Some outhouses are even sub-let as offices or craft workshops.

RELIGIOUS BUILDINGS

The Cathedrals

Cathedrals are churches which contain the seat or throne of a bishop. A few British cathedrals are also called 'minsters', a word derived from the Greek 'monasterion' meaning monastery. Some of England's cathedrals, like those in Sheffield and Manchester, started out as churches but were promoted to cathedrals and extended accordingly as the local population grew. Although Britain also has Roman Catholic and Scottish Episcopal cathedrals, the most architecturally interesting and therefore the most popular with tourists are the Anglican cathedrals which have the longest history.

England alone has forty-eight Anglican cathedrals. Although Truro, Coventry and Liverpool cathedrals were built in the 19th and 20th century, the majority date back at least in part to the Middle Ages.

Since most cathedrals don't charge for admission, approximate visitor figures must be drawn from sales of tickets to visit towers and crypts, guidebook sales, etc.

The top three cathedrals' popularity is easy to explain: St. Paul's is in London, and benefits from publicity generated by events like the 1981 royal wedding; Canterbury is within day trip reach of London and is famous both because of the story of St. Thomas Becket and as the seat of one of England's two archbishoprics; York is the UK's second biggest tourist centre and seat of the second archbishopric. Both Canterbury and York cathedrals are also magnificent examples of medieval architecture, while

St. Paul's is the work of England's most famous architect, Sir Christopher Wren.

TABLE 50 THE MOST VISITED CATHEDRALS IN THE UK 1988

1.	St. Paul's Cathedral, London	2,500,000
2.	Canterbury	2,125,000
3.	York Minster	2,100,000
4.	Chester	625,000
5.	Norwich	500,000
6.	Salisbury	500,000
7.	Coventry	400,000
8.	Winchester	400,000
9.	Wells	360,000
10.	Durham	352,713

Of the other 'most visited' cathedrals Norwich, Salisbury, Wells, Winchester and Durham are particularly beautiful. However, beauty on its own doesn't always guarantee lots of visitors; Southwell Cathedral is one of England's finest examples of Early English architecture and yet drew only about 85,000 visitors in 1988, presumably because it is in a small town on the way to nowhere. Chester cathedral is not as impressive architecturally. However, it's in a town which is very popular with tourists because of its Roman remains and Tudor buildings, and because it's conveniently positioned to act as a stopping place for coach tours heading north or south. Salisbury was the first English cathedral to introduce charges but they don't seem to have deterred tourists, perhaps because they are drawn by memories of Constable's painting of the cathedral and because Salisbury can be linked with Stonehenge for day trips. Coventry Cathedral is a fine example of modern architecture and probably attracts visitors because of the romantic story of its creation out of the ruins of a building destroyed in the Second World War. Were it not for the cathedral there would be little reason for anyone to visit Coventry, while only a third of tourists who go to Chester take in the cathedral. Ironically Coventry Cathedral only received the protection of listed building status in 1988.

Problems Facing the Cathedrals

By their very nature cathedrals are usually ancient and in constant need of repairs, many of them of an expensive specialist nature. Apart from the natural effects of wear and tear, some cathedrals were also damaged in the war and needed partial rebuilding. Others stand at the heart of modern cities, exposed to constant traffic fumes and industrial pollution.

Unexpected disasters, like the 1984 fire in York Minster which destroyed much of the south transept, can also necessitate expensive restoration. By 1990 it could cost £1,500 to restore a single buttress, £4,000 to repair one 18th century monument, £65,000 to restore and overhaul an organ and £70,000 to repair a major stained glass window. The work is largely funded from donations and there have been many spectacular appeals for funds since the end of the Second World War. For example, Canterbury Cathedral raised £3.5 million, much of it to repair its world famous stained glass.

TABLE 51 CATHEDRALS OF ENGLAND, SCOTLAND AND WALES

ANGLICAN CATHEDRALS OF ENGLAND AND WALES			
Bangor	Birmingham	Blackburn	Bradford
Brecon	Bristol	Bury St. Edmunds	Canterbury
Carlisle	Chelmsford	Chester	Chichester
Coventry	Derby	Durham	Ely
Exeter	Gloucester	Guildford	Hereford
Leicester	Lichfield	Lincoln	Liverpool
Llandaff	London (St. Paul's)	Manchester	Newcastle
Newport	Oxford	Peel (Isle of Man)	Peterborough
Portsmouth	Ripon	Rochester	St. Alban's
St. Asaph	St. David's	Salisbury	Sheffield
Southwark	Southwell	Truro	Wakefield
Wells	Winchester	Worcester	York
ROMAN CATHOLIC CATHEDRALS OF ENGLAND AND WALES			
Arundel	Birmingham	Brentwood	Cardiff
Clifton (Bristol)	Lancaster	Leeds	Liverpool
Middlesbrough	Newcastle	Northampton	Nottingham
Plymouth	Portsmouth	Salford	Shrewsbury
Southwark	Westminster	Wrexham	
CATHEDRALS OF SCOTTISH EPISCOPAL CHURCH			
Aberdeen	Dundee	Edinburgh	Glasgow
Inverness	Millport	Perth	
ROMAN CATHOLIC CATHEDRALS OF SCOTLAND			
Aberdeen	Ayr	Dundee	Edinburgh
Glasgow	Motherwell	Oban	Paisley

Research conducted at Rochester Cathedral in 1989 suggested that the average visitor only gave 8p voluntarily. In 1987 all the English cathedrals between them only managed to raise £5 million from their visitors, although estimates of the amount needed for repairs varied between £70 and £170 million. Consequently much time and energy has had to be spent on fund-raising, some of it, like Hereford's attempt to sell the unique Mappa Mundi in 1989, decidedly controversial.

Because of these difficulties a 'National Trust' for cathedrals which would aim to raise £20 million a year has been suggested. Recognition of the cathedrals' difficulties came in May 1990 when the National Heritage Memorial Fund agreed to grant Ely Cathedral £500,000 to repair the 14th century octagon which had been damaged in storms. The NHMF doesn't normally fund repairs, and the size of this single grant meant it would have difficulty meeting other demands in the year. A few cathedrals have also obtained financial help from the European Regional Development Fund; Coventry was given money to strengthen the ruins of the old building, while Lichfield was helped with restoration costs.

The cathedrals are still owned by the Church and although most of them are Grade I listed buildings government repair grants used not to be available to them. However, in 1990 it was finally agreed that English Heritage would help finance essential repairs. About £70 million a year will be made available for this purpose.

Cathedrals as Money Generators

Charging for admission to British cathedrals has never been popular, although by the late 1980s the idea was becoming more acceptable. By 1990 Ely had a fixed admission charge of £2.30 except on Sundays and during services which was bringing in about £150,000 a year. In 1991 even St. Paul's Cathedral introduced an admission fee. Elsewhere visitors are usually asked to donate a specified amount.

However, even without a fixed entrance fee cathedrals can raise money by charging people to visit towers, crypts, triforia, chapter houses, cloisters and any special exhibitions being staged in the cathedral; in 1989 York Minster was charging £0.50 for admission to the chapter house, £1.00 for the tower and £1.30 for the crypt, with another £1.00 fee for photography. In 1990 the revenue from these charges came to £250,000, with another £600,000 gained from voluntary contributions.

In addition bookstalls sell guidebooks, postcards and religious books; quite often there is a more substantial souvenir shop as well. By 1990 major cathedrals like Durham and York also had full-scale restaurants in their cloisters or chapter-houses. Others, like Bristol, had smaller-scale tea shops.

The cathedrals' great musical heritage also offers scope for making money. Almost all cathedral buildings have wonderful acoustics, and some also have marvellous organs and/or choirs. Consequently cathedrals often host concerts, not all of them free. There are also cathedral music festivals. For example, Gloucester, Hereford and Worcester Cathedrals have held the Three Choirs Festival every August since the early 1700s.

It isn't only the cathedrals that profit from their visitors. In 1975 a SAVE Britain's Heritage survey in Canterbury suggested that more than a million tourists, 45% of them foreign, were already visiting the city, and 93% of those questioned said that they had visited or would be visiting the cathedral; in fact 77% said they were visiting Canterbury specifically to sightsee, while 58% gave the cathedral as their main reason for visiting. The average guest was spending £3 a day on snacks, gifts, meals, drinks, guidebooks, clothes and groceries in Canterbury; only 3% of visitors came and went without buying anything. Perhaps 14% of all shopping in the city was being done by tourists. The shops doing best from tourists were those in the streets nearest to the cathedral, where 25% of the shopping space was taken up with shops selling things like souvenirs. A similar trading pattern was obvious in York in 1990, with shops in The Shambles and Stonegate catering almost exclusively for tourists.

Facilities for Cathedral Visitors

Many cathedrals have 'Ministries of Welcome', using volunteers as guides and general assistants. Most also sell guidebooks, ranging from glossy Pitkins to detailed studies of the stained glass, roof bosses, misericords, etc. Often guidebooks are also available in French, German, Spanish and Italian. Ground plans with the age of different parts of the structure shaded in different colours are usually provided as well.

Some cathedrals provide large mirrors on wheels which allow visitors to study roof vault details without getting a crick in the neck. Many now have wooden ramps at their main entrances to allow wheelchair access.

The Churches

In 1988 the UK had 16,518 Church of England churches, 8,500 of them dating from before the Reformation. Including the cathedrals, there were 12,719 listed churches, 2,894 of them Grade I. Most listed churches are wholly or largely medieval and 47% of them are in remote areas of the East Midlands, East Anglia and the West Country. There are also 2,500 listed Roman Catholic churches, most of them Victorian. Of the listed churches 588 were redundant in 1988.

Marcus Binney and Max Hanna have described churches as the 'Cinderellas of tourism', and certainly, when compared with other historic buildings, little has changed in their presentation to make them appeal to a wider audience, perhaps because many people feel uneasy about introducing commercialism into buildings which still have religious significance.

Visiting the Churches

It's difficult to know exactly how many people visit churches since free admission means there are no convenient ticket stubs. Many churches have visitor books, but surveys suggest that only between one in four and one in fifteen people actually sign them. Nevertheless in 1982 there were probably 10 million visits to Anglican churches in the UK, with two-thirds of those visits being to 200 particular churches. In 1988 the ETB estimated that 3.2 million visits were made to 73 specific churches, with 22 of them probably receiving more than 50,000 visitors each.

TABLE 52 THE MOST VISITED CHURCHES IN ENGLAND IN 1988

1.	Bolton Abbey	400,000
2.	St Mary the Virgin, Oxford	300,000
3.	Tewkesbury Abbey	189,000
4.	St Mary in the Castle, Dover	175,889
5.	Christchurch Priory	168,000
6.	Holy Trinity, Stratford	125,000
7.	Great St. Mary, Cambridge	101,000
8.	Waltham Abbey	100,530
9.	St. Lawrence, Eyam	100,000
10.	St. Winwaloe, Gunwalloe	100,000
11.	Lancaster Priory	100,000
12.	St Mary the Virgin, Rye	100,000

Once again architectural significance alone is not enough to guarantee visitors. Beverley Minster and St. John's, Cirencester are much more impressive architecturally than Dover and Eyam churches but seem to have received fewer visitors. Dover drew a high proportion of overseas visitors probably because it's situated in a major Channel port, right inside the grounds of a highly visible and much visited castle (Lancaster Priory is also next door to a prominent Castle). Eyam is in the popular Peak District National Park and is associated with the romantic story of a village sealing itself off from the world to prevent plague infecting its neighbours. The Oxford and Cambridge churches undoubtedly benefit from the number of tourists attracted to the towns by the colleges, while Holy Trinity, Stratford owes its popularity to the fact that Shakespeare is buried there. The church at Gunwalloe has an unlikely setting right on a Cornish beach, while Rye is a village renowned for its prettiness, to which the church contributes. Only Bolton, Tewkesbury and Waltham Abbeys, and Christchurch Priory seem to owe their popularity purely to their intrinsic qualities. Even then Christchurch probably profits from being within easy reach of the seaside resort of Bournemouth, while Bolton Abbey is part of a larger ancient monument in a particularly picturesque setting.

Churches as Tourist Attractions

In many ways churches have great potential for attracting visitors. They are often the most interesting buildings in a town or village and hold the key to interpreting local history. What's more the fittings are sometimes as interesting as the building itself. However, not all churches can be supervised, and security problems mean that valuable items often have to moved to safe keeping elsewhere. Many country churches, including some of the most beautiful like Salle and Walpole St. Peter in Norfolk, are also hard to reach without public transport which immediately limits the likely number of visitors.

Visitor numbers can be boosted by better signposting and publicity in the media (especially on TV), particularly after an appeal for restoration funds. Holy Trinity in Hull, England's largest parish church, is well placed to receive visitors in the Old Town conservation area; extending its opening hours in 1988 brought an 82% increase in the number of visitors. Ironically, many churches which would once have been open round the clock are now locked because of theft and vandalism. This is mainly a problem in towns, but even country churches are increasingly likely to be closed.

Most churches provide only minimal facilities for visitors. Guidebooks range from simple leaflets to glossy Pitkin booklets. In most cases churches rely on visitors' honesty to pay for these, with safes often set into the wall near the door. In many cases guidebooks are not expected to produce a profit. A few churches have printed information pasted on to boards which can't be taken away.

Some churches also sell postcards of the building and its fittings and/or religious publications. Larger churches sometimes have volunteer stewards to look after the book-stalls, answer visitors' queries and sell souvenirs like bookmarks. Sometimes there are even small restaurants. At St. Paul's in Jarrow, a church linked with Bede and early Christianity in England, monastic robes hang at the back of the nave; visiting school children wear them for history lessons aimed at making the church more interesting to them.

Since the 1970s churches with memorial brasses have been able to reap extra income from people wishing to rub them. To avoid the risk of damage to the most popular brasses because of the number of people wishing to do this some churches now provide facsimiles which can be rubbed instead. This facsimile process has spawned purpose-designed Brass-Rubbing Centres where visitors can rub copies of brasses from all around the country.

A few churches also charge visitors for taking photographs. Like cathedrals, some also charge for climbing their towers, and Holy Trinity, Stratford, charges for access to the area containing Shakespeare's memorial. However, churches have limited opportunity to make extra charges, since most are small buildings without crypts or private chapels.

It is hard for church authorities to sanction more forceful courtship of tourists since commercialism sits uneasily in buildings which are still primarily places of prayer. Nevertheless Thames and Chilterns Tourist Board publishes a leaflet listing 100 of its most interesting churches, while Northumbria has a Christian Heritage leaflet.

Churches don't make much money from tourists. In 1988 75 told the ETB they had made £764,048 from their visitors. Of this 50% was from the sale of guidebooks and souvenirs, 38% from donations and 12% from catering, brass-rubbing, charges to visit the tower, etc. Only three churches had an income of more than £70,000.

Special Events

Churches can attract more vistors by hosting temporary exhibitions or special events. Many country churches organise flower festivals when the building is decorated with flower arrangements The work is usually carried out by volunteer parishioners, so most of the extra money raised from entrance fees, sales of guidebooks, etc. is profit. Recently some tourist authorities have organised more imaginative events to attract tourists. So in 1990 visitors to Shropshire churches were offered tea in the local vicarage in return for a donation to church funds.

Problems Facing Britain's Churches

The biggest problem facing UK churches is the falling number of church-goers. Many of the most beautiful, like the 'wool' churches of East Anglia and the Cotswolds, were built by wealthy patrons at a time when there were large congregations to fill them. Over the centuries industry has moved away, leaving them isolated in villages with small church-going populations unable to cope with the cost of maintaining them. The congregation's religious needs could often be met more cheaply and efficiently by moving into smaller, purpose-built accommodation which would cost less to heat. But that leaves the beautiful medieval building to be maintained without a congregation. Even in towns the fall in the number of church-goers has left many Victorian churches without a function.

With more than 8,500 Anglican churches dating back to the Middle Ages, repairs bills are mounting up. In 1913 when the Ancient Monuments Act offered financial aid to many historic buildings the Church opted to exclude its own buildings. This let it keep absolute control over them, but also deprived it of useful repair grants from the Historic Buildings Council. However, since 1978 English Heritage and Cadw have administered £8 million of government money for grants to the finest churches when they face bills in excess of £5,000. The Historic Churches Preservation Trust and the Incorporated Church Building Society can also help out with grants and interest-free loans.

Abbeys and Priories

When Henry VIII broke with the Roman Catholic church and dissolved the abbeys and priories in 1536 he brought to an abrupt end a life-style which had endured for centuries and left its mark on the landscape in the form of innumerable ecclesiastical settlements, often in remote parts of the countryside. Much of the land was sold to private owners and the buildings were left to collapse, their roofs stripped of lead and their bricks removed to be reused elsewhere.

The ruins were rediscovered by the 18th century Romantic Movement. However, the remote setting of many abbey ruins made them almost inaccessible until the advent of the private car. By the 1980s most abbey and priory ruins were cared for by English Heritage or its equivalents and some received large numbers of visitors every year.

TABLE 53 THE MOST VISITED ABBEY RUINS IN THE UK IN 1988

1.	Beaulieu Abbey	537,750
2.	Fountains Abbey	274,414
3.	Glastonbury Abbey	160,000
4.	Battle Abbey	127,772
5.	Whitby Abbey	117,972
6.	Tintern Abbey	105,509
7.	Rievaulx Abbey	79,291
8.	Lindisfarne Priory	50,420
9.	Melrose Abbey	46,303
10.	Jedburgh Abbey	34,714

Having something 'extra' certainly helps attract the visitors. In the case of Beaulieu the abbey ruins are a very small part of what is on offer; on their own they would probably receive few visitors. Glastonbury has the lure of the legend that it was King Arthur's burial place, while Battle is linked with stories of the Norman Conquest and King Harold's death. Whitby has a wonderful position on a cliff above the winding shopping streets of a fishing port. But whereas Tintern is a convenient stopping point for anyone travelling along the M4 to South Wales, few people would bother to travel to the remote island of Lindisfarne unless they intended to visit the abbey (and castle) ruins.

Protection and Presentation of Abbey Ruins

Some abbeys have few visitors, and in his book on the presentation of ruins M.W. Thompson points out that they are particularly difficult for most people to understand because the monastic life is so uncommon now. Once taken into guardianship abbey ruins must be made safe and intelligible for visitors and also protected from further decay. Vegetation must be removed from the walls which may have to be reset and repointed. Disguised steel rods set in concrete may be needed to secure crumbling masonry. Sometimes mouldings have to be reconstructed to prevent them vanishing. Mullions may have to be reconstructed so they can be reglazed.

Fallen rubble is usually cleared away from the lower walls so they can be secured and the ground plan excavated. During this process old tiled floors are sometimes uncovered. Unfortunately tiles (particularly decorative ones) weather badly once exposed to the open-air and may have to be moved into a museum. Later additions to the building may also be removed unless they are regarded as attractive and historical in their own right, as at Fountains Abbey.

Where the ground plan of previous buildings has been excavated it can be marked out on the ground in brickwork or tile. Ruins are also easier to understand if those parts which would once have been indoors are floored with gravel, while those which would have been outdoors are grassed over.

INDUSTRIAL HERITAGE

In the late 18th century Great Britain was the first country to experience what is now called the Industrial Revolution. Consequently although heavy industry now plays a smaller and smaller part in the UK economy, the country is littered with reminders of the industrial past in the form of redundant buildings and obsolete machinery.

Ever since the Great Exhibition in 1851 there has been an awareness that the best industrial artefacts deserved preservation, a belief that originally led to the creation of the Science Museum in South Kensington in 1899. However, in general people were slow to appreciate the many surviving mills, mines and factory buildings. The growth of interest in industrial archaeology in the 1960s may have been inspired by emotional reaction to highly publicised demolitions like that of Euston Arch and the London Coal Exchange at Billingsgate in 1962 which drew attention to the lack of protection for such buildings.

The expressions 'industrial archaeology' and 'industrial heritage' are usually taken to refer to the physical remains of the following:

* power sources...wind and watermills, steam engines, nuclear power stations, etc.

* extractive industries...quarries, mines and associated buildings.

* manufacturing industries...agricultural produce, clothing, chemicals, potteries, etc.

* public services...gas, electricity, water, drainage, sewerage, post, telecommunications, etc.

* commercial buildings...shops, corn exchanges, etc.

* associated buildings and model towns...workers' houses, factory owners' mansions, docks, etc.

The relics of the transport infrastructure, including the preserved railways and canals, are also part of the industrial heritage. However, because their remains are so extensive and because they have distinctive new leisure uses these are examined in Chapter Three.

Location of Industrial Heritage Sites

Some industrial heritage sites cannot, by their nature, be evenly distributed around the country. For example old tin and copper mines are mainly restricted to Cornwall, while lead mines are concentrated in Derbyshire, Northumbria, Somerset, Scotland and Wales. Coal mines used to be widely distributed around the country except in South and South West England and in East Anglia. However, during the 1980s many of them closed and even in the once-flourishing South Wales coalfields 'heritage tourism' now offers more hope for future income than mining itself.

Potteries tended to develop around good sources of suitable clay, as in the Staffordshire region, while cloth mills grew up in sheep-rearing areas like Yorkshire and South Lancashire with plenty of water for industrial processes and transportation. The original canals were built to transport materials from the new industrial sites, but once they were in place factories tended to open all along their banks to take advantage of the improved transportation.

Some power sources were only available in restricted areas of the country. So there are many more redundant windmills in the flat, open countryside of East Anglia than in hillier parts of the UK. Watermills are only found by Britain's many fast-flowing rivers and streams. The development of electricity removed the crucial link between industry and localised power supplies, and 20th century factories are more evenly distributed around the country, often in towns with easy supplies of labour. Towns also contain many relics of old public utilities.

TABLE 54 EXAMPLES OF INDUSTRIAL HERITAGE SITES IN THE UK

Type of Site	Examples
Flint mine	Grimes Graves, Thetford, Norfolk
Coal mine	Big Pit Mining Museum, Blaenafon, Gwent
Gold mine	Dolaucothi, Dyfed
Lead mine	Killhope, Weardale, Durham
Silk mill	Derby Industrial Museum
Textile mill	Quarry Bank, Styal, Cheshire; Manningham Mill, Bradford; Salt Mill, Saltaire, Bradford
Windmill	Berney Arms Windmill, Reedham, Norfolk
Watermill	Flatford Mill, Suffolk
Waterwheel	Lady Isabella Wheel, Laxey, Isle of Man
Pumping Station	Ryhope Museum, Sunderland
Gasworks	Fakenham, Norfolk
Power Station	Battersea, London
Model villages	Saltaire; Port Sunlight; New Lanark
Industrial Museums	Bristol Industrial Museum; Camden Works, Bath; Abbeydale Industrial Hamlet, Sheffield

Presenting Industrial Heritage Attractions

There are some specific difficulties when it comes to presenting industrial heritage attractions. In the first place many of the artefacts are too large to be moved to conventional museums, a problem which can be solved by creating museums around them instead. So the Leicester Museum of Technology was created around the Abbey Pumping Station, an old sewage works.

Industrial processes were also dynamic and a machine that may be fascinating in use can seem dull when stationary, a problem often resolved by putting it to use again particularly when it is being displayed in its original setting. This has the added advantage that machine produce can be sold to visitors to raise extra revenue and that people can learn more about the actual processes involved. However, moving industrial machinery is frequently dangerous so extra safety precautions will be needed. Clearly this also applies when people are taken into old mine shafts, quarries, etc.

Increasingly industrial heritage sites are 'living museums' which attempt to show how people lived and worked alongside the artefacts. Costumed attendants are often on hand to explain what visitors are seeing, as at Quarry Bank Mill and Ironbridge Gorge.

Curators putting together an industrial exhibition have the advantage that few technological objects are unique or priced for their intrinsic beauty. Consequently they rarely fetch high prices at auction. Exhibits can also be treated more roughly.

LISTED BUILDINGS AND CONSERVATION AREAS

While castles and stately homes usually become tourist attractions in their own right, many other buildings of historic or architectural interest can contribute to the generally pleasant environment that draws tourists to an area even though they can't be visited individually. Tourists would probably still come to Bath to visit attractions like the Roman Baths even if it wasn't such a beautiful town. However, many come specifically for the elegant ambience created by the many Georgian buildings. Similarly Chester's popularity springs more from its generally attractive streets than from its specific tourist sights.

The 1947 **Town and Country Planning Act** enabled the Secretary of State for the Environment to 'list' buildings which could not then be altered or demolished without specific permission. Listed buildings are divided into three separate categories:

a) Grade I buildings are of national importance.

b) Grade II* buildings are of regional or special local importance.

c) Grade II buildings are of historic or architectural interest, including some which are of value only within a group.

Most buildings are listed because of their external features, but some are protected for their interiors or because of links with historical events or characters. All buildings dating from before 1700 in anything like their original condition should be listed, as should most of those built between 1700 and 1840. Only buildings of definite character and/or quality and the principal works of important architects erected between 1840 and 1914 are likely to be listed. An increasing number of inter-War buildings (including Battersea Power Station) are now listed. In 1988 eighteen post-War buildings, including Coventry Cathedral and the Royal Festival Hall (both Grade I), were listed. Since 1987 any building more than thirty years old has been eligible for listing. In exceptional circumstances ten-year-old buildings can also be listed; such buildings are likely to reflect changing building technologies like the first use of concrete, or to be street furnishings like telephone boxes.

In 1989 England had more than 500,000 listed buildings, including 6,056 Grade Is. In 1990 Wales had 13,324 listed buildings and Scotland about 36,800.

Conservation Areas

Just as the scheduling of specific monuments has been broadened to cover entire 'archaeological areas', so the 1967 **Civic Amenities Act** widened listed building protection to cover 'conservation areas'. These may contain or be centred on specific listed buildings, but this is not always the case where it is felt that it is an area's overall appearance that needs to be protected. So although individual buildings in Bath's Royal Crescent are listed in their own right the entire street is also protected as a conservation area, limiting the changes owners of individual houses can make, particularly to their properties' exteriors. In 1989 the Department of the Environment started designating 'views' as well, offering protection to nine London skylines including those round St. Paul's Cathedral and the Palace of Westminster.

By December 1988 England had about 6,300 conservation areas, 60% of them in rural areas, and about 200 town centres with special planning controls over them. In 1990 Wales had 362 conservation areas and Scotland 578.

Presenting the Past to Visitors

Local authorities sometimes attach information plaques to the walls of properties once owned or lived in by famous people to help tourists learn more from buildings which can only be examined from the outside. London's system of **blue plaques** identifies the homes of the famous. English Heritage decides which building of many that may have links with any one individual should bear the plaque. Those commemorated must have been dead for more than twenty years, unless the centenary of their birth has passed. In 1990 London had 572 blue plaques. Twelve more are added each year.

By 1989 68 English towns also offered guided walks for visitors. Some are simply tours of buildings of architectural or historic interest, but others bring together sites with specific themes. So London, Bath, York and Edinburgh all had 'ghost walks', with guides bringing the gorier episodes of their past to life again.

Some towns and villages also have self-guided 'town trails', with sign-posts, plaques, guidebooks or tape recordings giving additional information about buildings and monuments along the way. By 1989 there were 931 trails in 595 English towns and villages.

CHAPTER EIGHT
COUNTRYSIDE AND WILDLIFE ATTRACTIONS

Historic buildings may be the mainstay of the UK tourist attractions industry, but the countryside is also very important despite the fact that the British climate puts it out of bounds for much of the year. Countryside attractions are particularly important to the Highlands and Islands area of Scotland, parts of Wales and the Lake District.

COUNTRYSIDE ATTRACTIONS

Developing Appreciation of the Countryside

The countryside's appeal may seem obvious in the 1990s, but this hasn't always been the case. In fact it wasn't really until the Romantic Movement of the late 18th century that people started to think of the countryside as intrinsically interesting. Appreciation of the countryside gradually increased throughout the 19th century as the railways brought it within the reach of more of the population. But it wasn't until the second half of the 20th century that private cars gave everyone who wanted it access to as much of the countryside as they liked.

Countryside Conservation

For people to enjoy the countryside it must be protected against the constant threats from redevelopment, destructive farming practices, etc. In the UK most land, even in the remotest areas, is privately owned. Its preservation depends on control of development and incentives to encourage beneficial use of it. The basis for protecting the most scenically beautiful areas of England and Wales is the **1949 National Parks and Access to the Countryside Act** which authorised the creation of ten National Parks, mostly in upland areas, and established National Park Direction Areas in Scotland. In addition the act allowed for the designation of Areas of Outstanding National Beauty (AONBs), National Nature Reserves (NNRs), Local Nature Reserves (LNRs) and Sites of Special Scientific Interest (SSSIs). The Nature Conservancy Council (NCC) was also set up to look after nature conservation throughout the UK.

The National Parks

The International Union for the Conservation of Nature and Natural Resources (IUCN) uses the expression 'National Park' to refer to wilderness areas not materially altered by human exploitation or occupation and which are owned or managed by governments.

FIGURE 64 THE NATIONAL PARKS, AONBS, NATIONAL TRAILS AND HERITAGE COASTS OF ENGLAND AND WALES, 1990

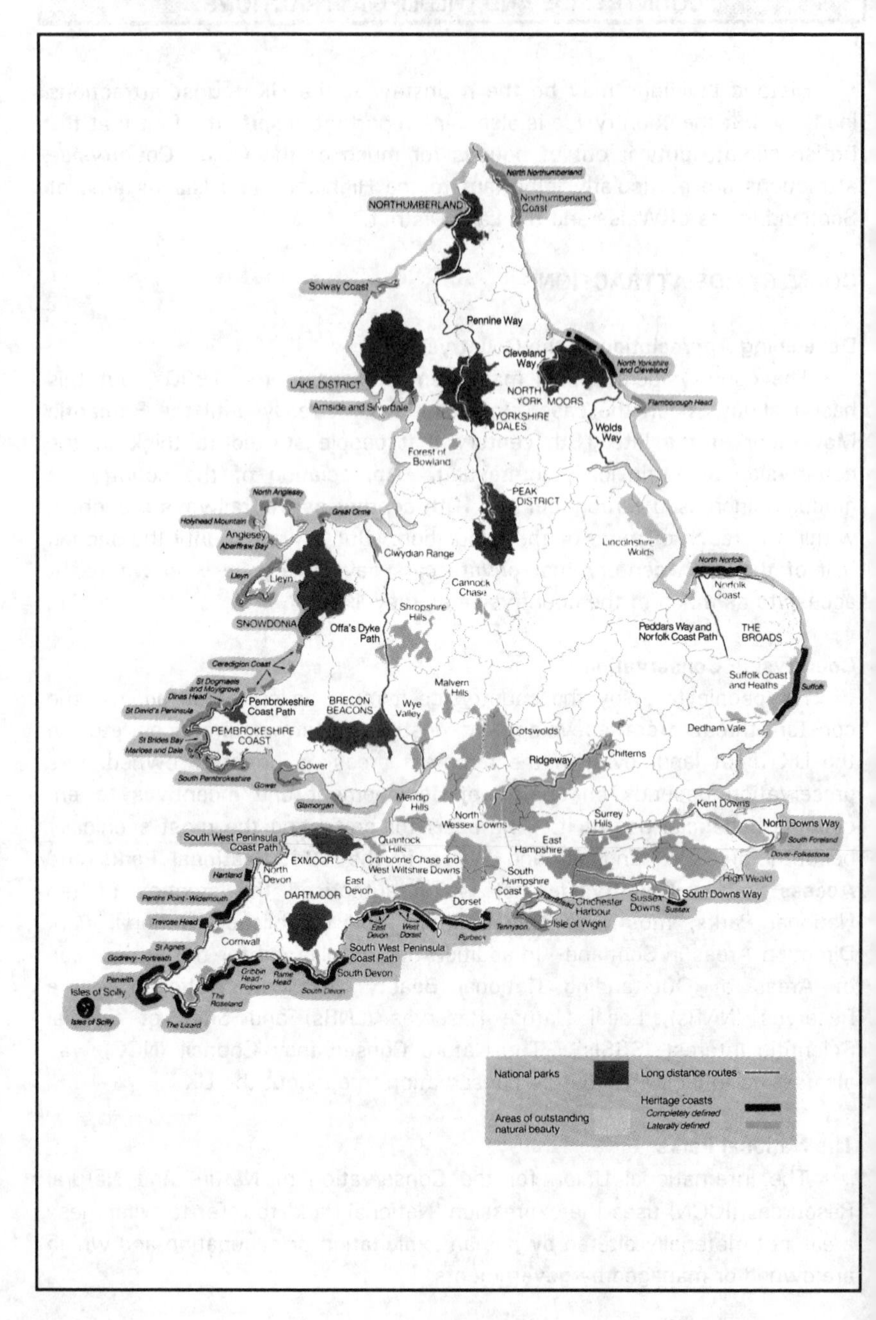

The ten National Parks of England and Wales were designated by the Countryside Commission under the authority of the 1949 National Parks and Access to the Countryside Act. They are extensive areas of beautiful and relatively wild country where the characteristic beauty of the landscape is strictly protected and where the wildlife and historic buildings are conserved. However, existing farming is allowed to continue and facilities for public access and enjoyment are provided so they are not strictly wildernesses according to the IUCN definition. In 1987 the ten parks covered 13,745 square kilometres between them.

TABLE 55 THE NATIONAL PARKS OF ENGLAND AND WALES

Name	Established	Area (sq.kms)	Visitor Days (millions)
Dartmoor	1951	945	7.80
Lake District	1951	2280	12.00
Peak District	1951	1404	20.00
Snowdonia	1951	2170	7.50
North Yorkshire Moors	1952	438	11.00
Pembrokeshire Coast	1952	583	12.50
Exmoor	1954	686	2.50
Yorkshire Dales	1954	1761	8.50
Northumberland	1956	1031	1.00
Brecon Beacons	1957	1350	7.00

No new National Parks had been created since the 1950s. In 1973 an application to designate the Cambrian Mountains was rejected. However, in 1987 the Broads Act gave the Norfolk Broads Authority statutory control over activities in the area, and the Broads became a National Park in all but name. The New Forest in Hampshire is administered by the Forestry Commission under a mandate from the Ministry of Agriculture and is also a National Park in all but name. No National Parks have ever been established in Scotland or Northern Ireland.

Since 1974 each park has been administered by a National Parks Authority. However, only the Lake District and Peak District authorities have sole control; the other park authorities work together with local councils. All the authorities are overseen by the Countryside Commission and 75% of their running costs come from central government. The National Park Authorities make planning decisions and offer help, grants and advice on land management, public access, etc. to landowners within the parks. Their statutory duties are:

a) to protect and enhance the character of the landscape,

b) to enable the public to enjoy the parks as recreation areas, and
c) to protect the social and economic well-being of the local communities.

Despite their legal protection the National Parks still face threats, particularly from the changing nature of agriculture, but also from:

* military use
* quarrying (a particular threat in the Peak District)
* housing and office development
* increased afforestation with non-indigenous species of tree
* new roads. In 1972 the A66 which runs through the Lake District National Park from Penrith to Workington was widened to provide better access to the park. Afterwards the Sandford Report said that where the preservation of natural beauty and public enjoyment of the Park came into conflict, priority should be given to conserving the Park's natural beauty. The Report's recommendations were accepted in 1976 and plans to route the Manchester to Sheffield motorway through the Peak District National Park were dropped. However, in 1985 permission was granted for the Okehampton by-pass to be built on Dartmoor.

Areas of Outstanding Natural Beauty (AONBs)

The 1949 National Parks and Access to the Countryside Act also authorised the Countryside Commission to designate Areas of Outstanding Natural Beauty in places of particularly fine landscape quality. Thirty-eight AONBs now cover 17,084 square kilometres or 11.3% of England and Wales. The Tamar and Tavy valleys, the Berwyn Mountains and Nidderdale Moors may also be designated eventually.

Designating an Area of Outstanding Natural Beauty makes it easier for planning authorities to justify turning down unsuitable large-scale development proposals like new roads and reservoirs. Sometimes extra money for conservation also becomes available. Local authorities are not obliged to set up special administrative procedures for AONBs but are encouraged to set up management plans for them.

In Northern Ireland the **1965 Amenity Lands Act** authorised the Department of the Environment to designate Areas of Outstanding Natural Beauty, the country's only category of protected landscape. In doing so it was advised by the Ulster Countryside Commission and the Committee for Nature Conservation. As a result of the Nature Conservation and Amenity Lands Order (NI) of 1985 there was a major revision of AONBs.

In Scotland the **1978 Town and Country Planning (Scotland) Act** authorised the Secretary of State for Scotland, advised by the Countryside

Commission for Scotland, to designate forty **National Scenic Areas.** Most are in north and west Scotland and the islands; altogether they cover 12.9% of the land and inland waters of Scotland. Once an NSA has been designated special planning procedures apply and most medium and large-scale proposals must be vetted by the Countryside Commission for Scotland.

FIGURE 65 NATIONAL SCENIC AREAS IN SCOTLAND IN 1990

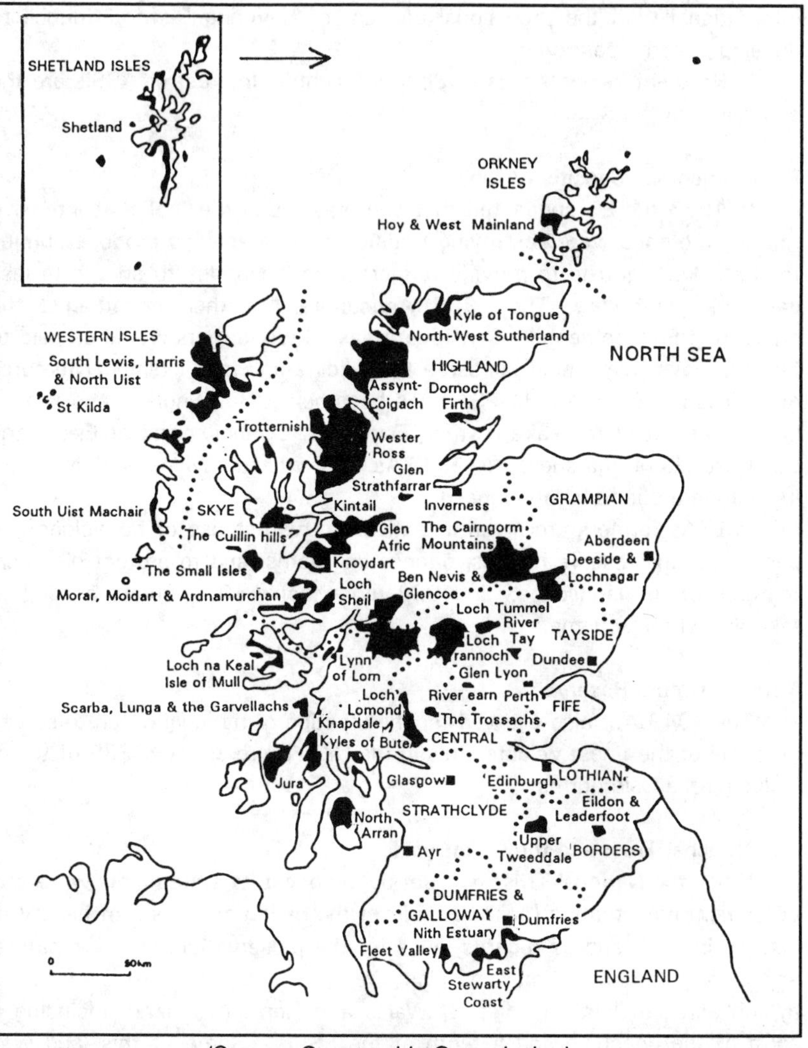

(Source: Countryside Commission)

Sites of Special Scientific Interest (SSSIs)

The 1949 Act also allowed the Nature Conservancy Council to designate areas of land which were of special interest because of their flora, fauna, geological or physiographical features. Once it had selected such sites the NCC was to advise their owners on care of them; the owners were then to give the NCC at least three month's notice of changes which were likely to damage the sites. The **1981 Wildlife and Countryside Act** (amended in 1985) strengthened the legislation. However, it is still proving rather ineffective. Rainham Marshes in Essex is an SSSI, but MCA International won the provisional consent of Havering District Council to develop a theme park on it.

In **Northern Ireland** Areas of Special Scientific Interest or ASSIs are the equivalent of the SSSIs.

Environmentally Sensitive Areas

In 1985 the EC suggested that one way round the fact that intensive farming methods were destroying traditional landscapes to produce surplus food stocks might be to provide farmers with incentives to switch to less damaging methods. The **1986 Agriculture Act** then encouraged the creation of Environmentally Sensitive Areas where farmers would be paid to farm in ways that would conserve the wildlife and archaeological features of their land. By 1991 31 ESAs had been selected in England and Wales, including most of the Lake District, Dartmoor, Exmoor, parts of Essex and the North Kent marshes. New ESAs in Scotland, Wales and Northern Ireland were due to be announced.

In ESAs farmers are given incentives to restrict use of herbicides and pesticides, to preserve hedges, ditches and barns, and to protect historical features of the landscape. In 1988 more than 1400 farmers applied to take part in the scheme.

National Nature Reserves

The 1949 Act also allowed for the creation of national nature reserves on some of the finest wildlife sites in the UK. There are now 235 of them, including the Cairngorms.

The National Trust and the Countryside

When the National Trust was set up, amongst its stated aims were 'the permanent preservation for the benefit of the nation of lands....of beauty or historic interest and as regards lands for the preservation...of their natural aspect features and animal and plant life'. By 1990 it owned over half a million acres of land in England, Wales and Northern Ireland, including a sixth of the coastline and a tenth of the SSSIs. Some of this land was attached to historic houses, but much had been acquired purely for its landscape value. After the Forestry Commission and the Ministry of Defence the National Trust is the UK's biggest single landowner. The National Trust for Scotland owns another 100,000 acres of land, including important battlefield sites like Culloden and Bannockburn.

Country Parks

The **1968 Countryside Act** authorised the creation of country parks for recreational purposes on the outskirts of large towns. Many have now been established, especially in northern England and the Midlands; Center Parcs in Sherwood Forest is technically a country park on old Ministry of Defence land. Many are on abandoned industrial land or in old quarries and reservoirs which now have picnic facilities, nature trails, etc.

Country parks are especially popular in Northern Ireland where 41% of all visits to tourist attractions in 1989 were to country and forest parks. All but one of Northern Ireland's country and forest parks are owned by the government or local authorities. Between them they provide 11% of all employment in tourist attractions in the province. In 1989 the most popular were Crawfordsburn, Scrabo, Roe Valley and Castle Archdale Country Parks and Tollymore Forest Park.

THE COASTLINE

Heritage Coasts

Some of Britain's most beautiful countryside is to be found along its undeveloped coastlines. However, this scenery is threatened by industrial development, new marinas, intensive farming, housing schemes, caravan parks and land reclamation schemes. In 1970 the Countryside Commission suggested the designation of 'heritage coasts'. In 1972 the government authorised local authorities to develop plans and produce management plans for the stretches of coast suggested by the Commission. To date 43 'heritage coasts', mostly within National Parks, AONBs or SSSIs, have been designated; the Exmoor coastline may soon be added. The protected areas cover 1,460 kilometres or 33% of the coast of England and Wales.

Like SSSIs, 'heritage coasts' have proved vulnerable to developers. In 1989 it was agreed that the new A20 should be routed along the top of the White Cliffs of Dover, regardless of their supposed protection.

Some individual coastal features are very popular tourist attractions. In Northern Ireland the single most visited tourist attraction (other than Crawfordsburn Country Park) is the Giant's Causeway which received about 300,000 visitors in 1989. St. Michael's Mount in Cornwall was visited by 175,815 people in 1988. In 1987 Peter de Savary bought Land's End, a stretch of rocky coastline which the National Trust had hoped to acquire, and developed a theme park there. Statistics show that visitors who used to spend an average twelve and a half minutes at Land's End now stay for four or five hours. Of 5,000 people questioned in 1989 98% thought their visit good value for money.

FORESTS AND WOODLANDS

In prehistoric times most of Britain was probably heavily wooded; areas like the Midlands may have been entirely covered in trees. Although the word 'forest' is often thought of as synonymous with woodland, in the Middle Ages it referred specifically to land which belonged to the king and was controlled by the 'forest law', which prohibited the killing of game. Forests were certainly wooded, but were not necessarily covered in trees; the New Forest, for example, was probably never entirely wooded. A 'chase' was a noble's hunting ground.

As the population grew the forests came under pressure from the land-hungry. By the start of the 20th century only 5% of the UK was still covered by trees. In 1919 the Forestry Commission was set up to plant 1,770,000 acres of new woods by 1999.

However, between 1947 and 1980 half the trees which had survived from the 16th century were felled. In the 1970s Dutch Elm disease killed a further 11 million trees, while farmers continued to uproot single trees that got in the way of intensive farming methods. By 1979 the Nature Conservancy Council was warning that all remaining broadleaved woods could soon be lost.

Various tax and grant schemes to encourage tree planting have been tried. Most have been criticised for encouraging foresters to plant quick-growing conifers even in environmentally fragile areas like the Scottish Flow Country. However, by 1990 almost 10% of the UK was once again covered in trees, two-thirds of them conifers. The hurricane-force winds that ripped across southern England in October 1987 toppled 15 million trees and damaged many more. The Countryside Commission responded by creating a special task force to help repair the damage.

Forest Parks

Since 1935 the Forestry Commission has created many forest parks. The first was at Argylls in Scotland and there are others in Snowdonia and the Wye Valley. The New Forest is also a forest park. The Forestry Act of 1967 said that the Forestry Commission should provide recreational facilities on its land and protect and enhance the environment, so within the parks the Commission provides picnic areas, camp-sites, forest and nature trails, museums and information centres, and forest drives. One of the Forestry Commission's most popular attractions is Westonbirt Arboretum (a tree garden) in Gloucestershire, visited by about 180,000 people in 1988.

Community Forests

Research carried out on the continent suggests that the countryside's popularity with holidaymakers springs as much from desire to escape the cities as from real love of nature. Given the pressures that rural tourism can cause, one solution is to bring the countryside closer to the towns. Country parks and city farms already attempt to do this. The Countryside and Forestry Commissions now plan that by the year 2000 every major town and city will have a community forest on its doorstep.

These forests will contain both deciduous and coniferous trees, often planted on areas of derelict wasteland. Funding will come from a variety of sources, including European Community grants. The first forests will be in South Staffordshire, South Tyne and Wear, East London, Cleveland, Manchester, Liverpool, Sheffield, Bristol, Neath/Port Talbot, North Nottingham, Swansea and Cardiff.

TABLE 56 RECREATIONAL FACILITIES IN FORESTRY COMMISSION FORESTS IN THE UK, 1986

Facility	Number
Forest walks/nature trails	646
Picnic sites	624
Forest cabins/holiday homes	191
Youth camps	51
Camping/caravan sites	32
Arboreta	20
Visitor centres	17
Forest drives	8

(Source: Forestry Commission)

ACCESS TO THE COUNTRYSIDE

Public Rights of Way

Most land in the UK is in private hands and there is no assumption in favour of public access except in Scotland where there is no crime of trespass for people passing through. In fact at the start of the 20th century very little land could be walked on, even in areas which are now National Parks. In 1932 a group of ramblers were actually jailed after a 'mass trespass' on Kinder Scout in the Peak District to assert the public's right to access. Even now the public only has absolute right of access, even in the National Parks, on public footpaths and bridleways and some stretches of common land (Fig. 66). There is de facto right of access to areas like the Lake District fells and mountains simply because no one is likely to be around to complain. Elsewhere access depends on agreement with farmers, some of them more obliging than others who regularly plough up public paths. Where access is granted the National Parks Authorities have the right to enact by-laws to control public behaviour which can be enforced by rangers. The situation is not helped by the fact that the Ministry of Defence owns 850,000 acres of land, including some in Dartmoor, the North Yorkshire Moors, the Dorset Coast and Salisbury Plain, where access is often restricted for safety reasons.

In 1990 England and Wales had 140,000 miles of footpaths. According to the 1980 Highways Act these must be maintained in the same way as bridges and road surfaces. Ideally they should be signposted and kept clear of undergrowth; the Health and Safety at Work Act also means that dangerous animals like bulls shouldn't be kept in fields containing public rights of way.

Permitted Rights of Way

In addition to the public rights of way there are also permitted rights of way where access has been negotiated with a landowner. Charges can be made for using these routes although they are often low and don't seem to deter visitors.

National Trails

The Countryside Commission has negotiated access along ten long distance footpaths or national trails which extend through 1,742 miles of England and Wales. It funds the maintenance and signposting of these paths. The existing national trails are:

* The Pennine Way
* The Cleveland Way
* The Wolds Way
* Offa's Dyke Path
* Pembrokeshire Coast Path
* Peddars Way and Norfolk Coast Path
* The Ridgeway
* South West Coast Path
* The North Downs Way
* The South Downs Way

In 1990 the Countryside Commission was planning an eleventh national trail, the Thames Path, which would follow the river from its source in Gloucestershire to the Thames Barrier at Greenwich.

Scotland also has several long distance footpaths: the Millennium Way, the West Highland Way and the Speyside Way. In Northern Ireland the Ulster Way extends for 500 miles around the coast and there are several informal paths, like the Apple Blossom Trail in Armagh. The Isle of Man also has a Millennium Way, and two other long-distance footpaths: the Herring Road and the Road of the Gull.

FIGURE 66 THE COUNTRYSIDE ACCESS CHARTER

YOUR RIGHTS OF WAY ARE
Public footpaths - on foot only. *Sometimes waymarked in yellow*
Bridleways - on foot, horseback and pedal cycle. *Sometimes waymarked in blue*
Byways (usually old roads), most 'Roads Used and Public Paths' and, of course, public roads - all traffic.
Use maps, signs and waymarks. Ordnance Survey Pathfinder and Landranger maps show most public rights of way.

ON RIGHTS OF WAY YOU CAN
Take a pram, puchchair or wheelchair if practicable
Take a dog (on a lead or under close control)
Take a short route round an illegal obstruction or remove it sufficiently to get past.

YOU HAVE A RIGHT TO GO FOR RECREATION TO
Public parks and open spaces - on foot
Most commons near older towns and cities - on foot and sometimes on horseback
Private land where the owner has a formal agreement with the local authority.

IN ADDITION you can *use* by local or established *custom or consent*, but ask for advice if you're unsure:
Many areas of open country like moorland, fell and coastal areas, especially those of the National Trust, and some commons
Some woods and forests, especially those owned by the Forestry Commission
Country parks and picnic sites
Most beaches
Towpaths on canals and rivers
Some private paths and tracks.
Consent sometimes extends to riding horses and pedal cycles.

FOR YOUR INFORMATION
Country and metropolitan district councils and London boroughs maintain and record rights of way, and register commons and village greens
Obstructions, dangerous animals, harassment and misleading signs on rights of way are illegal and you should report them to the council
Paths across fields can be ploughed; they must normally be reinstated within two weeks
Landowners can require you to leave land to which you have no right of access
Motor vehicles are normally permitted only on roads, byways and some 'Roads Used as Public Paths'
Follow any local bylaws.

AND, WHEREVER YOU GO, FOLLOW THE COUNTRY CODE
Enjoy the countryside and respect its life and work
Guard against all risk of fire
Fasten all gates
Keep your dogs under close control
Keep to public paths across farmland
Use gates and stiles to cross fences, hedges and walls
Leave livestock, crops and machinery alone
Take your litter home
Help to keep all water clean
Protect wildlife, plants and trees
Take special care on country roads
Make no unnecessary noise.

This Charter is for practical guidance in England and Wales only. Fuller advice is given in a free booklet 'Oout in the country' available from Countryside Commission Publications Despatch Department, 19-23 Albert Road, Manchester M19 2EQ.

(Source: Countryside Commission)

Presentation of Countryside Attractions

Presenting the countryside to visitors in such a way as to make it attractive without spoiling it is particularly tricky. Providing certain basic facilities (lavatories, car parks and rubbish bins) is essential to good management. Where more vistors are expected fences, seating, picnic sites and information boards may also be needed. Sometimes visitor centres and trails of various kinds may also be appropriate. However, where it is the unspoilt nature of the countryside itself which is the attraction care must be taken that none of these facilities detracts from what people have come to see. The more people are expected, the more likely it is that there will be problems.

Wherever possible seats, picnic tables, fences and rubbish bins should be made from natural materials which will not stand out. Sometimes treated logs will make adequate and natural seating. The positioning of fences needs careful thought. Clearly they are essential where there is a danger that people might fall; for example, along some cliff-tops. However, sometimes the presence of a fence would ruin the view people have come to see. A compromise may be to fence the stretch of cliff within ten minutes' walk of the car park which is as far as most people walk. Luckily some evidence suggests that the most apparently dangerous spots may actually be safest since people anticipate danger and behave accordingly. Where people must walk across wet or uneven ground, including sand dunes, wooden boardwalks can be laid; these blend in with the scenery but make walking much easier.

Ideally litter bins and picnic tables should be placed round the edge of fields rather than in the centre where they will mar the view. Fortunately research suggests that people tend to hug the edges of open spaces anyway. The ideal picnic sites are on light, well-drained soil, particularly near water. Lavatories and litter bins should always be within easy reach of picnic sites.

Sites without visitor centres still need information boards which say who owns the land, the times and dates when it is open and any relevant by-laws. Ideally there should be site maps showing points of interest. Again, they should be as unobtrusive as possible, and preferably attached to pre-existing buildings. Alternatively they can be secured to posts reaching as much as three feet into the ground to resist wind and vandals. The ground around the post should be covered with compacted gravel or slope downwards to prevent water collecting around the base. Ideally signs should be legible from three feet away.

The best nature trails are no longer than one mile, and laid out in a figure of eight with spurs so people can turn back early if they want to. Perhaps thirty items should be highlighted. Paths should be wide enough for two people to walk side by side; winding paths also mean that it will not be necessary to see people ahead all the time. Where the trail leads to viewpoints a firmly secured telescope can be supplied.

GARDENS OPEN TO THE PUBLIC

Many country houses have beautiful grounds to match the building's grandeur, and some of these are now popular tourist attractions. At Stourhead, Athelhampton and Hever Castle nearly as many visitors visit the grounds alone as visit both the house and grounds. Even a non-traditional tourist attraction like Alton Towers has beautiful gardens that add to its appeal by providing something for those who don't like the rides.

In the UK historic gardens are not eligible for scheduling or listing so it is difficult to say precisely how many there are. However in 1977 the International Council on Monuments and Sites (ICOMOS) suggested that there were 179 in England, 45 in Scotland and 12 in Wales. English Heritage also maintains a *Register of Parks and Gardens of Special Historic Interest* which includes 1,085 entries. Of the many country houses open to the public in the UK 735 also have gardens. The National Trust owns 50 historic gardens and the National Trust for Scotland a further 23.

By 1988 ICOMOS estimated that almost 10 million people were visiting the gardens in its provisional schedule. Another half a million visited gardens open through the National Gardens Scheme. Figures had risen only slightly from those for 1987, probably because the hurricane of October 1987 did great damage to many of the gardens, forcing some of them to close temporarily.

The National Gardens Scheme

In 1927 the National Gardens Scheme was set up as a memorial to Queen Alexandra. Garden owners were asked to open to the public on specific days in the year and give the money to charity. In the first year 600 gardens held open days and the number has grown ever since. In 1988 2,200 gardens in England and Wales collected £600,000 from open days. There are similar schemes in Scotland and Northern Ireland.

Ownership of the Gardens

Under the terms of the 1983 National Heritage Act the Royal Botanic Gardens at Kew are funded by a grant from the Ministry of Agriculture, Fisheries and Food (MAFF) and administered by a board of trustees. Until 1988 the buildings were maintained by the Property Services Agency (PSA) but the Trustees now have responsibility for them as well. Other gardens belong to the National Trust along with their houses. Kew's southern offshoot, Wakeham Place, is owned by the National Trust but leased to the

Royal Botanic Gardens for research work. Many of the gardens open to the public through the National Garden Scheme are privately owned. Yet others, including Westonbirt Arboretum, belong to the Forestry Commission. The Gardens of the Rose at St. Albans are owned by the Royal National Rose Society, a registered charity.

TABLE 57 THE TEN MOST VISITED GARDENS IN BRITAIN, 1988

1.	Kew Gardens, London	1,181,245
2.	Hampton Court Gardens, London	1,000,000 *
3.	Stapeley Water Gardens	1,000,000 *
4.	Royal Botanic Gardens, Edinburgh	756,405
5.	Risley Gardens	500,000
6.	Glasgow Botanic Gardens	300,000
7.	Stourhead	214,464
8.	Westonbirt Arboretum	180,000
9.	Blenheim Palace Gardens	162,599
10.	Bodnant Garden, Colwyn Bay	149,796

(* approximate number)

Opening Gardens to the Public

Gardens are very popular with the public, but most only open during spring, summer and autumn. In 1988 the average English garden opened for only 185 days in the year and 72% of visitors were received between April and September (in Scotland nearly 92% of people time their visits for the warmer summer months).

Some gardens, like those at Hampton Court, are open free so it is difficult to tell exactly how many visitors they receive. Well-known gardens like those at Stourhead attract large numbers of visitors every year. Figures elsewhere can be boosted by specific, short-term considerations. So Arley Hall and Gardens in Cheshire won the 1987-8 Christies/Historic Houses Association Garden of the Year Award, thereby attracting extra press attention. Not surprisingly it was visited by 45,699 people in 1988, a 32% increase on the 1987 figure.

While visitors to gardens are usually drawn by a love of flowers and scenery, many such properties offer more than natural beauty. Some are, for example, the work of distinguished landscape gardeners like Capability Brown at Burton Constable and Humphrey Repton at Sheringham Hall. Kew Gardens also contain an imitation Chinese pagoda, several museums and a gallery devoted to flower paintings.

Gardens can contain general collections and be of many different dates. However, some are more specialist; the Gardens of the Rose obviously concentrate on roses and the Rococo Gardens at Painswick on special winter displays of snowdrops. Physic gardens like the one planted at Chelsea in 1673 were originally developed to grow a wide range of medicinal plants for research purposes.

WILDLIFE ATTRACTIONS

Wildlife attractions range from zoos and safari parks to the many specialised collections around the country. Within the UK they are increasingly popular despite an increasing number of opponents; 5% more people visited wildlife attractions in 1990 than in 1989.

Zoos

The word 'zoo' as an abbreviation for 'zoological gardens' was first used to refer to Clifton Zoo in Bristol in 1847 and gradually replaced the term 'menagerie' which was previously used to refer to collections of captive animals. According to the 1981 Zoo Licensing Act zoos are 'establishments where wild animals are kept for exhibition to the public'.

The Development of Zoos

Menageries existed throughout the Middle Ages. In the early 12th century Henry I kept animals, many of them gifts from other rulers, at Woodstock. Henry III moved this collection, which included a polar bear, to the Tower of London where it stayed until 1828. England's first elephant arrived in London in 1254 as a gift from Louis IX to Henry III.

However, in 1826 there were only three real zoos in England. One was at Chiswick House, another at the Exeter Exchange in the Strand and the third in the Tower of London where the public was already being admitted in the 18th century in return for payment of 1½d. They could also buy cats and dogs to feed to the lions. There were also several travelling zoos.

In 1826 Sir Stamford Raffles founded the Zoological Society of London, based on a collection of animals he had brought back from Malaya. The Society was like a private club for scientists and a few aristocrats with an interest in animals. Women were not admitted as members until 1827.

London Zoo started with a griffon vulture, a white-headed eagle, some deer and a few monkeys. In 1831 it acquired a quagga (now extinct), while in 1834 it bought an Indian rhino. In 1835 the zoo got its first chimpanzee which only survived for six months. By 1839 it also had some gibbons. However, in 1836 Charles Darwin felt that it was in too poor a condition to house the specimens he brought back from his voyages. In 1850 the first hippopotamus was acquired, and in 1887 the first male gorilla arrived. Some animals were bought, others given by members of the royal family after visits overseas.

In 1849 London Zoo's old carnivores' house was turned into the world's first reptile house. In 1853 the Zoo also opened a 'Marine and Fish Water Vivarium', the world's first public aquarium. This was closed in the 1870s and other zoos didn't copy the idea until the 1920s.

The Zoological Society of London now runs two zoos; London Zoo in Regent's Park, and Whipsnade Wild Animal Park which opened in 1931 on 500 acres of farm and downland suitable for animals that could be left to roam in paddocks. London Zoo now displays over 8,000 animals. In 1988 it was the most popular wildlife attraction in the UK with 1,326,000 visitors. Numbers dropped slightly to 1,221,000 in 1989 but it remained the top choice with visitors, probably because of its convenient position in the heart of London.

The Purpose of Zoos

Until the 17th century most zoos were seen as objects of curiosity. Research students tended to use common animals for their studies; when something more exotic was called for it was rarely obtained from a zoo.

However, in the 18th century a more scientific approach was taken to animal studies, particularly after Linnaeus produced his plant and animal classification in 1735. This new approach was reflected within the zoos so that the Zoological Society of London's charter, granted in 1829, gave the Regent's Park Zoological Gardens' purpose as 'the advancement of zoology and animal physiology and the introduction of new and curious subjects of the animal kingdom'. London Zoo was particularly successful in establishing its credentials as a scientific establishment, no doubt helped by its proximity to other academic institutions.

Once zoos were seen as scientific establishments they were quickly thought of as educational as well. Most modern zoos now label all cages with details of where the animal comes from, what it eats, etc. and provide teaching materials for schools. Some also have 'talking labels', allowing people to listen to a commentary through head-sets. Others have 'Meet the Keeper' sessions when the public can ask the experts questions.

But in the late 20th century many zoos see their primary function as conservation, particularly of endangered species. During the 1980s an animal species was probably being lost every hour; even previously common ones like the African elephant were threatened. In such circumstances zoos can provide places where endangered species can be protected. However, it is not enough simply to keep individual specimens in zoos. Several species finally became extinct inside zoos: for example, the quagga died out in 1883 in Amsterdam Zoo. To safeguard a species an organised breeding programme is required and recognition of this fact has radically altered some zoos. Traditionally they were places where a wide variety of species were on display. Now many good ones prefer to keep a larger number of animals from a smaller range of species which can be reared in breeding colonies. Thus in 1966 London Zoo kept 120 different species of animal but by 1978 the number had fallen to only 72 species.

Jersey Zoo, set up in 1959 by Gerald Durrell, doesn't even call itself a zoo any more; instead it is a 'wildlife preservation trust'. In 1963 it became a charity, dedicated to keeping only endangered species. When deciding which animals to show the Trust gives priority to those that might otherwise disappear entirely because of the loss of their habitat, and to the zoo's ability to manage them properly. Currently two-thirds of the animals on show have been bred in the Trust's grounds. Amongst its success stories are the rare pink pigeons, some of which have been returned to their native home of Mauritius.

The Zoo Licensing Act, 1984

Since 1970 the National Federation of Zoos had been pressing the government to introduce a bill to license zoos. When the Zoo Licensing Act was finally introduced in 1984 it had been drawn up after consultation with the Federation and with the RSPCA, the British Veterinary Association and other animal welfare organisations. The Act covers all aspects of animal welfare and husbandry as well as health and safety regulations to protect zoo staff and their visitors. In detail, it specifies that:

a) All zoological collections, including bird gardens, safari parks and aquaria, must have a licence to operate.
b) These licences must only be issued after a thorough inspection by government-approved inspectors and representatives of the local authority within which the attraction is based.
c) Licences will last for four years, during which time there may be periodic inspections by local authority representatives.
d) At the end of the four years establishments must be reinspected. If they meet all the required standards new six year licences can be issued.

Presentation within Zoos

Those in charge of designing zoos face a fundamental conflict between what is good for the animals and what is good for the public. Ideally animals require large enclosures with secluded areas offering them privacy. In contrast the public want smaller enclosures which make easy viewing possible, together with restaurants, shops and entertainments.

The first zoos were designed with little thought for the needs of their animal occupants. Thus London Zoo's original Lion House, designed in 1876, gave the big cats no privacy at all. Many were also bleak places and it was obvious that if they were to attract visitors they would need to be redesigned with that in mind.

In 1907 Carl Hagenbeck opened a private zoo near Hamburg in which, for the first time, he used moats to create enclosures without bars. He made them even more attractive by building up artificial hills, etc. Paths and fences kept predators away from their prey in such a way that the public saw only unbroken panoramas. London Zoo copied some of his ideas when the Mappin Terraces were built in 1913. Now zoos often use concrete, epoxy resin and other artifical materials to create natural-looking environments which are more appealing to visitors. Armoured glass, also protects the public from the animals, keeps the animals warm and creates an illusion of openness.

Originally zoos were laid out taxonomically i.e. with the animals grouped according to their biological classification into families. However some zoos are now laid out zoogeographically i.e. according to the animals' place of origin. This enables visitors to see how different animals co-exist at different levels within the same environment. To make it easy for the public to see the animals exhibitions can be designed to be long and shallow. Monorails also let them view animals from above.

New zoos are at an advantage when it comes to creating attractive settings since they don't have to start by removing the old cages (some of London Zoo's buildings, like the 19th century Camel House, are listed buldings and can't be simply demolished). They are therefore well-placed to take advantage of everything that hi-tech now makes possible.

Visitors are often upset by the repetitive behaviour of bored animals. Several zoos have tried to overcome this problem by providing distractions for the animals, usually related to feeding, that will also entertain on-lookers. In London Zoo marmosets burrow into artifical trees in search of gum, while in Glasgow Zoo Himalayan bears have to search for food scattered around the hillside. However, while the public will happily watch animals catching and eating fish and insects, they're more squeamish about watching carnivores hunting for their food which restricts what can be done for them.

London Zoo's Snowden Aviary which opened in 1965 was one of the first aviaries designed to let birds fly freely. Walk-through humming-bird exhibitions are now also commonplace, with double entrance and exit doors to make sure birds can't escape into the cold outside. Finding new ways to display birds of prey has taken longer but in late 1990 London Zoo opened an Africa Aviary with synthetic African landscapes in place of bare concrete floors, and 'invisible' mesh to create an illusion of openness.

One particular presentational problem has been that many animals are nocturnal; under normal conditions day-time visitors either don't see them at all or see them sleeping. Many zoos have resolved this problem by building special dimly-lit houses in which day is turned into night where people can see little known animals going about their normal lives. In 1967 the Charles Clore Pavilion for Small Mammals at London Zoo was designed with just such a 'Moonlight World'.

Some animals are much more naturally popular with visitors than others. Research has suggested that visitors to reptiles and amphibians spend only seconds in front of each display, so extra effort is needed to interest visitors in them. In 1989 London Zoo's plans for a £35 million facelift included a walk-through vivarium featuring spiders, insects, etc.

In zoos where entertainment is seen as important animal shows still take place. However, in 1972 London Zoo stopped the popular chimps' tea parties. In order to take part in them chimps had to be hand-reared. Unfortunately at puberty they became too unruly to continue play-acting but couldn't be returned to the captive troop because they were not used to living with it.

Funding Zoos

Many zoos around the world have their capital costs paid either by central or local government. However, running costs must often be met from entrance fees and these can be very high. For example, London and Whipsnade Zoos employ about 500 staff, half looking after the animals and half dealing with the public. They also run a library, two reserach laboratories, a hospital, a pathology department, a quarantine station and an education centre. The cost of keeping different animals varies, with carnivores costing the most in food bills and gorillas the most in medical fees. London Zoo in particular is also hampered by a backlog of costly maintenance work needed to make its listed buildings more appealing; the estimated cost of demolishing the listed Mappin Terraces which have outlived their useful live is £6 million. Since most zoos are outdoor attractions they are rarely financially viable all year round.

Where zoos depend on admission fees for their income this can influence the animals they choose to keep. Whipsnade Zoo's financial problems meant that a commercial partner was sought in 1989. However, the changes that would have been needed to produce an adequate return on the capital invested would not have been in keeping with the Zoological Society's overall aims in which conservation and education feature prominently.

Attendances at Zoos

When it was first set up London Zoo was popular and fashionable. In 1831 there were 250,000 visitors, and until 1836 never fewer than 210,000 a year. After that visitor numbers declined and by 1843 there were less than 100,000 a year. However, the arrival of a new animal could double numbers, as happened in 1850 when the first hippopotamus was bought from Egypt for £350. The birth of a particularly appealing baby animal could have the same effect; when the polar bear, Brumas, was born in 1950 it pushed London Zoo's visitor figures back up to 3 million. In general in the late 20th century conventional zoos had more difficulty attracting visitors, partly because of competition from safari parks and partly because of changing attitudes towards keeping animals in captivity.

FIGURE 67 THE MOST POPULAR WILDLIFE ATTRACTIONS IN THE UK, 1989

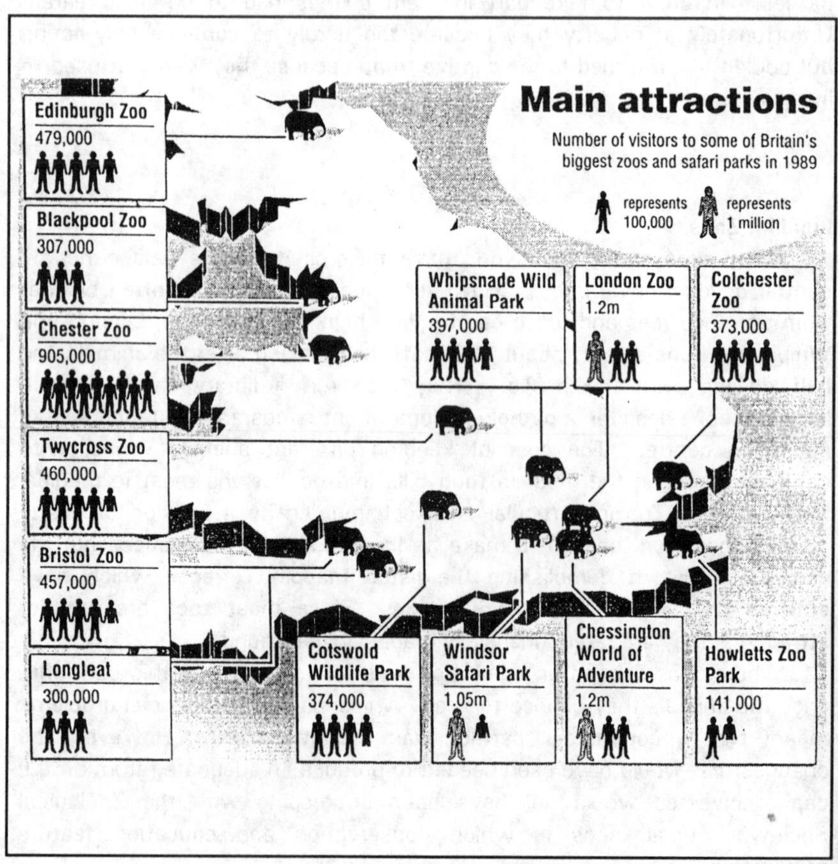

(Source: *The Guardian*, 1989)

Safari Parks

Some people have always objected to caged animals. For example, during the French Revolution the crowds demanded the release of the animals in the Versailles Menagerie; the least dangerous were freed, the most dangerous eaten. However, it wasn't until the 1960s that such demands really began to bear fruit. Conventional zoos experimented with more imaginative ways to keep animals while other people turned their minds to alternatives. Safari parks built both on the popularity of real safaris and on the success of the African game parks in conserving surplus giraffes, zebras, lions and antelopes which could be shipped to England for show in more 'natural' surroundings than a zoo.

England's first safari park was set up in the grounds of Longleat House in 1966 when Lord Bath collaborated with Jimmy Chipperfield (of Chipperfield's Circus) to bring lions from various different zoological collections to the grounds of his stately home, then receiving an average 135,000 people a year. The original 'Lions of Longleat' were quickly joined by giraffes, zebras, camels, elephants, baboons, rhinoceroses and other wild animals. Visitor numbers soared to an average 500,000 a year.

TABLE 58 OTHER WILDLIFE ATTRACTIONS

Type of Attraction	Examples
Aquaria	Brighton; Sea Life Centre, Blackpool
Wildfowl Trust reserves	Slimbridge; Martin Mere; Arundel; Washington; Peakirk; Welney; Caerlaverock; Richmond-upon-Thames (planned)
Bird sanctuaries	Minsmere
Falconry centres	Newent; Weyhill
Swannery	Abbotsbury
Rare breeds farms	Cotswold Farm Park; Croxteth Home Farm; Graves Park, Sheffield
Heavy horse attractions	Horse at Work exhibition in Halifax; Norfolk Shire Horse Centre at West Runton; Courage Shire Horse Centre
City farms	Kentish Town, London; Windmill Hill, Bristol
Trout farms	Bibury, Gloucestershire
Butterfly farms	Tropical Butterfly Garden, Cleethorpes; Butterfly Centre, Newent; Great Yarmouth Sea-front Butterfly Farm; World of Butterflies, Whitchurch.
Specialist wildlife attractions	Earsham Otter Trust, Norfolk; Seal Sanctuary, Gweek; Woolly Monkey Sanctuary, Looe; Birdland, Bourton-on-the-Water, Gloucestershire

Safari parks allow visitors to drive through countryside and view animals from their cars. Safety precautions are meticulous, with notices reminding people to stay in their car and sound the horn if they are in trouble. So far the parks have an admirable safety record.

The boundary between safari parks and leisure parks is often blurred, and visitors to Longleat can also explore a maze, visit a Dr. Who exhibition, shop in a garden centre and souvenir shop, while away a few hours in an amusement arcade, and tour the House and gardens.

In addition to the safari parks, Britain also has **zoo parks** and **wildlife parks** which exhibit animals in traditional zoo fashion but in more attractively rural surroundings. Zoo parks include Howlett's and Drusilla's, and the zoo at Port Lympne. There are wildlife parks at Cricket St. Thomas and Burford (Cotswold Wildlife Park).

CHAPTER NINE
THE ARTS

Many tourists are attracted to the UK by its great cultural traditions, by the many art galleries, theatres, concert halls, opera houses, etc. Despite government reluctance to subsidise the arts there is growing recognition that they make a valuable contribution to the gross national product, albeit one that is sometimes difficult to quantify. By the late 1980s the arts were estimated to have had an annual turnover of roughly £10 billion, or 2.5% of all spending on goods and services in the UK. The arts were increasingly seen both as a catalyst for urban renewal (as in the case of the Alhambra Theatre in Bradford) and as a stimulus to tourism (as with the creation of the brand-new Tate of the North in Liverpool's Albert Dock). It was even suggested that 100,000 visitors to a temporary exhibition at the Royal Academy could benefit the economy to the tune of £6 million. In 1985 Sir William Rees-Mogg, then Chair of the Arts Council, commented that 'the arts are to British tourism what the sun is to Spain'.

What are 'the Arts'?

In its broadest sense the term 'the arts' encompasses not only the creative arts, crafts, art galleries and the art trade, but also theatres and concerts, the music industry, publishing, broadcasting and the museums. Museums have already been considered in Chapter Seven. The other arts of particular relevance to tourism are the *visual arts* which include fine arts (painting, sculpture, etc.) and decorative arts (textiles, furnishings, porcelain, etc.), and the *performing arts* (drama, concerts, etc.).

The Arts and Tourism

Surveys suggest that cultural attractions are high on the list of reasons overseas visitors give for coming to the UK. This is particularly the case with those who come to London, and many arts venues in the capital receive a high percentage of overseas tourists; in 1985/6 37% of audiences at West End theatres came from overseas, while in 1989 50% of visitors to the National Portrait Gallery were foreigners. The bias towards London is probably most pronounced because the best known national art collections are in the capital, as are most of the world-famous theatres, opera houses and concert halls. However, overseas visitors seem less likely to attend concerts, ballets and plays while in the UK, perhaps because music sounds the same at home, while plays present a language barrier to some of them. Outside London tourists probably only make up 5% to 10% of visitors to arts venues. Places like the Royal Shakespeare

Theatre in Stratford and the Aldeburgh Festival, with an international reputation, are the exception. However, in the late 1980s there were signs of a growth in regional arts tourism to places like Glasgow.

Domestic tourists make up a high percentage of visitors to art galleries and other arts attractions; in 1985/6 26% of audiences at West End theatres were from elsewhere in the UK, while 60% of a typical Royal Shakespeare Theatre audience has usually travelled more than fifty miles to get there.

Some money is made out of tourists directly from admission charges to art galleries, theatres, concerts, etc. However, even more is made because most of them buy food and drinks, guidebooks, postcards and other items during their visit.

Art Galleries

In Britain the fine arts are usually displayed in art galleries, although the decorative arts may be shown in museums. However, this divide is not absolute; paintings from non-European traditions also tend to be kept in museums. So the National and Tate Galleries display the best European, British and North American paintings, while the Victoria and Albert Museum shows Moghul Indian paintings alongside other *objets d'art*, like bronzes, pottery and statues.

Evolution of Art Galleries

During the Middle Ages churches and monasteries were the main repositories of works of art, which were viewed by the public as part of religious observances rather than as beautiful objects in their own right. Then in the late 15th century the Renaissance brought a new interest in art for its own sake; wealthy patrons like the Medici in Florence sponsored the production of works of art and built up their own private collections. Paintings came to be valued purely as works of art, set apart from any other context. Artists also began to be valued for their talents.

The Grand Tour encouraged both a wider interest in art and more private collectors. By the 18th century some of them were already showing their collections to the public. Just as many museums started life as private collections, private art collections often formed the basis for later public art galleries. However, their survival was sometimes precarious, particularly when the original collector died; in the 18th century Robert Walpole's Houghton Collection was sold to Catherine the Great. Collections at Stowe and Marlborough were also sold abroad. In 1824 the government bought John Julius Angerstein's collection for £57,000. In 1838 it was moved to Trafalgar Square to form the nucleus of what is now the National Gallery. When Henry Tate gave sixty modern British paintings to the

National Gallery in 1890, a brand-new gallery for modern art was created to house them; the Tate Gallery opened in 1897. Private collectors continue to influence the art world today, partly because individuals can build up collections of works that only become fashionable later on. In 1973 Sir Robert and Lady Sainsbury bequeathed their entire collection of modern and non-European art to the University of East Anglia. Their son David also provided a £3 million endowment to build the Sainsbury Centre for the Visual Arts.

Like museums, art collections were seen as having an educational purpose. So when the Victoria and Albert Museum opened in 1852 it aimed to promote good design and improve standards of public taste. However, as the concept of 'art criticism' evolved in the 19th century it tended to build a barrier between ordinary people and works of art, elevating art into something remote from everyday experience.

The 1989 Arts Review Yearbook listed 593 art galleries in England, 105 in Scotland and 37 in Wales (in Northern Ireland most paintings are displayed either in the Ulster Museum or the Belfast Gallery). Some of these galleries, particularly in London, are commercial ventures offering short-term exhibitions while also selling works of art. About 150 of Britain's stately homes also contain major art collections.

In addition to the full time galleries London in particular has several venues offering regular temporary art exhibitions, including the Hayward, Royal Academy and Barbican Galleries.

TABLE 59 THE TEN MOST VISITED ART GALLERIES IN THE UK, 1988

1.	National Gallery, London	3,228,153
2.	Tate Gallery, London	1,581,467
3.	Victoria and Albert Museum, London	997,000
4.	Royal Academy, London	987,018
5.	Glasgow Museum and Art Gallery	926,804
6.	National Portrait Gallery, London	639,795
7.	Birmingham Museum and Art Gallery	598,856
8.	Burrell Collection, Glasgow	580,357
9.	Nottingham Castle Museum and Art Gallery	500,512
10.	Tate of the North, Liverpool	500,000

Although half of England's population lives in the North and the Midlands, three-quarters of the art galleries are concentrated in East Anglia and Southern England, with 46% of them in London. However, while the number of galleries open to the public has increased since 1979 in Scotland

and Wales, it has decreased in London; most of the closures have been commercial galleries.

Types of Art Gallery

Just as the national museums mainly started life as comprehensive collections, the national art galleries tend to show a wide range of paintings of all dates and by a variety of artists. However, there are some more specialist collections. For example, several galleries, including the Tate, specialise in modern art. Portrait galleries, which were a relatively recent development, concentrate on pictures of famous people. Other galleries focus on individual artists: for example, the Marianne North Gallery at Kew and the Stanley Spencer Gallery in Cookham. Photographic galleries can also be seen as a form of modern specialist art gallery.

Ownership of the Art Galleries

Several art galleries have 'national' status and are funded directly by the government, through the Office of Arts and Libraries. These are:

The National Gallery
The Tate Gallery
The National Portrait Gallery (offshoots at Montacute House, Beninborough Hall and Bodelwyddan Castle)
The Victoria and Albert Museum (branches at Apsley House (the Wellington Museum), Ham and Osterley Park Houses, the Theatre Museum in Covent Garden and the Bethnal Green Museum of Childhood)
The National Museums and Galleries on Merseyside
The Wallace Collection
The National Gallery of Scotland

Others are owned by local authorities and are often housed in the same building as the local museum (the Castle Museum and Art Gallery, Nottingham; the City Museum and Art Gallery, Stoke, etc.); in 1988 the most popular local authority gallery was Glasgow Art Gallery and Museum which received 927,000 visitors, probably because of the Garden Festival. Some galleries are independently owned and run, perhaps by a group of trustees like the Stanley Spencer Gallery in Cookham. Others are owned and run by private individuals or companies as purely commercial ventures.

Art Galleries and Display

Like museums, many art galleries are housed in old buildings which are not necessarily well adapted to modern presentation techniques and may even make conserving the collections difficult. When the Victoria and

Albert Museum took over the running of its building from the Property Services Agency in 1988 it inherited wiring that presented a fire hazard, leaky central heating, poor drainage, leaking roofs and inadequate fire exits. Its trustees estimated that it would cost £50 million just to put right these problems and that £125 million would be needed to maintain the building over the next decade. In 1988 the Museums Association believed the national museums and art galleries would need an additional grant of £200 million between them to make good past problems.

Art galleries are completely unnatural places. Almost all works of art were designed as individual entities and were meant to be appreciated as such rather than gathered together with other competing works. Many items that now hang in art galleries were not even created as works of art but as religious objects, perhaps for medieval church altars. Removing such items to an art gallery can alter their relationship with the viewer, turning what was once an emotional experience into an intellectual one.

Like museums art galleries have had to adapt their display techniques to take account of changing tastes. In the 19th century art gallery walls were literally papered with paintings, a layout which can still be seen in the Marianne North Gallery in Kew Gardens. During the Second World War the National Gallery stayed open showing just one picture at a time which helped bring about a change in attitudes towards picture display that has endured. Now the preference is for fewer pictures, individually displayed and lit. Ideally some paintings should be displayed alongside decorative art items like furnishings as they would have been in their original homes. So stately homes often make more natural settings for pictures, although they may attract less attention because of competition from the architecture, fittings and historical connections of the building.

Inevitably the more pictures are spaced out on the walls the more display room is required. Most of the big national collections own more items than they can put on show, but the National Gallery has almost all its paintings on display. In 1988 a government report criticised the Tate Gallery and the Victoria and Albert Museum for not displaying all their possessions. However, they argue that many of the pictures are of mainly academic interest and can be seen by scholars on request. Some of the Tate's reserve collections are now on show at the Tate of the North Gallery in Liverpool which opened in 1988, while the Victoria and Albert Museum plans a branch gallery in Manningham Mills, Bradford, where its South Asian collections will be suitably displayed. The opening of the Theatre Museum in Covent Garden in 1987 enabled the V & A to put another, specialised collection on public display, albeit it in a different building.

Traditionally paintings have been displayed according to different 'schools' in accordance with Vasari's *Lives of the Artists*. So Dutch and

Italian paintings of the 16th century would appear in different areas of the gallery. However, in 1990 under the directorship of Neil MacGregor, the National Gallery broke with this tradition and rehung its paintings in a continuous time line running from 1260 to 1910.

Art Galleries and Security

Like museums, art galleries must be designed and laid out with security in mind. As the price of paintings has risen on world markets there have been more thefts, sometimes of well-known paintings, many of them apparently by thieves with a specific hit list. The risk can be minimised by fitting adequate alarms, keeping custodians in each room and hanging small pictures away from doors and windows.

Pictures also need to be protected against physical attack by people with grievances. Paintings in the National Gallery and National Portrait Gallery have been slashed, and Leonardo da Vinci's famous cartoon in the National Gallery was actually shot. Guarding against such attacks is particularly difficult and may require the installation of special security devices.

Paintings must also be protected against damage both from changes in humidity and from the elements. Modern galleries usually have de-humidifiers in all the rooms to remove excess moisture from the air. Air conditioning may also be installed. Pictures also need to be kept away from direct sunlight which can lead the colours to fade and the paint to crack. Some paintings are protected by glass, but this can cause problems of reflection, making it difficult for visitors to appreciate them

Art Galleries and Funding

Traditionally the national art collections didn't charge for admission. However, since the 1983 National Heritage Age gave them 'trustee status', their annual grants have been frozen. In 1988 they were also required to take over the running of the buildings from the Property Services Agency. By March 1989 the Victoria and Albert Museum calculated that the real value of its grant had fallen by 90% over the previous five years, at a time when staff salaries were rising at more than the rate of inflation and art prices at auction were soaring.

In 1988 a system of three year rolling funding was introduced; museums and galleries were to be given a grant for one year and told what they could expect over the next two, with allowance being made for rising costs. At the end of each year a new third year was to be added to make forward financial planning easier. However, the inflation rate was under-estimated, leaving little for running costs once this had been taken into account; in 1989 grants rose by 2.9%, even though salaries (linked to Civil Service pay scales and agreed with the Treasury) rose by 10%.

Local authorities have been entitled to use money from the rates (the community charge since 1989) to support art galleries since the passing of the 1948 Local Government Act. By 1987/8 they were spending £93 million to support roughly 750 museums and art galleries. The Victoria and Albert Museum also administers a government-backed Purchase Grant Fund with an annual budget of £1,114,000 to help local museums and galleries purchase suitable items. However, there is not enough money to meet all the requests for assistance.

The Arts Council

In 1967 the Arts Council of Great Britain's royal charter stated that its aims were:

a) to develop and improve knowledge, understanding and practice of the arts
b) to increase public access to the arts
c) to advise and co-operate with government departments, local authorities and other bodies over arts' issues

The Arts Council is funded by the Office of Arts and Libraries but provides 'arm's length' funding, rather than direct government funding which is what happens with the national art galleries. It tends to support the performing arts and avant garde art in particular. In 1991 the Arts Council received an unexpected 14% increase in its grant to enable it to help its clients cope with the effects of the recession and the fall-off of tourism after the Gulf War.

Many local galleries receive support from the Arts Council or its equivalents, the Scottish and Welsh Arts Councils. The abolition of the Greater London Council and the Metropolitan Authorities in 1984 left the Arts Council to pick up the funding of many arts organisations, although its grant did not increase in line with what had been lost. Subsequently it published a report called *The Glory of the Garden*, laying out a strategy for subsidising local arts ventures. It said that funding was disproportionately slanted towards London and proposed that more money should be diverted to the regions. Although galleries like Bristol's Arnolfini received more money, in 1987/8 the per head subsidy to the arts in London still worked out at £7.92 compared with £1.94 in Merseyside.

Other local art galleries in England and Wales receive money from Regional Arts Associations (RAAs) which are, in turn, funded by the Arts Councils, local authorities, the Crafts Council, the British Film Institute and the Welsh Office. In 1989 more Arts Council-funding was devolved to the Regional Arts Association which were renamed Regional Arts Boards (RABs).

Other Sources of Funding

Arts Council figures show that art galleries, like museums, are raising more of their income from sources other than public subsidy. In 1988 only 28% of the income of visual arts associations came from box office receipts or other earned income; by 1989 the proportion had risen to 42%. In 1988/9 the National Gallery made more than £1 million from its bookshops and publishing ventures. But charging for admission to art galleries is controversial. In 1985 the Victoria and Albert Museum's 'voluntary' charges brought in £400,000 in the first year, rising to £700,000 in 1989. However attendances plummeted by about 700,000. Charging for temporary exhibitions is less controversial; the Royal Academy and Tate Gallery routinely do this, even though entry to the main Tate collections remains free. Some local art galleries, particularly the privately owned ones, also charge for admission.

In 1976 an **Association for Business Sponsorship of the Arts (ABSA)** was established. In 1980 the government gave ABSA £25,000 to encourage its work, and in 1984 it set up a **Business Sponsorship Incentive Scheme.** ABSA administered this scheme but the government matched money given by new sponsors on a pound for pound basis, and by old sponsors on a one pound to three pounds basis upto a total of £25,000. By 1987/8 the Office of Arts and Libraries was providing £1.75 million in matching grants through the Scheme. By 1989 business sponsorship of the arts had risen to £33 million, although this was still only about 5% of the visual and performing arts' total income.

However, it's easier to attract sponsorship for specific, high profile exhibitions or for capital projects than it is to get companies or individuals to underwrite annual running costs. So the new Gallery of Japanese Art and Design at the V & A was sponsored by Toshiba International Ltd, but no one has offered to make up the shortfall in its wages bill. Nor do corporate sponsors usually act out of kindness or from a love of art; instead they see sponsorship as a relatively cheap and cost-effective form of advertising. Consequently their choice of what to sponsor is likely to be conservative and London-centred. In 1988/9 the largest single sponsorship of the visual arts came from IBM UK who provided financial support for the Hayward Gallery's Leonardo da Vinci exhibition which was guaranteed to attract large audiences. It's much harder to attract sponsorship for modern, innovative work for which there may be a smaller audience or for exhibitions in the provinces. So no large sponsors could be found for the

1991 Royal Academy exhibition of the work of Egon Schiele, seen as controversial because of his sexually explicit pictures. Business sponsors can also have too much say over the content of an exhibition. Thus when Coca Cola sponsored the 'Designing A Megabrand' exhibition in the V & A's Boilerhouse Gallery critics argued that it became little more than a showcase for the company. What's more, during a recession sponsorship tends to dry up just as it is most needed.

Figures published by the Policy Studies Institute in 1990 show that public subsidy to the arts in the UK is much lower than in other European countries. In the UK the subsidy worked out at £9.80 a head, compared with £17.50 in Sweden, £20.50 in The Netherlands, £21.40 in France and £24.00 in Germany.

The Purchase Problem

Since 1985 the national art collections have seen their purchase grants (the annual sums available to buy new items) frozen. Although some already own more items than they can display, there are still gaps in their collections which need filling. The purchase of contemporary art also needs to be an on-going process. Major art works in private collections still occasionally come on to the market and ought to be bought for the public collections. At the same time prices for works of art have soared to ridiculous levels. Between 1830 and 1880 only one sale per decade at Christie's raised more than £50,000. Between 1880 and 1914 fifty sales raised more than £50,000. Since then prices, particularly for 19th and early 20th century paintings and Old Masters, have soared. In 1987/8 64 works of art were sold for more than £1 million, including van Gogh's 'Irises' which was sold for $53 million (about £31 million) at Sotheby's.

THE NATIONAL ART COLLECTIONS FUND

The National Art Collections Fund is a charity which was set up in 1903 and which gives grants to museums and art galleries to help them buy works of art. In 1905 it bought Velazquez's *Rokeby Venus* for the National Gallery and in 1929 it helped it buy the *Wilton Diptych*. In 1988 it dispensed 75 grants totalling £1,619,490. One of its largest ever grants was the £250,000 it gave to the National Gallery and National Gallery for Wales to buy a Poussin, but in a typical year it now spends about £2 million. By 1991 it had helped save over 10,000 works of art. It has no government grant and depends on donations and membership subscriptions.

The market seemed to peak in 1989, but the combination of static purchase grants and soaring art prices has almost frozen the public collections out of the market.

Temporary Exhibitions

Temporary exhibitions are particularly important to the visual arts and attract the sort of publicity which makes them appeal to business sponsors. Several of London's main art galleries hold regular temporary exhibitions which are a useful source of funding, particularly because they generate spin-off sales of catalogues, postcards and other merchandise. The Tate Gallery usually has three big temporary exhibitions a year which can be very well-attended; for example, in 1984 224,759 people paid to see the Pre-Raphaelite exhibition.

Other galleries like the Hayward and the Royal Academy of Arts are primarily temporary exhibition halls. Every year the Royal Academy hosts major exhibitions which attract queues and many overseas visitors (it now sells timed tickets to get round the queuing problem). In addition it hosts the annual Summer Exhibition of work by contemporary artists which has drawn more than 100,000 visitors a year since 1983 and produces sales worth over £1 million a year. The Hayward Gallery, opened in 1968, is run by the South Bank Board and regularly hosts popular temporary exhibitions.

One problem for patrons of temporary exhibitions is the cost of insuring borrowed items against damage or theft. However, the Museums and Galleries Commission runs a government indemnity scheme for non-national galleries to save them from the prohibitive cost of commercial insurance.

THEATRES

The word 'theatre' can be used to describe either a type of performance (drama, opera, etc.) or the place where it takes place (theatre, opera house, etc.). It is also used in descriptive phrases like 'mainstream theatre', 'alternative/fringe theatre', 'commercial theatre' and 'subsidised theatre'.

Some theatre buildings have regular companies attached to them, like the Royal Shakespeare Company at the Barbican Theatre. Other theatre companies don't have permanent bases and tour a lot using theatres all round the country. Finally some theatre buildings don't have companies based in them but are available for use either by touring companies or by casts brought together for specific commercial plays.

Evolution of the Theatre

Theatres have existed since Classical times when the Greeks staged plays in semi-circular outdoor arenas. However, it wasn't until 1576 that London got its first real playhouse, an unroofed, circular building called simply 'The Theatre'. In 1597 this was pulled down and some of its timbers reused to build the Globe Theatre in Southwark where Shakespeare later performed. During the Commonwealth period theatres were closed down as frivolous, only to open again in 1660 with the restoration of the monarchy. It wasn't until the 18th century that most theatres took on the horseshoe shape with tiered balconies which is now standard.

In the 18th century theatres became very grand, a trend which continued in the 19th century when many were built with impressive exteriors, complete with porticoes and colonnades. Inside plush velvet and gilt fittings became the norm. Sometimes decoration even got in the way of the purpose, with pillars obscuring the stage view from some seats.

In Britain many local seaside theatres opened in the late 19th/early 20th centuries as part of a policy to lure tourists to the resorts. Some have since been taken over by local authorities.

In the 20th century theatre design has become simpler, if more adventurous. Some theatres, like the New Victoria in Newcastle-under-Lyme, stage plays in the round with minimal scenery, while others have done away with the proscenium arch in favour of more open stages. New theatres have also been designed without the sort of balconies and steep upper circles that could induce vertigo and often offered only partial views of the stage; when the Barbican Theatre opened in 1982 its three circles only had two rows each and these jutted forward towards the stage for easy viewing, rather than sloping backwards as in traditional theatres. Both the Lyttelton Theatre (at the National) and the Barbican were designed without permanent space in front of the stage for an orchestra but with adaptable stall seating which could be removed to provide a pit when necessary.

By 1990 the UK had about 300 theatres, seating between 200 and 2,300 people. Most were owned by local authorities and were non-profit-making. Just over thirty had resident companies. In 1989 237 product-ions opened in London's West End and there were 10,944,760 paid attendances at 16,436 performances in 42 theatres.

Theatres and Tourism

London theatres in particular attract many overseas visitors with an interest in drama. However, theatres also serve as tourist attractions in other ways:

a) Active modern theatres like the National Theatre in London and the Old Vic in Bristol offer guided tours of their buildings.

b) Famous historical theatres may even by rebuilt. The Globe Theatre is being reconstructed in Southwark and is bound to be very popular with tourists.

In 1985/6 Society of West End Theatres, (SWET) figures suggested that visitors to London theatres spent the following on incidental items:

TABLE 60 INCIDENTAL EXPENDITURE BY THEATRE VISITORS, 1985/6

	£(millions)
Eating out and restaurants	68.0
Accommodation for trip	13.0
Public transport	10.5
Taxis	5.0
Parking/petrol	4.4
Drinks/sweets	3.0

London's Theatres

Some of London's theatres are major tourist attractions. In the West End (bordered by Oxford Street to the north, Strand to the south, Kingsway to the east and Regent Street to the west) there are more than forty theatres. In 1987 SWET estimated that 37% of their audiences came from overseas, while a further 26% came from outside London, making it unlikely that so many could be supported without the tourists. Overseas visitors also seem to be making up an increasing proportion of the audience; between 1982 and 1985 ticket sales to overseas visitors grew by 68%. Many theatres had a particularly tough year in 1986 when fears of retaliation after the Libya bombing and worries over Chernobyl caused many Americans to stay at home. Most overseas theatre-goers come from the United States (18%), followed by Canada and Sweden.

The Provincial Theatres

Outside London theatres generally rely on a local clientele. The Royal Shakespeare Theatre in Stratford-upon-Avon is exceptional in being as dependent on tourists as the West End theatres. Nevertheless a successful provincial theatre can help create a climate in which cultural tourism will flourish. Thus the rehabilitation of the Alhambra Theatre in Bradford was important in the city's strategy to attract tourism. Glasgow's Citizen's Theatre is also thought to have played a part in the revival of the city's fortunes, culminating in its being declared European City of Culture in 1990. (See page 260).

Some theatres are run as charitable trusts, with unpaid directors and representatives of those providing the funding on their boards. Trust theatres are usually established as limited companies by guarantee and the trustees have only limited liability. They are normally eligible for a range of tax benefits.

Many provincial theatres are funded and administered by local authorities, and may be more expensive to run than trust theatres because local authority pay scales tend to be higher. By 1990 many such theatres were struggling. In the 1980s they were expected to generate more money from box office receipts and sponsorship as subsidies were frozen or reduced. The community charge also forced many authorities to look for economies and arts budgets were particularly vulnerable. The European Regional Development Fund has helped the Plymouth Theatre Royal, Bradford's Alhambra and Newcastle's Theatre Royal.

The Plays

On any one night in London a wide choice of theatrical entertainments will be on offer, ranging from Shakespeare and serious drama at the Barbican and National Theatres, to long-running farces like *No Sex Please, We're British*, thrillers like *The Mousetrap*, and musicals like *Joseph's Amazing Technicolour Dreamcoat* and *Cats*. The cost of staging serious plays, particularly with large casts, means that few commercial theatres can afford to take the risk. Consequently most of the innovative and experimental plays will be at the subsidised theatres: the National, Barbican and Royal Court. After a successful run some plays then transfer to West End theatres, as happened in 1986 when the Royal Shakespeare Company's production of *Les Liaisons Dangereuses* transferred from The Pit (Barbican) to the Ambassadors Theatre. This phenomenon led the 1987/8 Cork Report to conclude that the subsidised theatres were offering a research and development operation for the English theatre. At the same time, the subsidised theatres are staging more commercial plays, including musicals, in an effort to become self-supporting.

Musicals have always been important to the West End but got a new lease of life in 1972 when Tim Rice and Andrew Lloyd Webber staged *Jesus Christ Superstar* at the Palace, introducing a new, younger audience to the medium. They are now the most popular box office events and did well even in 1986 when other theatres were struggling.

The Mousetrap, adapted from Agatha Christie's *Three Blind Mice*, has been running since 1952. The longer a play runs the more likely it is that much of its audience will be from outside London. *The Mousetrap* is now a tourist attraction as much because of its fame as the world's longest running play as because of its intrinsic dramatic merit.

Funding the Theatres

Theatres are expensive to run. Although wages are relatively low, theatres are labour-intensive with not just the actors, actresses and producers but all the stage designers, make-up artists, costume-makers, musicians, stagehands, etc. to pay. Rehearsal time must also be financed. Buildings, particularly the older ones, may be expensive to maintain and heat. Theatres that depend on tourists will still have to bear fixed maintenance costs during winter despite smaller audiences.

Costs can be divided into:

a) Overheads - rent, utility costs, administration, costs related to the public, general stage costs which are not tied to a specific production, contingencies, etc.
b) Production costs - scenery and other physical production costs, fees, advert-ising and publicity, rehearsal expenses, scripts and other miscellaneous costs.
c) Running costs - fees to stars, authors, designers, the Performing Rights Society, etc.

FIGURE 68 COST OF MOUNTING THE NEW PRODUCTION OF *CHILDREN OF EDEN*, 1991

Where the money goes

Cost of mounting production	£2,200,000
	£
Rehearsal wages and salaries	246,000
Fees and expenses	260,000
Transport, travel and subsistence	30,000
Set, wardrobe, lighting etc.	1,000,000
Running expenses	75,000
Marketing and promotion	230,000
Administration	70,000

Cost of running show per week	
Wages and running expenses	94,000
Royalties to composer and theatre	25,000

To make a profit the show needs
100 per cent business for 24 weeks
90 per cent business for 29 weeks
80 per cent business for 38 weeks

(Source: *Independent on Sunday*, 1991)

The Subsidised Theatre

England's main subsidised theatres are those used by the Royal Shakespeare Company (the Royal Shakespeare, Other Place and Swan Theatres in Stratford; the Barbican, Pit and Mermaid Theatres in London; and the Theatre Royal, Gulbenkian Studio and People's Theatre in

Newcastle), the National Theatre (Olivier, Lyttelton and Cottesloe Theatres) and the Royal Court. However, few theatres can be run on totally commercial lines; most local theatres receive grants from their local authority or arts council.

In addition to the money taken at the box office and from ancillary sales, the subsidised theatres also receive government funding. In 1984 it was agreed that the value of its grant to the RSC (then 41% of its costs) should be maintained. Nevertheless, by 1989 it had fallen by £2.2 million in real terms (to 27% of its costs). Over the 1989/90 season it fell by another estimated £855,000 in real terms. The RSC is lucky to have received sponsorship worth £2.9 million from Royal Insurance to help it widen its activities. But in the 1989 Arts Council report the Group's Chief Executive emphasised the limitations on this sort of sponsorship when he said his company was only interested in sponsoring a well-established company with an international reputation to which its name could be linked for publicity purposes.

TABLE 61 SOURCES OF RSC'S FUNDING, 1987/8

	£
Box office	8,681,000
Central government grant	5,686,000
Other trading	1,954,000
Sponsorship/donations	494,000
Local authority grants	45,000
Total:	**16,860,000**

By 1990 the RSC was attracting audiences of more than a million a year to the Barbican. Since 1985 it had increased its income from sponsorship by 25% and from transfers by 403%. In 1989 it received £5,882,000 in government grants but paid back £5,989,000 in VAT and indirect taxes. Faced with a deficit of £2 million by the end of 1990/1 it closed the Barbican Theatre for the winter.

Commercial Theatres

The SWET theatres are the closest to pure commercial theatres in the UK. However, the land they stand on would probably be worth more to developers than can be made from staging plays. They stay open mainly because planning restrictions make it difficult to demolish theatres and because of philanthropic leaseholders.

Plays at commercial theatres are usually financed as individual entities. A producing management assembles a cast and finds investors to put up the production costs for the first few weeks. The producer is paid a weekly fee but doesn't make real money until the production costs have been covered. The first profits are returned to the investors until the break-even point is reached; then they are split, with 40% going to the producers and 60% to the investors. By the start of 1990 investors in *Les Miserables* had netted a £6 million profit, but in general new plays are high risk investments.

Commercial theatres must make most of their money from box office takings and ancillary sales. Since 1979/80 ticket prices have risen faster than the retail price index as theatres moved away from dependence on grants to greater self-sufficiency. However, by 1987 the average UK theatre still raised only 48% of its income from the box office.

Constant price rises above the rate of inflation present potential problems. Although there is some evidence that the average age of audiences is falling, particularly because of the number of overseas visitors under the age of forty-five, there is a danger that younger people won't be able to afford tickets and won't develop the theatre-going habit. Theatres try to get round this problem by offering a range of tickets to suit most pockets. Thus those in the stalls indirectly subsidise those in the 'gods' (the upper circle). The subsidised theatres also offer stand-by student concessions, while other theatres sell cheaper 'view-impeded' or 'standing' seats. SWET also sells same-day half-price tickets from a booth in Leicester Square; theatres would prefer to sell unfilled seats at the last minute for half the price rather than lose 100% of their value if the curtain rises with the seat still empty.

When capital needs to be invested (for example, for computerising lights or the box office), a theatre may be able to get help from a local authority or the Arts Council. They may also be able to run up a temporary deficit on the strength of the assumed savings that will result from the investment.

Theatres can also hope for money from sponsorship deals, although this is still on a small scale; for example, although Scottish theatres dramatically increased their number of sponsors in 1987/8, sponsorship still only provided about 2% of their income. In general sponsors prefer to back individual productions rather than the theatre itself.

For the bigger theatres selling television and production rights to successful plays is an increasingly important source of revenue. When a play transfers from the subsidised to the commercial theatre transfer rights must also be paid; so in 1987/8 the Royal Court made £75,000 out of the rights to *Serious Money*.

Historic theatres may also be eligible for grants from conservation bodies. In 1990 the management of Margate's Theatre Royal decided to sell shares to raise the £1.25 million for redevelopment. The local authority and English Heritage were expected to make up the shortfall.

However, despite all these varied sources of income most theatres were struggling by 1989. Faced with difficulty in making ends meet theatre managers have several options:

* They can raise ticket prices (although if they lose some of their audience the increase in revenue may not be as great as they hope).
* They can increase the number of performances they put on.
* They can market their productions more effectively.
* They can choose tried and tested popular plays.
* They can choose plays with smaller casts.
* They can extend the popular Christmas pantomime season into November and February.

However, such decisions strike at their artistic credibility and are unlikely to be popular with directors. Price rises which cut into audience numbers also lead to a lower income from ancillary sales of programmes, drinks, etc.

In the past theatres only came to life half an hour before the afternoon (matinee) or evening performance and so were not designed with space for other activities. Those that want to extend their catering to make more money may need to extend the building, buy up an adjacent site or reorganise the existing space. A few, like the National, have enough space to stay open all day. However, as all-day cafés they face stiff competition from other venues.

Theatre licences require usher/ettes for safety reasons, so they usually double as sales-staff in the intervals. Bar sales can be tricky because intervals are so short that there is barely time to serve everyone before the curtain rises again. Most theatres now let people place their drinks orders before the play starts so they can be prepared in advance.

The Theatre Box Office

In most theatres the box office is usually a glassed-in booth in the foyer which acts as the point of sale for tickets. People can either call into the theatre in person to book or can phone up.

Some theatres still operate manual booking procedures. A plan in the box office shows the situation of each seat. Once one has been sold it is crossed off on a master plan, with different colours indicating if the sale was over the phone, by credit card, etc. Seats which have been reserved over the phone but not paid for are initially pencilled on to the plan and then inked in when payment is received; they must usually be collected by a specific time before the performance starts. The ticket itself often comes in three parts, each with the number of the seat and its row (usually indicated by a letter) on it; one is kept by the box office, one by the customer and the third is given up to the usher/ette.

Some box offices have 24-hour answerphones for enquiries. Discounts are offered to school groups, pensioners, playgoers' societies, etc. Occasionally free tickets are distributed to help fill what might otherwise look like an empty theatre. To make the theatre look fuller ticket sales may be scattered around the building rather than grouped together.

Some theatres now have computerised box offices, with several telephonists having access to the same master plan. Printers can be attached to the computers to print not only the tickets, but accounts and statistics as well. Some companies have remote selling points for their computers and access to other systems as well.

Space for selling tickets in theatre foyers is often very limited. The growth of the megamusicals in the 1980s put particular pressure on them and by 1990 most theatres also sold seats through agencies. In 1991 the oldest agency, Keith Prowse, went into liquidation. Producers may offer the agents 'inside commissions' so they can sell tickets at their face price. However, the client is usually charged a booking fee or commission; the mark-up can be as high as 25%.

The importance of running an efficient box office operation was highlighted in 1990 when Dave Clark successfully sued Rank Theatres, claiming that losses on his musical, *Time*, were partly due to an under-manned and inefficient box office

MUSICAL ENTERTAINMENT

Once again it is mainly London Classical music venues and London-based companies that are patronised by tourists. However, even in London audiences are mostly local; figures from the South Bank concert halls suggest that only 7% of their audiences is from overseas and 20% from outside London. Nevertheless audience figures declined in 1986 when American visitors stayed away, implying that tourism does play a role, especially since few concert venues ever play to capacity audiences.

The most popular Classical music venues are the South Bank concert halls (the Royal Festival Hall, Queen Elizabeth Hall and Purcell Room), the Barbican Centre and the Royal Albert Hall where the 'Proms' concerts, in particular, are favourites. Opera at the Royal Opera House in Covent Garden and at the Colisseum where performances are always in English is also increasingly popular.

All the big Classical music venues in London are subsidised by the government via the Arts Council. However, like the theatres, they are under pressure to become more self-supporting and ticket prices have risen much faster than the rate of inflation. Perhaps surprisingly there is evidence that audiences have been growing, possibly because of better publicity. Opera companies have been particularly tightly squeezed since the Arts Council's *Glory of the Garden* report (1984) suggested that they received a disproportionately large amount of subsidy. However, although they have increased their revenues from sponsorship this still brings in on average only 8% of their income (1987/8). The symphony orchestras have also courted sponsorship fairly successfully; the Royal Philharmonic increased the amount of revenue drawn from that source from £236,000 in 1984/5 to £630,000 in 1987/8. However, the majority of funding for the orchestras comes from recording rights and sales of recorded music.

Following the demise of the GLC the Arts Council-funded South Bank Board took charge of the three South Bank concert halls and the Hayward Gallery in 1987. Efforts have been made to increase the audience sizes (Table 62); in 1989 the Royal Festival Hall introduced an 'open foyer' policy to attract passers-by into the building (even if they don't stay for concerts they may spend money on food, drink and other merchandise). Themes have also been used to link activities at all the South Bank venues. However, these have met with varying success; RFH audiences may even have failed in 1989 when Schoenberg was the theme.

TABLE 62 AVERAGE AUDIENCE CAPACITY AT LONDON AUDITORIA, 1987/8

National Theatre (all 3 auditoria)	76%
Royal Festival Hall	69%
Queen Elizabeth Hall	54%
Purcell Room	47%

The Schoenberg experience suggests that, like theatres, music venues can increase their takings by picking tried and tested favourites and avoiding experimentation. However, in the long-term this is likely to lead to stagnation.

Concert audiences tend to be older and from higher socio-economic groups. Up to 59% may also be regular visitors, a figure more typical of leisure facilities in general than of other tourist attractions. Audiences for popular music concerts obviously tend to be younger. Concerts at Wembley Stadium may attract non-Londoners and a few overseas visitors but pop concerts are usually primarily local affairs. Surprisingly the 1986 General Household Survey suggested that only ½% of UK residents had been to any kind of concert, even a pop concert, in the preceding four weeks.

DANCE COMPANIES

Britain's major dance companies are the Royal Ballet, the Sadlers Wells Royal Ballet (Birmingham), the Ballet Rambert, the English National Ballet, the London Contemporary Theatre, the Scottish Ballet (Glasgow) and the Northern Ballet Theatre (Manchester). No ballet companies are based in Wales or Northern Ireland.

Dance companies attract a predominantly female audience, with 'modern' dance drawing younger people than classical ballet. Audiences also tend to come from higher socio-economic groups. However, tourists make up only a small part of audiences, even in London. Outside London dance companies are just one of the many features that help to make a town attractive to cultural tourists.

CHAPTER TEN
MISCELLANEOUS TOURIST ATTRACTIONS

Some of the UK's attractions don't fit easily into the categories so far examined. These include attractions as diverse as Madame Tussaud's Waxworks, Alton Towers Theme Park and the many event attractions which take place around the country every year.

THE ROYAL FAMILY

Royalty has a great appeal to tourists, particularly those from overseas who find their past history and modern life-style fascinating. This is so much the case that the part they play in tourism and the revenue they generate are sometimes given as reasons why tax-payers should continue to support the Royal Family. The importance they play in UK tourism is highlighted by looking at 1977, the year of the Queen's Jubilee, when the UK received a record 9% of worldwide tourist arrivals and when expenditure by overseas visitors rose not just in actual terms but also in real terms.

The figures for visitors to palaces and houses associated with royalty are impressive: in 1988 699,836 people visited the State Apartments at Windsor Castle, 532,955 went to Hampton Court Palace, 247,873 to Osborne House on the Isle of Wight (a favourite with Queen Victoria) and 152,993 to Carisbrooke Castle where King Charles I hid during the Civil War. Buckingham Palace, perhaps the best known of all the royal homes, is not open to the public, but 59,786 people visited the Royal Mews where the state carriages, including the Coronation Coach, are displayed.

The Historic Royal Palaces agency, a branch of the Department of the Environment, cares for Hampton Court Palace, the Tower of London, Kew Palace, Banqueting House and Kensington Palace.

TABLE 63 VISITORS TO THE HISTORIC ROYAL PALACES IN 1988

Tower of London	2,181,707
Hampton Court Palace	532,955
Kensington Palace	166,100
Kew Palace	43,318
Banqueting House	15,400

Royal Pageantry

Ceremonies associated with royalty also have considerable touristic pulling power; there are always crowds for both the daily Changing of the

Guard and the Trooping of the Colour in June when the Queen herself can be seen. These events are, of course, free. However, local shops and restaurants do better business as a result of them. Despite the high cost of staging such ceremonies it is probable that fewer people would choose London as a holiday base without them.

Modern Tourist Attractions Associated with Royalty

By their very nature attractions associated with royalty tend to be old and traditional. However, in the 1980s there were attempts to create new 'royal' tourist attractions to cash in on this popularity. Most successful was the 'Royalty and Empire' exhibition, created by the Madame Tussaud's group in 1983 in Windsor and Eton Central Station. The exhibition is within easy reach of London and relieves some of the pressure on the Castle, offering a secondary attraction in keeping with what brought people to Windsor in the first place. However, the Castle itself is so appealing that Royalty and Empire may attract fewer vistors than if it was on its own.

The original Brunel station has been returned to its appearance in 1897 when Queen Victoria celebrated her Diamond Jubilee. The Madame Tussaud's studio team have created models of everyone who would have been waiting when the Queen arrived, right down to the organ-grinder and the station porters. Despite its 19th century subject matter this is very much a 20th century production: in the 250-seater theatre visitors can watch an audio-visual performance during which twenty projectors dissolve 800 slides on to a nine-metre screen; computers control the projectors, music, lighting, curtains and exit doors. More models reenact scenes from Victoria's reign. They actually move and appear to speak, a process known as 'audio animatronics' which was introduced to Europe here.

In 1988 385,634 people visited Royalty and Empire. However, the site is too small to accommodate limitless visitors and its very precise theme precludes adding the sort of new features that bring repeat visits. In 1990 Pearson sold the site to L & R Leisure.

The slide show at the Royalty and Empire exhibition provides information about the 19th century, and there's also an excellent loose-leaf teacher's pack about life in Victorian Windsor. However, the educational value of such exhibitions can be limited since it tends to lean on the anecdotal and picturesque, by-passing tricky questions or in-depth analysis.

The Royal Parks

Tourists also benefit from another royal legacy in the form of the Royal Parks: Hyde Park, Kensington Gardens, St James Park, Green Park, Regent's Park, Richmond Park, Hampton Court Gardens, Bushy Park, Greenwich Park and Windsor Great Park. Some are relics of the 11th century when one-sixth of England was reserved as royal hunting grounds. Others, like Hyde Park, were developed on ex-monastic land by Henry VIII.

With no charges for going into the Parks it's difficult to assess how many people visit them and how many are tourists as opposed to Londoners taking lunch breaks. However, more than 100,000 people may pass through Hyde Park on a summer Sunday, and perhaps 750,000 gathered there to enjoy the free firework display preceding Prince Charles' marriage to Lady Diana Spencer in 1981.

The Royal Parks have been adminstered by the State since the reign of George III, and there is a special Royal Parks Department of the Department of the Environment, with a Central Parks sub-division to look after most of them. A special constabulary looks after all the parks except Hyde Park which has been policed by the Metropolitan Police Force since the Reform League Riots there in 1866, which also led to the creation of Speaker's Corner to provide a legitimate outlet for voicing grievances.

Until 1990 the Royal Parks Department looked after the parks infrastructure, providing litter bins, lavatories, chairs and deck-chairs. It also provided the special green and white, crown-topped signposts which direct people round the parks, and employed the park gardeners. However, the deckchair and catering operations have now been privatised, the gardening is being put out to contract, and in 1991 a government review body was examining Hyde Park and Kensington Gardens to see what further changes could be made.

With no admission charges to the parks, no direct profits can be made from them. Even special events like concerts are usually free. Nevertheless most of them now have cafes or restaurants and some sell guidebooks to recoup part of their running costs. During the summer there are regular performances of Shakespearean plays in Regent's Park open-air theatre.

LEISURE AND THEME PARKS

Leisure parks are primarily outdoor entertainment attractions which offer many different activities, including hair-raising rides, safari parks, animal shows, children's play areas, boats, replica buildings, shops, restaurants and live entertainment. They are usually enclosed and owned by one company rather than a group of concessionaries. There is normally one entrance price covering all the activities inside.

The term *theme park* is often used loosely to cover a range of attractions from urban fun-fairs like Blackpool Pleasure Beach to the Elizabethan entertainments which were to be staged in the grounds of Avebury Manor. However, there is a world of difference in size and atmosphere between such places and purpose-designed theme parks like Alton Towers, Thorpe Park and the American Adventure Theme Parks.

True theme parks are leisure parks within which all the activities are linked by a common theme: Disneyworld and Disneyland are the prime examples. Few leisure parks in the UK are true theme parks, although Granada (owners of the Camelot and American Adventure Theme Parks) is attempting to turn nominal themes into real ones at its properties.

The UK Theme Parks

In the UK leisure parks are a relatively recent development, perhaps because the seaside piers, pleasure beaches and many parks and gardens fulfilled some of the same functions; Thorpe Park which opened in 1979 is usually regarded as England's first theme park. Unlike on the continent there has never been a tradition of building leisure amenities on the outskirts of large towns; in general Britons were used to travelling for their leisure entertainment, a fact which may have helped somewhere like Alton Towers which is not particularly easily accessible.

More and more leisure parks have opened in the last ten years, but competition may actually increase the potential market for this type of attraction rather than dilute it as might have been expected. In southern England a big increase in the number of visitors to Windsor Safari Park and Chessington World of Adventures between 1985 and 1988 didn't significantly damage Thorpe Park's visitor figures even though all three attractions were increasing their entrance fees faster than the rate of inflation. Nevertheless, the opening of the Channel Tunnel will make it easier for British visitors to get to the new Euro Disney just outside Paris and many tourist attractions in southern England see this as potential competition. When MCA bid to build on Rainham Marshes in Essex they argued that unless they obtained a site near London their intended market might be lured away by Euro Disney.

What makes a leisure park successful?

A new park is by no means guaranteed success. For example, Britannia Park in Derbyshire, which was intended to celebrate the theme of 'British Genius', opened to the public in June 1985 and closed again in September 1985. Delays in getting planning permission from Derbyshire County Council meant that work on the site didn't actually start until 1984. A Marketing Director wasn't appointed until December 1984 which meant he had only six months instead of the ideal two years to get his message across. The original plans grossly underestimated the cost of work on the site, and the banks were reluctant to lend more money so that the Park was still incomplete when it opened. That the problem didn't lie with the site itself has been proved by the success of the American Adventure

Theme Park which Granada later developed on it; this received 660,000 visitors in 1988.

To be successful a park needs something to appeal to everyone. Alton Towers has a beautiful, peaceful garden for those guests not in search of white-knuckle thrills, and a selection of gentler rides for younger children. Thorpe Park has a small farm. Ideally the parks should be within two hours' drive of 12 million residents, or within one hour's drive of a major holiday destination and two hours' drive of 5-6 million people. Many of Britain's theme parks are concentrated in the Midlands where they are within easy reach of the bulk of the population and where the collapse of industry in the 1980s meant alternative sources of employment were eagerly sought. Dobwalls Theme Park at Liskeard in Cornwall might seem off the beaten track but is in one of Britain's most popular holiday areas and attracted 190,000 people in 1988. Ideally the park should also be within fifteen minutes of a main road for easy access and signposting.

Upto 95% of visitors may arrive by car or coach so a large site is crucial. Roughly 180 cars can be accommodated on an acre of land but to cope with peak periods enough space for 5-8,000 cars and 250 coaches at any one time will be needed. Parking must be provided free to avoid traffic jams forming as people queue to pay. Of course with that volume of traffic theme park owners may need to pay for improvements to local traffic arrangements as well. Sites with water are particularly popular. Both Alton Towers and the American Adventure Theme Park have vast lakes offering boat rides. Thorpe Park was built around a series of flooded ex-gravel pits.

The site will also need impressive rides. Unfortunately these are expensive to create and new ones must be constantly added to attract repeat visits. So in 1990 Alton Towers invested £2 million in a new rollercoaster. Enthusiastic and suitable staff must be recruited; Thorpe Park has a rigorous code of conduct for staff which even lays down which shades of eye make-up are acceptable. Scrupulous site cleanliness is essential; at Alton Towers cleaning buggies constantly tour the grounds.

In the UK the 'theme' itself doesn't seem particularly important; Thorpe Park's theme is England's maritime heritage and Alton Towers does have Henry Hound whose image appears on everything down to the sugar sachets. However, in neither case is the theme the most important or memorable feature of the site. There are Camelot and Gulliver's Kingdom theme parks, but by far the most popular 'theme' in the UK is the American West which has inspired three parks; American Adventure at Ilkeston, Pleasurewood Hills at Lowestoft and Frontierland at Morecambe.

Problems for Leisure Parks

One of the biggest problems facing someone planning a new theme park in the UK is likely to be getting planning permission for large-scale development of potentially noisy facilities; it took Thorpe Park six years and more than 150 planning applications before the site could open to the public. Britannia Park's problems were at least partly due to difficulty in obtaining planning permission. Even when a park is well-established permission is still needed for new rides and this too can be problematic as local people often fear the noise and traffic that will be generated. In 1989 Alton Towers built its new 'Beast' rollercoaster after planning permission had expired; the 'Mouse' had no permission at all. Local people objected both to the extra noise and to the fact that both were visible above the trees, so Staffordshire Moorland Council initially said they must be taken down again. Eventually it relented and granted retrospective planning permission on the understanding that both would eventually be replaced by a new 'Gravity Ride'.

Cost is also a problem. A new theme park will require internal roads, sewage pipes and pumps, perimeter fencing, electricity, water, gas, telephone lines and landscaping, in addition to the costly attractions themselves, restaurants, shops, etc. Total costs may rise as high as £220 million. Some of the running costs are also fixed and must be covered even during the low season; in 1991 running Alton Towers during the first three months of the year cost £3.5 million.

Safety is also very important. In the UK rides must be inspected daily, with independent experts examining them at least once a year. Since 1986 the Health and Safety Executive and British Association of Leisure Parks, Piers and Attractions have had codes of good practice for owners of theme parks. At Alton Towers each ride has a radio link to the main control centre so any problems can be quickly notified. Most parks have attractively-designed signs warning of rides which may not be suitable for those with heart and other health problems and stipulating height requirements for admitting children to rides. Water attractions have been responsible for the most accidents.

Queuing for popular rides is a difficulty which parks try to get round by providing wandering entertainers to prevent people getting bored. Notices are also posted telling visitors how long they can expect to wait from a particular point in the queue. As far as practicable rides must be designed to carry large numbers at once to keep queuing time to a minimum.

Entrance tickets for most UK leisure parks are inclusive and cost between £3 and £8, with only small discounts for children. This sounds expensive but doesn't seem to deter visitors, perhaps because at a site like Thorpe Park there are more than fifty separate attractions. Most parks provide free transport, often by monorail or train, around the site so people can visit as much as possible in one trip.

Access can also be a problem. Most British theme parks are in the countryside where they can be difficult for non-car owners to get to. In London there were fears that the planned Battersea Theme Park would add to traffic congestion even though there was to be a British Rail link from Victoria.

Nor were UK parks helped by the cheap price of holidays in Florida in the late 1980s. By 1989 almost 8% of south-east England's population had visited one of the Florida parks, often in glorious sunshine, and could compare the high standards they found there with those at home.

TABLE 64 THE MOST VISITED THEME PARKS IN ENGLAND, 1988

1.	Blackpool Pleasure Beach (free entry)	6,500,000
2.	Alton Towers	2,509,736
3.	Dreamland Theme Park, Margate	*2,000,000
4.	Pleasureland, Southport	1,500,000
5.	Thorpe Park	1,028,000
6.	Frontierland, Morecambe	1,000,000
7.	Drayton Manor Park, Staffs.	984,500
8.	American Adventure Theme Park	660,000
9.	Needles Pleasure Park, Isle of Wight	*600,000
10.	Pleasurewood Hills American Theme Park	533,623

(* approximate number)

Shops

Shopping is often high on the average tourist's list of planned holiday activities, but shops are not normally thought of as tourist attractions per se. However, there are some exceptions, amongst which Harrods in London is the best example. Flagship of the House of Fraser chain of stores, Harrods opened in Knightsbridge in 1905 and quickly established a reputation as a shop which sold everything. It is visited by thousands of overseas visitors and non-Londoners every year. Other shopping areas in London which are particularly popular with visitors include Oxford Street and Regent Street, and King's Road in Chelsea.

Carnaby Street's continuing popularity is harder to explain and illustrates tourism's tendency to turn attractions into parodies of themselves. In the 1960s and early '70s Carnaby Street was where fashionable Londoners went to buy their hippy clothes. It became so famous that overseas visitors still include it in their itineraries even though it is now just a drab annexe to Regent Street.

In contrast in Covent Garden the provision of shops with an eye to tourists has brought new life to a run-down area. When the fruit, vegetable and flower stalls were moved out to Nine Elms in 1974, they left empty warehouses and halls, many of them dating back to the 19th century. The site had obvious tourist potential because of its situation, squeezed in between the Royal Opera House, the Strand and Leicester Square. The GLC therefore invested £2½ million in restoring the buildings and turning them into small shops.

Covent Garden now offers novelty shops on three levels interspersed with mainly out-door cafés and restaurants. A crafts market takes place on stalls in the shopping alleys, and there are licensed buskers and street entertainers. Similar shops and restaurants have since spilled into the surrounding streets as well. The London Transport Museum and the Theatre Museum occupy the Old Flower Market building at one corner of the Piazza, and the Jubilee Hall, a Grade II listed building, now houses a conventional clothing market alternating with an antiques fair. But despite its success Covent Garden is still vulnerable to insensitive development. In 1990 the Royal Opera House had to drop plans for a theme park-style scheme on the site of the listed Floral Hall after a public outcry.

Outside London few shops are tourist attractions in their own right although Gateshead's new Metro Centre is likely to prove a big pull for domestic tourists in the north-east. Nevertheless in popular tourist areas individual town centre shops often reflect the needs of visitors rather than local people. Towns like Bath, York and Canterbury which receive millions of visitors every year have lots of novelty shops similar to those found in Covent Garden. In York the main tourist shopping streets are the picturesque Shambles and Stonegate. Until the new uniform business rate and steep rent rises caused problems for small businesses like these shops, Stonegate was regarded as the most successful shopping centre in the whole of Europe.

Combined Shop and Attraction Complexes

An idea which was developed in North America and has now spread to England is the vast mall incorporating shops, restaurants and conventional tourist attractions, often on the outskirts of town where providing car parking is easiest.

Unlike Covent Garden, London's Trocadero Centre is an all-weather, undercover development and the building itself is of no interest, although its position, on the road linking Leicester Square to Piccadilly, is perfect for picking up passing tourists. Although the Trocadero looks like a standard shopping centre it also houses several attractions, including the Guinness World of Records exhibition which brings the record book to life, with models of the shortest, tallest and fattest people ever to live. The London Experience tells London's history using five screens, thirty automatic slide projectors and a wide-screen movie projector programmed so that its images merge with those of the slides. The success of the Trocadero inspired the restoration of the London Pavilion building on the corner of Shaftesbury Avenue and Piccadilly which is now home to the Rock Circus as well as to a range of shops.

THE GRANADA STUDIOS

Although the Hollywood film sets and the MGM Studios in Florida had long been open to film fans, when Granada Studios opened in 1988 it was unique in showing the sets of popular television programmes like Coronation Street which is still filmed there. 'That's Entertainment' cost £9 million to develop, and the Engish Tourist Board helped with a grant of £750,000.

Tourists can visit television sets of Downing Street, Checkpoint Charlie and Baker Street, a state-of-the-art cinema, the Rover's Return pub and a selection of themed eating places. A reproduction House of Commons can even be hired as a novelty conference venue.

INDUSTRIAL TOURISM

The success of industrial heritage sites in interesting people in technological processes has led an increasing number of companies to consider industrial tourism as an additional money-spinner. While *industrial heritage tourism* is concerned with presenting redundant machinery, processes, buildings and ways of life, *industrial tourism* is about contemporary manufacturing processes. Sometimes the two may even overlap; a modern factory may decide to open an on-site museum about the history of the industry while also inviting visitors to tour the existing factory as well.

By 1988 the BTA estimated that there were about 5 million visits to industrial tourism attractions in the UK, and that the market was likely to grow rapidly to between 8 and 9 million visits. As early as 1964 sixty-nine British companies had some sort of museum on their premises. However, these were rarely actively promoted; development of industrial tourism was generally demand- rather than product-led. In 1988 the ETB and CBI started promoting industrial tourism more actively. In 1990 the BTA also published *Visit Britain at Work* to publicise work places open to visitors.

Companies become involved in industrial tourism for a variety of reasons. In the case of a company like Wedgwood producing a world-famous product there was always interest in the production process, so much so, in fact, that at one stage there was a two year waiting list for factory tours. The new Visitor Reception Centre was therefore designed as a central feature of the Barlaston site even though there would have been more space for parking, etc. on the periphery. It was also designed to be all on one level to suit disabled visitors and mothers with pushchairs. Sixty staff are now employed specifically to deal with tourists, although those working in the craft demonstration hall are ordinary factory workers whose piece-work rates have been adjusted to allow them time to talk to visitors.

Breweries, too, have always drawn thousands of curious visitors. Since 1974 the Carlsberg plant in Northampton has been open to visitors who are provided with free refreshments during their tour. Little advertising is done except to coach tour operators and yet there were 15,000 visitors in 1988, mainly drawn by word of mouth recommendation.

In contrast some industrial tourism has developed partly as a public relations exercise. For example, in 1980 the visitor centre at the Sellafield nuclear fuel plant was opened to try and reassure the public and improve the industry's image. In 1988 157,842 people visited Sellafield, one of the more surprising success stories of UK tourism.

In 1983 Austin Rover at Cowley also opened its factory to visitors. Cars are obviously interesting to many people and Germany's most popular industrial tourism attraction is the Munich BMW plant. However, the Cowley plant is not so glamorous and was primarily opened to improve morale in a factory with a history of strikes and to restore public confidence in the company.

Finally, some companies open their doors to tourists as an alternative to closing them altogether. For example, by 1978 the Walkley Clog Factory at Hebden Bridge (which dates from 1870) faced closure because the market for its products had virtually vanished. Instead it started admitting visitors to watch the clog-making process. In 1988, after an organised publicity drive, helped by the Yorkshire and Humberside Tourist Board and the local council, it received about 100,000 visitors. Craft workshops, a pine showroom, a puppet theatre and bee museum have since been added to guarantee its future as an attraction.

Some industrial tourism attractions open to the public free of charge and rely on sales of merchandise to make a profit; the Calsberg Brewery reckons to sell several hundred pounds worth of goods to coach groups although it then donates the money to industry-linked charities. It is also assumed that people who are impressed by what they see on their visit may become future customers, so that an indirect profit may be generated. However, the Wilton Royal Factory which couldn't expect to sell many carpets to passing visitors charges £1.60 for a tour.

Industrial tourism also helps to generate visitors for other local attractions, hotels and restaurants; the sucess of Sellafield is credited with having drawn more visitors to the Ravensglass and Eskdale Railway and to Muncaster Castle. Many potential industrial tourism centres are in towns which didn't traditionally attract many visitors and have the advantage that they can be marketed as year-round, all-weather attractions. What's more when company profits are squeezed, they offer a way to boost revenue at relatively little cost, although a reception centre becomes essential once visitor numbers start to rise. Additional staff may also be needed to act as guides/interpreters, and extra safety precautions will be needed to protect visitors from dangerous machinery.

ENGINEERING PROJECTS AND TOURISM

Just as workplaces that had nothing to do with tourism originally have nevertheless become attractions, so several engineering projects also draw large numbers of visitors each year. The Eurotunnel Exhibition Centre in Folkestone, set up to explain the project and allay the concerns of local people, drew 100,000 people in 1988, its first year of opening. The Thames Barrier, built to improve London's flood defences, also has a Visitors' Centre which attracts tourists. Perhaps more surprisingly the London Docklands Light Railway also seems to be attracting tourists. During the summer it carries an average extra 5,000 people every day, suggesting that it is not just being used to get tourists to Greenwich but also as an attraction in its own right.

EVENT ATTRACTIONS

Tourists may also be drawn to a place not by its fixed natural or man-made attractions but by special events, some of them one-off, but many of them regular or at least annual occasions. Some such events, like the Changing of the Guard in London, have long histories. Others, like Glasgow's Mayfest, are recent innovations which, it is hoped, will gradually attract more attention.

Requirements for Successful Event Attractions

Like other attractions events won't attract visitors unless they are readily accessible. Drivers will need adequate, reasonably priced and secure parking near the site. If groups are to be attracted there must also be plenty of coach parking space. The AA and RAC play a vital role by providing temporary signposts to direct people to event sites.

There must also be suitable site amenities; plenty of public lavatories, a range of food and drink to suit all budgets, promotional materials like programmes and postcards, and clear signposting to guide people round the site. The site must also be safe for children, with suitable play areas. Preferably the needs of disabled visitors will also have been taken into account when it was chosen.

In addition, if event attractions are to attract a non-local clientele there must be adequate accommodation to suit all budgets. This is one of the trickiest problems facing the organisers. Since by their very nature events are shortlived, they lead to sudden peaks in demand for accommodation which may be under-occupied for the rest of the year. This may not be a problem in cities like London where there are many other year-round attractions to take up slack capacity. However, for smaller towns, it is very frustrating to see potential tourist revenue lost to neighbouring towns, villages and camp-sites because it isn't possible to provide enough hotel rooms for everyone. A similar problem faces those in charge of public transport; while extra long-distance coaches and trains can usually be laid on to coincide with the rush, local bus companies may find it harder to cope with sudden extra numbers, leading to long queues and over crowding.

Event attractions, especially new ones, are particularly dependent on well-placed and well-timed publicity; it's no use people hearing about the Lord Mayor's Show the weekend after it takes place. For this reason it helps if the event is held at the same time each year so that it becomes part of the social calendar, like the Wimbledon Lawn Tennis Championships. To generate publicity it also helps if the event is unique or especially colourful and exciting.

Problems Facing Organisers of Event Attractions

While attendances at all attractions are influenced to some extent by the weather, event attractions, particularly those that take place outdoors, are uniquely vulnerable to bad weather. Even if people still attend because they have already paid and made their travel arrangements they are less likely to linger and spend money when it's pouring with rain. Insurance against bad weather is available but expensive. This means that countries like Great Britain with poor climates are at a disadvantage when it comes to organising events. Consequently they tend to be crowded into the short summer period when there is a better than average chance of sun. In such circumstances events can end up competing with each other for visitors.

Security can also be difficult since large numbers of people will be crowding into relatively small areas. Because they can be a magnet for pickpockets, drug dealers and other crooks, extra policing often has to be organised. Where alcohol is available fights may also break out, making policing even more tricky.

With the emphasis on excitement some events are intrinsically dangerous even without the crowding. In such circumstances organisers must try to ensure the safest conditions possible but they are likely to face constant challenges over their right to continue with the event.

TABLE 65 TYPES OF EVENT ATTRACTION

Type of Event Attraction	Examples
Traditional Ceremonies	The Changing of the Guard, outside Buckingham Palace; the Trooping of the Colour; Mounting of the Guard, Whitehall; Well-dressing in Youlgreave and Tissington, Derbyshire
Sports Events	Wimbledon All-England Lawn Tennis Championships; Derby, Epsom; Royal Ascot; Goodwood Races; St. Leger, Doncaster; Oxford and Cambridge Boat Race; Henley Royal Regatta; Veteran Car Race from London to Brighton; Scottish Highland Games (Braemar, Fort William, Nairn, etc); T.T Races, Isle of Man
Festivals of Music, Drama & Film	Aldeburgh Festival, Suffolk; Glyndebourne Opera, Sussex; Henry Wood Promenade Concerts, Albert Hall, London; Royal National Eisteddfod, Wales; International Musical Eisteddod, Llangollen; Chichester Drama Festival; Malvern Drama Festival; Bath Festival; Edinburgh Festival; Mystery Plays, York
Flower Festivals	Chelsea Flower Show, London; Floral Carnival, St. Helier, Jersey
Illuminations	Blackpool; Skegness; Christmas Lights in Oxford St. and Regent St.
Carnivals	Notting Hill, London; St. Paul's, Bristol; Trowbridge, Somerset
Food and Drink Festivals	Good Food Fair, Jersey
Miscellaneous events	May Day parades (all over England)

EUROPEAN CITIES OF CULTURE

Since 1985 the European Community has nominated one city to be 'European City of Culture' each year. This is not strictly a festival but must be promoted in much the same way and has much the same effect in terms of attracting extra visitors to the city. What's more festivals them-selves play an increasing part in the activities planned by the reigning city. Glasgow was the City of Culture in 1990 and used the opportunity to build on the success of its *Glasgow is Miles Better* campaign and of the 1988 Garden Festival. Despite the success of the year in attracting more attention to Glasgow, there were complaints from some Glaswegians about the type of culture that was promoted and arguments over the actual long-term benefits to local people.

CIRCUSES

The word 'circus' refers to the circular shape of the site where circus performances take place but also suggests an entertainment or spectacle consisting of animal acts or feats of human daring. The 1981 Zoo Licensing Act defined circuses as 'places where animals are kept or introduced wholly or mainly for the purpose of performing tricks or manoeuvres.'

During the Middle Ages jugglers and other artistes we now associate with circuses wandered the trade fairs of Europe. Then in 1768 an Englishman, Philip Astley, discovered that centrifugal forces made it possible to stand upright on a horse's back and ride in a circle on it. Astley erected a roof over a ring and provided seats to show off his new-found skill. In 1782 one of his riders, Charles Hughes, set up a 'Royal Circus', the first modern use of the word. Travelling players gradually deserted the fairs in favour of the circuses and may have brought the idea of the big top tent with them. The first known circus big top was used in the United States in 1826.

In the early 19th century Isaac van Amburgh introduced wild animals to the performances and was probably the first man to put his head in a lion's mouth. In 1874 the first group of performing elephants seems to have appeared in a London circus.

After the First World War circuses declined. Those that traditionally toured the continent had difficulty obtaining passports and clearing quarantine. In England Bertram Mills revived circuses, using Olympia in London as a showcase and taking his troupe on tour by train. However, inflationary pressures meant expenses rose faster than income. Nowadays circuses are thought of as outdoor attractions. However, there were some permanent purpose-built indoor circuses (or 'hippodromes') where companies could perform all year round in London, Liverpool, Brighton and Great Yarmouth. There was even a circus inside Blackpool Tower.

Since the 1960s the public seems to have lost its taste for performing animals and even the famous Bertram Mills circus had to close. By the 1980s most British circuses were seasonal events which took place on commonland. Those without animals (like Ra-Ra Zoo and Circus Archaos) were at least as popular as those with them.

Local authorities must give consent for circuses (or fairs) to take place, and they are controlled by the terms of the 1961 Public Health Act and the 1976 Local Government (Miscellaneous Provisions) Act. The 1971 Animals Act made site owners liable for harm caused by dangerous animals.

Table 66 lists some of the UK's most important event attractions. Those in Bristol are also listed as typical of what may happen in one specific locality. Neither of these lists is comprehensive.

TABLE 66 EVENTS CALENDAR

Month	National	Bristol
January	First Footing	Festival of One Act Dramas
	Burns Night	
February	Shrovetide Festivals	
	Cruft's Dog Show	
March	St. David's Day	
	Universities' Boat Race	Bristol Eisteddfod
April	Well-dressing	
	Battersea Easter Parade	
	Pilgrimage to Walsingham	
	Grand National, Aintree	
May	Spalding Tulip Parade	Bristol Proms
	Minehead Hobby-Horse	
	Founder's Day for Chelsea Pensioners	
	Milk Race	
June	Trooping of the Colour	Women's World
	Bath Festival	Bristol to Bournemouth
	Highland Games	Vintage Vehicle Run
	Good Food Fair, Jersey	Festival of the Sea
	Garter Ceremony, Windsor	
	Solstice Ceremonies at Stonehenge	
	Derby	
	Royal Ascot	
	TT Races, Isle of Man	

July	Royal Tournament	St. Paul's Carnival
	Llangollen International Eisteddfod	Ashton Court Festival
	Swan Upping on Thames	Wine Fair and Festival
	Battle of Flowers, Jersey	Charities Fayre
	Royal National Eisteddfod	Steam Weekend
	Wimbledon Finals	
	Manx National Day	
	Royal International Agricultural Show, Stoneleigh	
	Henley Regatta	
	Dressing of Buxton Wells	
	Racing at Silverstone	
	Goodwood Races	
August	Notting Hill Carnival	Harbour Regatta
	Sidmouth Folk Festival	International Balloon Festival
	Cowes Week, Isle of Wight	Flower Show
	Grouse Shooting starts 12 August	
September	Braemar Gathering	Kite Festival
	Edinburgh Festival	
	St. Giles' Fair, Oxford	
	St. Leger Races, Doncaster	
	Farnborough Air Show	
	Manx Classic Car Race	
	Manx Grand Prix	
October	Blackpool Illuminations	
	Horse of the Year Show	
	Nottingham Goose Fair	
November	State Opening of Parliament	Carnival Procession
	Lord Mayor's Show	
	Remembrance Sunday	
	Bridgwater Carnival	
	London to Brighton Veteran Car Run	
December	King's College Carols	Water Carnival
	Royal Smithfield Show	
	Trafalgar Square Christmas Tree	
	Hogmanay	

WORLD HERITAGE SITES

In 1972 UNESCO (the United Nations Educational, Scientific and Cultural Organisation) drew up an International Convention for the Protection of the World, Cultural and Natural Heritage to provide the framework for protecting worldwide sites of 'outstanding universal value'.

The Convention had two underlying principles: that each country must recognise its own duty to preserve its heritage, and that it must acknowledge the need to co-operate with other countries to conserve the world's heritage.

The result was the creation of a World Heritage Committee whose representatives meet once a year to update a **World Heritage List** of cultural or natural sites of outstanding universal value. By 1991 337 sites had been designated. Some were chosen for historic or aesthetic reasons, while others were picked for their scientific merits or because of their great natural beauty. In every case the site was assessed on its intrinsic value rather than on whether it was in particular need of help.

Once somewhere has been added to the World Heritage List the site owner can display a special logo with a square representing the man-made heritage set inside a circle to represent the natural heritage, with the two linked to represent the world heritage transcending time and borders (Fig. 69). The country in which the site is found is then morally obliged to undertake its care and conservation. However, the last owner of Avebury Manor in England was only narrowly prevented from developing it as an Elizabethan theme park only minutes away from the delicate prehistoric Avebury Stone Circle.

A country's world heritage sites can be seen as its most valuable tourist attractions. In 1991 Britain had thirteen of them (Table 67).

TABLE 67 WORLD HERITAGE SITES IN THE UK, 1991

Giant's Causeway & Causeway Coast	Ironbridge Gorge
Durham Castle & Cathedral	Studley Royal Park including the Ruins of Fountains Abbey
City of Bath	Stonehenge, Avebury & Associated Sites
Canterbury Cathedral	Castles & Town Walls of King Edward in Gwynedd
Westminster Abbey & Palace	St Kilda.
Tower of London	
Blenheim Palace	
Hadrian's Wall	

FIGURE 69 SYMBOL OF A WORLD HERITAGE SITE

CHAPTER ELEVEN
THE IMPACT OF TOURISM ON THE UK

Tourism affects receiving countries in many different ways. Most obviously it brings in money and creates jobs. It may also result in the conservation of items, buildings and landscapes seen as likely to attract tourists. Facilities provided for visitors may also be available for local people as well. However, tourism can also lead to increased congestion on the roads, overcrowding of popular areas, damage to the landscape and the degradation of cultural traditions to suit the needs of those to whom they are unfamiliar. As the tourist industry grew to maturity in the 1980s these potential and actual problems were increasingly recognised, and by the 1990s 'sustainability' (i.e. finding forms of tourism that would not self-destruct) was the buzz-word of much of the industry.

This chapter looks at some of the economic, socio-cultural and environmental results of tourism in Great Britain. For a more detailed consideration of the theoretical aspects of calculating tourism's impact, see Patrick Lavery's *Travel and Tourism,* Second edition, Elm Publications, 1990.

THE ECONOMIC IMPACT OF TOURISM IN THE UK

Tourism is now one of the UK's most profitable industries, earning more than either the car or aerospace industries. According to the OECD the only countries earning more from tourism in 1988 were the United States, Spain, France and Italy. In London it is the third most important economic activity, after financial services and the public sector, while in Scotland it is the single largest enterprise. In Devon, too, tourism is now more important to the local economy than traditional agriculture. Overall, tourism probably benefits the UK economy by more than £200 per head of population.

However, calculating tourism's precise value to the economy is very complicated. In general three different types of expenditure must be taken into account. These are:

a) the money spent directly by tourists on goods and services in hotels, shops, restaurants, tourist attractions, etc.

b) the money spent by tourist enterprises on goods and services to run their businesses.

c) the money spent by hoteliers, restaurateurs, etc. on discretionary goods as a result of their profits from tourism.

Economists use the concept of the tourism multiplier to calculate the true worth of the money actually spent by the tourist and then respent by the recipient and so on. In the case of the city of York in the late 1980s, Cambridge Economic Consultants calculated a multiplier effect of 7.14, meaning that for every £2.5 million spent on tourism by visitors, £17.5 milllion was actually generated in the local economy.

In addition economists take into account any 'leakage', whereby money spent by the tourist leaves the economy again, usually to pay for goods and services not locally available and which must therefore by bought in for visitors. 'Leakage' also occurs when tourists pay their money to hotels and other businesses whose owners are not British and who will repatriate their profits. This is less likely to happen when tourists stay in bed and breakfast-type accommodation than when they stay in large chain hotels. Although there is relatively little 'leakage' from the UK national economy, local 'leakage' for taxes, interest paid on loans, money respent outside the local area and so on is common.

In 1989 tourism was estimated to have generated a total £22.4 billion for the British economy. This was 4% of the Gross Domestic Product. Of this total, 48.7% (or £10.9 billion) was spent by domestic tourists on trips involving at least one night away from home. Another 13.4% (or £3 billion) came from day trips by domestic residents. Overseas visitors spent £6.9 billion, or 30.8% of the total, on their visits. The remaining £1.6 billion, or 7.1%, was received by UK carriers as payment for transportation (Fig. 70).

FIGURE 70 VALUE OF TOURISM TO THE UK, 1989

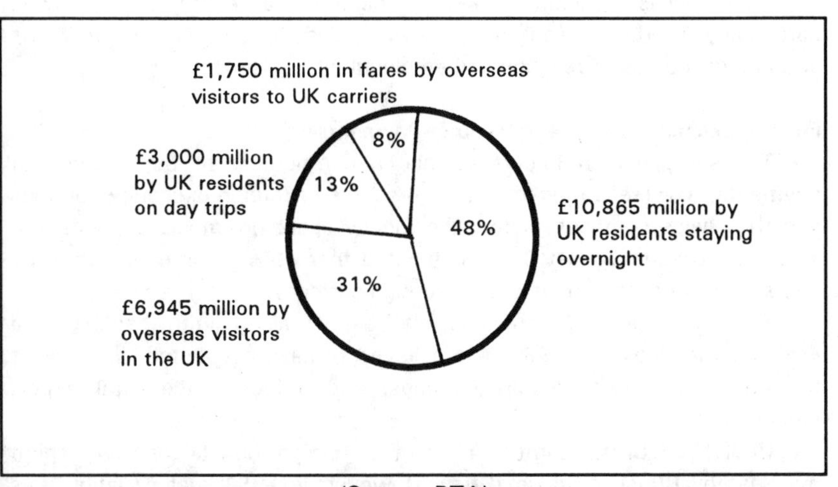

(Source: BTA)

In 1989 the ETB estimated that tourism to and within England, the most popular destination with visitors, was generating £13 billion a year.

Depending on their preferences different types of tourists are worth more or less to the economy. Business travellers are renowned for being big spenders, as are the Japanese. Those staying in hotels and holiday camps also tend to spend on average three times as much as campers and caravanners. Thus, depending on the different types of business they attract, different parts of the country will benefit from tourism to different degrees. Marketing strategies need to take these different patterns of expenditure into account.

Apart from the impact they have on the national economy tourists also affect local economies. In areas with a developed tourism industry local authorities used to benefit from the rates paid by tourism businesses. However, since the introduction of the uniform business rate central government has had more say over exactly how much of the amount collected stays in the local authority area. Because of tourism local authorities may incur extra costs for litter collection, street cleaning, providing public lavatories, etc. For example, Windsor Borough Council estimates that it spends an additional £1 million a year on services for its visitors. The Department of the Environment takes the number of staying visitors into account when working out the annual Standard Spending Assessments (SSAs) on which decisions about support grants to local authorities are based. However, it doesn't consider the extra cost of providing for day trippers who usually outnumber staying visitors, particularly in heritage towns, putting greater strain on facilities even though they usually contribute less to the local economy.

Nevertheless tourism can also benefit fragile local economies, particularly in rural areas or areas of industrial decline, by providing alternative sources of revenue and employment.

Foreign Exchange and the Balance of Payments

Tourism plays an important role in contributing to the balance of payments. Overseas tourism is a vital source of foreign exchange earnings and thus helps compensate for the money spent on imported goods. In 1991 the London Tourist Board estimated that 80% of all expenditure by overseas visitors to London was in foreign currency.

Tourism counts as an 'invisible' export along with banking and insurance services. In 1990 it is believed to have accounted for 30% of the country's service export earnings, and 4.4% of the total export earnings.

Until 1981 Britain earnt more from its foreign tourists than was spent overseas by British holidaymakers. However, in 1981 that situation was reversed, and ever since then the British have spent more overseas than visitors have spent here. Thus the contribution of tourism to the balance of payments has tended to be in deficit.

Employment

There are three main areas of employment which can be seen as directly or indirectly tourism-related:

* employment in businesses that sell goods and services directly to tourists, like hotels and tourist attractions.
* employment in manufacturing and wholesale distribution companies that supply goods and services to the tourism businesses e.g. those selling furniture and fittings to hotels.
* employment in construction companies working on tourism projects e.g. new hotels or tourist attractions.

However, it is difficult to calculate exactly how many people are employed in the tourism industry, partly because the industry itself is so diverse and partly because some of the services provided for tourists (restaurants, attractions, etc.) are available to the local population as well. What's more some employment statistics omit the self-employed, thus 'losing' tourism's many small family businesses.

FIGURE 71 EMPLOYMENT IN TOURISM-RELATED INDUSTRIES, 1979-1989

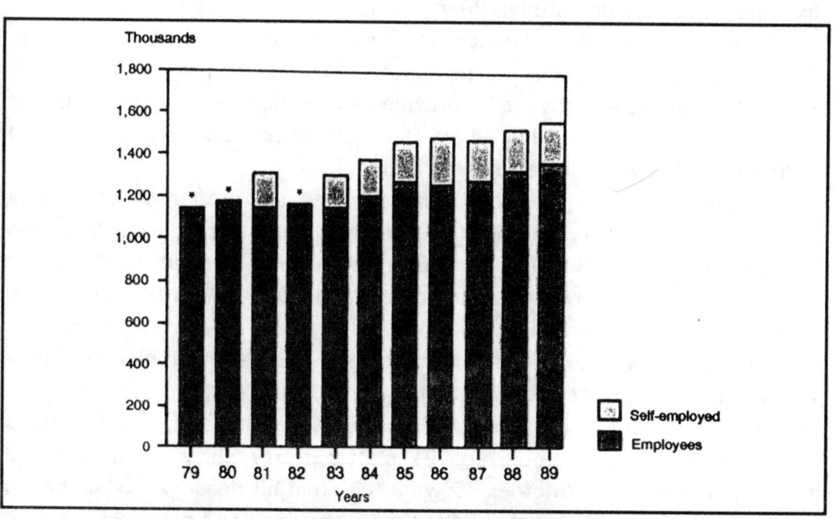

(Source: Quarterly Survey of Employers & Labour Force)

In 1990 the Department of Employment estimated that 1.5 million people, or 6% of the total employed work force, had jobs directly related to domestic and overseas tourism. In addition there were probably about 191,000 self-employed people working in tourism-related jobs. Since the figures were collected in June they probably underestimated the total numbers involved since many tourism jobs are linked to the July/August peak season. If travel and passenger transport-related jobs are also included a figure nearer to 2.4 million jobs would be reached. In Scotland tourism-related jobs employed about 150,000 people in 1989. In Wales there may be 95,000 full-time jobs in tourism-related industries.

Between 1979 and 1989 the number of jobs in tourism-related industries rose by 18.8%, compared with a rise of 15.6% for other service industries and a fall of 1.8% in other industries. The steepest rise in new jobs was in restaurants and cafés, precisely the area where it is hardest to separate the effect of tourism from that of leisure in general. Some regions experienced a particularly steep rise in the number of jobs in hotels and catering in the decade to June 1989; in the East Midlands the number of these jobs grew by 49%, while in East Anglia it grew by 34%. In 1990 7% of the working population of London were working in tourism-related jobs; another 50,000 jobs are expected to be created by the end of the century. Twenty per cent of all jobs in Stratford-on-Avon are believed to stem from tourism, and it is estimated that tourism will be the main source of jobs in heritage towns like Chester (which already has 4,000 tourism-related jobs) by the end of the century.

Tourism is also an important source of secondary employment. For example, the London Tourist Board estimated that projects worth £625 million were underway in London between July and December 1990. In that same period projects worth another £161 million were completed. Work on this scale obviously provides large numbers of jobs in the construction industry. The Albert Dock supports 459 on-site jobs and perhaps another 285 jobs elsewhere in the city.

However, like tourism itself, tourism-related jobs are not spread evenly throughout the country. In hotels and catering the majority, or 33% of the total, are in London and the South East. A further 11% are in the South West and 10% in the North West and Scotland. Only 3% of the total are in East Anglia, and 5% in Wales.

Unfortunately tourism-related jobs have a number of problems. Many are seasonal and therefore only suitable for people who don't need year-round employment. For example, in 1988 Frontierland, Morecambe's American theme park, employed 137 staff but only 35 of them were full time and permanent. Another 85 were full time but seasonal, while seven were permanent but part time and ten were part time and seasonal.

The employment pattern also varies around the country. For example, jobs in the accommodation and catering sectors in seaside resorts are particularly likely to be seasonal, whereas similar posts in London or other large cities may be permanent. In Looe in Cornwall there is little unemployment in summer but 40% of the locals are jobless in winter. In 1989 Scottish tourist attractions employed 5,642 people. Only 1,613 of these people had full time, year-round jobs, a fall of 46% since 1988; the number of full time, seasonal jobs had risen by 99% in the same period. In Northern Ireland 1100 people were employed in tourist attractions in 1989, but only half of them had full time, year-round jobs.

Many tourism jobs are notoriously poorly paid. For example, in 1985 60% of women working in hotels and catering were earning less than the then DHSS's 'poverty line'. Until recently they have also been unskilled and offered few opportunities for training or a proper career structure. Consequently there has often been a high staff turnover, especially in the hotel and catering sectors which had a 70% annual turnover in 1987.

As a result tourism jobs are often seen as less prestigious than other jobs. An ECTARC survey carried out in Wales in 1986 found that local inhabitants rated jobs in tourism at the bottom of a scale topped by employment as doctors, nurses, teachers, police officers and even house-wives.

More positively, creating a new job in tourism is believed to cost only £15,600, compared with £23,400 for the average new job. The pattern of employment may also suit those who want to be their own bosses or to work for only part of the year. Tourism also continues to offer a range of jobs for those with few skills in a world where those are rapidly vanishing.

Traditionally tourism has depended on a steady flow of young people prepared to work for low wages. However, in London alone the number of sixteen to twenty-four year olds is expected to drop by 20% by 1995, a pattern which will be repeated around the country. Employers may be forced to try harder to keep staff by offering better pay and conditions. This may in turn lead to higher standards and a better image for the industry as an employer.

ENVIRONMENTAL IMPACT OF TOURISM IN THE UK

In the late 1980s the growing 'green' movement focused attention on the environmental problems created by tourism. In 1990 the government set up a Task Force to look into the whole subject of tourism and its impact on the environment. In May 1991 it produced its report, *Tourism and the Environment: Maintaining the Balance*, which examined the problem in detail.

The Task Force looked at the impact of tourism on the environment of:

* Heritage sites which it defined as a 'wide range of places of cultural and historic significance' including 'cathedrals, churches, historic buildings of all shapes and sizes, museums, galleries, ancient monuments and gardens'.
* Historic towns, including cathedral cities like Wells and Salisbury, spa towns like Leamington and Tunbridge Wells, market towns like Ludlow and Shrewsbury, and university towns like Oxford and Cambridge.
* The countryside.

It constructed a diagram showing the relationship between the visitor, the host community and the place where the two meet (Fig. 72). In doing so they acknowledged that external influences (the mass media, population movements, etc.) also affect all aspects of these relationships with the result that it is not always easy to decide how much influence can be attributed to the impact of tourism alone.

FIGURE 72 THE RELATIONSHIP BETWEEN THE VISITOR, THE PLACE AND THE HOST COMMUNITY

The visitor, the place and the community

A helpful way to look at the relationship between tourism and the environment is to examine the interaction of the visitor, the place and the host community. This is expressed in the diagram below.

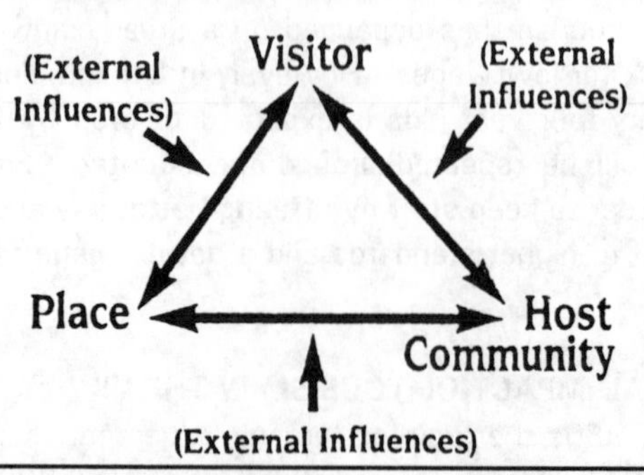

(Source: Task Force on Tourism and the Environment, 1991)

Undoubtedly tourism has safeguarded the future of many heritage sites whose fate would have been uncertain otherwise. In the first place tourist visits provide a tangible reason for preserving old buildings. Then the revenue from gate admissions can provide at least some of the money needed to preserve them. Tourism may also provide a spur to the conversion of old buildings for new uses, as at Wigan Pier, or of derelict landscapes, as at Thorpe Park.

However, the number of tourists can result in **overcrowding,** particularly at the most popular, or 'honeypot', destinations. For example, some heritage sites are too small to absorb large numbers of visitors and quickly become overcrowded. When this happens there may be actual risk to the structure and contents, and increased costs for wear and tear. Visitors may also enjoy their visits less; for example when the crowds in front of a painting make it impossible to step back and appreciate it, or when a cathedral nave is so crowded with tour groups that quiet contemplation is impossible. Luckily, in most places overcrowding is mainly a seasonal problem; there may be too many visitors from July to September, at weekends and over bank holidays, but the site may be comfortable to visit outside those times.

Structures vary in their capacity to handle large numbers of people: The Shambles in York can often feel uncomfortably crowded, while the Albert Dock can handle five million visitors a year without difficulty. A village may have trouble absorbing extra tourist cars without damage to the landscape, while in historic towns tourists may only worsen an already existing traffic problem.

Tourists may also add to the **litter** problem. A recent London Tourist Board survey discovered, not surprisingly, that tourists are put off by the quantities of rubbish littering London streets. Since then the LTB has linked up with the Tidy Britain Group and the British Incoming Tour Operators Association to campaign for improved standards of cleanliness.

Tourists can also aggravate problems of **traffic congestion**. The worst damage is often done in rural areas where the lack of public transport may mean that almost all visitors arrive by car and where the tranquillity which cars destroy may be the main reason for visiting in the first place. For example, 98% of all visitors to Flatford Mill in the low-lying Constable Country of Essex arrive in cars which clog the narrow country roads. In small villages cars also pollute the atmosphere and make for a generally noisy and less enjoyable experience for the visitor. Historic buildings are also damaged and blackened by exhaust fumes. Tourists often crowd into historic towns, like Canterbury and York, whose medieval street plans are ill-equipped to deal with the crush of cars. In Cambridge various ways of keeping cars and coaches out of the city centre have been tried. In Bath a draconian parking system backed up with a park and ride scheme keeps at least some cars out of the centre.

Coaches cause some of the worst problems. Although they are a cheap and efficient way of transporting tourists and reduce the number of individual cars, they are often too large for the narrow streets they pass through. Coach parties tend to arrive and leave sites at similar times, making the congestion worse. The Task Force on Tourism and the Environment also highlighted problems in enforcing regulations on coach drivers, especially those from overseas.

Parking is another difficulty associated with tourism by car. Yellow lines painted along village streets to prevent parking can be an eyesore, while large car parks (and caravan parks) often spoil the views people have come to see. In particular the fine sea-fronts of many of Britain's older resorts are now marred by rows of cars parked in front of them. Providing adequate coach parking in built-up city centres where land prices are at a premium is an even worse problem; the LTB has highlighted this as a particular difficulty for London.

The visual environment can also be spoilt by proliferating signposts. Fortunately this problem has been acknowledged by the Department of Transport which has comprehensive guidelines for permitting white on brown tourist signs to be erected (see Chapter Six). These were tightened up in 1991; vague signs saying 'historic town' when there are only a few 18th century houses are no longer permitted.

Large numbers of tourists inevitably lead to **wear and tear** which can take the form of damage to floors in churches and cathedrals; to paintings, textiles and carpets in historic houses; to grassed areas in parks and gardens; to riverbanks in waterside attractions; and to paths and fragile natural environments like sand-dunes and peat bogs in the countryside. The cost of making good the damage can be enormous; by 1991 the National Trust had probably spent £1.25 million just to repair soil erosion in upland areas of the Lake District.

The environment can also be damaged by **inappropriate development**, often to provide facilities like shops, toilets and car parks for visitors. Sometimes the damage is done by buildings which are out of proportion to what is already there; so many of the objections raised to a planned extension to the Haworth Parsonage Visitor Centre were because the facilities for visitors would then overwhelm the scale of the relatively small house they had come to see. Alternatively they can be out of keeping with what is already there; so Prince Charles' famous reference to the planned National Gallery extension as a 'monstrous carbuncle on the face of a much-loved friend' was mainly because it didn't blend with existing Trafalgar Square buildings (unlike the new Sainsbury Wing, opened in 1991, which mirrors the surrounding architecture). When Peter de Savary was given the go-ahead to build a theme park at Land's End many people thought it was unsuitable for what was in essence a piece of wild and romantic coastline. In contrast in 1986 the National Trust bought a shop, café and house at Kynance Cove, also in Cornwall, and demolished them to improve the landscape.

Towards Sustainable Tourism in the UK

The Task Force on Tourism and the Environment concluded that sustainable tourist development was most likely to occur where it was part of a properly thought through management strategy with clearly worked out objectives and a thorough understanding of the ways in which tourist destinations interact with each other. Before drawing up a tourist strategy they saw the following as essential:

* a detailed knowledge of the number and type of tourists already visiting.
* plans for regular monitoring of the situation since it would inevitably change over time.
* that managers should have a thorough knowledge and understanding of their specific sites and how they would be affected by tourists, rather than a general knowledge of the subject.
* that managers should have access to information about good practice, perhaps provided by the tourist boards.

Tourism development strategies should then take the following into account:

The tourist-bearing capacity of individual sites/destinations

Sites vary in their ability to absorb visitors. So some beaches in big resorts can absorb hundreds of visitors without anyone minding the crowding. They will also be washed clean by the tide twice a day. In contrast during the breeding season some nature reserves may only be able to handle a few visitors if nesting sites are to be protected. In assessing an individual site's capacity managers should bear in mind:

a) the number of visitors above which its ambience would be damaged
b) the point at which physical damage to it might occur
c) the point at which irreversible damage would occur
d) the point at which the host community would also suffer unacceptable side effects

Where a site is deemed to be overloaded it can be protected by closing it altogether. This has happened at Stonehenge where the number of visitors was thought to threaten the fragile prehistoric structures. Alternatively, it can be temporarily closed, as sometimes happens at

Osborne House on the Isle of Wight during the peak summer season.

The number of visitors can also be reduced or controlled by:

a) limiting road signs to deter casual visitors, as at Lacock Abbey
b) reducing the size of the car park, as at Dovedale in the Peak District
c) insisting everyone takes a guided tour, as at Dove Cottage in the Lake District
d) using 'time cars' as at Jorvik or headphones as at the Oxford Story to limit how many people can be inside the building at one time
e) selling tickets with specific admission times, as at Chartwell where people are admitted at fifteen minute intervals with roughly sixty tickets available for each fifteen minute period
f) insisting on advance booking for groups
g) providing alternative attractions in the grounds to spread people away from the centre point, as at Warwick Castle
h) charging for admission to over-popular villages

Transport management

Signposts can be used to direct tourists away from fragile areas and along the routes least likely to become congested. Attractions can also help by indicating preferred access routes in advance publicity.

Cars and coach parks should be clearly signposted from likely access points. In very popular areas pedestrian signs may also be needed to direct tourists from the car parks to the actual attractions. Car park prices can also be used to 'direct' tourists; in Oxford city-centre car parks are more expensive than those on the outskirts. Coupled with a park and ride scheme, such a strategy should reduce the number of cars in the city centre. Ideally there should be specific planning for coaches as in York and Windsor where coach routes are specially signposted and separate parking areas are provided.

In extreme cases roads can be closed to traffic altogether, as is the case in the small Devon village of Clovelly. Many towns and cities now have pedestrianised areas, although these are usually in the main shopping centres.

Marketing and information provision

If a site is thought to have too many visitors the best policy may be to stop actively promoting it. Thus the National Trust has considered removing Lacock Abbey from its Members Handbook, while the Ordnance Survey no longer marks the overwalked Lyke Wake Walk in the North York Moors National Park on its maps.

The Regional Tourist Boards are trying to persuade more tourists to visit out of the peak periods. An important part of this process are the *Places To Visit In Winter* brochures, listing winter opening hours. Reducing prices in midweek or in winter may also persuade some people to visit in the low season.

Some tourism development plans like the one for the Eden district of Cumbria specifically aim to direct visitors to less popular areas of a county. However, it's hard to persuade first-time and overseas visitors to miss out the best known sites.

Marketing can be targeted at specific groups of 'preferred' visitors; for example, walkers and cyclists, staying visitors who contribute more to the local economy, users of public transport, etc.

Carefully sited Tourist Information Centres, like those in the car parks at Canterbury and Stratford, can play an important role in helping to channel visitors as required. Pedestrian signposting can also help. Visitor Centres also have a role to play in teaching visitors more about the significance of what they have come to see and of the reasons for preserving and protecting it.

Control and design of all tourist development

Ideally local planning authorities should ensure good design for developments especially in sensitive areas. In particular developers should be encouraged to use materials in keeping with the surrounding area and to camouflage potentially intrusive new buildings, as has been done particularly well at Center Parcs in Sherwood Forest. Increasingly existing old buildings with character are being reused, for example to provide cafés, so that a new building need not mar an area's appearance.

Where tourism projects are used to regenerate decaying urban or industrial areas, as in Liverpool's Albert Dock or the Wigan Pier Heritage Centre, their contribution to improving the environment can be immeasurable.

Conservation and adaptation of sites

Wear and tear can be minimised at sites with guides or wardens to keep an eye on things but there are also more specific ways to protect structures and landscapes. So footpaths and riverbanks can be artificially reinforced to make them last longer; carpets can be laid over floors which are likely to be damaged; and decorative railings can be put round monuments to protect them, as in Westminster Abbey. Occasionally original structures can be protected by replacing them with exact replicas as in many churches with brasses which people want to rub.

The Task Force concluded that the various agencies concerned with tourism need to be better co-ordinated if tourism is to be prevented from damaging the environment. There also needs to be an agreed strategic framework at local, county and regional levels if conflicts are not to arise. Care must also be taken to ensure that efforts to protect one site don't simply shift the problem to another nearby. It recommended a partnership approach as the best way to ensure that tourism action policies, tourism development action programmes and statutory land use plans don't end up in conflict with each other. The Task Force also emphasised that protection of the environment was difficult unless adequate funding arrangements could be guaranteed and drew attention to a particular need for funding of Town Centre Management Schemes. It also recognised that the problems faced by London were on a completely different scale and needed more specific research.

Inner City Tourism and Urban Decay

In the 1980s tourism was identified as a way to restore the decaying centres of many Britain's cities. Not only could new jobs be created cheaply, but the improvements undertaken to make the sites attractive would obviously make them more appealing for local residents too. The innumerable schemes to redevelop abandoned docks around the country in the 1980s are one of the best examples of this process in action.

Rural Tourism

Just as turning derelict inner city areas into tourist attractions was seen as one way to handle the problems of urban decline in the early 1980s, so turning farms into tourist attractions began to be seen as a way of handling the increasing problems facing British farmers by the end of the 1980s. As concern over the adverse impact of tourism in 'honeypot' destinations grew, planners decided that developing rural tourism could help to spread the load. By 1989 the ETB had produced its *Visitors in the Countryside: Rural Tourism...A Development Strategy* and the Countryside Commission its *Principles for Tourism in the Countryside*. The Rural Development Commission had also appointed a national Rural Tourism Development Officer. Many district councils in rural areas also appointed tourism officers. Some farms have always offered bed and breakfast or allowed caravans and camping on their land. Now many more have set up small craft centres, provide facilities for sports or offer farm open days and demonstrations of farm techniques like ploughing matches and sheep dog trails.

Surveys suggest that of British tourism nights spent away from home 21% are passed in the country, with 20% of all visits being to the West Country. During 1990 73% of the British population were estimated to have taken at least one day trip to the countryside. 77% of rural tourists reach their destinations by car and 24% will have travelled more than thirty miles from their home. Rural tourism may be worth about £3 billion a year to the British economy. However, the countryside seems to appeal mainly to the ABC1 socio-economic groups and better educated segments of the market, limiting the likely expansion which can take place.

However, the development of tourism in the countryside presents potential problems. Not all small communities can absorb increasing numbers of visitors without irreparable damage being done to their social fabric. In the most popular areas tourists can do great damage to what they have come to see. In the Lake District footpaths and lake edges have been worn away and litter carelessly dropped. During August Bank Holidays twelve mile traffic jams can build up between Kendal and Ambleside at the heart of the Lakes, and ugly yellow lines now mar the appearance of Glenridding in an effort to stop people blocking the streets. The Friends of the Lake District have suggested levying a bed tax on visitors to pay for repairs but this would be unpopular with hoteliers and is not currently seen as a realistic solution to the difficulties. Some farmers also resent tourists walking across their land, blaming them for damage done to crops, open gates, etc.

In 1990 the ETB and the Countryside Commission agreed a six point plan for future development in the countryside to limit further damage. It said that:

* tourism promotion should emphasise those activities in keeping with the country's character, history, culture, etc.
* tourism development should assist with conservation; for example, by providing new uses for historic buildings.
* the design, siting and management of new developments should be in keeping with/enhance the existing landscape.
* tourism investment should support the local economy, but encourage a wider geographical and seasonal spread of visitors.
* those who gain from rural tourism should play a full part in countryside conservation, etc.
* the tourism industry should try to widen the public's understanding of countryside issues through its marketing, etc.

However, in 1989 the government introduced plans to remove some of the planning restrictions on the development of equestrian centres, canoeing and caravan sites, and theme and amusement parks in the countryside.

Good conduct in the countryside can be summarised in the Tourism Concern slogan:

Take nothing but photographs.
Leave nothing but footprints.

FIGURE 73 THE TRADITIONAL COUNTRYSIDE CODE

Enjoy the countryside and respect its life and work.
Use gates and stiles to cross fences, hedges and walls.
Keep your dogs under close control.
Protect wildlife, plants and trees.
Help to keep all water clean.
Make no unnecessary noise.
Leave livestock, crops and machinery alone.
Keep to public paths across farm land.
Take special care on country roads.
Guard against all risk of fire.
Take your litter home.
Fasten all gates.

SOCIAL AND CULTURAL IMPACT OF TOURISM IN THE UK

As Fig. 72 shows, visitors also have an impact on the host communities of the places they choose to visit. In some ways this impact is the hardest of all to quantify since other outside influences will be affecting the same communities which are living, changing entities. Deciding how much any individual change is the result of tourism rather than the influence of, say, television, can be extremely tricky.

In general tourism may enrich local communities by putting them in touch with a range of external views, life-styles and opinions. In rural areas where communities are small the social benefits of tourism may be particularly important. However, not all forms of tourism actually result in much contact between the visitors and their hosts. This is more likely when people take self-catering holidays or stay in local bed and breakfasts than when they stay in large hotels. Day trippers arriving at heritage sites in their cars may not speak to any local people at all during their visit.

Tourism may also make it possible for marginally profitable businesses like village post offices to stay open when local trade alone would not justify this. In larger towns it may mean that a wider range of quality shops can be supported. Facilities largely provided for tourists will also be available for locals to use. For example, people living near large theme parks may make more visits to them then those living further afield. There is also evidence that local people visit local attractions more frequently when they themselves have visitors; in other words, the existence of local attractions makes their jobs as hosts much easier. Some public transport services used by local people would also be withdrawn as unprofitable were it not for the extra tourist traffic.

FIGURE 74 THE ENGLISH TOURIST BOARD'S GREEN TOURISM CODE

20

TIPS FOR VISITORS

1. Always remember you are the guest: show consideration for residents and their environment. Respect local laws and customs.

2. Leave beaches, parks and public places as you would like to find them.

3. Put litter in a bin or take it home: don't expect others to clean up after you.

4. Keep noise levels down, especially at night or in quiet places like churches and the countryside.

5. Show respect for nature: keep to proper footpaths, don;t feed wildlife and don't pick flowers or shrubs.

6. Remember that many people find smoking offensive, and careless smokers may cause countryside fires.

7. Don't carve your initials on trees and historic monuments or spoil them with graffiti.

8. Complain if you have just cause, but do it politely.

9. Don't argue with staff who seek to enforce rules: they are only doing their jobs.

10. Avoid the temptation to touch valuable objects such as paintings, tapestries and vases.

11. Keep an eye on your children to see they don't indulge in destructive or annoying behaviour.

12. If you want to photograph other people, ask them first.

13. Behave towards others as you would wish them to behave towards you: don't push, shove or jump queues.

14. Good manners are always appreciated: don't forget to say 'please' and 'thank you.'

15. Dress properly to visit places of worship: remember they are not holiday playgrounds.

16. Wear suitable footwear to visit historic buildings: high-heeled shoes can cause a lot of damage.

17. Be enterprising: visit parts of the country off the usual 'tourist trail'.

18. If you live in Britain, try to visit our popular attractions in off-peak periods; you will enjoy them much more .

19. Use public transport whenever possible. If you take your car, park in a designated space, not just where you please.

20. Help the local economy: buy locally grown or made goods wherever possible.

(Source: ETB, 1991)

The interests of tourists can also ensure the survival of skills and crafts that might otherwise fade away, and in the 1980s many attractions opened craft workshops as additional lures for visitors. Sometimes crafts can be degraded by mass production for an undiscerning market. However, in general in the UK the craft revival has been of high quality, relatively expensive goods. The needs of tourists may also ensure a wider range of cultural and entertainment facilities than the local population alone could justify.

In London many services and amenities available to Londoners might not be viable without the financial contribution of tourists. So 25% of passengers on the London Undergound are visitors, 25% of all taxi journeys are by tourists 17% of the spending in Oxford St shops is by tourists and 40% of all West End theatre tickets are bought by visitors. Many restaurants and entertainment facilities, especially in Central London, also depend on tourists for much of their income; a decline in the number of visitors would threaten their viability.

Tourism can also help improve an area's image which might encourage companies to move there when they might not otherwise have done so, bringing jobs and greater prosperity for local people. For example, the report of the Tourism Study carried out for Merseyside Tourist Board in 1986 states that: 'Generally, pleasure visitors to Merseyside developed more positive attitudes towards Merseyside during their stay showing that the image of Liverpool did not match reality. For example, 26% of staying vsiitors indicated that they thought Liverpool was a rough, violent and depressing place before their visit but only 2% felt that way after their visit.' Glasgow, too, has seen its image improve by leaps and bounds since the Greater Glasgow Tourist Board actively set out to promote it as a tourist destination.

However, problems can easily arise when the **number of visitors** exceeds the number of local residents. This regularly happens in small villages like Lacock which has a resident population of about 200 but receives about 500,000 visitors a year to view the Abbey and Fox Talbot Photography Museum. Clovelly, with a resident population of about 400, receives about 370,000 visitors a year who swarm down the steep main street in summer, peering through villagers' windows and making them feel as if they live in a goldfish bowl. To reduce this problem a 'typical' fisherman's cottage is to be opened to the public so that they can see a cottage interior without disturbing the villagers. Even towns like Windsor can feel swamped when they are visited by a hundred tourists for every single resident each year.

The sheer number of tourists can result in the **transformation of villages** in other ways, as traditional shops give way to souvenir shops and tea rooms. The problem may be less obvious in places like Welsh and Cornish coastal settlements with a long established tourist trade. However, tourism has also been blamed for the transformation of many Cotswold villages. While the changes at Bourton-on-the-Water and Broadway may well be primarily the result of tourism, in other villages they may really be the result of ex-city dwellers moving permanently to the countryside, or of second-homers who leave villages virtually empty during week-days and in the winter.

Another difficulty that can arise in small communities visited by large numbers of tourists is that the **value of land** and the **cost of housing** can rise steeply as speculators and developers buy land to build tourist facilities and houses to turn into hotels or self-catering accommodation. Local people may then be forced out of the market for affordable local homes which inevitably causes resentment. In Wales this has resulted in political activists actually burning down houses bought by outsiders, although often these are second homes and it is debatable whether they are truly part of the tourism industry or part of a more general pattern of social change. To resolve these difficulties in the Lake District there has been talk about setting aside some housing which can only be sold to young local couples. In Lacock village which is owned by the National Trust, priority is given to local people when houses become vacant.

To keep conflicts between tourists and local people to a minimum all development strategies must try to involve the host community in the decision-making process, however hard it may be to decide how this should be done. Normal planning procedures already allow for public participation in development decisions, but local forums can also be used to allow everyone affected by a project to get involved. The tourism development action programmes already pull together many local tourism interests although it is usually businesses rather than individuals who become involved. A simple method of acknowledging local people is to let local community chargepayers into attractions at a preferential rate, as already happens in Bath.

CHAPTER TWELVE
SPECIALIST MARKETS FOR TOURISM IN THE UK

During the 1980s business travel became increasingly important to the UK. Many tour operators also offer special interest holidays aimed at specific segments of the holiday market. This chapter looks at some of these specialist markets in more detail.

BUSINESS TRAVEL

In 1991 business tourism made up 15% of total tourist trips to the UK and accounted for 23% of the spending. In 1989 overseas business travellers made 4.4 million trips to the UK and spent £2,032 million on their travels. UK residents made another 14.5. million business travel trips, spending £2,050 million in the process. In the period from 1979 to 1988 business travel seems to have grown three times faster than other forms of tourism, with overseas business travel showing the fastest rate of increase of all.

The typical business traveller tends to be male, from socio-economic groups ABC1, and aged between 25 and 54. He spends more than the average visitor, but stays for roughly half the average length of time. Overseas business travellers are the highest spenders of all and tend to stay longer on their trips than their domestic counterparts, perhaps because some take advantage of the opportunity to add a holiday on to the end of their trip. Seventy per cent of all overseas business travellers are from Western Europe. They are more likely than other tourists to travel by plane or train, and less likely to use cars or buses.

The destinations of general business travellers tend to be dictated by the pattern of economic activity within a given country. So about half of all UK business travel is focused on London. Eighty-two per cent of domestic business travellers stay within England, the most frequent destinations being in London, the Heart of England or the North West. They are least likely to visit Cumbria and Northumbria. Business travel also tends to be strongly city- and town-centred.

Business travel is more evenly spread throughout the year than holiday tourism, offering considerable benefits to towns like Blackpool, Brighton and Bournemouth which have been able to attract a flourishing business market to supplement the traditional seaside holiday pattern.

Because 66% of business travellers stay in hotels (compared with 23% of tourists as a whole) their needs have had a great influence on British hotel development. Three and four star hotels may draw 80-90% of their clientele, especially mid-week, from business travellers. Even lower grade hotels may be 50% filled with business travellers, including travelling salesmen.

Visitors to conferences and exhibitions make up an important part of the UK business travel market. These markets may also be growing faster than business travel as a whole. Conference and exhibition attenders spend more on average than already high-spending general business travellers. However, although incentive travel is a growing area of business travel worldwide little of it currently finds its way to Britain.

The Conference Market

Perhaps 700 large conferences (involving more than 500 delegates) take place in the UK every year. However, there are also many smaller corporate meetings for sales conferences, product launches, seminars, training sessions, etc. These conferences, most of them held in hotels, probably make up 85% of the UK total. In 1988 domestic visitors made 1.35 million trips to conferences, staying for an average 3.9 nights and spending a total £113 million. Overseas visitors made 0.26 million trips, staying for an average 1.5 nights and spending a total £135 million. In 1990 conference travel probably accounted for about 6% of the total business travel market.

The largest purpose-built conference centres in the UK are:

The Queen Elizabeth II Centre, London

Bournemouth International Centre

Barbican Conference Centre, London

Birmingham International Convention Centre

In addition to the purpose-built conference centres and the hotels catering for this market, conferences are also held in university and polytechnic buildings, town halls and concert halls, and increasingly in more unusual venues like museums and historic houses.

The Exhibition Market

In 1989 707 exhibitions were held in major exhibition spaces in the UK. In 1988 domestic visitors made 1.19 million trips to exhibitions, spending a total £158 million. Overseas visitors made 0.18 million trips, staying for an average 0.9 nights and spending a total £100 million. In 1990 the exhibitions market probably accounted for about 6% of the total business travel market.

Trade shows should be seen as a sub-section of the overall exhibitions market. They tend to attract fewer people but from a wider area. Visitors to trade fairs tend to be particularly high spenders.

The largest exhibition centres in the UK are:

Olympia, London,

Earls Court, London,

National Exhibition Centre (NEC), Birmingham

SPECIAL INTEREST HOLIDAYS

Most types of holiday can be taken in the UK, although obviously the climate means that those focusing on sightseeing are likely to be more popular than simple beach holidays.

Boating Holidays

Each year an estimated 420,000 to 440,000 people, 87% of them British, take boating holidays in the UK, mainly between Easter and late October. These holidays usually last for seven or fourteen days, which is no longer typical of domestic holidays. However, there are an increasing number of three or four day short breaks as well. The value of these holidays is probably about £44 million. Boating holidays seem to be particularly popular with the younger age ranges (18 to 45) and attract a lot of repeat business. About 200 companies offer boats for hire, although many of them are very small. Boating holidays can be taken on Britain's river and canal network and on large expanses of inland water like the Broads. Hoseasons and Blakes are two of the largest UK operators of boating holidays. Fig. 75 shows the most popular areas for UK boating holidays and Table 68 describes the type of boating most popular in each area.

Holidaymakers can opt for *self-skippering*, sailing their own boat and taking responsibility for their itinerary. Alternatively they can choose hotel boats, or floating hotels where a crew does all the work. On rivers most people use motorised *cabin cruisers* fitted with hot and cold water, electricity, sanitation, central heating, etc. On canals they often choose *narrowboats*, based on traditional designs. On a few canals it is even possible to travel by horse-drawn barge. Most boats sleep between two and twelve people.

FIGURE 75 HOLIDAYS ON INLAND WATERWAYS

(Source: BTA)

For non-sailers Britain's waterways are attractive as places to walk, birdwatch, sketch, go fishing or visit industrial heritage attractions. In 1991 the National Tourist Boards and the British Marine Industries Federation were particularly promoting the following 'Seven Wonders of the Waterways':

* Anderton Vertical Lift in Cheshire
* Pontcysyllte Aqueduct on the Llangollen Canal
* Standedge Tunnel on Huddersfield Narrow Canal
* Barton Swing Aqueduct which carries the Bridgewater Canal over the Manchester Ship Canal.
* Bingley Five Rise Locks in Yorkshire
* Burnley Embankment on the Leeds-Liverpool Canal
* Caen Hill flight of locks on the Kennet and Avon Canal

TABLE 68 BOATING HOLIDAYS IN THE UK

The South Coast
Offshore cruising & powerboat racing events.

The West Country
Cruising for sailing and motor yachts.
Sea fishing.

Bristol Channel
Boating on strong tidal waters.

The Midlands
Inland dinghy sailing. Canal and river cruising. Traditional narrowboat holidays.

Fenlands
Waterway linking Cambridge, Bedford, Ely, Northampton & The Wash.

The Broads
Miles of river & open water linked to the sea. Holiday cruisers, dinghy sailing, small yacht racing. Hydroplane racing.

East Coast
Cruising and catamaraning from Orfordness to North Foreland in the Thames Estuary. Thames barges and Essex smacks.

Home Counties
Motor cruising on the Thames. Dinghy sailing on the Medway, inland reservoirs, rivers and lakes.

North West England
Sailing at Ullswater and Windermere. Powerboats on Windermere. New marina on Mersey. Twin keels and catamarans.

North East England
Sturdy boats can use traditional fishing harbours.

Wales
Sailing round North Wales coast and Anglesey. Boating on Welsh lakes and reservoirs. Canoeing on the Wye.

Scotland's West Coast and Islands
Cruising along the coast for experienced sailors.

Scotland's East Coast
Yacht racing on Firth of Tay & Firth of Forth.

Firth of Clyde
Yacht & dinghy clubs. Miles of sheltered water.

Scottish Lochs
Motor cruising on Loch Lomond and Caledonian Canal.

(Source: Ship and Boat Builders National Federation, 1991)

When asked why they chose a boating holiday people cited the freedom, informality and relaxation it offered. Eleven per cent said they had fancied a change, and 23% mentioned the novelty value. Birdwatching, fishing and country walking are popular secondary activities with boating holidaymakers.

Golfing Holidays

The UK currently has about 2,350 golf courses. However, there are about two million regular players and another three million casual players. In addition some overseas tourist groups, including the Japanese, Americans and Australians, are particularly keen on golf. Consequently courses, especially in the south-east, are increasingly congested and waiting lists for club membership are growing. In the past most golf courses were owned by clubs which jealously safeguarded their exclusivity with high subscription fees and demanding conditions for membership. However, in the 1980s several companies realised that adding a golf course to other leisure facilities, particularly hotels, could make those facilities more attractive. In such circumstances users play on a 'pay-as-you-play' basis more appropriate to tourism.

The UK is thought to need another 700 courses to satisfy demand over the next ten years. However, it costs about half a million pounds to develop an eighteen hole course and planning permission can be hard to obtain. One possibility is for farmers to turn some of their excess land into courses suitable for beginners.

The ETB estimates that 2,675 hotels, or 12% of the total, offer their guests access to golf courses even if they don't actually own them. The higher the accommodation grade, the more likely it is to offer golfing facilities; perhaps 50% of all five crown hotels offer access to golf courses. In particular County Club Hotels, which is largely owned by Whitbread, has opened nine hotels with golf courses attached to them. Where the golf course is owned by the hotel there is usually a private membership scheme as well, so that the course generates revenue from outside too. Outside users may also utilise the hotel bar and restaurant, thus bringing in even more revenue. However, problems can arise if too many outsiders want to use the course at the same time as hotel residents.

Golf hotels seem most popular with the business/conference market, with people on short breaks and with the ABC1 end of the domestic market. Because their appeal is so upmarket, golf hotels must offer a quality product with golf shops, the services of a professional to advise players and a range of driving ranges and practice holes, as well as at least one full eighteen hole course.

Britain's best known golfing centre is at St. Andrew's in Scotland, home of the Royal and Ancient Golf Club.

Activity Holidays

In his analysis of the activity holiday market Steve Beioley argues that it includes: hobby holidays, adventure holidays, summer programmes, working holidays and themed breaks like 'murder weekends'. Perhaps two million holidays a year can be described as 'activity holidays' by this definition. The ETB publication *Let's Do It* lists 59 different types of activity holiday. The most frequently offered are multi-activities, holidays for children, painting, horse activities, sailing and heritage holidays, but operators disagree over which are most popular. Indeed, the most popular activities may change with general fashions.

Most such holidays are taken by domestic holidaymakers, many on repeat trips. Activity holidaymakers may be of any age, but tend to come from the ABC1 socio-economic groups. Activity holidays also seem to be particularly popular with single holidaymakers, seeking company in safe circumstances as much as the chosen activity itself. If walkers, boaters, fishers and those on heritage holidays are excluded more than a million activity holidays may still be taken each year, involving an expenditure of about £250 million. Circumstantial evidence suggests that this is a growth market; 65% of activity holiday operators only entered the market in the last ten years.

Activity holidays are offered by hotels and other accommodation providers, like the YHA and Pontin's, as a way of filling surplus bedspace and generating publicity. Hotel activity holidays tend to appeal to the older, wealthier, more passive end of the market. Embassy Hotels, Countrywide Hotels, Consort Hotels and Forte have all been successful in this market. Several public schools, colleges and universities also offer activity holidays during the summer holidays. They are particularly well positioned to offer short study courses, many of them organised by the National Institute for Adult Continuing Education. Millfield School in Somerset and the University of East Anglia have been particularly successful in marketing themselves as holiday centres. More active holidays tend to be offered by the specialist activity holiday operators and by outdoor pursuit centres and field study centres.

Several companies offer activity holidays aimed at children, mostly for the two peak summer months and Easter, and mainly in the wilder, remoter parts of the country like Scotland and Wales. PGL Young Adventure Ltd started business in 1957 offering canoeing and camping holidays on the River Wye. In the 1960s and '70s it expanded to offer sailing and pony trekking in the Brecon Beacons National Park. Increasingly it drew its market from schools. By 1991 PGL had ten multi-activity centres in the UK offering seventy different sports or activities from archery and abseiling to waterskiing and pigeon shooting. A PGL Family Adventure company now offers similar holidays for entire families.

Surprisingly, UK legislation currently allows anyone to set up an activities centre, even when it will be involved with potentially dangerous pursuits like caving and rock-climbing. The British Activity Holiday Association was set up in 1986 to monitor safety standards and the quality of holidays offered. It now has eighty inspected and approved members.

Walking Holidays

Walking holidays have long been popular in the UK, both with individuals who travel to remote parts of the National Parks and stay in camp-sites or youth hostels, and with those who prefer to walk in groups, often organised by the Ramblers Association. There may be as many as five million annual walking holidays in the UK, and walkers are estimated to spend about £600 million a year. Most Tourist Information Centres produce and stock brochures with details of local walks suitable for all levels of ability.

Motorsports

Motorsports, whether in cars or on motorbikes, are also very popular with holidaymakers, although local residents often dislike them because of the noise and crowds they generate.

The Isle of Man has had a particularly intensive programme of motorsports since 1907 when the first Tourist Trophy Race for motorbikes took place on a fifteen and a quarter mile circuit run on normal roads and starting and finishing in St. Johns. In 1911 the race circuit was moved to the Mountain Course; it is now run along a 37.73 mile circuit finally established in 1920 and there are seven different races for sidecars, light-weight bikes, vintage bikes and junior and senior riders.

TABLE 69 ISLE OF MAN - ISLE OF SPORT

late May	T.T. Practice Week
June	T.T. Races (motorbikes)
late June	Manx International Cycling Week
July	Southern 100 Course (motorbikes)
September	Manx Grand Prix (motorbikes)
September	Manx International Rally (cars)
late September	Manx Classic Car Pursuit

Ornithological Holidays

Many birdwatchers also like to take holidays which let them pursue their hobby. The Royal Society for Protection of Birds (RSPB) has a network of 98 sanctuaries around the country, covering many of the most important sites like Minsmere in Suffolk, Grassholm in Wales and Bempton Cliffs in Northumbria. It also offers its own programme of specialist holidays which let birdwatchers stay with other like-minded souls. Other specialist tour operators featuring birdwatching holidays advertise in its magazine, *Birds*.

Health Holidays

Health holidays have a long history, with spa towns attracting some of the earliest known tourists. Much of the appeal of seaside resorts originally came from their association with health-giving sea breezes. After the First World War the traditional spas mostly fell from favour. Their place has been taken to some extent by health farms like Grayshott Hall which offer the client the opportunity to relax and take part in both active and passive activities in luxurious surroundings.

Health farms are usually large hotels offering saunas, massages, aerobics, yoga, meditation, nutritional advice and beauty treatments, although they may also have tennis courts, golf courses and other sports facilities as well. Water-based treatments are particularly popular and one of England's newest spa hotels, Hoar Cross Hall in a converted stately home, offers hydrotherapy and thalassotherapy. There are also a few 'New Age' health farms, usually on a much smaller scale; so the Middle Piccadilly Natural Healing Centre in Dorset, in a 16th century farmhouse, caters for no more than eight guests at a time and offers organic vegetarian meals, Shen Tao acupressure, aromotherapy and other holistic treatments.

Traditionally health farms had a very upmarket image. However, some of their wealthiest clientelé now prefer to travel to the Bahamas or even the continent and health farms have had to become less exclusive. A few are also exploring the potential of the business market; Champneys, for example, has a meeting room alongside the gyms and pools.

USEFUL ADDRESSES

Arts Council of Great Britain, 14 Great Peter St, London SW1P 3NQ; tel: 071-333 0100

BAA plc, 130 Wilton Rd, London SW1V 1LQ; tel: 071-834 9449

Blakes Holidays, Wroxham, Norwich NR12 8DH; tel: 06053 2141

Brecon Beacons National Park, 7 Glamorgan St, Brecon, Powys LD3 7DP; tel: 0874 4437

British Activity Holidays Association, Norton Terrace, Llandrindod Wells, Powys LD1 6AE; tel: 059782 3902

British Association of Leisure Parks, Piers and Attractions, 25 Kings Terrace, London NW1 0JP; tel: 071-383 7942

British Holiday and Home Parks Association, Chichester House, 31 Park Rd, Gloucester GL1 1LH; tel: 0452 26911

British Incoming Tour Operators Association, 18A Coulson St, London SW3 3NB; tel: 071-581 4101

British Marine Industries Federation, Boating Industry House, Vale Rd, Oaklands Park, Weybridge, Surrey KT13 9NS; tel: 0932 854511

British Railways Board, Euston House, 24 Eversholt St, PO Box 100, London NW1 1DZ; tel: 071-928 5151

British Spas Federation, Norbury House, Droitwich Spa, Worcs WR9 8EE; tel: 0905 795155

British Tourist Authority/English Tourist Board, Thames Tower, Black's Rd, Hammersmith, London W6 9EL; tel: 081-846 9000

British Waterways, Greycaine Rd, Watford, Herts WD2 4JR; tel: 0923 226422

Broads Authority, Thomas Harvey House, 18, Colegate, Norwich, Norfolk NR3 1BQ; tel: 0603 610734

Bus and Coach Council, Sardinia House, 52 Lincoln's Inn Fields, London WC2A 3LZ; tel: 071-831 7546

Butlin's, Bognor Regis, West Sussex PO21 1JJ; tel: 0243 860068

Caledonian Macbrayne Ltd, Ferry Terminal, Gourock PA19 1QP; tel: 0475 33755

Camping and Caravanning Club Ltd, Greenfield House, Westwood Way, Coventry CV4 8JH; tel: 0203 694995

Caravan Club, East Grinstead House, East Grinstead, West Sussex RH19 1UA; tel: 0342 326944

CAA, CAA House, 45-59 Kingsway, London WC2B 6TE; tel: 071-379 7311

Cumbria Tourist Board, Ashleigh, Holly Rd, Windermere, Cumbria LA23 2AQ; tel: 09662 4444

Cyclists Touring Club (CTC), Cotterell House, 69 Meadrow, Godalming, Surrey GU7 3HS; tel: 0203 417217

Dartmoor National Park, Parke, Haytor Rd, Bovey Tracey, Devon TQ13 9JQ; tel: 0626 832093

East Anglia Tourist Board, Toppesfield Hall, Hadleigh, Suffolk IP7 5DN; tel: 0473 822922

East Midlands Tourist Board, Exchequergate, Lincoln, Lincs LN2 1PZ; tel: 0522 531521

Exmoor National Park, Exmoor House, Dulverton, Somerset TA22 9HL; tel: 0398 23665

Farm Holiday Bureau of the UK, National Agricultural Centre, Stoneleigh Park, Kenilworth, Warks CV8 2LZ; tel: 0203 696909

Great British Cities, Greater Glasgow Tourist Board and Convention Bureau, St. Vincent's Place, Glasgow G1 2ER; tel: 041-221 0049

Guild of Guide Lecturers, 2 Bridge St, London SW1A 2JR; tel: 071-839 7438

Haven Holidays, Swan Court, Waterhouse St, Hemel Hempstead, Herts HP1 1DA; tel: 0442 230300

Heart of England Tourist Board, 2-4 Trinity St, Worcester, Worcs WR1 2PW; tel: 0905 613132

Highlife Value Breaks, PO Box 139, Leeds LS2 7TE; tel: 0532 439111

Holiday Care Service, 2 Old Bank Chambers, Station Rd, Horley, Surrey RH6 9HW; tel: 0293 774535.

Holiday Club Pontins, PO Box 100, Sagar House, The Green, Eccleston, Chorley, Lancs PR7 5QQ; tel: 0257 452452

Holimarine, 171 Ivyhouse Lane, Bilston, West Midlands WV14 9LD; tel: 0902 880100

Hoseasons Holidays, Sunway House, Lowestoft, Suffolk NR32 3LT; tel: 0502 500505

Hoverspeed Ltd, International Hoverport, Western Docks, Dover CT17 9TG; tel: 0304 240101

Inland Waterways Association, 114 Regents Park, London NW1 8UQ; tel: 071-586 2556

Isle of Man Tourist Board, Sea Terminal, Douglas, Isle of Man; tel: 0624 686800

Lake District National Park, Brockhole National Park Centre, Windermere, Cumbria LA23 1LJ; tel: 09662 6601

London Tourist Board, 26 Grosvenor Gdns, London SW1W ODU; tel: 071-730 3450

London Transport, 55 Broadway, London SW1H 0BD; tel: 071-222 5600

National Association of Holiday Centres Ltd, 10 Bolton St, London W1Y 8AU; tel: 071-499 8000

National Express/Caledonian Express, Ensign Court, 4 Vicarage Rd, Edgbaston, Birmingham B15 3ES; tel: 021-625 1122

National Gardens Scheme, Hatchlands Park, East Clandon, Guildford, Surrey GU4 7RT; tel: 0483 211535

Northern Ireland Tourist Board, River House, 48 High St, Belfast BT1 2DS; tel: 0232 235906

North Sea Ferries, King George Dock, Hedon Rd, Hull HU9 5QA; tel: 0482 795141

Northumbria Tourist Board, Aykley Heads, Durham DH1 5UX; tel: 091-384 6905

North West Tourist Board, The Last Drop Village, Bromley Cross, Bolton, Lancs BL7 9PZ; tel: 0204 591511

North York Moors National Park, The Old Vicarage, Bondgate, Helmsley, York YO6 5BP; tel: 0439 70657

Northumberland National Park, Eastburn, South Park, Hexham, Northumberland NE46 1BS; tel: 0434 605555

Olau Line (UK) Ltd, Ferry Terminal, Sheerness ME12 1SN; tel: 0795 580010

P & O European Ferries (Dover) Ltd, Channel House, Channel View Rd, Dover CT17 9TJ; tel: 0304 223000

Peak National Park, Aldern House, Baslow Rd, Bakewell, Derbys DE4 1AE; tel: 0629 814321

Pembrokeshire Coast National Park, Haverfordwest, Dyfed SA61 1QZ; tel: 0437 764591

PGL Young Adventure Ltd, Alton Court, Penyard Lane, Ross-on-Wye, Herefordshire HR9 5NR; tel: 0989 764211

RADAR, 25 Mortimer St, London W1N 8AB; tel: 071-637 5400.

Rainbow Holidays and Shortbreaks, Ryedale Building, Piccadilly, York YO1 1PN; tel: 0904 643399

Ramblers Association, 1-5 Wandsworth Rd, London SW8 2XX; tel: 071-582 6878

Sally Line Ltd, Argyle Centre, York St, Ramsgate CT11 9DS; tel: 0834 595566

Scandinavian Seaways, Scandinavia House, Parkeston Quay, Harwich CO12 4QG; tel: 0255 241234

Scotland Holidays Afloat, Room BA, Marine Parade, Dundee DD1 3JD; tel: 0382 21555

Scottish Tourist Board, 23 Ravelston Terrace, Edinburgh EH4 3EU; tel: 031-332 2433

Sealink Stena Line, Charter House, Park St, Ashford, Kent TN24 8EX; tel: 0233 622558

Shearings Holidays, Miry Lane, Wigan, Greater Manchester WN3 4AG; tel: 0942 48777

Snowdonia National Park, Penrhyndeudraeth, Gwynedd LL48 6LS; tel: 0766 770274

South East Tourist Board, 1 Warwick Park, Tunbridge Wells, Kent TN2 5TA; tel: 0892 540766

Southern Tourist Board, 40 Chamberlayne Rd, Eastleigh, Hants SO5 5JH; tel: 0703 620006

States of Guernsey Tourist Board, PO Box 23, White Rock, St Peter Port, Guernsey, CI; tel: 0381 26611

States of Jersey Tourism Committee, Weighbridge, St Helier, Jersey, CI; tel: 0534 78000

Superbreak Mini Holidays, 305 Gray's Inn Rd, London WC1X 8QF; tel: 071-278 5724

Thames and Chilterns Tourist Board, The Mount House, Church Green, Witney, Oxon OX8 6DZ; tel: 0993 778800

Wales Tourist Board, Brunel House, 2 Fitzalan Rd, Cardiff CF2 1UY; tel: 0222 499909

Wallace Arnold Tours Ltd, Gelderd Rd, Leeds LS12 6DH; tel: 0532 636456

Warner Holidays, Swan Court, Waterhouse St, Hemel Hempstead, Herts HP1 1DS; tel: 0442 230300

Waterway Holidays, Penn Place, Rickmansworth, Herts WD3 1EU; tel: 0923 770040

West Country Tourist Board, Trinity Court, Southernhay East, Exeter, Devon EX1 1QS; tel: 0392 76351

Yorkshire and Humberside Tourist Board, 312 Tadcaster Rd, York YO2 2HF; tel: 0904 707961

Yorkshire Dales National Park, Colvend, Hebden Rd, Grassington, Skipton, North Yorkshire BD23 5LB; tel: 0756 752748

Youth Hostels Association, Trevelyan House, 8 St. Stephen's Hill, St Albans AL1 2DY; tel: 0727 55215

BOOK LIST

Chapter One: Introduction to Tourism in the United Kingdom

Holidaymaking in the British Isles 1988-9...An Overview, M. Wood, ETB Insights, 1989

Tourism Intelligence Quarterly, BTA/ETB, October 1990

Pleasure, Leisure and Jobs: The Business of Tourism, Cabinet Office (Enterprise Unit), HMSO, 1985

Tourism into the '90s: Summary of Key Facts, Department of Employment, 1991

The UK Tourist, NTBs, 1990

BTA National Facts of Tourism, BTA, 1990

Britain Welcomes Japan: Caring for the Japanese Visitor, BTA, 1991

The Japanese Visitor Market, M. Montgomery, ETB Insights, 1989

The Japanese Tourist in London, T. Webb, ETB Insights, 1989

Tourism in the British Economy, Wales Tourist Board Factsheet 5, 1990

Overseas Visitors to Wales, Wales Tourist Board Factsheet 4, 1990

Isle of Man Passenger Survey Annual Report 1990, Economic Affairs Division, Isle of Man Treasury

Holiday 1991, Mintel, 1991

The Business of Tourism, J. Christopher Holloway, Pitman, 1989

The Tourist Market for Older People, J. Bailey, ETB Insights, 1989

Marketing to the Over 50s: A Problem or an Opportunity? A. Ritchies, ETB Insights, 1989

Good Companions: A New Product Development for the Grey Panthers, B. Daykin, ETB Insights, 1990

Travel and Tourism, P. Lavery, Elm Publications, 1989

The Disabled Visitor, R. Denman and S.Clarkson, ETB Insights, 1991

Educational Visits to Tourist Attractions, C. Cooper and J.Latham, ETB Insights, 1989

Tourism and the Tourist Industry: Latest Statistics, B. Baty, Employment Gazette, September 1990

The Case For and Against Using Travel Agents to Sell Domestic Tourism Products, V. Middleton, ETB Insights, 1989

Schemes of Financial Assistance, Welsh Tourist Board, 1990

European Community Funding for Tourism Projects, G. Downie, ETB Insights, 1991

The Leisure Environment, A. Cheers/A.Sampson, Macmillan, 1991

The BITOA Yearbook, 1990

Chapter Two: Tourist Geography of the United Kingdom

Regional Tourism Fact Sheets, 1989, Regional Tourist Boards, 1989

Travel Geography, R. Burton, Pitman, 1991

Annual Report to the States and Statistical Digest for Jersey, 1990

Isle of Man Passenger Survey Annual Report, 1990, M.Kelly, Economic Affairs Division

Seaside Resorts, V. Middleton, ETB Insights, 1989

The Future for England's Smaller Seaside Resorts, V. Middleton, ETB, 1991

Great British Cities Marketing Group Chairman's Report, 1991

Chapter Three: The British Transport Networks

Transport Statistics for Great Britain, 1978-1988, Department of Transport, Scottish Development Department and Welsh Office

British Airports, A. J. Wright, 1988, Ian Allan Ltd

The Channel Tunnel, J. Maning-Shaw, ETB Insights, 1990

A History of British Motorways, G. Charlesworth, 1984, Thomas Telford Ltd.

Metro: Ten Years of Service in Tyne and Wear, D. Howard, Tyne and Wear Passenger Transport Executive, 1990

London Transport Fact Sheets, 1991

London Underground Ltd. Fact Sheets, 1991

National Express Fact Sheets, 1991

Marketing to the Bus and Coach Industry, L. Fitzpatrick and C. Milburn, Bus and Coach Council, 1991

London Port Handbook, 1991

The River Thames for Tourism, Leisure and Pleasure, P. Chambers in Port of London Magazine, 1989.

Chapter Four: Accommodation in the UK

Wales Tourist Board Factsheets 3, 7 and 8, 1990

It may be less fun but a set menu can prove appetising, Roger Cowe, The Guardian, 19 April 1991

The Best method of winning, Tourism Enterprise, 1990

The Butlin's Story

Holiday Cottages, S. Beioley, ETB Insights, 1990

Bed and Breakfast, ETB Product Development Dept, ETB Insights, 1991

Touring Caravans and Camping, S. Beioley, ETB Insights, 1990

Hotel Product Segmentation in Europe, Pannell Kerr Forster Associates, ETB Insights, 1990

Leisure, the Hotel Bedfiller, A. Bolt, ETB Insights, 1990

Four and Five Star Hotel Ownership in the UK, L. Lennon, ETB Insights, 1990

Center Parcs, P. Lavery, ETB Insights, 1989

Polurrian Hotel, G. Lazenby, ETB Insights, 1989

Budget Hotels...Which Way Forward?, S. Durrell, ETB Insights, 1990

Chapter Five: The Public Sector and Tourism

Travel and Tourism, P. Lavery, Elm Publications, 1989

Promoting Tourism to Britain: How the BTA Can Help, BTA, 1986

Wales Tourist Board: its Role, Objectives and Structure, WTB, 1990

Tourist Information Centres in Britain 1990/1, BTA 1990.

The National Network of Tourist Information Centres in England, A. Clark, ETB Insights, 1991

TICs...An Identity Crisis?, K. Davies, ETB Insights, 1991

Chapter Six: The UK Tourist Attractions Industry

Sightseeing in 1988, ETB/BTA

English Heritage Monitor, ETB, 1988

Visitor Attractions Survey: 1989 STB

Visitors to Tourist Attractions in Wales 1989, WTB

Visitor Attraction Report 1989, NITB

From Tourist Attractions to Heritage Tourism, P. Yale, Elm Publications, 1990

Tourism Law, J. Corke, Elm Publications, 1987

Tourism Development Action Programmes...An Approach to Local Tourism Initiatives, B. Bramwell & G. Broom, ETB Insights, 1989

Visitor Attractions and the Commercial Sector, Dr. J. Seeley, ETB Insights, 1989

What Makes a Successful Attraction? B. Martin & S. Mason, ETB Insights, 1990

Tourist Signing: Minimum Qualifying Criteria for White on Brown Tourist Signs in England, ETB, 1991

The Heritage Industry, R. Hewison, Methuen, 1987

Britain's Heritage: The Creation of the National Heritage Memorial Fund, A. Jones, Weidenfeld & Nicolson, 1985

Treasures for the Nation: Conserving Our Heritage, BM Publications, 1989

Loot...The Heritage of Plunder, E. R. Chamberlin, Thames & Hudson, 1983

Chapter Seven: Historical Attractions

The British Museum...Purpose and Politics, D. M. Wilson, BM Publications, 1989

That Noble Cabinet: A History of the British Museum, E. Miller, Deutsch, 1973

The Museum Time Machine, R. Lumley (ed.), Routledge, 1988

Palaces of Discovery: The Changing World of Britain's Museums, S. Tait, Quiller, 1989

What's Happening to Our Museums? Holiday Which?, 1990

Preserving the Past, E. R. Chamberlin, Dent, 1979

Priceless Heritage...The Future of Museums, I. Finlay, Faber & Faber, 1977

Museums and Galleries in Great Britian and Ireland, British Leisure Publications

The North of England Open-Air Museum at Beamish, K. Harrop in 'Travel and Tourism', Business Education Publishers Ltd, 1989

Ruins: Their Preservation and Display, M. W. Thompson, Colonnade, 1981

A History of Country House Visiting, A. Tinniswood, NT/Blackwell, 1989
National Trust Handbook 1990
Historic Houses Directory, Historic Houses Association
Caring for Country Houses, National Trust, 1990
Change and Decay: The Future of Our Churches, M. Binney & P. Burman, Studio Vista, 1977
Historic Churches Preservation Trust Report 1989
Highgate Cemetery: Victorian Valhalla, J. Gay & F. Barker, John Murray, 1984
Underneath English Towns: Interpreting Urban Archaeology, M. Carver, Batsford, 1987
Past Imperfect: The Story of Rescue Archaeology, B. Jones, Heinemann, 1984
English Heritage: Facts and Figures, 1989
Introduction to the Ancient Monuments and Archaeological Areas Act 1979, DOE, 1985
Listed Buildings: The Law and Practice, R. Suddards, Sweet & Maxwell, 1982
Great Britain, H. Cleere in 'Approaches to the Archaeological Heritage', H. Cleere (ed.).
Archaeology and Planning...a Consultative Document, DOE, 1990
Visitors Welcome, HMSO (for English Heritage), 1988
The Jorvik Viking Centre: An Experiment in Archaeological Site Interpretation, P. Addyman & A. Gaynor, International Journal of Museum Management and Curatorship, 1984
BP Book of Industrial Archaeology, N. Cossons, David & Charles, 1987
The National Trust Guide to Our Industrial Past, A. Burton, NT, 1983
John Broome's Fawlty Towers, M.Tomkinson, The Independent, 1990
Visitor Survey Report for the Ironbridge Gorge Museum Trust 1985

Chapter Eight: Countryside and Wildlife Attractions

A Future for Our Countryside, J. Blunden & N. Curry, Blackwell, 1988
Protected Landscapes: The UK Experience, D & J Poore, ISCN, 1987
A National Park in the Balance? Lake District National Park Authority, GCSE Resource Guide
Designed for Recreation: A Practical Handbook for All Concerned with Providing Leisure, E. Beazley, Faber & Faber, 1969
The Future for Rural Tourism, B. Lane, ETB Insights, 1989
National Trust Annual Report, 1989
National Trust for Scotland Annual Report, 1990
Forests for the Community, Countryside Commission, 1989
Great Zoos of the World: Their Origins and Significance, Lord Zuckermann (ed.), Weidenfeld & Nicolson, 1977
Zoo 2000, J. Cherfas, BBC, 1984
International Zoo Handbook 1988

The Zoological Society of London Annual Report, 1989-90
Gardens of England and Wales Open to the Public 1989, National Gardens Scheme

Chapter Nine: The Arts
Arts Council Report 1988-9
Cultural Trends Quarterly, 1989, Policy Studies Institute
Victoria and Albert Museum Report of the Board of Trustees, 1986-9
The National Gallery, M. Wilson, Orbis, 1982
The Arts and the People, R. Shaw, Cape, 1987
The Great Exhibition of 1851, HMSO, 1981
Theatre Administration, F. Reid, A & C. Black, 1983

Chapter Ten: Miscellaneous Tourist Attractions
The Royal Parks, D. Edgar, W. H. Allen, 1986
Madame Tussaud: Waxworker Extraordinary, A. Leslie & P. Chapman, Hutchinson, 1978
Madame Tussaud's: Chamber of Horrors, P. Chapman, Grafton, 1985
Pearson Annual Report and Accounts, 1989
Britannia Park: Showcase of Britain, R. Quick, ETB Insights, 1989
Managing Inland Water for Leisure and Recreation...An Example from Southern England, D. Oliver, The Environmentalist, 1985
A Seasoned Traveller, C. Wright, Christoper Helm, 1989
King of the Castles, S. Bowen, in Leisure Opportunities, July 1991
Our World's Heritage, National Geographic Society, 1987

Chapter Eleven: The Impact of Tourism on the UK
The Tourism Strategy for London, London Tourist Board, 1987
A Tourism Strategy for Bristol, City Planning Dept., 1990
Tourism and the Tourist Industry, B. Baty, Employment Gazette, September 1990
Tourism and the Environment...Into the '90s, Department of Employment, 1991
Tourism and the Environment: Maintaining the Balance, ETB/Department of Employment, 1991
Tourism: Environment and Development Perspectives, P. Mason, WWF, 1989
Tourism in National Parks: A Guide to Good Practice, Countryside Commission & NTBs, 1991
Preservation Pays, M. Hanna & M. Binney, SAVE Britain's Heritage, 1979
Industrial Tourism, A. Menzies, ETB Insights, 1989
Portsmouth Harbour, Tourism Development Action Programme Background Document, 1986
Visitor's Guide to the Potteries, 1989
Britain at Work, BTA

Study of the Social, Cultural and Linguistic Impact of Tourism In and Upon Wales: A Report to the Wales Tourist Board, ECTARC, 1988

Chapter Twelve: Specialist Markets for Tourism in the UK

Business Tourism, S. Beioley, ETB Insights, 1991
Boating Holidays, J. Hoseason, ETB Insights, 1990
Holidays Afloat, National Tourist Boards and British Marine Industries Federation, 1990
Norfolk Broads Case Study, P. Mason in Tourism: Environment and Development Perspectives, WWF, 1990
Activity Holidays, S. Beioley, ETB Insights, 1991
Golfing Hotels, ETB Insights, 1991
Golf Development for the Nineties, L. McLellan, ETB Insights, 1991

INDEX

INTERACTIVE MANAGEMENT SIMULATIONS

Editor: Humphrey Shaw
Programmers: Jon Carter, Brian Dakin, Wayne Griffiths

3 new interactive management simulations on IBM compatible computer disk (3½" or 5¼"). Specially written for trainee managers and students of business and commerce. Designed to improve manager's decision making and presentation skills, they allow trainees to work together in groups managing a simulated business in competition with each other.

Restaurant Manager

Groups make decisions on all the major aspects of a new restaurant business including site, staff and supplies. Their goal is to establish and run a successful business by making necessary financial, marketing and human resource decisions.

Football Manager

Allows groups to make decisions on buying or selling players, investing in new amenities and saftey equipment, and managing the finances of a football club. Their main aim is to build a skilled team with stamina and high morale and for the club to be profitable and successful in the league.

Property Manager

Groups of trainees make decisions on land purchase, what style and size of houses to build, what price to sell them at and how to promote and sell them effectively. They receive details of their sales, profits and bank loans from the tutor before being asked to make another round of decisions.

From Tourist Attractions to Heritage Tourism

Pat Yale

A comprehensive survey of tourist attractions - from museums to stately homes, castles, palaces and gardens, religious buildings, archaeological sites and ancient monuments, industrial and transport heritage. The Arts, wildlife and the countryside, events and the marketing and management of national and international heritage.

Book - Illustrated with maps, charts & diagrams. Index
isbn 1 85450 016 3 1991

Tutor's Manual with case studies, notes and overhead projection transparencies
isbn 1 85450 094 5 1991

Tourism Law

Jim Corke

The first text specially written on the law relating to tourism and travel. Designed for people who are not law specialists, and for students of hospitality, travel, recreation and leisure on courses from BTEC to degree level.

Book (large format paperback) isbn 0 946139 95 4
(Second edition February, 1993)

Tutor's Manual - case studies and notes, references to relevant statutes £59.00 isbn 0 946139 96 2
(Second edition March, 1993)

Travel and tourism - second edition

Patrick Lavery

An introduction to the main sectors of the tourism industry, which defines and outlines its development in Britain, Europe and the United States.
It includes transport deregulation, Tourism Development Action Plans and innovation in tourism development in Britain and Europe.

Book - large format paperback - isbn 1 85450 120 8

Tutor's Manual (Second Edition) of workable and tested exercises, notes and overhead projection transparencies
isbn 1 85450 021 6

Travel and Tourism: a North American/European Perspective

Patrick Lavery and Carlton Van Doren

An overview of the characteristics and operations of the travel and tourism industry and the role of the private and public sectors in developing tourism. A contemporary comparison of North America, the U.K. and Europe.

Book - large format paperback - isbn 1 85450 125 9 US $17.95

Travel company Business Simulation

Ray Garnett

The **Travel Company Business Simulation** is an IBM compatible computer based non-interactive business simulation - not just a game, it is a cleverly put together learning exercise based on the real world and using real data. Requiring no prior understanding of business concepts, it can be used as a platform to develop some highly sophisticated ideas.

The exercise is easy to learn and, for the tutor, easy to run. It also provides easy to mark assessment methods.

Working in groups, each with their own company name, participants operate a newly-established travel business offering weekend coach trips from London to the Lake District. Each decision time span is 1 month and the usual period of operation 1 financial year - run over a six-hour period (ideally split into two blocks of 3 hours each). In planning each month, a group must take into account tourism habits for the time of year, booking hotel accommodation in advance, advertising expenditure, bank loans, coach hire, refunds from cancellations, overheads, wages and then pricing the package competitively. To reflect the real world, various unforeseen extraneous activities occur as the simulation progresses.

Especially suitable for 1st year business studies, accounting and leisure and tourism students the **Travel Company Business Simulation** has been tested on a wide range of courses. Used early on it acts as an excellent "ice-breaker" involving the students in team work as well as inter-group rivalry.

The package contains: A computer floppy disk (3½ "or 5¼") and instructions; Tutor's Manual with full detils of market research data, easy to mark assessment methods (group & individual), OHPs, chapter on discussion points & learning platforms explored in the exercise, a simple step-by-step set of instructions on how to work out the accounts generated by the simulation model, permission to copy freely participants' handouts (a master set is supplied), full details of all extraneous activities generated during the running of the exercise.

Interactive demo disk supplied on request

1992 Tutor's Manual - isbn 1 85450 035 X